THE TRANSITION COMPANION

Making your community more resilient
in uncertain times

"Get ready for a smaller world. Soon, your food is going to come from a field much closer to home, and the things you buy will probably come from a factory down the road rather than one on the other side of the world. You will almost certainly drive less and walk more, and that means you will be shopping and working closer to home. Your neighbours and your neighbourhood are about to get a lot more important in the smaller world of the none-too-distant-future."
Jeff Rubin, *Why Your World is About to Get a Whole Lot Smaller* (2009)[1]

"Maybe all this [Transition initiatives] sounds a bit goody-two-shoes to you – a bit ecofreaky – but what's wrong with that? We've been here before. When our food supplies were threatened in the last war the government urged us to dig for victory . . . and we did. Never in our history have we had a more healthy diet. And the fact is that people are responding to Transition schemes. They're packing town and village halls around the country to support them. You don't believe there's any need even to think about this sort of thing? You reckon this latest oil crisis is just another scare and the danger of global warming is being exaggerated? Well maybe you're right. I hope you are. But if you're wrong, doesn't it make sense to think local rather than rely on politicians at national and world level to get us out of the mess they've helped create?"
John Humphrys, *Sunday Mirror*, 25 November 2007

"It was a funny little path, winding here and there, dashing off in different directions, and sometimes even tying a knot in itself from sheer joy. [You don't get tired of a path like that, and I'm not sure that it doesn't get you home quicker in the end.]"
Tove Jansson, *Comet in Moominland* (1946)

THE TRANSITION COMPANION

Making your community more resilient
in uncertain times

Rob Hopkins

Chelsea Green Publishing
White River Junction, Vermont

green press
INITIATIVE

Chelsea Green Publishing is committed to preserving ancient forests and natural resources. We elected to print this title on FSC`-certified paper containing at least 10% postconsumer recycled paper, processed chlorine-free. As a result, for this printing, we have saved:

23 Trees (40' tall and 6-8" diameter)
10,692 Gallons of Wastewater
9 million BTUs Total Energy
678 Pounds of Solid Waste
2,371 Pounds of Greenhouse Gases

Chelsea Green Publishing made this paper choice because we are a member of the Green Press Initiative, a nonprofit program dedicated to supporting authors, publishers, and suppliers in their efforts to reduce their use of fiber obtained from endangered forests. For more information, visit www.greenpressinitiative.org.

Environmental impact estimates were made using the Environmental Defense Paper Calculator. For more information visit: www.papercalculator.org.

Originally published in 2011 by Green Books, Dartington Space, Dartington Hall, Totnes, Devon TQ9 6EN, UK.

Designer: Jayne Jones

First Chelsea Green printing October, 2011
Printed in the United States of America
10 9 8 7 6 5 4 3 2 1   11 12 13 14 15

Our Commitment to Green Publishing

Library of Congress Cataloging-in-Publication Data

Hopkins, Rob, 1968-
  The transition companion : making your community more resilient in uncertain times / Rob Hopkins.
      p. cm.
  Includes bibliographical references and index.
  ISBN 978-1-60358-392-3 (pbk.) -- ISBN 978-1-60358-393-0 (ebook) 1. Community development--Environmental aspects. 2. Sustainable development. 3. Sustainable living. 4. Energy consumption--Social aspects. 5. Energy conservation--Social aspects. 6. Energy conservation--Citizen participation. 7. Energy policy--Citizen participation. I. Title.
    HN49.C6H664 2011
    307.1'4--dc23
                                            2011035859

Chelsea Green Publishing Company
Post Office Box 428
White River Junction, VT 05001
(802) 295-6300
www.chelseagreen.com

MIX
Paper from
responsible sources
FSC® C101537

To my family, Tessa, Mum, Dad, Jo, Ian, Jake, Archie, Steve, Hilary, Robert, Harriet and Helen.

To Colin Campbell, Richard Heinberg, David Holmgren and Howard Odum for sowing the seeds of this concept.

To the Transition Network team and to everyone testing the Transition model out, doing extraordinary work and having so much fun in the process.

To Geshe Jampa Gyatso, who taught me everything that really matters.

To my wonderful sons, Rowan, Finn, Arlo and Cian: take this world by the horns, boys.

To Emma: companion, lover, friend and wife.

Finally, to two of the twentieth century's great geniuses lost to us in 2010/11: the dear David Fleming, and Captain Beefheart – both brilliant in *very* different ways, but brilliant nonetheless.

Contents

Acknowledgements

Trailblazers and assorted sources of inspiration

Christopher Alexander, Peter Bane, Albert Bates, Graham Bell, David Boyle, Lester Brown, Colin Campbell, Fritjof Capra, Alec Clifton-Taylor, Phil Corbett, Martin Crawford, Chris Day, Charles Dickens, Dr Carlo DiClemente, Chris Dixon, Richard Douthwaite, Matt Dunwell, Paul Ekins, Ianto Evans, Simon Fairlie, David Fleming, Masanobu Fukuoka, Clive Hamilton, James Hansen, Stephan Harding, Tim and Maddy Harland, Peter Harper, Lea Harrison, Robert Hart, Emilia Hazelip, Richard Heinberg, Colin Hines, Arthur Hollins, David Holmgren, Barbara Jones, Ken Jones, Martin Luther King, Naomi Klein, Satish Kumar, John Lane, Andy Langford, Jeremy Leggett, Aldo Leopold, Bernard Lietaer, Richard Mabey, Joanna Macy, Marcus McCabe, Bill McKibben, Dennis Meadows, Bill Mollison, George Monbiot, Sterling Morrison, Helena Norberg-Hodge, Howard and Elisabeth Odum, Harrison Owen, Rosa Parks, Jonathan Richman, Dr Stephen Rollnick, Mark Rudd, Kirkpatrick Sale, E. F. Schumacher, John Seymour, Vandana Shiva, Michael Shuman, Andrew Simms, Chris Skrebowski, Linda Smiley, Gary Snyder, Sufjan Stevens, Ruth Stout, Tom Vague, Don Van Vliet and Meg Wheatley.

Collaborators, idea-shapers and co-conspirators

Gary Alexander, Paul Allen, Bart Anderson, Teresa Anderson, Sharon Astyk, Tom Atkins, Sophy Banks, Steph Bradley, Ben Brangwyn, Julie Brown, Lou Brown, Adrienne Campbell, Dave Chapman, Jo Coish, Matthieu Daum, Catherine Dunne, Michael Dunwell, Emma, Adam Fenderson, Simon French, Naresh Giangrande, Brian Goodwin, Jennifer Gray, Mike Grenville, Stephan Harding, Matt Harvey, Polly Higgins, Nicola Hilary, Colin Hines, Patrick Holden, David Johnson, Chris Johnstone, Mike Jones, Tessa King, Helen La Trobe, William Lana, Alan Langmaid, Peter Lipman, Noel Longhurst, Caroline Lucas, Tim Lunel, Ed Mitchell, Gavin Morris, Emilio Mula, Sasha Nathanson, Aaron Newton, Sarah Nicholl, Frances Northrop, Anna O'Brien, Iain Oram, Dave Paul, Jules Peck, Davie Philip, Catrina Pickering, Tamzin Pinkerton, Amber Ponton, Adrian Porter, Hilary Prentice, Sarah Pugh, Julie Richardson, Thomas and Ulrike Riedmuller, Tom Rivett-Carnac, Simon Roberts, Louise Rooney, Alexis Rowell, Mary-Jayne Rust, Chris Salisbury, Schumacher College, Molly Scott Cato, Mike Small, Simon Snowden, David Strahan, Graham Strouts, Mark Thurstain-Goodwin, Jill Tomalin, Nigel Topping, the people of Totnes, Robert Vint, Fiona Ward, Nick Weir, Patrick White-field, Carole Whitty.

Others – without whom you wouldn't be reading this

John Elford, Amanda Cuthbert, Jayne Jones, Alethea Doran and the team at Green Books.

Louise Rooney and Catherine Dunne, who first coined the term 'Transition Town'.

Martin Tepper, who suggested the first part of this book's title.

Thanks also to . . .

I'd like to thank all the organisations and people who have funded the work of Transition Network and Transition Town Totnes so far, and made possible so much of our work:
Artists Project Earth, Ashoka, Calouste Gulbenkian Foundation, Carnegie UK Trust, Curry Stone Design Prize, Economic and Social Research Council, Esmée Fairbairn Foundation, Grundtvig Programme, Keep the Land Foundation, LUSH, Marmot Charitale Trust, Polden-Puckham Charitable Foundation, Prairie Trust, Roddick Foundation, Roger Ross of Lots Road Auction, Tanner Trust, The Network for Social Change, Theresa Field, Transition Tyndale, Tudor Trust, and many individuals to whom we are very grateful.

Those who contributed to the process of creating the ingredients

The readers of TransitionCulture.org, the ever-patient Helen La Trobe, Amber Ponton and Ed Mitchell, workshop participants at the Transition Network conference and the Diverse Routes to Belonging conference, Gary Alexander, Bart Anderson, Patrick Andrews, Ria Baeck, Sophy Banks, Jade Bashford, Justin Bere, Rachel Bodle, Ben Brangwyn, Vicky Briggs, Jim Brown, Nathan Burlton, Shaun Chamberlin, Tom Chance, Chris Chapman, Dave Chapman, Kenrick Chin, Danielle Cohen, G. Collins, Dan, Charlotte Du Cann, Matt Dunwell, Chloe Farmer, Naresh Giangrande, Chrissie Godfrey, Gordon from Vinegar Hill, Nigel Grant, Jo Hardy, Lisa Heff, Mark Hodgson, Shane Hughes, Justin Kenrick, Trish Knox, Helmut Leitner, Peter Lipman, Alex Loh, Lucy, Dan McCallum, Anna McIvor, Scott McKeown, David McLeod, Dan McTiernan, Cara Naden, Lucy Neal, Sara Neuff, Sarah Nicholl, Nick Osborne, Bob Patterson, Catrina Pickering, Joanne Porouyow, Adrian Porter, Hilary Prentice, Janet Rawlings, Teen Ross, Alexis Rowell, James Samuel, Eva Schonveld, Carin Schwartz, Richard Shore, Michael Shuman, Judy Skog, Sophia, Nick Temple, John Thackara, Mark Thurstain-Goodwin, Graham Truscott, Tully Wakeman, Penny Walker, Fiona Ward.

Photographers and illustrators

All photos and illustrations by the author, apart from those by:

Artgym™, Gabriele Baldazzi, Dan Ball, Sophy Banks, Jeremy Bartlett, bere:architects, Tulane Blyth, Philip Booth, Rose Bridger, Vicky Briggs, Lou Brown, Katy Bryce, Nathan Burlton, Peter Campbell, Iva Carrdus, Joel Catchlove, Dave Cockcroft, Chris Croome, Mick Dean FCUM Matchday Photography, Chris Dixon, Charlotte Du Cann, Denise Dunn, May East, EcoLabs, Suzan Fiskin, Jan Forsmark, Future Proof Kilkenny, Hilary Gander, Geofutures, Chrissie Godfrey, Jonathan Goldberg, Andy Goldring, Amelia Gregory, Mike Grenville, The Handmade Bakery, Tim Harland, Deanna Harrison, Trathen Heckman, Jonny Helm, Fredrik Hjerling, Mark Hodgson, M. King Hubbert, Kenn Jordan, Ann Lamot, Mary Linley, Robert Logan, Loudphoto/Barcelona-en-Transición, Simon Maggs, Filipe Matos, John McLennan, Samagita Misha, Yannick Molin, Emilio Mula, Cara Naden, Lucy Neal, New Forest National Park Authority, Sarah Nicholl, Jan O'Highway, PEDAL, Davie Philip, James Piers Taylor, Jane Price, Janet Rawlings, Philip Revell, Tish Rickard, Chris Rowland / OVESCO, Sandpoint Transition Initiative, Eva Schonveld, Carin Schwartz, Paul Shepherd, Small World Theatre, Chris Smedley, Jonathan Smith, James Southwick, Shelby Tay, TEIA, John Tikotsky, Christine Tope, Totnes Image Bank and Rural Archive, Totnes Renewable Energy Society, *Totnes Times*, Transition Belsize, Transition Cambridge, Transition Edinburgh University, Transition Linlithgow, Transition Malvern Hills, Transition Stoke Newington, Transition Town Dorchester, Transition Town High Wycombe, Transition Town Lewes, Transition Town Totnes, Aiofe Valley, Michael Vin Lee, Marina Vons-Gupta, Jon Walker, Chris Wells, Laura Whitehead, Wycombe District Council.

Artists one and all.

The speech bubbles . . .

. . . at the start of each section were responses by readers of my blog, www.TransitionCulture.org, to the question "Why do you do Transition?"

Tran · si · tion [tran – zish – uhn]

*n. 1. passage from one form, state, style
or place to another
2. a period of transformation*

Forewords

When Transition arrived in Brasilândia (a favela in São Paolo, Brazil) I felt a wave of renewal in my heart and the hearts of my friends who joined the meetings. It cheered us up! A great example is Dona Luzia, an old-time resident . . . she is now sharing what she is learning in the practical workshops and became a proud member of the community. She knows she is part of the transition. Long life to Transition Brasilândia!

Sr Quintino Jose Viana

When Transition arrived in Brasilândia my life started to change. I've learnt simple facts which changed old habits. For example, at home we used to throw everything in one bin – we now discard less and even get some money by selling sorted garbage. I learnt garbage is the right thing in the wrong place! One of our abandoned public squares has been cleaned and re-owned by the community. Now it is a meeting spot for the old, the new and the tribe of young graphiteurs [graffiti artists]. Transition is changing the consciousness of our simple people, many struggling to survive, who now feel valued by who they are. My mother, who was leading Brasilândia Filmes, died a few weeks ago. I realised what we most have to sustain in Transition is care and affection . . . here and now . . . between us and the planet.

Japa, a young rapper from Brasilândia

Observing the growth of the Transition movement over the past five years has been inspiring in so many ways. While governments and big business struggle (to put it politely) to tackle the enormous environmental issues that face us, this movement has forged ahead with its collective bid to find a creative, passionate response to the question "Where do we go from here?" Spreading outwards from its inception in the towns of Kinsale and Totnes, Transition has become a remarkable network with global reach. There are now practical projects under way on the ground all over the UK, and beyond. They demonstrate beyond doubt that the strengthening and diversification of local economies, underpinned by a commitment not to squander the Earth's finite resources, is a highly effective strategy for the uncertain times we live in. They help take the fear out of the future, while offering people a renewed sense of belonging; of shared experience and goals; of a life that makes sense again.

Four years after the publication of *The Transition Handbook*, Rob Hopkins has now completed this second volume. The former explored the theory of Transition, and asked what an international movement based on it might look like. This new book draws on five years of practical experience that go a long way towards answering that question. Here, Rob sets out an exciting, much-expanded idea of what Transition is and could become; one that is rich with hard-won insights and practical advice. It's a work full of bold answers, inspirational ideas and daring solutions. Although profoundly serious at heart, it's never sombre. In fact, it's a great deal of fun, frequently demonstrating how Transition is a highly creative, stimulating and even playful process.

I am struck by the way Rob describes each Transition undertaking as unique – like the community in which it thrives. While always rooted in a set of crucial principles, every example will reflect the specific needs and qualities of an individual place. It's rather like giving a great cake recipe to a dozen different cooks and watching how their particular ingredients, techniques and creative ideas produce subtly different results. Rob argues that a Transition community never will, or should, look quite the same twice – and in that flexibility lies the strength of this movement. He makes the wholly convincing point that community strategies to tackle peak oil, climate change and all the other pressing environmental issues that face us should emerge organically from the community itself, rather than being imposed from the top down. It's a vital insight of the movement that this kind of bottom-up process is far more likely to result in real change that is rooted in local knowledge, creativity and passion. It's what gives Transition its enduring resonance and relevance.

My first experience of Transition came in 2008, when I travelled to Totnes to film a sequence about Garden Share, a project that matched people who wanted to grow food but had nowhere to do it with people who had unused or under-used gardens around the town. It was a brilliantly simple initiative, and above all a practical one that was getting a great response. It inspired me, and colleagues from the production company, to set up our online Landshare scheme, which aims to match would-be growers with land and garden 'donors' all over the country. There's no question that we owe the success of Landshare to that inspiring day I spent in Totnes, among Transition pioneers.

Pretty much everything I do, as a writer and broadcaster, is predicated on the idea that families and communities can gain huge pleasure and satisfaction from taking more responsibility for the food they eat, and sourcing it closer to home. Rob holds to the same faith, expanding this nourishing self- and community-reliance to all aspects of our lives. His view is that an extraordinary and historic shift in how this country feeds, powers and houses itself is on the horizon, and we can all play a part in it. It will be a shift, or transition, that future generations will remember and celebrate. The practical aspects of this – the solar panels, the vegetable beds, the low-carbon buildings – are the easy bit. As Rob says, "If we wait for the governments, it'll be too little, too late; if we act as individuals, it'll be too little; but if we act as communities, it might just be enough, just in time." It is the working together, rediscovering how to build community and to support each other, that is the harder thing to get right. That is where *The Transition Companion* comes in. It offers an extraordinarily rich yet highly accessible model for drawing together the people around you, and describes the tools needed to start an economic and social renaissance in the place you live. It's a book that is unashamedly ambitious and far-reaching in its scope and vision. But, if we are to successfully navigate what's coming towards us, and hold on to our identity, our community and our shared optimism for the future, that is exactly what we need.

Hugh Fearnley-Whittingstall, River Cottage, September 2011
To find out more about Hugh's latest project, energyshare, log on to www.energyshare.com.

Introduction

This book seeks to answer the question:

"What would it look like if the best responses to peak oil and climate change came not from committees and Acts of Parliament, but from you and me and the people around us?"

It's a big question, which is why it requires this relatively big book to address it, but I think you're going to enjoy the pages ahead, and the journey they will take you on. For the first *The Transition Handbook*, published in 2008, this was pretty much a speculative question, but for this new book we are able to draw from what has, in effect, been a five-year worldwide experiment, an attempt to try to put the Transition idea into practice. I think it is one of the most important social experiments happening anywhere in the world at the moment. I hope that by the end of this book you will agree, that if you aren't involved you will want to get involved, and if you are already involved, it will affirm, inspire and deepen what you are doing and give you a new way of looking at it.

Supported by some simple principles, ingredients and tools – which I'll introduce you to later – and by a global network of self-organising initiatives, many thousands of people in cities, islands, towns and villages, from the US to New Zealand and from Brazil to Norway, are coming together to ask, "For all those aspects of life that this community needs in order to sustain itself and thrive, how do we significantly rebuild resilience (to mitigate the effects of peak oil and economic contraction) and drastically reduce carbon emissions (to mitigate the effects of climate change)?"

While the overriding cultural response is to duck that question and to pop our heads into the sand of denial, these people are responding with creativity, compassion and a deep commitment. They're also having fun, lots of it, connecting with people they'd never met before, and together creating something far greater than the sum of its parts. What they're doing is telling a new story about the place they live and about what it could be like in the future.

This book is called a 'Companion' because that is exactly what it is intended to be. It is a move away from 'The 12 Steps of Transition' that has underpinned the work of Transition initiatives up to this point, towards a more holistic, more appropriate

Transition Town Kingston using big maps for a community visioning exercise.
Photo: Hilary Gander

model. It will act as a very useful companion as you try to address the questions set out above. It imagines the work involved in transforming the place you live from its current highly vulnerable, non-resilient, oil-dependent state to a resilient, more localised, diverse and nourishing place, as a journey. It is a companion in the sense that it doesn't tell you which way to go or what your journey will look like, but suggests some of the especially good views along the way, and provides a rough sense of the different types of terrain you will find yourself travelling across. But the journey itself and where you end up – that's up to you.

The analogy of the journey is a useful one. Throughout history, we have told stories of heroes who undertook extraordinary journeys, which combined an inner and an outer journey. Often they go something like this: a likeable but flawed character (Frodo, Harry Potter, Jason of the Argonauts) is faced with a challenge/problem that seems impossible and for which they feel hopelessly unequipped. They set out on a journey (either literal or metaphorical), overcome the problem and in the process discover they are a hero. To do this they have to go on a journey that transforms them, and on which they are required to take on challenges they feel unprepared for and find new strengths and inner resources. The process of shifting our society on

the scale it needs to shift, in the time that we have available, requires a story of such magnitude. At the moment it looks impossible, yet the situation demands courage, commitment and intention from us. In those stories, our heroes don't have a clear sense of where they are going, but they know which general direction to head in and some of the key stages their journey will need to pass through. This book is designed as the companion for a hero, such as yourself, setting out on such an adventure, one that we need to be embarking on in our millions, and not as solitary heroes but working with others. We can't do this alone. The idea of the solitary hero can be quite an unhealthy one, and we need to pool our efforts and be heroic together!

Here's a story of my own, which will hopefully give a flavour of how this journey might unfold. Sometime in 1992, I travelled from Bristol to the Snowdonia National Park with my friend Mark, who had borrowed his mother's car for the day. We left the city, first passing through suburbia, then through industrial estates, then into the open flat country as we headed to the Severn Bridge. Once in Wales we headed up through the valleys, the landscape becoming more mountainous, before entering a very different landscape of small fields and rolling hills. Finally we entered the national park, with its forests and rocks, as we neared our destination. The reason

By 1993, after six years of regeneration, Tir Penrhos Isaf is already starting to feel more like woodland. Today it is thick woodland – a thriving ecological community that has grown naturally on this site.
Photo: Chris Dixon

for our trip was Tir Penrhos Isaf, an emerging perma-culture (see page 98) project that had recently set an interesting planning precedent, having success-fully argued that their practising permaculture was a valid reason for them to live on their smallholding.

On a damp afternoon with leaden grey skies, we were greeted by Chris and Lynn Dixon, who showed us round the site and told us about what they were doing there over a cup of tea next to their woodstove. Although there was much that impressed me about what they were doing, what was most fascinating to me, and what I took away with me most, was what they weren't doing. When they had taken on the piece of land, which had been heavily overgrazed by the former owner, they soon fenced off one-third of the site from deer and rabbits to allow it to regener-ate naturally. Chris showed us a series of photos taken of the area year after year, showing what then happened. After just three years, the pioneer plants, gorse, broom and bracken, were well established, with young trees emerging. After six years, some substantial trees were established, and the place was starting to look like real woodland.

Most land wants to be forest. If left, grassland will pass through stages, with the arrival of gorse, bracken and brambles, followed by the pioneer trees such as rowan and birch, then the trees that will make up the final woodland, such as oak and hazel. The photos of the evolution of the land showed the process unfolding. Chris felt that the best way to create new woodlands was not to plough the site, plant trees, fit plastic guards to protect them from rabbits, mulch them, apply herb-icides to keep the weeds down and then thin the trees to create the desired final spacings; rather, it was just to protect the site from grazing and allow natural regeneration.

I remember Chris and Lynn's woodland (which is by now a well-established woodland) when I consider the results of the self-organising response to peak oil and climate change that we are starting to see. Are we talking about an imposed, centrally coordin-ated response that starts with a detailed plan and which takes little account of local culture and topography, or should we enable self-organisation and the emergence of something more specific to the site? While there is a need for support from central government, and the statutory removal of obstacles that stand in the way of communities creating their own responses and initiatives, well-organised and inspired community groups can do extraordinary things.

There is another useful analogy in that story too. A journey from one place to another can take a number of different routes, but will usually pass through a series of distinctly different landscapes. You don't necessarily notice when you leave one and enter another, but there are moments when you realise you are in a very different place. The Transition Journey is similar. You find that you move from raising awareness, showing films and trying to interest people, to noticing that you seem to have created an organisation that has different needs from those it had originally, and then later to starting to think about what new businesses and infrastructure your community needs. Each stage is like finding yourself in a distinct landscape. What follows in these pages also tries to capture that aspect of creating Transition.

This book is our best attempt at creating as useful a companion on that journey towards community res-ilience as possible. It is rich with stories of ordinary people doing extraordinary things, of tried-and-tested tools, as well as some more experimental ones, and offers many of the ingredients you may find you need to create this process where you live.

The way it has been created has embodied this sense of collaboration and creativity. Each of the 'tools' and 'ingredients' was written in draft and posted to my blog, TransitionCulture.org, as well as on the Transition Network's site. Comments and feedback were invited. Transition initiatives around the world were invited to send in their stories and photos, which abound in this book. The photo-shopped images here were done after I put up a post asking for help with images. Even the title was thought up by Martin Tepper when I put a post on Transition Culture asking for ideas as to what this book should be called.

You will find not just my voice throughout this book, but the voices of many people who are actively trying out these ideas and sharing their experiences. You will hear from Transition trainers, community activists, brewers, bakers, people who have organised a few film screenings in their communities, people who have set up energy companies and local currencies or who have got together to share skills. I am grateful to them all for sharing their insights.

In any journey, there are times when it looks impossible, when we need to rest and recapture why we set out on this mad venture in the first place. There are also times when the view and the journey are so exhilarating that we feel our hearts might burst. Transition initiatives all have very different experiences: they have moments when they can feel the world around them shifting in unimaginable ways, and other moments where it all feels flat and becalmed. This book offers an honest look at the work of Transition initiatives around the world, in the hope that it will inform and inspire you to pick up and run with this approach.

The format for this book arose from wanting to better show how Transition has evolved since it was first suggested, and the insights from the work of many hundreds of initiatives. Initially it was modelled on Christopher Alexander's 'Pattern Language' approach,[1] a great inspiration to me over many years. I began, through TransitionCulture.org, to suggest that Transition might make a good pattern language, and to draft some initial patterns, and over time these different aspects of Transition began to be called 'ingredients', which people found far more engaging. It then became clear that some of them were more like tools, and so the structure of this book began to come into focus.

Being in the privileged position of hosting conversations and being sent stories, photos, posters, ideas and feedback that have shaped this book has reinforced why all this matters to me. Transition has grown up very fast within just four years into a rich, deep movement that has developed a unique approach. I will speculate at the end of the book as to where I imagine it might go from here, but one of the qualities I hope will come through in this book

is Transition's rigour. In some ways it is an appeal to the environmental movement to get serious about creating a new more localised economy, to create projects and infrastructure that are economically viable, and to engage rigorously with these issues.

It also, I hope, provides a context. You may be helping with a small project: a school vegetable garden, an allotment, the community bus, a community group, or setting up a website. This book aims to set out how all of this might fit together in a spirit of not waiting for permission but just getting on with it, being part of the whole; part of a historic process of rethinking how our communities, our economy and many aspects of our daily lives work. As our economies wobble and contract, the oil price becomes increasingly volatile and the climate breaks record after record, there is no avoiding the fact that now is the time and we are the ones to do this. We may feel like Harry Potter in the cupboard under the stairs, unequipped to even start on this journey, but hopefully this companion will inspire a sense of heroism and an opportunity. We can do this. As my friend Chris Johnstone says, "life is a series of things we are not quite ready for".

I remember once reading online about a young couple in the US who built themselves a strawbale house. When they got married, they invited all their family and friends and had a clay plastering party. Everyone came along, ate, danced, drank, got filthy, and plastered the inside of their house. "What we love most about our house", the newly weds said, "is that it has been patted all over by all the people we love." This book is very similar. It has been patted all over by many hundreds of people who have as much day-to-day experience of Transition as I do, and it is infinitely the better for it. My deepest gratitude to them all and to the amazing team at Transition Network, who support the ongoing spread of Transition. Enjoy the journey.

Rob Hopkins
Dartington, September 2011

You can follow Rob on Twitter at @robintransition, or read his blog at www.transitionculture.org.

A Cheerful Disclaimer

Transition is not a known quantity. We truly don't know if Transition will work. It is a social experiment on a massive scale.

What we are convinced of is this:
- If we wait for the governments, it'll be too little, too late.
- If we act as individuals, it'll be too little.
- But if we act as communities, it might just be enough, just in time.

Everything you will read in this book is the result of real work in the real world, with community engagement at its heart. There's not an ivory tower in sight; no professors in musty oak-panelled studies churning out erudite papers; no model carved in stone.

This book, like the Transition model, is built around the stories and experience of the people achieving Transition around the world. People who are learning by doing – and learning all the time. People who understand that we can't sit back and wait for someone else to do the work. People like you, perhaps . . .

Image: Joel Catchlove

"**Honestly,** I don't really see many other ways of ensuring a **better world** for our children ..."
Miguel Leal

"... it provides a **positive, creative** and **challenging** place to apply my energies to those challenges ... and it's **fun.**"
Hilary Jennings

"The Transition movement **invites us to re-imagine** and **bring to life** a new story about how we live as members of the Earth family. **Using less, respecting more.**"
Kyla

PART ONE:

Why the Transition movement does what it does

CHAPTER ONE

The emergence of an idea: a potted history of Transition

I am often asked "So how did this whole Transition thing start?" So often, in fact, that I often consider having the following couple of paragraphs printed on a T-shirt. The poor souls who share an office with me have heard this so many times that I can see their eyes glaze over when they hear someone ask me. Anyway, given that what follows is a history of how the Transition idea emerged and evolved, I must start at the beginning. If you too have heard it dozens of times, do leap forward a few paragraphs to the highlights on pages 21 to 26.

I was a teacher of permaculture at a wonderful, very progressive adult education college in Kinsale, Ireland, where I had set up and taught the world's first two-year full-time permaculture course. The course[1] proved to be, and still is, wildly popular, turning one of the largest areas of lawn in the town into a mixture of ponds, gardens, polytunnels, forest gardens, a cob-and-cordwood amphitheatre and much else, while producing many inspired and enthusiastic students. At the start of term in October 2004, I showed the students the film *The End of Suburbia*, and the following day Dr Colin Campbell[2] came in to talk to them about peak oil. This combination put a bomb under both me and the students, and so I set the second-year students a project to create a plan for the intentional weaning of Kinsale off its oil dependency (for more about permaculture see Tools for Transition No.1: Permaculture design (page 98).

The resulting document, entitled 'Kinsale 2021: an Energy Descent Action Plan',[3] a compilation of the students' work and a few other bits and pieces, was finished in time for a conference we held in June 2005 at the college, called 'Fuelling the Future'. We didn't see that we had created anything especially meaningful, and the document wasn't even formally launched; rather, it was almost apologetically on sale at the back of the room. Luckily, others, including Richard Heinberg, who spoke at the event, picked it up and saw something of importance in it.

The 500 printed copies were rapidly sold (I remember over 100 going off in one box to Australia), and the pdf was downloaded many thousands of times. A few months later, Kinsale Town Council unanimously voted to support the plan and its findings.[4] In the meantime I had moved to Totnes in Devon, where I met Naresh Giangrande, a fellow peak oil educator, and the two of us set about investigating what a better and deeper version of the Kinsale EDAP in Totnes might look like. We began showing films together and giving talks, and they generated a great deal of interest. Other people started getting involved and bringing pieces from systems thinking, psychology, business development and the power of the internet to spread ideas. The right people seemed to turn up at the right time. In

he could imagine". He offered to help set up an organisation designed to support the other places where Transition was emerging. The idea of something called 'Transition Network' emerged, and within a short time we had secured core funding to get it under way – just in time, as it turned out, as pretty soon after that everything started going bonkers. Over the four years since then, there have been regular events or occurrences that have made us stop and go "wow!" Anyone reading this who

Members of the audience meeting each other at the Unleashing of Transition Town Totnes, September 2006.

Some of *The Transition Handbook*'s Dutch translators celebrating at the launch of the book. *Photo: Ann Lamot*

September 2006, after eight months of awareness raising and networking, we held an event called the 'Unleashing of Transition Town Totnes', where over 400 people turned up at Totnes Civic Hall to launch a process that had barely been designed in any detail. At that event were people from a few other communities, including Falmouth, Penzance and Lewes, who went back home and tried to figure out if this might work there too.

Shortly afterwards, at Schumacher College in Dartington, a course was held called 'Life After Oil', whose teachers included Dr David Fleming and Richard Heinberg, and I also taught a day about Transition. One of the participants, Ben Brangwyn, described me as looking like "a man standing under a tsunami that was building faster and higher than

has been involved in Transition will have his or her own list, but here are some of my highlights.

The first crowd-translation of *The Transition Handbook*. In the Netherlands a group of around 50 people decided there needed to be a Dutch translation of *The Transition Handbook*, so they divided the book into 50 bits and collectively translated it. The result, *Het Transitie Handboek*, has helped greatly in establishing a thriving network of Transition initiatives across the Netherlands.

The passing of the Transition Somerset resolution. We got a call one day from Somerset County Council, saying they had just passed a resolution supporting their local Transition initiatives (of which there are many) and pledging to support them, which caused great excitement and inspired others to follow suit. Somerset has since had a change of administration and abandoned much of its sustainability work (see *Daring to dream* 1: Policies for Transition, page 281), but at the time this felt like a very significant development.

The spread of Transition Training. Naresh Giangrande and Sophy Banks designed Transition Training as a two-day total immersion course. Since the first course in Totnes in October 2007, 106 training courses worldwide have been organised by Transition Training, with local organisers, and presented by members of a dedicated team of 16 UK trainers to over 2,500 participants. Courses have been run throughout the UK, as well as in Eire, Sweden, Brazil, Portugal, Italy, Germany and Flanders. Dozens more are being organised and run by local organising hubs in the US, Canada, Australia, New Zealand, Europe, parts of South America and Asia, led by a team of multilingual trainers.

The Lewes Pound Launch. I have been to many extraordinary events put on by Transition groups across the UK, but one that most sticks in my memory is the launch of the first Lewes Pound.[5] It

was a celebration of Lewes, of its independent nature, of its local traders, and of the potential of its Transitioned future. Hundreds of people and traders packed the town hall, and the moment when the notes were first unveiled nearly took the roof off. The 10,000 notes they had printed were sold out within three days and were selling on eBay for as much as £50 each! The scheme settled down again after a few days and the currency is now accepted by well over 100 traders in Lewes. The launch of the Brixton Pound, about a year later, was a similarly rousing occasion (see Tools for Transition No.19: Tools for plugging the leaks, page 257).

In Transition 1.0. The film *In Transition 1.0* was conceived as a 'wiki' film, where people doing Transition across the world were invited to send us their tapes. Over 100 hours of footage were contributed, from which producer Emma Goude painstakingly edited a wonderful film.[6] The collaborative nature of the project also continued after completion of the film, with a crowd-translation process which saw people around the world subtitling it into many different languages. *In Transition 2.0* tells the next part of the story, and will be released shortly after this book.[7]

Sophy Banks (front row, centre) and Naresh Giangrande (middle row, blue shirt) with participants on a Transition Training in Newcastle.
Photo: John McLennan

The launch of the Lewes Pound. (Clearly the notes weren't actually that big in reality.)
Photo: Mike Grenville

'Keynote Listeners'. Ed Miliband, then Secretary of State for Energy and Climate Change, requested an invitation to the 2009 Transition Network conference in Battersea Arts Centre. We told him that he could come on the condition that he attended as a 'Keynote Listener' – as in being there to listen, but most definitely not to give a speech. This proved a great success, with the now Labour leader spending subsequent months raving about the experience in a number of speeches. This story symbolises the approach Transition takes to politics, of leading by example and of trying to get politicians to experience the buzz being created by Transition initiatives, rather than just protesting. Reflecting later on the experience, Miliband wrote: "Thank you to all the people I met for taking the time to talk to me, and thank you for continuing to be the vanguard of that persuasion."[8]

The conferences. The word 'conference' is often enough to send most people to sleep. It is probably not the best word to describe the annual gatherings of Transition folks to share ideas, insights, tools, concerns and stories. So far these gatherings have been at Nailsworth, near Stroud (2007); Royal Agricultural College, Cirencester (2008); Battersea Arts Centre, London (2009); Seale Hayne, Devon (2010) and Liverpool (2011). They have been remarkable events, with usually over 350 people, lots of Open Space sessions and self-organising conversations, workshops, plenty of downtime and relaxation, and often group processes which take the whole thing to deeper levels.[9]

The first US Unleashing. An 'Unleashing', as you will discover later in these pages (see Tools for Transition No.10: Unleashings, page 184), is a launch event for a Transition project – the moment when it announces its arrival on the local scene and celebrates what it has already done, and what it hopes to go on to do. While there had been several Unleashings in the UK, the first in the US felt like a landmark. The Sandpoint Transition Initiative (STI) held their Unleashing event in a local theatre on 14 November 2008. It was packed, they streamed it live on the internet, and by all accounts it was an amazing event. Since then there have been many more US Unleashing events, each extraordinary in its own way and each a celebration of place, people and possibility.

The 2010 Transition Network conference at Seale Hayne, Devon. *Photo: Mike Grenville*

The Sandpoint Transition Initiative Unleashing, November 2008. *Photo: Sandpoint Transition Initiative*

Transition Ambridge. In March 2008, the UK's longest-running radio soap opera ran a storyline where one of the characters set up a Transition initiative in the fictitious village of Ambridge. Pat Archer, an organic farmer, told her friend Kathy: "The Transition movement says we've got to do something about climate change, and we've got to reduce our dependence on oil." Kathy replied "Everyone's been saying that for ages," to which Pat responded "Yes, but Transition communities are actually doing it."[10] The group set up a local currency which is still in circulation, having survived Joe Grundy's attempts to use it for his own profit.

The Monteveglio Resolution. Transition in Italy began in the town of Monteveglio, and a year or so later its Comune (local authority) passed an amazing resolution committing the town to responding to peak oil and climate change, to building resilience and optimism and to seeing challenges as opportunities. It included a commitment to "inform the community on the limits of a concept of development based on unlimited resources, on the need to reconvert an economy based on the massive use of fossil fuels and other non-renewable resources, and on the benefits of a more frugal and sustainable lifestyle". You can read more about this in *Connecting* 2: Involving the council (page 204), but I had to sit down when I first read about it . . . quite amazing.

Transition in Brazil. We had often been asked what we thought Transition should look like in the developing world, to which we usually responded that we had no idea; it wasn't for us to design that, but for the people who live there. Some things had started in Chile and China, but the momentum generated in a short time in Brazil has been amazing. Transition Trainings have been held in a range of settings, from the wealthy neighbourhoods to the favelas (as has already been seen in the Forewords). The first Unleashing in a favela, in December 2010, saw residents, shamen, rappers and local elders gathering to celebrate the potential of Transition for their community (see Tools for Transition No.10: Unleashings, page 184).

Social enterprises emerging. It has been fascinating to see the emergence of social enterprises in the area of Transition – businesses designed to address a social need and to create employment as well as revenue for the wider Transition process.

Leopardo Kaxinawá, from Kaxinawá Indigenous Village in Acre, and members of Recanta and Transition Brasilândia, at their Unleashing, December 2010. *Photo: May East*

Transition Heathrow hosting the Sipson Golden Conker Championship, October 2010. *Photo: Robert Logan*

The art of identifying business opportunities and starting local enterprises in response has now begun in earnest and, as this book sets out, is seen as the next key stage in the evolution of the Transition movement (for more see *Building* 2: Social enterprise and entrepreneurship, page 239).

Media interest. One of the most remarkable facts about Transition Network is that it has only ever done one press release, and that was in the summer of 2009.[11] In spite of this, Transition has featured in all the main newspapers, in *Elle* magazine, the cover of *The New Yorker* magazine, on Michael Portillo's *Great British Railway Journeys*, and on BBC's *The One Show*, which included the bizarre spectacle of Westlife handing each other Totnes Pounds . . .

Malvern's MP Harriett Baldwin speaks about what Transition means to her at the Unleashing of Transition Malvern Hills.

Transition Heathrow. The interface between Transition and the protest movement, especially around climate change, has been often discussed. A remarkable example emerged in Heathrow where, following the cancelling of the proposed third runway, a group of climate activists occupied a derelict market garden, turning it into a community resource and once again growing food in the glasshouses. A statement provided by Daljinder Bassi of the Safer Neighbourhood Team, Heathrow Villages and Metropolitan Police Hillingdon, in support of the group when they were threatened with eviction, stated that "there is evidence to show that crime has reduced since the Grow Heathrow Group has occupied the neglected Berkeley Nurseries. Possibly the presence of the group acts as a deterrent for crime in the surrounding area. Positive feedback has been received from local residents regarding the group, and that the local residents feel safer knowing that there are people staying there. The evidence shows a reduction in motor vehicle crime in the area by **50 per cent** and a general reduction in crime of **25 per cent**."[12]

Energy Institute / Department of Energy and Climate Change event. In March 2010, the soon-to-be-outgoing Labour government held a seminar at the Energy Institute, the first event where government began to explore the potential impacts of peak oil and their mitigation. Around 25 people were invited, from industry, academia, business and government, and also two of us from Transition Network, which felt like an amazing acknowledgement of Transition's work.[13] Asked to give a presentation, we began with discussing Elizabeth Kubler-Ross's 'Five Stages of Grief', which suggests that people pass through stages of denial, anger, bargaining, depression and acceptance when they encounter grief. Whereas the government is stuck at denial, Transition initiatives have passed through depression and arrived at acceptance, showing what is possible; as such, they are significantly ahead of government thinking on the matter.

Transition 'endorsements'. Some of the most fascinating new developments in Transition appear when you least expect them. In May 2010 I travelled to Malvern for the Unleashing of Transition Malvern Hills, and halfway through that amazing event, a short session called 'Transition Endorsements' brought on to the stage 11 local people to say what Transition meant to them. They were the local MP, the head of the local police, the CEO of the local council, the principal of the local school, and so on. It was a remarkable testament to how deep the work of Transition Malvern Hills had gone in such a short time, and the regard with which they are viewed (see Tools for Transition No.17: Speaking up for Transition, page 231).

A community garden in Mölndal in Sweden run by members of Transition Gothenburg.
Photo: Jan Forsmark

Diversity conference. One of the key challenges for Transition initiatives is to make them as inclusive as possible. This is explored in more detail in *Starting out* 2: Inclusion and diversity (page 94), but one of the key developments in this was a two-day conference in Edinburgh in November 2010 called 'Diverse Routes to Belonging', which explored issues of diversity, what it means to be indigenous and how Transition initiatives can ensure they appeal to and include as broad a cross section of their communities as possible (see page 94) .

Sweden and France. Sweden is an interesting example of Transition spreading very fast. In 2010, Transition Sweden saw its website attract over 2,000 members, and over 90 Transition initiatives were set up across the country. Transition Sweden ran 30 seminars across the country about Transition, attended by over 1,200 people. Transition Network also recently received an email from France that read: "There's a real frenzy about Transition right now. The public and media interest is growing fast, there must be around 15 established groups and one or two dozen more mulling across the country . . . two national meetings (one for the north and one for the south) and many conferences are to take place this month." This is not centrally controlled or coordinated; rather, a fascinating example of self-organisation in practice.

These, as I say, are just my own highlights. Each individual Transition initiative will have its own moments that made it pause and say "whoa!" This, for me, is one of the most rewarding things about Transition – how it never does what you expect it to but it delights and amazes in many unexpected ways. The idea of 'letting it go where it wants to go' is central to Transition. Transition can be very challenging for control freaks . . . it develops its own momentum and, because it builds on what those involved feel passionately about, it tends to head off in many unexpected, but usually delightful, directions . . .

"The change in direction represented by the Transition movement is as profound as any intentional change experienced by a civilisation."
Dr David Fleming

CHAPTER TWO

Why Transition initiatives do what they do

People get involved in their local Transition initiatives for a range of reasons. Although when Transition started it was framed very much as a response to peak oil and climate change, as time has passed and the idea has taken root in more and more places, it has been fascinating to see the wide range of reasons why people get involved. They include the following.

Because it feels way more fun than not doing it

Many people get involved because it is fun, because they get to meet and do stuff with new people, and because it is more exciting, nourishing and rewarding than not doing it. There's the man in Lancaster who told me that even if nothing else ever came from his Transition group, he now knows 200 people he didn't know before he got involved. There's the woman in Tooting who told me "I've lived in Tooting for 22 years, but I think I've lived more in Tooting in the past two years since I've been involved in Transition than I have in the last 20 years." There's the experienced retired market gardener who found, through his local Transition group, an opportunity to pass his skills on to a new generation of young people . . .

When Steph Bradley of Transition Network walked around the UK visiting Transition initiatives,[1] again and again she heard tales of people engaged in Transition because they felt part of something really dynamic happening in their community. Very few people wanted detailed discussions about oil depletion rates or the latest reports on climate change; instead, they wanted to tell their stories about how their work with Transition was exciting them. The aim of this book is to capture and draw together some of these stories.

> "It is best to think of this as a revolution, not of guns, but of consciousness, which will be won by seizing the key myths, archetypes, eschatologies and ecstasies so that life won't seem worth living unless one is on the transforming energy's side."
> Gary Snyder[2]

There is a palpable buzz that emerges from Transition projects. I have been to events in town and village halls or city venues, where hundreds of people have come together to celebrate the

Transition can lead to the production of beautiful things, such as these tickets for a Marsden and Slaithwaite Transition Towns (MASTT) event in 2009. *Photo: Rose Bridger*

Transition Belsize transforming the corner of their local Premiere Inn hotel car park into a raised-bed food-growing bonanza.
Photo: Sarah Nicholl

possibilities a more localised, lower-energy world could offer. Local currency launches, where local people, dignitaries and traders come together to celebrate the launch of the community's own money. 'Unleashings' – big launch events that celebrate the place, its culture and a vision of the town's future, featuring stories, choirs, food, dance, speeches and the sharing of hopes and visions, and where the sense of excitement is evident for all.

Because of wanting a fairer world

There is a strong argument[3] that the more equal a society becomes, almost all desirable social indicators, such as literacy and life expectancy, rise, while undesirable ones, such as teenage pregnancies and mental illness, fall. The gulf between rich and poor continues to rise, with many damaging impacts on global society. Many people are motivated to engage in Transition because a more local economy, in which assets and key enterprises are owned and managed by and on behalf of the local community, offers a far better route to social justice, as well as local economic resilience, than business-as-usual does. This is particularly pertinent in the current economic climate of austerity, with deep cuts and closure of services leading increasingly to a sense of injustice and unfairness.

Because of peak oil

One of the key concerns underpinning the Transition approach is peak oil. Oil, as Tony Blair once noted, is the 'lifeblood' of Western economies. Producing oil from a single oilfield follows a particular pattern. About halfway through its lifespan, production starts to tail away. Whether it actually looks like a peak or a more gently downward plateau, this

"How might greater equality and policies to reduce carbon emissions go together? Given what inequality does to a society, and particularly how it heightens competitive consumption, it looks not only as if the two are complementary, but also as if governments may be unable to make big enough cuts in carbon emissions without reducing inequality."
Richard Wilkinson and Kate Pickett[4]

"... we don't know when exactly the oil is going to start peaking and production is going to start running down, but ... we don't as a nation want to be putting ourselves in hock ... to these sorts of markets ..."

Chris Huhne, UK Energy Secretary, December 2010, interviewed on BBC Radio 4's *Today* programme

– energy output / energy input = 100:1, a remarkable return. Now it is somewhere around 20:1.) As we pass into the downward half, we find the 'easy' oil is gone. We are finding fewer and fewer new oil fields. Those we do find are smaller and in less accessible places, the energy we get back compared to what we put in is far lower, and the resultant oil is more expensive. It is a very different new world.

"By 2012, surplus oil production capacity could entirely disappear and, as early as 2015, the shortfall in output could reach nearly 10 MBD [million barrels per day]."

The US Joint Operating Environment 2010 report, February 2010

pattern is seen over and over in individual oilfields, and indeed in the oil production of whole nations. Of the 105 current or former oil-producing nations, 65 are thought to have passed their geologically imposed production peak.[5] When might the world pass its overall peak in production?

It is not a question, as is often misunderstood, of 'running out of oil'. We started running out of oil, of course, the moment we started using it (in the same way as you started 'running out of' this book when you started reading it). In that regard, peak oil makes little difference. However, why it does matter, and matters very much, is because it marks a historic shift from the world's economy having more oil available every year globally to having less. In a world fixated with the idea of perpetual growth, we don't tend to do very well at having less of things, especially of things on which we are so dependent.

Also, one side of the peak is very different from the other. On the upward side of the past 150 years (or the 'Age of Cheap Oil', if you like), oil has mostly been relatively inexpensive. It has been easy to produce, has been extracted from accessible places and relatively little energy has been needed to make it possible to extract far more energy. (In the 1930s, one unit of energy put into oil production could harvest 100 units of energy in the oil produced

It is important here to distinguish between 'conventional' and 'unconventional' oil. Conventional oil – the sweet crude that comes gushing out of the ground under pressure – defined the last 150 years. The International Energy Agency (IEA), which had spent many years previously deriding the idea of peak oil, announced in one sentence tucked away in its 2010 World Energy Outlook[6] that "crude oil output never regains its all-time peak of 70 million barrels per day reached in 2006", and that output is now rapidly depleting. What is now making up the shortfall is what is referred to as 'unconventional oil', which includes deep-sea oil production, tar-sands oil production and making oil from coal. These unconventional oils make conventional oil production look 'green'. They have far higher carbon emissions, use much more water, produce a lot more pollution and lower-grade fuels and often give us an energy return closer to 5:1 or less. Although some people argue that improving technology means that what are currently 'unconventional' fuels will one day become the new 'conventional' fuels (e.g. gas from coal), this is still a long way from reality, if indeed it is possible.

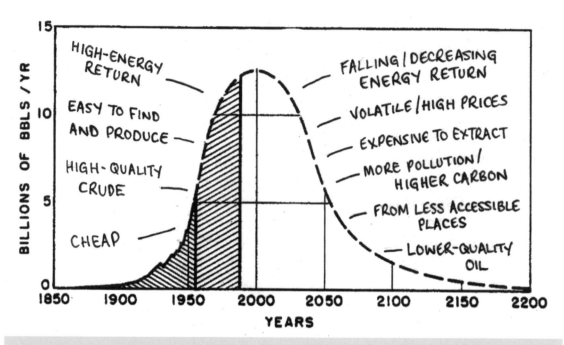

The Oil Age: a game of two halves! (With apologies to M. King Hubbert's classic 1956 peak oil graph.)

Globally, oil production has largely been on a plateau since May 2005, and, in early 2011, as the price of oil started to rise again, concerns have been raised by the IEA that economic recovery will be very difficult in a world of high or volatile oil prices. The exact date of the peak is often debated, but in reality it is something we will only be able to see in hindsight. The forecasts of most relevant organisations have been steadily moved from further in the future back to nearer the present, many putting the date at any time between now and 2015. Others have expressed concern that stated world oil reserves could have been exaggerated by up to a third,[7] and documents made available by WikiLeaks in February 2011[8] suggested that Saudi Arabia's reserves may have been overstated by as much as 300bn barrels – almost 40 per cent.

A 2005 report that looked in detail at how much time the US economy would need to prepare for the peak[9] argued it would need 20 years, or 10 if the response were akin to a wartime mobilisation. Given this timescale, whether peak oil happens now or in five years is neither here nor there. We rely hugely on the unreliable, moving from a time where our sense of success and who we are is directly linked to how much oil we consume, to a time where our oil dependency is a key vulnerability.

"Oil prices are entering a dangerous zone for the global economy. The oil import bills are becoming a threat to the economic recovery. This is a wake-up call to the oil-consuming countries and to the oil producers. It is not in the interest of anyone to see such high prices. Oil exporters need clients with healthy economies but these high prices will sooner or later make the economies sick, which would mean the need for importing oil will be less."
Fatih Birol, International Energy Agency, January 2010[10]

Because it means they can do that project they have always dreamed of

Transition creates a space and a context within which people are invited to get going on projects they are passionate about, with the support of a larger organisation and with connections to other projects. Events such as Open Space (see Tools for Transition No.15: Community brainstorming tools, page 220) let people meet others who share the same passions, to create an environment in which it feels natural to start and make things happen. Start a community bakery? A farm? An energy company? A food garden on the roof of your local supermarket? Why not?

Because of climate change

The basic notion of climate change, that carbon dioxide and water vapour trap energy from the sun in the Earth's atmosphere and stop it being bounced back out into space, was established in the mid-nineteenth century. Without that process, our planet would be 20-30°C colder than it is today. Since then, due to the combustion of fossil fuels, the average temperature of the planet has risen by 0.8°C, and due to the time lag between greenhouse gases being released and their impact, we know that a further 0.6°C rise is unavoidable regardless of what we do today.

The body of scientific evidence supporting the idea that human activity, largely through the combustion of hydrocarbons, is changing the climate is overwhelming. This is not intended to be a comprehensive guide (for some good primers and sources of up-to-date information on climate change, see Resources section). I am going to focus on the science that emerged in 2010, a year that provided alarming new data and broke many climate records.

Pressing apples on the Scilly Isles.
Photo: Jonathan Smith

"What is happening now in our central regions is evidence of this global climate change, because we have never in our history faced such weather conditions in the past."
Russian President Dmitry Medvedev, December 2010

- December 2009 to November 2010 was, according to NASA,[11] globally the hottest year on record. Nineteen countries broke their all-time temperature records,[12] with Pakistan recording a temperature of 53.3°C, and record temperatures in Russia leading to the country's worst-ever forest fires.

- The Earth's warmer atmosphere is now able to hold 4 per cent more water vapour than before, resulting in more storms and floods, and an increase of total global rainfall of 1.5 per cent a decade.[13] On this evidence, it is impossible to absolutely attribute to climate change individual events such as the Australian, Brazilian or Sri Lankan floods of early 2011, but, as James Hansen puts it, "would recent extreme events have occurred if atmospheric carbon dioxide had remained at its pre-industrial level of 280 parts per million? The appropriate answer is 'almost certainly not'."[14]

- East Siberia's vast stores of undersea methane, containing 1.5 trillion tonnes of carbon – twice that presently in the world's atmosphere – have begun to melt and release methane.[15]

- Warming of the world's soils means they are releasing CO_2 at much greater rates than had been predicted. "There's a big pulse of carbon dioxide coming off the surface of the soil everywhere in the world," said ecologist Ben Bond-Lamberty of the US Department of Energy's Pacific Northwest National Laboratory.[16] One 2005 study[17] that looked at soils in England and Wales found they had become a net emitter of CO_2, losing 13 million tons of carbon per year, regardless of the form of land use, which suggested that warming was to blame.

- Sea ice in the Arctic continues to decline in both extent and thickness, and by December 2010 had reached the third lowest extent ever recorded. Mark Serreze, Director of the US National Snow and Ice Data Center, was quoted as saying "all indications are that sea ice will continue to decline over the next several decades. We are still looking at a seasonally ice-free Arctic in twenty to thirty years."[18]

- 2010's drought in the Amazon rainforest meant that the forest, usually expected to be a net absorber of carbon dioxide, emitted more CO_2 than the whole of the United States. The previous drought on such a scale, in 2005, was said by scientists to have been a once-in-a-lifetime drought. The Amazon's becoming a net emitter of greenhouse gases has been predicted in many climate models, and would appear to be rapidly becoming a reality.[19]

Climate change is often talked of in a future tense, that we need to do things now to prevent future disasters, but for those who have suffered from fire, drought and flooding on a Biblical scale over the last few years the impacts of climate change have already arrived.

"It may seem impossible to imagine that a technologically advanced society could choose, in essence, to destroy itself, but that is what we are now in the process of doing."
Elizabeth Kolbert[20]

So if we are to reduce our carbon emissions in order to avoid runaway climate change, what scale of cuts are we looking at? One of the most detailed studies of this[21] concluded that the world's emissions will need to have peaked by 2020 and that a 72 per cent cut by 2050 will give us an 84 per cent chance of avoiding runaway climate change. In practical terms, this means that where we are heading in terms of personal emissions is somewhere between an 86 and 92 per cent reduction on 1990 levels by 2050. It is worth stopping to read that twice.

To put that figure in perspective, it is roughly the per-capita emissions produced by Mozambique today. On top of this, there are those who argue that our current emissions are deceptively low because they don't take into account all the goods we import, and the emissions caused by their manufacture and transportation.[22] Creating a low-carbon economy is, after all, much easier if you no longer manufacture anything. It is estimated that around a quarter of China's emissions come from producing goods for export. With the average UK carbon footprint being 9.7 tonnes, our imports of goods add another 4.7 tonnes per person, amounting to nearly 50 per cent.[23] It is clear that the challenge of climate change is about far more than low-energy bulbs, solar panels and slower driving speeds. It is about a profound shift in what we do and how we do it; a complete adjustment of what we imagine to be lying in front of us, of our expectations of the future. Many people would think it is completely unachievable. But let's move forward into this book, keeping the option open that it might actually just about be do-able, and see where it gets us.

> "The only plausible explanation for the rise in weather-related catastrophes is climate change."
> Munich Re Insurance[24]

Because of fear

Fear is a natural, reasonable and powerful motivator. It is hard to look at the data on peak oil and climate change, as we have just done, and not feel fearful in the pit of your stomach. For some, engaging in Transition is their way of acting in order to stay sane. Sitting on our own feeling fearful is a wretched state that I wouldn't wish on anyone. While engaging in Transition may not make the fear go away, working with others and sharing your fears and hopes can be a lifesaver, and a way of avoiding feeling overwhelmed. This is one of the reasons that the idea that Transition is also an inner process has been hard-wired into the concept.

Because of the economic crisis

The crisis most in the public eye since 2008 hasn't been peak oil or climate change. It has been the economic crisis: the mountain of debt we have accumulated during the huge party that the Age of Cheap Oil made possible. This intense period of economic unravelling has been fascinating, terrifying and enlightening. The issuing of money as debt means that economic growth has become necessary just to stand still. This has spiralled debt to levels that can never be fully repaid. Governments can borrow money on the financial markets only because those markets have faith that they will be repaid. That faith is in turn based on the expectation that taxes will be paid on income from increased future GDP.

One of the pillars of economic growth is cheap energy, which enables economic growth. As Jeff Rubin, Chief Economist at CIBC World Markets, puts it, "virtually every dollar of world GDP requires

energy to produce".[25] I have yet to see a convincing argument as to how economic growth will be possible in a world of volatile oil prices. Indeed, Fatih Birol of the International Energy Agency warned in 2011 that oil prices are entering the 'danger zone', which could derail any fragile economic growth under way.[26]

> "Conventional economic growth and cheap oil have marched hand in hand for the best part of 60 years; within just a few years, it will have become increasingly apparent that both are on their last legs."
> Jonathan Porritt[27]

Part of the reason for the current economic crisis has been the excessive risks bankers have taken with our money. Risk-taking is endemic in the financial services sector, where money is made by gambling on currencies rising or falling, making

Using local materials, such as straw bales, to retrofit homes, could help revive local economies. *Photo: Yannick Molin*

In uncertain times, which offers communities more protection and makes them more resilient: a vibrant diverse economy of local shops, or a dependence on supermarket chains? *Photos: Lou Brown*

unstable economies more lucrative than stable ones. This instability can be disastrous. A boom economy is highly destructive, leading to over-consumption and debt; a bust economy leads to great uncertainty and misery.

Pursuing economic growth at all costs is proving to be our undoing. A growing economy by necessity consumes more resources, and produces more carbon emissions, pollution and debt, yet doesn't necessarily make us any happier. If the economy manages 3 per cent per year growth over the next 100 years, it will mean a doubling of economic activity every 23 years.[28] By 2100, which many children born today will see, global consumption will have increased by around 1,600 per cent. And this on a planet already groaning under the weight of industrial activity and the over-exploitation of

> "If we want to thrive, we need to move from a growth imperative to a resilience imperative."
> Thomas Homer-Dixon[29]

resources. Professor Roderick Smith of Imperial College London argues that at those rates of growth, between now and 2100 we will have used 16 times as many economic resources as humanity has used since it mastered the arts of fire and flint knapping.[30]

Although the idea is often touted that a low-carbon economy with economic growth is possible, experience indicates that it is only when economies stop growing that carbon emissions fall. For example, the UK's carbon emissions fell for the first time in 2009 by 8.7 per cent, as a result of the economic downturn.[31] The idea of an economy that doesn't grow any more is usually presented as a disaster. Yet is there life beyond growth? Professor Tim Jackson of the University of Surrey has called for a shift from quantitative to qualitative growth. He argues that the term 'prosperity' needs redefining,[32] and that levels of education, equity, happiness and well-being, amongst other things, are better indications of prosperity than GDP. Japan's economy, for example, hasn't grown since the mid-1990s. Although it can't be called a 'steady state economy' (it is not a 'one planet' economy by any means), Japan was, before the catastrophic earthquake and tsunami of 2011, perhaps one of the first 'post-

> "The politicians know just how cata-strophic it is going to be, and just think well there's nothing we can do so we're just going to not bother telling them … fiddle around, drop the interest rate … I believe we are heading towards The End of Days, economically speaking, and that you'd better get yourself an allotment, personally."
>
> Jeremy Clarkson, speaking on BBC Radio 5 Live, 4 December 2008[33]

growth' nations; the trains ran on time, unemployment was only 5 per cent, literacy was high and it had the highest life expectancy in the world.[34]

Governments are still talking about getting 'back to growth', while debates grow as to whether that is a good thing. The UK government has introduced 'well-being indicators' alongside others, but is still wedded to the concept of growth. It is possible (depending on the theory) that our economies can return to growth. However, it is reasonable to ask whether what we are going to see isn't growth, or a 'double-dip' recession, but rather what Richard

> "It is not like an ordinary reces-sion where you lose output and get it back quickly. You may not get it back for many years, if ever, and that is a big long-run loss of living standards for all people in this country."
>
> Mervyn King, Governor, Bank of England, March 2011[35]

Heinberg has termed an 'L-shaped' recovery – a continued contraction until we reach a stable point.

I don't know whether economist Nicole Foss ('Stoneleigh') is right when she talks of an imminent economic crash,[36] or whether Herman Daly is right when he argues that a 'steady-state' economy is a possibility.[37] I do know that businessman Martin Sorrell was wrong in 2008 when he told the BBC that 2009 would be a tough year but that the economy would recover in 2010 due to the World Cup football and the Winter Olympics in Vancouver.[38] Economies, he smoothly told millions of listeners across the UK, are cyclical, moving from one state to another. Economic cycles are a natural phenom enon – underpinned, presumably, by the occurrence of major international sporting events. Well, at least we know that prognosis was wrong.

Given the events of the years since 2008, when bankers' risk-taking brought the economy to the brink of collapse (or, in Ireland's case, over the brink), and while we struggle with the huge debts they created (and they are paying bonuses again), I take talk of 'economic recovery' with a large pinch of salt. For me, the best place to invest in is your local community. The best debts are those that are as small as possible. Economic growth and renewed prosperity will come in a large part from diverse, vibrant and robust local economies. The best response we can make to our economic instability is to shift our support to an economy based on social justice, resilience and protection of the biosphere. Nothing else makes sense.

Because it feels like the most appropriate thing to be doing

This is what blogger and writer Sharon Astyk calls 'The Theory of Anyway'. She argues that what Transition promotes – living more simply, using less, reconnecting to our local economy and to more seasonal foods – are what she would still be doing 'anyway', even if climate change proved to be no longer a problem, or peak oil was 'solved'. She says this because "they are the right thing to do on many levels", connecting us more with place, with each other and with ourselves.

> "We are living in extraordinary times: 2008 is likely to be seen by our children as a watershed moment – the end of a glittering party, when we consumed, celebrated and indulged ourselves like we were guests at a table groaning with good things that would never end. Circumstances demand we become wiser now."
>
> Paula Reed, fashion journalist for *Grazia* magazine[39]

Transition Town Totnes's Transition Streets project (see page 201) was built on fun and community-building. *Image: Transition Town Totnes*

The aspects of Transition I am involved with where I live are some of the most exciting things in my life. As well as the social side, the new friendships and connections I have made, what excites me is the changes happening around me. Already in my community, after four years of the Transition process here, I can walk the streets and see trees we have planted, food gardens that exist because of our work and solar photovoltaic panels on the town hall and on many homes in streets across the town. Friends of mine have cut their carbon emissions and met new people thanks to projects we have run. Then there are the larger-scale, longer-term projects – the community energy company I now own shares in; the proposed community farm; the project aiming to bring a large site in the town into community ownership and to develop it as a community asset.

There is a palpable sense that something is turning, a momentum is building; and people come from around the world to visit this place because of the stories of what it has achieved. In that sense, whether you believe in climate change or peak oil is neither here nor there (although an understanding of them clearly helps shape the work that Transition initiatives do). Rather, Transition is an invitation to be part of changing the place you live, to be part of a process of making it more entrepreneurial, better connected, happier and healthier. Do we make change happen by striving to shock or depress everyone into action, or by creating a thrilling, fascinating process that people can put their shoulders to if they wish?

> "In our view, things have to get better before they can get better. Immiseration theory – the view that increasing suffering leads to progressive social change – has been repeatedly discredited by history."
>
> Ted Nordhaus and Michael Shellenberger[40]

"Because it gives me hope ..."

Hope is in pretty short supply these days. Constant grim news about climate change, the economy, a wide range of environmental issues, job losses, inflation and so on, can leave people feeling hopeless. A sense of powerlessness can take over and leave people feeling numb, that nothing's going to change, no one cares and it's all too late. Transition, for many people, is a way back into feeling that it is possible to make a difference.

A study in 2009 of Transition Norwich[41] found that around a third of those involved had at some point been involved with environmental or community initiatives, but had left feeling burnt out and ineffective. Transition had re-energised and brought them back in (although as we shall see, burnout is still a risk, as it is in any field of activism). We often underestimate the power of hope – what in Transition we call 'engaged optimism'. Getting started and making change in our lives is a hopeful activity that touches people deeply.

Two ways of thinking about our predicament

At the heart of Transition is a concern about energy. We can use terms like 'energy security' and 'vulnerability'; 'peak oil' or 'peak gas', but no one has yet come up with a better term than I saw in an email, translated not very well from French into English, from a conference in Paris I had been invited to speak at. They had entitled the session 'Energetic Precariousness', which captured it beautifully. So when we look at energetic precariousness, especially of peak oil and climate change, the following two illustrations of mine may help. They show how Transition shifts the thinking around these issues.

This classic peak oil graph of M. King Hubbert, the man who first coined the concept of 'peak oil', shows world oil production peaking and declining. I have added a few embellishments ... In the bottom left-hand corner is our intrepid mountaineer: you or I. Between 1850 and now, we have valiantly and

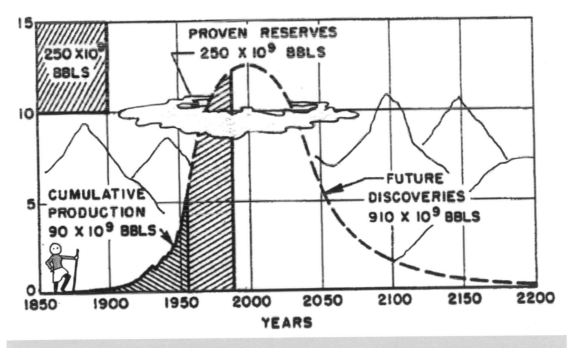

Should we view the oil age as a vast mountain we have valiantly conquered? (With repeated apologies to M. King Hubbert; I hope he would have approved of my doodling on his graphs.) ...

heroically climbed to the top of the energy mountain. It now takes around 86 million barrels of oil a day just to keep everything working, to keep the global economy ticking over, and to enable those of us in the global north to remain fed, clothed and generally provided for.

Standing at the top of this energy mountain means we can, in effect, see further than previous generations and have had experiences they could only dream of. We have power at our fingertips that our great-grandparents could never have imagined. We can pop to New York to go shopping, eat apples from the other side of the world and drive at well over 100mph (although that's not something this book is advocating). Looking at this as a mountain gives us a sense of the dizzying heights we have scaled in a short time, as well as a clear sense of the huge challenge ahead as we meet the change from more cheap energy every year to less.

The Age of Cheap Oil has been an extraordinary time. I feel remarkably fortunate to have experienced some of the luxuries and opportunities it

presented. But while seeing this era as a mountain is useful in understanding where we are, it is less useful in helping us design a safe way forward. This is where, as a society, we get stuck; where our politicians appear paralysed.

When trying to work out a safe way down, there is a psychological problem with the perception of moving away from something somehow irreplaceable. We can feel we are leaving behind something that can never be recaptured. Moving towards a lower-carbon, less-energy-intensive future becomes a move away from something better, from 'what might have been'. I liken it to trying to persuade a child to come home at the end of a birthday party where he or she has consumed far too many sugary cakes and drinks. The child has to be coaxed and dragged along. It is this very perception that moving beyond the peak means moving away from something irreplaceable that paralyses government responses, that means that so many of us dismiss peak oil and climate change or stick our heads in the sand. So in Transition we ask how might it be if we were, instead, to turn that picture upside down . . .

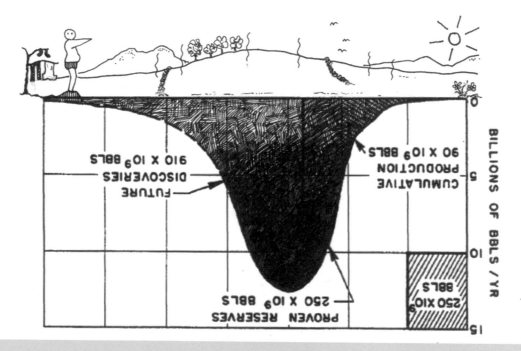

. . . or as a deep, dark lagoon we are currently plumbing the depths of?

Recognitions underpinning the Transition response

- Climate change and peak oil require urgent action.
- Life with less energy is inevitable. It is better to plan for it than to be taken by surprise.
- Industrial society has lost the resilience to be able to cope with energy shocks.
- We have to act together, now.
- Infinite growth within a finite system (such as planet Earth) is impossible.
- We demonstrated great ingenuity and intelligence as we raced up the energy curve over the last 150 years. There's no reason why we can't use those qualities, and more, as we negotiate our way up from the depths back towards the sun and air.
- If we plan and act early enough, and use our creativity and cooperation to unleash the genius within our local communities, we can build a future far more fulfilling and enriching, more connected to and more gentle on the Earth, than the life we have today.

. . . and instead look at the Age of Cheap Oil as being like a deep, dark, fetid lagoon (apologies once again to Mr Hubbert for my continued desecration of his lovely graph). We dived into it 150 years ago because we were told that if we dived deeply enough, we would find great wealth that would bring us great happiness, like Aztec gold in a mountain lake. The fossil fuel age promised so much: holidays on the moon, hoverboards, a leisure society, the 'trickling down' of great wealth to everybody.

Over the years, we have dived deeper and deeper, yet, the deeper we have gone, more and more indicators have been telling us this is not a good idea. Climate change, the wide range of other environmental effects, the depletion of non-renewable resources, and the fact that consuming more and more stuff has failed to make those in the UK happier since 1961[42] are all signs we should radically change how we live.

We are now the most indebted generation ever. Total UK personal debt at the end of January 2010 stood at £1,463bn, and the average owed by every UK adult was £30,306 (including mortgages).[43] In September 2010, UK public sector net debt was £952.8 billion (or 64.6 per cent of National GDP),[44] and it is estimated that UK national debt will rise close to 100 per cent of GDP by 2012.

As we have gone deeper and further into the gloom, it has become harder for us to see each other and we begin to feel more and more isolated, lonelier, less nourished.[45] Now we find ourselves rooting around in the sticky tar sands at the bottom of the lagoon, pursuing the illusory treasure that can never guarantee our happiness. Our climate is irrevocably altered with records being broken every year, and our economy's dependence on oil has left it vulnerable and fragile.

When we see it like this, the move away from oil dependency, from high-carbon living, is no longer a move away from something, but rather a push towards something.

A push towards clean air, sunshine, beauty, rediscovering each other; community and celebration. This is a key shift in our perception. The difference between change that feels like being torn away from something and change that feels like moving towards something is huge. This is the approach Transition takes. It suggests that collective intentional transition could lead us to a far better place than where we are today. Who's to say that the world we see today is the best we could ever do?

CHAPTER THREE

Where we might be headed: the power of future scenarios

Many people far more learned than I am have tried to look forward to what we might be moving into over the coming years. Taking an interest in peak oil, climate change and economics leads to one being introduced to a wildly eclectic mixture of opinions, models, world views and people, each with differing senses of what kind of future may lie ahead of us. One can identify three mindsets that underpin these scenarios:

- **Adaptation:** Scenarios that assume we can invent our way out of trouble.
- **Evolution:** Scenarios that need collective evolution, a change of attitude/heart, but which assume that society, more localised and more frugal with energy, will retain its coherence.
- **Collapse:** Scenarios that assume the outcome of peak oil, climate change and the end of economic growth will be fracturing and disintegration, sudden or gradual, of society as we know it.

There are those who believe that peak oil means we are about to see an imminent collapse, a rapid unravelling of civilisation, and the emergence of a new Dark Age. In such a scenario, the only thing one can do at this stage is to acquire survival skills and try to raise awareness about 'what's coming'.[1] There are those who believe that the contraction and fragmenting of society is inevitable, albeit over a longer time period, and that the best response is to gather and communicate those survival skills through networks of people who share that sense of desperation.[2]

Then there are those who believe technology can solve all our problems, that energy constraints stem merely from a lack of imagination, and that all challenges can be overcome by our collective brilliance. This school of thought assumes that design is our most powerful tool, that cities can be redesigned, reimagined and recreated as zero-carbon, lean, green, highly efficient urban centres, and that resource constraints are sufficiently distant to allow the radical overhauling of our infrastructure.[3]

It is important at this point to note that scenarios are not the same as predictions. They offer a choice of stories about the future, and are rooted in what is plausible, even though they may take us out of what is familiar. They help us to see that change is a necessity, and that we can anticipate it and plan proactively for it. Shell International, which does a lot of work with scenarios, in particular through its 'Signals and Signposts' research,[4] argues that:

> "Good scenarios are ones that explore the possible, not just the probable – providing a relevant challenge to the conventional wisdom of their users, and helping them prepare for the major changes ahead. They will provide a useful context for debate, leading to better policy and strategy, and a shared understanding of, and commitment to, actions."[5]

In *The Transition Handbook*, I reviewed many of the scenarios people have proposed in relation to peak oil, and arranged them in a continuum from the techno-escapist to the collapse scenarios, shown in the diagram on pages 42-43.

Of these, I find the clearest and most useful set of scenarios, which are used in Transition Trainings, are David Holmgren's.[6] They are:

- **Techno-explosion:** The idea that unimaginable new energy sources are discovered which allow colonisation of new planets and the overcoming of environmental constraints.

- **Green-tech stability:** A seamless transition to a steady-state economy that is powered by renewable energy.
- **Earth stewardship:** The impact of depleting resources on the economy lessens economic activity and a powering down of society, with increased localisation.
- **Atlantis:** Our complex, non-resilient economies cannot cope with fossil fuel depletion, economic contraction and climate change, and suffer rapid and chaotic collapse.

One aspect of these scenarios that is especially interesting is the tension between 'green-tech stability' and 'Earth stewardship', or energy descent. In trainings I have participated in with local authorities, you often hear people say things like "we're already doing Transition, because we recycle". Holmgren's scenarios are so useful because they help distinguish between a more business-as-usual sustainability approach, which attempts to reduce the carbon emissions of our current model, and the Transition approach of designing for a very different economic model – one based on resilience and localisation.

If pushed to pin down what I see as the most likely of these as we move forward, I would say that Transition designs for energy descent, seeing the first two of Holmgren's scenarios as unfeasible, and the last as avoidably pessimistic. A designed transition, an intentional powering down, is, in the long run, the only viable course of action, and the sooner we embark on it the greater our chance of success. There is, however, a fascinating and very live tension between the fact that in our current economic paradigm, techno-stability is undoubtedly attractive, and for existing businesses to leap into models designed for 'energy descent' scenarios would be a brave step indeed. It may be that there is a case for using existing organisations, in their pursuit of 'techno-stability' solutions, to put in place infrastructure that would be key to 'energy descent' scenarios.

For example, if an existing food retail chain were to decide that to lower its carbon footprint it could

> "If some of these answers seem radical or far-fetched today, then I say wait until tomorrow. Soon it will be abundantly clear that it is business as usual that is utopian, whereas creating something very new and different is a practical necessity."
> James Gustave Speth[7]

undertake to create a number of new market gardens around a city, and to plant new orchards, that infrastructure will be useful in the future regardless. It is my experience with councils, however, that once they understand the distinction between the two scenarios, creatively thinking about energy descent brings out inspired ideas. (This was also the experience of Transition Taunton Deane's visioning work with its local council – see page 115.) While planning and designing for the kind of intentional localisation that the energy descent scenarios call for, Transition also keeps one eye on collapse as a possibility. The degree to which it should be preparing in parallel for that is one of the livelier debates within the Transition movement.[8]

A visioning activity from the 2010 Transition Network conference.

SCENARIOS FOR LIFE BEYOND THE OIL PEAK [9]

Urban Colonies (Foresight)
A future of compact sustainable cities, with energy-efficient public transport systems, more isolated rural areas and reduced consumption.

Green-tech Stability (Holmgren)
Outlines the idea that business as usual can continue indefinitely, with renewable energy replacing conventional energy, hydrogen cars replacing existing cars, and so on.

Conventional Worlds (Gallopin)
This scenario is essentially business as usual, not deviating sharply from the present.

Business as Usual (FEASTA)
Puts oil peak at 2030, with the government doing nothing to pre-empt its arrival.

Waiting for the Magic Elixir (Heinberg)
A new energy source as abundant and versatile as oil is developed, such as cold fusion or the mythological 'free energy'.

Perpetual Motion (Foresight)
A zero-emissions hi-tech hydrogen economy; assumes that globalisation is still in place, with strong demand for travel.

Techno-explosion (Holmgren)
Technology solves every problem we are currently presented with, leading to a world of holidays on the moon, unlimited nuclear cold fusion, etc.

Last One Standing (Heinberg)
Describes a scenario where military force is used to secure remaining world hydrocarbon reserves; Dick Cheney's "war that will never end in our lifetimes".

Atlantis (Holmgren)
This scenario describes a sudden and catastrophic societal collapse.

Barbarisation Worlds (Gallopin)
Like Holmgren's 'Atlantis' scenario, this scenario projects a deterioration in civilisation, as problems overwhelm the coping capacity of both markets and policies.

Green-tech Stability
Urban Colonies
Conventional Worlds
Business as Usual
Waiting for the Magic Elixir
Perpetual Motion
Techno-explosion
Last One Standing
Atlantis
Barbarisation Worlds

ADAPTATION

COLLAPSE

Enlightened Transition (FEASTA)

Assumes that the government decides "to use energy which is much cheaper now than it will ever be again to develop Irish energy sources and to reduce the amount of energy required to maintain and run the Irish economy". This results in an economy much more prepared for the peak when it does eventually arrive.

Powerdown (Heinberg)

"The path of cooperation, conservation and sharing", a government-led strategy utilising all the resources at its disposal to reduce per-capita consumption and build the post-fossil-fuel economy and infrastructure.

Good Intentions (Foresight)

A world in which a system of rigorous carbon rationing has been introduced, leading to reduced traffic volumes and more mass transportation.

Fair Shares (FEASTA)

Assumes peak oil in 2007, but a rapid government response including the introduction of carbon rationing alongside a concerted effort to reduce energy use in all areas, and the relocalisation of most aspects of daily life.

The Great Transition (Gallopin)

This scenario "incorporates visionary solutions to the sustainability challenge, including fundamental changes in the prevailing values as well as novel socio-economic arrangements".

Earth Stewardship (Holmgren)

Here "human society creatively descends the energy demand slope essentially as a 'mirror image' of the creative energy ascent that occurred between the onset of the industrial revolution and the present day".

Enforced Localisation (FEASTA)

Assumes oil peak in 2007 leading to a drastic economic downturn. The economy contracts and then collapses, resulting in a very localised future, which over time becomes increasingly sophisticated, but only within much-reduced energy limitations.

Tribal Trading (Foresight)

A world that has been through a 'sharp and savage energy shock'. A global recession has left millions unemployed, and for most people, 'the world has shrunk to their own community'. Transport is typically by horse and bicycle.

Building Lifeboats (Heinberg)

Building Lifeboats "begins with the assumption that industrial civilisation cannot be salvaged in anything like its present form" and is a process of building community solidarity, creating a localised infrastructure and preserving and enhancing the essentials of life.

EVOLUTION

COLLAPSE

- Enlightened Transition
- Powerdown
- Good Intentions
- Fair Shares
- The Great Transition
- Earth Stewardship
- Enforced Localisation
- Building Lifeboats
- Tribal Trading

CHAPTER FOUR

Resilience and localisation

One of the concepts central to Transition is resilience. The former Crystal Palace football manager Ian Dowie described resilience as 'bouncebackability' – that when something happens to knock us off our stride, we can recover and resume our activities. Brian Walker and David Salt, in their seminal book Resilience Thinking, state:

> "at the heart of resilience thinking is a very simple notion – things change – and to ignore or resist this change is to increase our vulnerability and forego emerging opportunities. In so doing, we limit our options".[1]

We all experience resilience. When we have encountered crisis or calamity, we may have kept focused and got through it, or we might have gone under for a time, overwhelmed by events that felt out of our control. Likewise, we know people who at the first sign of difficulty start unravelling, seemingly unable to cope with difficulties, while others seem able to weather whatever life throws at them, able to adapt to new circumstances and to see challenge as an opportunity, not a calamity. Resilience is not a new and abstract concept; we all know what it looks and feels like.

People talk about resilience on a range of levels: societies, ecosystems, communities and individuals. The idea of resilience in socio-ecological systems is well established through a fascinating body of research. Less explored, though, is the resilience of communities. What would a resilient community look like? Neil Adger, one of the leading thinkers on resilience, sees community resilience as "the ability of a community to withstand external shocks and stresses without significant upheaval",[2] adding that a given community would have "a resilient and accessible resource base and a dynamic range of viable livelihood and responsive institutions".

Three factors determine the degree of a community's resilience.

Transition argues that a more resilient community is one that grows food everywhere . . . *Photo: Lou Brown*

. . . which teaches its young people basic life skills such as food growing . . . *Photo: Jane Price*

The first revolves around the extent to which communities can direct and shape decisions that affect them. As Adger puts it, "resilience also requires communities and societies to have the ability to self-organise and to manage resources and make decisions in a manner that promotes sustainability".[3] Increased local democracy and engagement are key.

The second is the ability of communities to learn and adapt. Being a resilient community means having the necessary skills, which may well not be skills taught in schools today. New skills and flexibility in education are key.

The third is the need for resilient communities to be planned. This intentional aspect, of building resilience being a collective design project, is central to Transition.

. . . and finds creative ways to deepen community engagement in decision-making.

Transition as a fresh take on resilience

Charlie Edwards, in 'Resilient Nation', a report about resilience written for the think tank Demos, came up with a description of resilience which is probably the most useful I have found: "the capacity of an individual, community or system to adapt in order to sustain an acceptable level of function, structure and identity".[4] This stresses how adaptability is at the heart of resilience. What would this explanation of resilience look like if we saw the need to be more adaptable not as a challenge but as an opportunity?

In Transition, we take Edwards' definition of resilience a few steps further. We look at resilience as more than 'sustaining' current models and practices. Rather, in the light of 'energetic precariousness', it becomes a rethink of assumptions about infrastructure and systems that should lead to a more sustainable, resilient and enriching low-carbon economy.

Making a community more resilient, if viewed as the opportunity for an economic and social renaissance, for a new culture of enterprise and reskilling,

should lead to a healthier and happier community while reducing its vulnerability to risk and uncertainty. In practice, a more adaptable community trains its young people in a wide range of skills, more decisions are taken at the local level, the community owns and manages more of its own assets and has access to some of the land adjoining it: it is the kind of community outlined in the next section of this book. Becoming more resilient is a positive and enriching step forward; resilience is reframed as a historic opportunity for a far-reaching rethink.

One of the key questions posed about resilience is "Resilient to what?" Are we building resilience in the face of peak oil and climate change, or of terrorism and pandemics? To weather-related disruption or interruptions to key supplies? What we see as the greatest potential disruptions will shape our actions. While it is clearly not an either/or situation, I would argue strongly that peak oil, climate change and the precarious economic situation are so far-reaching and destabilising that we really must give them precedence; the solutions that arise being markedly different from responses to the disruption of terrorism or pandemics. And, while solutions designed to boost resilience to peak oil (for example) might worsen climate change, being mindful of these three issues should enable a suitable response.

Would a community where the dominant form of urban land use is food production be a healthier and happier place to live? *Photo: Lou Brown*

This leads us to asking an important question: would a more resilient community be a happier one? While I was researching this book I interviewed the psychologist Tim Kasser,[5] and asked him if he saw an argument to support the claim that a more localised and resilient community would be a happier one. He replied:

> "All the research I've seen, all the thinking I've done, and all the people I've talked to, suggests to me that [localisation] will do a better job of meeting people's needs, they'd be happier and people will live in a more socially cohesive way and live more sustainably. Or at least it will *encourage* all those things. If my intuition about what a resilient community is is correct, then what you would hopefully find is that as time goes on, people would be experiencing more and more satisfaction of their needs and find that their community is providing them with more and more opportunities to enact those needs, and to enact those intrinsic values, and that they're experiencing less and less barriers to enacting the intrinsic values and satisfying the needs. On a psychological level, that's what I'd be looking at . . ."

So, how might the concept of localisation deepen our understanding of resilience in practice?

Localisation

In an interesting short article on the website Spiked,[6] Colin McInnes, Professor of Engineering Science at the University of Strathclyde, wrote a scathing critique of the idea of localisation, stating:

> ". . . at its core, localism is in many ways an indulgent form of self-interest. A self-sufficient community is exactly that. It is independent of the cares or needs of other communities and is unwilling to engage in the wider human enterprise . . . we should reject these new forms of localism. We should have as little interest in growing our own food or generating our own energy as we have in producing our own steel. If we leave energy to energy utilities and food to efficient large-scale farming, we can enjoy the products of both while undertaking myriad other productive tasks, and so ensure growing prosperity for all."

McInnes so profoundly misses the point about localisation that he provides a good starting point for a discussion about what the term means. For Peter North, one of few academics to actively explore the idea of localisation, this is not a discussion about what we collectively choose; rather, the volatility of oil prices and the urgent need to cut emissions mean we are rapidly entering a world where:

> "transport again becomes significant in terms of cost, resource use and emissions. Currently very cheap goods produced through globalised production networks will become, and remain, more expensive. The currently near will become further away, again, in a process of 'reverse globalisation'."[7]

This sense that the price volatility of oil will inevitably begin to reverse the assumptions that underpin the economics of globalisation is also picked up by Jeff Rubin:

> "...while there are certainly going to be losers as the eighteen-wheeler of globalisation is thrown into reverse, there are going to be winners too. In a world of triple-digit oil prices, distance suddenly costs money and lots of it. Many of those once-high-paying manufacturing jobs that we thought we had lost forever to cheap labour markets overseas may be soon coming back home. With every dollar increase in the price of the bunker fuel that powers the container ships that ply the Pacific, China's wage advantage becomes less and less important and Western workers once again become competitive."[8]

So, while volatile oil prices may prove to be globalisation's Achilles heel, localisation is an approach in its own right, and it differs greatly from the caricature McInnes paints of it. The table overleaf tries to set out what localisation is, and what it most certainly isn't. It is inspired by McInnes's characterisation of localisation as "a socially regressive slide back towards subsistence and poverty".

To reiterate, localisation is not something we choose. It is an inevitable change in direction as we pass the oil peak, as we decide to treat the climate issue with the urgency and practical response it requires. The late Dr David Fleming put this beautifully when he wrote: "Localisation stands, at best, at the limits of practical possibility, but it has the decisive argument in its favour that there will be no alternative."

Vitally, peak oil means that the economics change fundamentally. James Howard Kunstler, author of *The Long Emergency*, argues that peak oil will mean that the future will be "increasingly and intensely local and smaller in scale".[9] During 2008, when the oil price hit a record $148 a barrel, it became cheaper, for the first time for many years, for the US to manufacture its own steel rather than import it from China. As George Monbiot wrote in April 2010 when Mount Eyjafjallajökull erupted, grounding most European air travel (and noticeably reducing carbon emissions[10]), the eruption:

> "...made everywhere feel local, interchangeable. Nature interjects, and we encounter – tragically for many – the reality of thousands of miles of separation. We discover that we have not escaped from the physical world after all."[11]

The qualities of localisation in practice

When discussing how a localised community would differ from how we live today, I consider my own experience. I remember when I was 18, going into the school where I did my A-levels, collecting my, frankly, pretty poor results, and then sitting outside the school on the grass in the sunshine with a group of my friends, as we shared how we had done. I vividly remember looking around my friends thinking what a useless lot we were. None of us could really cook, none of us could sew, and none of us could build, grow food or repair anything. We didn't know how to use a saw, a hammer or a chisel. None of us had ever planted a tree, repaired a bicycle or fixed a shoe. If we were all to be washed up on a desert

What localisation is – and most certainly isn't

What localisation doesn't mean	What localisation means
Self-sufficiency.	Increased meeting of local needs through local production where possible (especially for food, energy and construction). Import substitution.
Complete energy independence ('off-the-grid' settlements).	Mixture of micro-renewables, greatly increased energy-efficiency and community ownership of grid-connected large-scale renewables.
Insular communities.	A global network of communities localising their economies but sharing their experiences and advice. A global process of resilience-building in a range of settings.
An end to trade.	Trading still happens but on a lesser scale. Where international trade happens, it is done fairly and in the lowest-carbon ways possible.
"A socially regressive slide back towards subsistence and poverty".	Localisation offers greater economic security and resilience than relying on more oil-vulnerable national and multinational businesses and an increasingly far-fetched 'return to growth'.
The driving out of multinational businesses and other employers.	The development, in parallel to existing businesses, of a more diverse, more robust local economy, promoting social enterprise and community ownership of key assets and businesses. Localisation does not start from an adversarial position, and indeed there may well be situations where collaboration with existing multinationals may be a skilful approach.
Harking back to some imagined 'golden age'.	The past was more resilient than today in some ways and less so in others (see page 51). Localisation is about combining the best of the old and the best of the new to design a response most appropriate to present-day challenges.
Dominance by a few powerful local families and landowners.	Localisation is designed with social justice and collaboration from the outset. Finding new models of land access will be key to its success.
A population forced to toil in the fields.	More localised communities will have a wider diversity of skills and more people will have more than one livelihood. Intensive food production, commercially or for personal consumption, will be a much more common skill and will be commonplace. Farming will regain the dignity and status it once enjoyed and become a much more respected career choice.
A rejection of modern medicine and healthcare.	Localisation is not about a rejection of progress and science. The challenge is to see how modern medicine can continue to do what it does best in a markedly lower-energy context.
Everybody hand-weaving their own underpants.	This is not essential, but each to their own. If using nettles, remember they need processing first.

island together, I doubt that any of us would even have had the wherewithal to eat each other.

I mention this because, for me, it illustrates how, as communities, we currently relate to each other. Let's imagine several towns or cities which are almost entirely dependent on imported food, which produce very few of their own needs, and which depend for their food, energy and most other necessities on cheap imports. The relationship between these neighbouring communities is one of mutual uselessness, as all are highly dependent and unresilient. While there is huge potential for entrepreneurship and creativity, this is unfulfilled.

Consider, instead, the relationship between an imaginary town/city and those around it if all are far more resilient, if they have vibrant local food economies, ownership of a percentage of their own energy generation, and more small scale manufacturing. These places then meet and interact in a very different way. There is a different quality to the relationship, as there is a difference between the meeting of two unskilled people as opposed to two people who feel confident in their ability to turn their hand to anything.

How local is 'local'?

So what degree of localisation might be possible? We are most likely not talking, as McInnes suggests, about each settlement "producing [its] own steel". Different things clearly work better (and worse) on, and are economic at, different scales (although, as we have seen, these economies of scale will change). It is not practical, for example, for every place to manufacture its own computers or its own frying pans. Different things work best at different scales, as the table overleaf, from the new economics foundation (nef), showing the minimum size units for adequate economies of scale, suggests.

This gives a useful sense of the kinds of scales we can be effective at, and where it is most practical to start. It leads to the question of what degree of localisation is possible in a city – the model of growing food as close as possible to where we live becomes far more complex when you live in the

> "The essence of localisation is to enable communities around the world to diversify their economies so as to provide for as many of their needs as possible from relatively close to home … this does not mean eliminating trade altogether, as some critics like to suggest. It is about finding a more secure and sustainable balance between trade and local production."
> Helena Norberg-Hodge[12]

middle of Manchester. Later in this book we'll look at how some people are starting to envisage how this might work. For now, the nef table gives us a good idea of the best areas for a Transition localisation initiative, and which aspects are most likely to be economically viable first.

Localisation also doesn't mean turning your back on the rest of the world in an insular retreat, as McInnes suggests. In an interview I did with Michael Shuman, he reasoned that the opposite is far more likely to be the case: "the wealth and the time and the resources that localisation provides to a community enables it to be a more powerful and effective participant in international affairs".[13]

Isn't this all just about romanticising the past?

Sometimes the accusation is thrown at those promoting Transition or localisation that what they are suggesting is about a romanticised version of a past that never existed, where everyone grew carrots, had roses growing over their front door and policemen stood on street corners laughing uproariously. As McInnes puts it, Transition's "vision of local production is a sustainable society filled with Saturday farmers' markets, forever. For some, this would be a welcome retreat from the uncertainties of modernity to a mythical golden era which never

How localisation works on a range of scales [new economics foundation 2010[15]]					
Unit	District	Region	Nation	Continent	Globe
Size (miles)	20	100	500	2,000	10,000
Population	100,000	2 million	50 million	1 billion	5 billion
Production	Food crops	Building materials	Clothes, textiles	Vehicles	Microchips
	Cash crops	Processed food	Small machines & components	Electronic systems	Pharmaceuticals
	Housing	Furniture	Electronic devices	Small aircraft	Large aircraft
		Hardware	Steel	Ships	
	Energy (micro-renewables)	Renewable energy (wind, hydro, solar)	Oil, gas, coal		
	Energy-efficiency, housing, retrofitting		Civil engineering		
			Books, films, bicycles		
Distribution	Fresh food	Groceries	Bulk commodities, e.g. grain	Oil, gas	
	Daily supplies	Clothes	Industrial machinery		
		Books			
		Cars			
		Household appliances			
		Seeds			
Services	Schooling	Universities	Insurance	Aviation	
	GP medical	Hospitals	Railways		
	House repair	Public health	News media		
	Restaurants	Safety	Telecom		
	Hotels	High street and local banking	Wholesale banking		
	Waste recycling	Buses	Electricity		
		Theatre/cinema			
		Water			

'Localism' or 'localisation'?

'Localism' is a term increasingly used by the UK government, to describe the transfer of political power towards local government and local communities, while also making central government smaller. 'Localisation' is something different: a wider, more far-reaching adjustment of economic focus from the global to the local; rebuilding local economies around the meeting of local needs. Although the terms are sometimes used interchangeably, localism and localisation are distinctly different concepts.

actually existed."[14] This point deserves some exploration, because there is a balance to be struck.

My sense is that over the last 40 years there has been a vilification of the more local approaches to doing many things, a condemning of things as being backwards and old-fashioned. Much of what we see around us today – out of town development, Clone Town high streets, the overbearing presence of the car – has been accepted as a natural progression of a culture. These things are, however, the result of a powerful process of rubbishing how things were before. "Smaller shops are more expensive and less efficient", "smaller farms are less efficient", and so on. In the UK, the process has occurred over a long period, but it is happening much faster today in parts of the developing world.

One of my favourite examples of this is an advertising campaign run in 2004 in Ireland by Sandtex, an exterior paint manufacturer. Ireland, at that point, was changing fast: the now-deceased 'Celtic Tiger' economy was in full roar, and bigger, better, shinier and more debt-generating was the order of the day. The ads were so stunning I had to go home and get my camera. They feature pictures of some of the world's oldest structures, including the Sphinx and some ancient Egyptian-looking walls, built thousands of years ago using hand tools and local

stone, which have stood the test of time far better than anything we build today. The caption read 'Should have used Sandtex'. The insinuation was presumably that had the Sphinx, when built 4,500 years ago, been given a nice coat of Sandtex paint, it would look much better than it looks now, and presumably its nose wouldn't have fallen off. This is, of course, nonsense, and an insult to those millions of buildings around the world made without any industrial building materials that have stood for many hundreds of years; the result of great skill and familiarity with local materials.

Yet this idea that everything about life before today was rubbish runs deep. C. S. Lewis referred to it as 'chronological snobbery'. But is it true? As part of helping create the Totnes Energy Descent Action Plan, I recorded interviews with people who remembered the town between the late 1940s and the early 1960s, the last time the place had a more localised economy and used significantly less energy than it uses today. I then looked at the work of Brian Walker and David Salt,[16] coiners of the term 'resilience thinking', and their 'aspects of resilience' – the qualities a more resilient community should have. What emerged was that there were some ways in which that period seemed more resilient than today, and other ways in which it didn't. In these respects it could have been argued to be more resilient:

- There was a greater range of shops, trades and crafts, employment opportunities and land uses, in and around the town.

An Irish advert for Sandtex paints in 2005. Would a coat of modern exterior paint really have made that much difference to the longevity of the Sphinx?

Totnes in the 1930s. Note the greenhouses and market gardens in the centre of the town. *Photo: Totnes Image Bank and Rural Archive*

- There was little need for cars, as most things were within walking distance, and public transport was good for longer journeys.
- There was far more local food production, in back gardens, on allotments and in commercial market gardens, which were part of the town.
- There were much stronger social networks and a higher level of people supporting and being dependent on each other.
- Local government was more representative, the town having its own borough council.

There were also some ways in which it was less resilient than at present:

- There was much less diversity of race, culture, sexual expression and orientation, faith and religion, or political allegiance. I was told "You were either Protestant or Catholic, Labour or Conservative."
- There was much less awareness that our actions had ecological consequences.
- It was a far more conservative community.

Localisation and Fair Trade

If developed nations were to localise their economies and become less dependent on imports, wouldn't it condemn much of the developing world to starvation and misery?

I don't believe this to be the case. Will the developing world really be lifted out of poverty by continuing to dismantle its own food resilience and becoming increasingly dependent on global trade, which is itself massively dependent on the cheap oil we can no longer rely on? Is the way out of poverty really an increasing reliance on the utterly unreliable?

It is not as though the developed world, even if it embarked on a powerdown crash course tomorrow morning, is going to be meeting a substantial majority of its food needs anytime soon. We are talking, after all, about a transition, and likewise, the transition for developing countries will be about moving towards far greater national food security and to smaller amounts of fairly traded produce for export. Rather than condemning anyone to starvation, such an approach is far more appropriate for an energy-scarce world, and would lead to greatly improved resilience across the board.

- Innovation and creative thinking were frowned on. I was told: "Anything innovative was suppressed . . . 'You've got an idea? Well keep it to yourself.'" The education system promoted learning facts and information rather than enquiry and creative thinking.

So, rather than romanticising the past, this exercise is very helpful in identifying what we might be able to learn from it. Of course, the period in question was one with much less money around, less expectation of owning material goods, much less cheap credit and personal indebtedness, a shared experience of austerity and a collective abhorrence of waste. It was also one far less bombarded by advertising, so people didn't know they 'lacked' certain goods or experiences. Yet, with Mervyn King of the Bank of England warning in March 2011 of "a big long-run loss of living standards for all people in this country", a new age of austerity may well be able to learn lessons from the previous one.

We learn, for example, that people in a more resilient society can live happy lives with fewer consumer goods than most of us do today, that food production can be central to our lives, that a local economy can be more robust, diverse and equitably owned than most of those in Western countries today, and that a far wider range of livelihoods and businesses is possible. When people criticise such a perspective as being about 'going back', they assume that such a thing would even be possible. What we are really looking at here is designing the best way forward, based on asking the right questions and keeping the best of what we already have, while also learning lessons from the past.

The hierarchy of responses

Given the scale of the challenge presented by peak oil and climate change, am I suggesting that local responses will be sufficient? Is localisation all we need? Not at all. Transition is one of many responses emerging around the world on a wide range of scales in response to the unprecedented scale of the challenges we face. It is what Paul Hawken refers to as the Earth's 'immune system' kicking into action. Any successful response needs to operate on a range of scales, shown in the table below.

While communities can inspire and lead by example, truly effective localisation and resilience-building will also need government support in different ways. Transition is not about a retreat from our need for engaged and visionary government; rather, it is designed to inspire that leadership. At the same time, change on the scale needed will struggle if enthusiastic communities do not seize the initiative.

It will require brave legislation, the support of inspired and visionary people in planning, education, business and local government, and pioneers to take risks and the first steps. Most of all, it will need us to realise that many of the obstacles to making this a reality lie with us, and that our willingness to change is central to success. Many of the challenges lie in our willingness to think big enough, to do things differently and to organise ourselves.

Politically, Transition is increasingly creating a culture where currently unelectable policies can become electable. This is a hugely important role.

How bottom-up and top-down responses intertwine		
International	National	Local
Strong international climate change protocols, Contraction and Convergence, a moratorium on biodiesel production, Oil Depletion Protocol, rethinking economic growth, biodiversity protection, a realistically high price on carbon.	Strong climate change legislation, Tradeable Energy Quotas, a national food security strategy, devolution of powers to local communities, support for the relocalisation of industry.	Transition initiatives, Energy Descent Plans, Climate Friendly Communities, Community Supported Agriculture (CSA), land trusts, credit unions, locally owned energy-supply companies (ESCOs).

CHAPTER FIVE

A taste of a powered-down future

"From nearly half a century of work in sustainable and natural systems agriculture, urban design, biomimicry, ecological engineering, green building, biophilic design, solar and wind technology, regenerative forestry, holistic resource management, waste cycling and ecological restoration, we have the intellectual capital and practical experience necessary to remake the human presence on the Earth."

David Orr, *Down to the Wire: Confronting climate collapse*[1]

"I wish it were a hundred years from today [I can't stand the suspense]."

Elliot Murphy (from the sleeve notes of *1969: Velvet Underground live*)

At this point this might all be feeling a bit abstract. It's all very well to suggest a future of stronger local economies, of needs being supplied by shorter supply chains and more local production, but what might that look like? A large part of our intention to bring this about arises from our being able to imagine it, having a vision of such a future – being able, on some level, to conceive of what it would look like, sound like, smell like and feel like.

The three areas that would most logically and easily lend themselves to localisation are food, energy and construction. This chapter aims to put a bit more flesh on the bones, exploring what our lives might look like in 20 years, as well as setting out for each of these areas what degree of localisation might be possible, based on projects and research already under way today.

Food

" . . . to draw in our economic boundaries and shorten our supply lines so as to permit us literally to know where we are economically. The closer we live to the ground that we live from, the more we will know about our economic life; the more we know about our economic life, the more able we will be to take responsibility for it."

Wendell Berry[2]

By 2030, the system that feeds us looks very different. There has been a food and farming revolution across the UK. The oil price volatility that began in 2011 focused the nation's minds; rebuilding the nation's food security became urgent. Just as in the early days of the Second World War, there was a national crash-training in intensive food gardening, with free courses across the country. Most colleges and schools made food growing a central part of the curriculum, and lots of self-organised groups trained and supported each other in learning how to grow food, sharing tools and saving seeds. Food hubs[3] popped up all over the country, which helped small-scale growers sell directly to the consumer, cutting out the middle man and helping to make small-scale growing viable.

It is a golden time for farming, and farms are quite different from how they looked in 2011. The landscape has more forest cover and more land uses. While livestock still graze on grassland,[4] there is

Who says growing vegetables is unsightly? State-of-the-art 'edible landscaping' at the Eden Project, Cornwall.

far more fruit production, more small-scale grain growing, and more land put aside, especially in the peri-urban areas, for intensive vegetable production. The high price of liquid fuels means farms have adapted as businesses. They now tend to be run as an umbrella for a range of small land-based businesses that support each other and specialise in local markets. Gourmet mushroom production, for both food and medicinal production, the on-farm adding of value to dairy produce (cheese, butter, etc.), fruit and a range of other produce, and the production of natural building materials are among the businesses now common on farms, which have been designed mostly to supply local markets.

A new generation of young farmers is now driving food and farming forward, enthusiastic about local markets and supported by a public keen to be part of the production of their own food. New variations on the Community Supported Agriculture model mean that people identify with 'their' farm or 'their' brewery, and, as shareholders, they are more involved in how the business operates.
During the 20 years to 2030, much research went into agroforestry, the combining of multi-layered tree plantings with other farming practices. Most

farms now include an element of agroforestry, which, as well as being very productive, is very effective at locking carbon into soils,[5] storing water, building biodiversity and providing shelter to the rest of the farm. The acceleration of agroforestry, supported by a change in payments to farmers, grants and free trainings, has contributed 10 per cent to the UK's arboreal landscape.

"Here's the bottom line: if the oil runs out, we won't be able to farm or trade this way any longer. And if we took global warming seriously, we'd stop doing it right now: compared with regional and local food systems, our national and international model releases five to seventeen times more carbon dioxide into the atmosphere."
Bill McKibben[6]

"Given the degree to which the modern food system has become dependent on fossil fuels, many proposals for de-linking food and fossil fuels are likely to appear radical. However, efforts toward this end must be judged not by the degree to which they preserve the status quo, but by their likely ability to solve the fundamental challenge that will face us: the need to feed a global population of seven billion with a diminishing supply of fuels available to fertilise, plough and irrigate fields and to harvest and transport crops."
Richard Heinberg and Michael Bomford[7]

In towns and cities, food production has become an integral part of the urban landscape. Most flat-roofed buildings now feature a roof garden, and raised beds adorn many of the now-newly-pedestrianised streets. Parks contain community gardens, and urban market gardening has now re-established itself, with entrepreneurial new growers competing to grow the most unusual or eye-catching produce. Most deliveries are done by bicycle or biogas-powered vehicle around the city, but the need for transportation is low, given that most such gardens serve very local markets. Many immigrant communities find the opportunity to reconnect with the edible plants they grew in their homelands, so the flat roofs of some of the more culturally diverse parts of London now feature a range of the more unusual vegetables and salads, the harvest of which is celebrated in a range of festivals and events.

On ground where only short-term access can be guaranteed, or where there is contamination, a booming market in freshwater fish production has emerged. Glasshouses are erected and freshwater fish are grown in tanks. Intensive salad production makes use of the fertility in the water. With a population eating less red meat, more fresh and seasonal fruit and vegetables and more fresh fish, as well as exercising more regularly, a number of key health indicators have improved markedly. In cities, urban agriculture has become a key feature of the local economy.

Most employers whose premises are surrounded by a significant amount of land, and most schools and hospitals, now have intensive edible landscapes surrounding them. Much of the food produced is available to the on-site kitchens or sold to employees. Very few lawns are now seen in towns and cities unless they can support grazing animals.

One of Growing Community's new urban market gardens in Hackney, London, producing salads for local vegetable boxes.

heat

18 November 2021

I can't rake it any more!

GARDENING FEUD PUSHES CHERYL'S MARRIAGE TO THE BRINK

Heat can reveal that Cheryl Cole and her husband Zak Friendly are to split. The couple, who met on the TV show *Strictly Come Mulching* three years ago, famously moved into a Bel Air mansion last year in order to create an edible garden, a process documented in the reality TV series *Cheryl and Zak Get Down and Dirty* on HBO.

In spite of an initial good start, things quickly soured as the couple's different approaches to gardening increasingly became a problem. Their spat was carried out through rival magazines, Cheryl tearfully telling *OK!* "I just don't see the point in growing flowers . . . for me it's all about growing vegetables in neat and productive rows. Some things are traditional for good reason." Zak confided to *Hello!* "I feel I'm losing her. Surely a garden needs flowers too, and curves. Cheryl's just veg, veg, veg. It's doing my head in, frankly."

Sources close to the couple told *Heat* that the final straw for Zak was Cheryl's being spotted in a cosy evening tête-à-tête with hemp-building guru Dane Schwim, and her confiding to *OK!* that she felt their mansion could never be energy-efficient no matter what they did, and that she

Cheryl at home in her garden yesterday.
Image: Aiofe Valley

wanted to build a hemp-and-cob cottage close to their garden. "Surely you can retrofit a mansion, for heaven's sake?" Zak stormed, as he moved his things out last week. Cheryl was unavailable for comment, but was believed to be on a seed-saving course in Sebastopol.

From the *Bath Chronicle* online, 15 June 2023

Midnight Aquaculture Revellers Infuriate Local Brewer

Bath publican and brewer John Straker has had enough. "You try and do your bit for your town's food security, put it on the map with something a bit innovative, and then this happens," he fumed yesterday. John runs the Turning Turbine pub in Bath, which is also home to the Turbine Microbrewery, a community-owned brewery launched in 2013 and now with ten years' brewing proudly under its belt.

Lansdown Road was one of ten of Bath's hilliest streets, which five years ago were pedestrianised and redeveloped as terraced fishponds and food production beds. Visitors to the city are invited to help themselves to salads (but not the fish), and 'The Hanging Gardens of Bath, Avon', as they've been dubbed, have become a major tourist attraction. Residents living alongside the gardens take turns in tending the pools and the beds, and in spite of initial resistance and concerns about infestations of slugs lowering house prices, the scheme has been a huge hit.

Last year John decided to try something new, using the waste hops from the brewery to produce biomethane and using the gas to heat ponds in an experiment to see what could be grown in the warmer waters. John received a small grant from Bath City Council's Urban Agriculture Department, which allowed him to start trialling rice crops and water chestnuts.

Last Saturday night, however, he had a

Bath landlord John Straker is not happy.

Image: Laura Whitehead

shock. "I came out of the pub after closing time, and there in my heated pools there were about 15 people, in various states of undress, carrying on and having a party as though it was a jacuzzi," he told a *Bath Chronicle* reporter. "I gave 'em a piece of my mind. I told 'em, 'this is a ground-breaking urban aquaculture research experiment, not a bloody 18-30s holiday.' I sent 'em packing with a flea in their ears." The pools are now fenced off while John decides what to do next, although he did tell the *Bath Chronicle* that he is considering trying to breed crayfish. "Something with a nasty bite," he told our reporter, with a twinkle in his eye.

Lawnmowers now hang from pub ceilings in the same way that old ploughs did 20 years earlier.

Increasing food supply resilience in Western nations has progressed alongside the increasing of resilience in the developing world. Volatile energy prices highlighted how depending on either imports or exports leaves a country equally vulnerable. It became clear that refocusing an economy to supply export markets, while dismantling small farmers, results in a major loss of food security, not an increase. This led to a change in international legislation, with national self-reliance in food once again accepted as a legitimate national objective. Farming and, in towns and cities, market gardening are now once again seen as 'cool' occupations, and there are now not one, but two, TV soap operas set in urban market gardens: BBC3's The Patch *and E4's* On Good Ground*, both of which are very popular.*

What degree of food self-reliance might be possible?

It is neither practical nor desirable for the UK to strive for complete self-sufficiency. It is a very long time since nothing was imported at all, and there are now rather a lot more of us, with rather more cosmopolitan tastes, than there were then. A certain amount of trade is healthy, but over-reliance on imports is a major vulnerability. Cheap oil has allowed us to rely on a massively wasteful food system. For example, in 2004 the UK exported 1.5 million kilos of potatoes to Germany while importing the same amount, and exported 9.9 million kilos of milk and cream to France, while importing 10.2 million.[8] In 2011 the UK imports 95 per cent of the fruit it consumes, and about a third of its food is actually thrown away. So if total self-sufficiency is out, as is depending heavily on imports because of energy consumption, what kind of system would work?

One of the most fascinating projects exploring this is the Fife Diet initiative in Scotland,[9] which supports people eating a more local diet. Their stated objective is an 80-per-cent local diet, with the remainder imported. I asked Fife Diet founder Mike Small where this ratio had come from. He said:

"It was about saying we didn't want the 'eat local' movement to be a parochial retreat inwards because we believe that eating locally is an act of solidarity with the developing world in terms of climate change and climate justice. We wanted to show solidarity by buying stuff that we just couldn't get here. We also wanted tactically to say to people 'look, this isn't too scary – you can do this!' Of course people say they couldn't give up things like bananas or chocolate or red wine. 80:20 per cent makes it seem less scary, that's the thinking behind it."

The Fife Diet has cleverly promoted local food production and the sourcing of seasonal local produce, as well as the rediscovery of traditional recipes. Julie Brown of Growing Communities, a fascinating local food social enterprise in Hackney, London,[10] also advocates an 80:20 per cent UK produced/imported ratio, but was less specific about why that figure was chosen, emphasising the work-in-progress nature of this debate:

" . . . it's a hypothesis, and it needs proving. It's an aspiration. It feels right. Broadly speaking, in terms of what we're sourcing

"Local food does not solve issues of food security. However, it creates a more resilient food chain in Stroud district, and consuming local food creates a multiplier effect in the local economy, supporting jobs and creating community viability. Developing local food production capacity is one of the ways to optimise food availability in the future."
From a report by Transition Stroud[11]

for our box schemes, which is all fruit and vegetables, that's what we manage to do, but we're playing around with that. I am struggling with how we measure this."

So although there is nothing fixed here, and it needs much more research, perhaps 80:20 seems a reasonable starting point for thinking about what an aspirational balance might look like.

Building

By 2011 there was a strong move towards greener building and zero-carbon housing. However, much of what was built was falling short of the targets set by government. Much of what did reach better performance levels, although producing buildings that used little energy once built, relied heavily on very energy-intensive materials. It was commonplace for the bulk of materials to be imported long distances, and it was at about this time that the concept of 'building miles',[12] akin to 'food miles', started to be looked at seriously.

A cob-builder's toolkit – a collection of tools we may become more familiar with? *Photo: Katy Bryce*

The construction industry began to move away from just building performance to also looking at the materials used. The priority was to create homes that reached or came very close to the Passivhaus standard (i.e. they require no space heating other than the body heat of the occupants) but were made from predominantly local, unprocessed, natural or recycled materials that could be used by less skilled labourers, often for self-/community-build projects. This shift, from energy-intensive, imported building materials to local, low-energy materials, revolutionised construction in the UK, and made a wide range of local, small-scale enterprises viable once more.

Vernacular building styles have once again come to dominate, with architectural designs being dictated by local materials. Whereas in 2011 new housing in Falkirk had twins in Portsmouth or Liverpool, by 2030 new housing helps to contribute to a strong sense of place and local identity. Materials that had passed into disuse have now gained a new lease of life (see box on pages 62-63).

By 2030 the existing housing stock (of the UK's 24 million homes in 2011, at least 87 per cent are still standing in 2050[13]) has been retrofitted to a high standard of energy-efficiency, increasingly using local materials, which have helped enhance the look of many of the less inspiring buildings created in the late twentieth century.[14] The rural economy now has stone and slate quarries operating again. Lime kilns produce lime plasters. Woodlands are managed for a range of building materials with efficient wood drying, grading and processing. Timber-frame buildings are manufactured to high levels of energy-efficiency off-site, and construction projects are designed to involve less-skilled labour and people new to building.

The construction of new homes now benefits local economies, creating work for builders and supporting a range of local industries. These homes are not just energy-efficient to live in but also healthy, life-affirming spaces that invite community. Most development is no longer carried out by private developers but by community trusts, who own land and buildings in the common interest and promote a wide range of other social benefits. This, again, means that new development strengthens and adds to the resilience of the community, rather than haemorrhaging money from the local economy. Builders' providers now offer a wide range of pigments, timbers, clay plasters and pre-made hemp/clay blocks, and most building projects now start with a look at what materials are locally available.

What degree of localisation in building materials might be possible?

At the moment, most of the buildings that fall into the category of 'natural building', as opposed to 'green building', tend to be self-build and one-off housing, rather than anything led by developers or on a commercial scale.

From the *Farmer's Journal*, 24 June 2018

"It's diversification, Jim, but not as we know it."

Local farmer now grows houses for a living

Woven willow wall image:: Small World Theatre

Unless they sell land for development, farmers usually have little to gain from new housing developments in their area. Jim Ashton, who farms near Woolston in Hampshire, is different.

When a nearby development of 120 houses was announced, Jim approached the developers, who were looking to build very low-carbon buildings and who were keen to support the local economy, and offered to provide some of the key ingredients for the buildings. He has now diversified out of dairy farming and into hemp, clay plasters, round-wood poles and willow production, all of which are certified by the British Natural Building Board.

"It has been amazing," Jim told the *Farmer's Journal*. "I now feel as though what I produce will be savoured, not just for one meal but for generations. It has enabled me to take on 20 new people, business is booming, and many other local builders and developers are now designing my produce into their buildings."

Can we say, as we suggested for a more localised, low-carbon diet, that by 2030 80 per cent of construction materials might be locally sourced? That sounds like a tall order in our present-day world of concrete blocks and PVC soffits. Yet there are some inspiring initiatives taking place that are indicating what might be possible. In 2010 North Kesteven District Council completed a development of strawbale council houses,[15] and in 2002 the Suffolk Housing Society built two hemp/lime council houses.[16] These materials are starting to be industrialised to some extent, through prefabricated strawbale panels[17] and aerated clay blocks, a fascinating construction system suited to areas

Building materials of the future

Roundwood timber: Rather than seeing existing woodlands purely in terms of the amount of straightwood that can be extracted from them, the revolution in building with roundwood that began in 2011 has led, in areas with good resources of roundwood timber, to a reskilled workforce and to beautiful buildings with a distinct sense of place.[20] Small-diameter coppiced roundwood can also be used for thatching spars, and for wattle-and-daub partitions.

Hemp: Hemp can be grown without the need for artificial fertilisers, produces a high-protein oil and seed, a strong fibre that can be used to make an insulating fibre and a central hurd that can be mineralised and used, with lime or clay, to make a very well-insulated wall or insulating plaster.[21]

Clay: Clay has a wide range of uses, from making durable, beautiful and breathable plasters; as the main ingredient in clay-based paints and finishes; as a binder in light earth (clay straw) construction; or, in its fired state, as expanded clay blocks, as underfloor insulating pellets, and roof or wall-hung tiles.

Wool: Sheep's wool makes an excellent insulation product, being breathable and non-toxic.

Lime: Lime is almost a carbon-neutral building material, as in order to set it reabsorbs carbon dioxide almost equivalent to that which was used in its manufacture. It can be used for breathable renders, mortars and plasters, limewashes and other finishes, hemp/lime walls or blocks, and in most ways that cement can be used.

Cob: Clay subsoil mixed with straw in the correct

Ben Law has pioneered roundwood pole building, such as in this structure at the Sustainability Centre, Hampshire. *Image: Tim Harland*

high in clay. A report in 2010 by the Prince's Foundation for the Built Environment[18] showed the benefits to local economies of such locally manufactured building materials:

- The simplicity of the systems means "it enables a local workforce to be used . . . this ensures that a greater proportion of economic value is captured in the local economy".[19]
- Jobs would be created by the manufacturing of the materials.
- It would also result in "professional skills development, a heightened sense of personal dignity and respect resulting from long-term professional

proportions produces a material rather like Plasticine, which can be used to sculpt both internal and external walls with excellent thermal mass properties and which enables the creation of a 'hand-sculpted house' like no other material.

Straw: Tightly baled straw makes an excellent, highly insulating building material, either as a load-bearing wall or as infill in timber-framed walls. Loose straw can be tossed in a clay slip and then tamped between shutters in a timber-frame wall to make 'light clay' or 'clay straw', a beautiful and well-insulated wall. Shredded straw is also a key ingredient in clay plasters.

Sheep's wool insulation behind timber laths, which await two coats of lime plaster.

Handmade cob blocks with a clay mortar form a curving internal wall within a newly built cob house in Dartington, Devon.

employment, enhanced social well-being, improved social capital, healthier buildings, a more resilient building supply chain, reduced CO_2 emissions, and increased longevity of the building stock".

The 'holy grail' in terms of the construction of new sustainable buildings is homes that reach the highest level of energy-efficiency while also using as high a proportion of locally sourced materials as possible – what we might call 'The Local Passivhaus'. Two buildings completed in 2011 in Ebbw Vale, known as 'The Lime House' and 'The Larch House', have moved this concept forward significantly.[22] As architect Justin Bere told me:

> "Local materials matter because they do two things. They reduce carbon emissions from transportation, and they increase local employment. Local employment, if it really is local, also requires less carbon emissions and travel from the factory or workshop to the site."

The final buildings used Welsh timber (used in an innovative way to make up for its poor quality compared to, say, Scandinavian timber), Welsh-made Rockwool insulation, Welsh-made slates, local stone and UK-made paint and sprinklers. Things that were harder to source included lime render (a Welsh company but a French lime) and woodfibre insulation, which was imported from Germany but could easily be made in Wales.

The last challenge was the windows, which need to be of very high quality. For the first house, they were imported from Germany. For the second house, a Welsh joiner produced them to a Passivhaus-certified design. I asked Justin if he had a sense of the local/imported proportions in the materials used. He said he thought the first house was probably

'The Local Passivhaus' project in Ebbw Vale. *Images: bere:architects*

The building industry of 2030   by Justin Bere

"One would be choosing a house from local companies, and there'd be in one's locality perhaps five or ten smallish companies, each with a proven track record of building wonderful, low-energy houses. Those organisations or companies would be buying raw materials locally and also employing people in the area, and there'd be a tremendous pride in the kind of results that are being produced. Some areas, such as Herefordshire and East Anglia, on opposite sides of the country, would have similar technologies in terms of timber-frame buildings. Somewhere else you'd have stone buildings. We'd be going forward to a new regional interest, attention to detail, producing buildings, results and products for local people.

You'd have a pride in doing something well. You don't want it to fall apart, and you want to do your best for the people you know and care for. We'll get a completely good culture, as I see it, just as we will with food. It's like farmers' markets – you're buying from people who are producing and they know who they are selling to each week, and they want to produce the best for regular friends that come to the market.

Yes, there probably will be some things that are transported around, but hopefully we'll need so little power going into our buildings that we'll be able to use some nice big wind generators to generate electricity for vehicles, so that when we do have to move things around, it's done by electrically run vehicles. It'll all be low-carbon, healthy and rewarding."

(From an interview with the author)

Local materials, such as timber and stone, will once again become the foundation (so to speak) of a more localised building industry.

Might it be that the future of construction in 2030 will emerge from hands-on research such as this? At a course at The Hollies Centre for Practical Sustainability in West Cork, Ireland, a wall is being built using 'bale-cob' – a hybrid combining straw bales and cob, maximising cob's thermal mass and strawbale's very high levels of insulation.

"Traditional materials, using vernacular technologies, are generally appropriate to local conditions, being drawn, for the most part, from available resources . . . Their use has important economic implications, being obtained with the minimum of transportation costs and, frequently, worked by hand, they involve relatively little use of high-energy-consuming fuels. Vernacular architecture is therefore ecologically sensitive and, with regional resources being carefully nurtured, is, as it has always been, economically and environmentally sustainable."

Paul Oliver[23]

around 80-per-cent Welsh, and the second house was closer to 90 per cent. Did he think, I asked, that an 80:20 per cent local/imported ratio could work for construction in a powered-down UK? "I think", he told me, "that in time people will be forced to do better than 80 per cent!"

Energy

The third area of our lives that has been transformed over the 20 years to 2030 is our relationship with how energy is generated. The first place where the difference is noticeable is regarding how much less energy is used today. Compared with 2011, the UK now uses 55 per cent less energy than it did; energy has been saved through the retrofitting and increased energy-efficiency of schools, homes, offices, public buildings and industrial premises, and increased transport efficiency.[24] Gone are the days of office lighting left blazing all night, shops pumping hot air into the street and energy-guzzling appliances. Expectations of thermal comfort are lower. In winter people rightly expect to be warm, but part of that warmth now comes from the jumpers they are wearing rather than from the gas they are burning.

Most communities now have their own community-owned energy company. It offers a range of energy services, from energy-efficiency advice and insulation to the opportunity to own shares and influence the development of large-scale renewable energy [explored in more depth in Tools for Transition No.18: Community renewable energy companies, page 246]. Given the amount of money that poured out of local economies in 2011 every time energy bills were paid, by 2030 the generation of energy, and the retrofitting of buildings, has become a key way for communities to fund the development of their own relocalisation processes, creating employment and a number of spin-off enterprises.

The exact technologies used by each company are place-specific and represent its best exploitable resources, but the principle is universal. Many people, by around 2012, as the momentum began to pick up nationally, began to see these emerging local energy companies as a better investment for their savings than many commercial opportunities. Some specialise in the creation of anaerobic digestion, turning waste food and other organic matter into biogas and fertilisers. Some, in areas with good forestry resources, focus on biomass. Those with significant hydro resources exploit that, and the majority have turned to wind generation. The level of community support for local energy companies means that there has been a sea change in the attitudes of local authorities to on-shore wind, with significant lobbying coming from the communities affected by the developments.

In some cases, local authorities have created energy companies in partnership with local Transition and other community groups. Some new developments have been created which have their own 'off-the-grid' grids, but the breaking of the national grid into smaller more localised grids, proposed by some earlier in the century,[25] failed to materialise given the scale of the engineering challenge and the need to be able to balance supply and demand nationally.

By 2030, the energy mix that powers the UK is almost entirely renewable, principally driven by wind. The oil shocks of 2013 accelerated existing work on a national renewable energy grid, after studies showed the huge potential of wind generation[26] and other technologies to contribute significantly to the mix. These include tidal energy, hydro, solar PV, biogas and biomass. Many more wind turbines are now visible in the landscape, but they have become as much of an unnoticed fact of people's lives as electricity pylons were in 2011. Most houses sport some kind of solar panel on the roof, and many have installed other renewable energy appliances, such as heat pumps.

Everyday culture is very focused on energy conservation, with each generation of schoolchildren more aware of energy use and how to reduce it. People look back to the levels of energy consumed in 2011 with disbelief, as well as amusement at the absurdity of the levels of waste, and anger that they are increasingly living with the resulting climate impacts. There is also a deep sense of collective pride about the new infrastructure that has been created.

What degree of energy relocalisation might be possible?

Trying to put a figure to how the localisation of energy might work is altogether more problematic than for food and building. One of the key constraints is that energy is mostly something that sits in the context of a national grid, and local, decentralised energy systems are very costly. What we are asking here is really what proportion of the new energy infrastructure that a powered-down economy will need might be directly owned by and managed for the benefit of communities.

I put this question to Simon Roberts, Chief Executive of the Centre for Sustainable Energy (CSE) in Bristol. In theory, he told me, a lot of it could be owned and managed in this way, but in practice most communities, even if they were very wealthy and had had spectacularly successful share launches and phenomenal levels of community investment, would raise only a few million pounds at most. This, in the scale of renewable energy projects, places them (according to work CSE did for the south-west of England), firmly in the '10MW and under' bracket, which constitutes only about 25 per cent of all the renewable energy installations that could potentially be installed.

In Austria, the woodpile has reached the level of a work of art.

The larger question, he suggests, is what happens to the rest of the money over which a community has some kind of control. If money held in ISAs, pensions and other longer-term investments were to be refocused into local renewable energy initiatives, it could have a huge impact. In short, a new renewable energy infrastructure will cost a lot of money, and communities, even the wealthier ones, don't have that kind of money. As Paul Allen of the Centre for Alternative Technology succinctly put it, "there is nowhere near enough money at community level to fund it all; we need the big money too".

The other obstacle to greater community ownership of significant-scale energy-generating capacity, Simon told me, is the fact that:

> " . . . management of the projects is just as important as the ownership. In other words, they take a lot of very skilled looking after. Even where that task has been contracted out, the contractor needs a lot of attention to make sure they are on the case, and that insurance claims are being made promptly if something doesn't work as it should. And the equipment manufacturer warranties don't offer recompense without a legal fight, etc. etc."

PEDAL (Portobello Transition Town) and Greener Leith are hoping to create Edinburgh's first community-owned urban wind turbine. *Image: PEDAL*

There is a great deal of microgeneration that can be owned by communities, and, for projects that lend themselves to it, such as anaerobic digestion and microhydro, it looks likely to always remain a vital part of the energy landscape in terms of local

Installing the UK's first community solar power station, Lewes. For the full story see page 249. *Photo: Chris Rowland /OVESCO*

economies, albeit a minority one. Now, if communities could get their local authorities and local businesses to look at investing their pensions and other investments differently, perhaps it might all able to step up a gear . . .

Reflections / meeting our needs

McInnes's critique of localisation discussed on page 46 could, at the time of writing, be seen as correct. Cheap and abundant energy (provided it is capable of generating close to zero-carbon emissions) makes the kind of future he sets out – of constant technological progress, global trade and technology able to solve any problem – reasonably feasible. If cheap energy will be a permanent feature of our lives, why change anything? On closer inspection, however, that doesn't appear to be an accurate assessment. The move away from small-scale production, from diverse local economies and high streets and independent local businesses, was intentionally driven by the interests of big business, the banking sector and international legislation. The small traders, farmers and producers who fell (and continue to fall) were (and still are) seen as the inevitable casualties of progress.

My sense is that over the next 10-20 years, the reality of economic contraction and energy price volatility will start to change the scale at which businesses are viable, so that localisation moves from being seen as "an indulgent form of self-interest" to being the lynchpin of vibrant local economies. However, this won't just happen by itself. Campaigning and lobbying are vital but, equally, we also need to start creating and implementing the economic models of the near future, right here, right now. This book is an attempt to set out how we might actually make that happen.

This leads to a question I will not seek to answer here, but which you might bear in mind as you travel through the book: might a more resilient world better meet our needs as human beings? It may seem like a wildly presumptuous question, but it is worth considering seriously. Psychologist Tim Kasser has identified four needs, which he argues are "basic to the motivation, functioning, and well-being of all humans."[27] These are:

- **Safety, security and sustenance:** the essentials of life – the food on our table, the roof over our head, our clothing, and also the need to feel emotionally secure and cared for.
- **Competence, efficacy and self-esteem:** refers to our ability to feel like a competent and worthy person capable of doing what we set out to do.
- **Connectedness:** the need to feel intimacy and closeness with others, and a part of the communities around us.
- **Autonomy and authenticity:** refers to our ability to pursue activities that provide us with "challenge, intent and enjoyment", and our ability to follow our own interests.

Our current way of doing things is unravelling community, pushing the biosphere to the edge of collapse, and leading to growing fragmentation, disempowerment and isolation. Might it be that the Transition approach, of creating vibrant local economies with increased community ownership, meeting practical needs from as nearby as possible, and living well while consuming far less energy than we do today, could actually better meet our needs?

" . . . it means nurturing locally owned businesses which use local resources sustainably, employ local workers at decent wages and serve primarily local consumers. It means becoming more self-sufficient, and less dependent on imports. Control moves from the boardrooms of distant corporations and back to the community where it belongs."
Michael Shuman[28]

"I thought it **could work,** and now I know it **will work.**"
Cristiano Bottone

"How can I not, you know? Once you acknowledge something is wrong **you must act.** It's what **being alive** and a part of community is all about."
Ken Eidel

" To stay sane . . . and to help me **make meaning** for my **children** and **my community.**"
Adrienne Campbell

PART TWO:

What the Transition response looks like in practice

CHAPTER SIX

Framing Transition

'The Head, Heart and Hands of Transition': display boards at the Cultivate Centre, Dublin.

"The sustainability revolution will be organic. It will arise from the visions, insights, experiments and actions of billions of people. The burden of making it happen is not on the shoulders of any one person or group. No one will get the credit, but everyone can contribute."

Donella H. Meadows, Jorgen Randers and Dennis L. Meadows,
Limits to Growth: The 30-year update[1]

So, what is Transition?

I've set out the why of Transition; now let's move on to the what. The Transition model is pretty straightforward. The first thing to get straight here is that the term 'Transition Town', often used to describe these initiatives, is really rather redundant. At the start, they mostly were towns. Now, there are Transition cities, villages, universities, hamlets, neighbourhoods, districts, and so on. Although 'Transition Towns' has nice alliteration, it is limited and no longer accurate.

The starting point for Transition is that the future with less oil, and producing less carbon emissions,

could be preferable to today. Its aim is to act as a catalyst, a pulse, an invitation; to galvanise the shift towards a more localised and resilient community. Transition can be thought of as many things. Different people and different initiatives may focus more on one of these things than others, but in reality, Transition is all of these:

Transition as . . . an inner process

Is the change we need to make external (new technologies, infrastructure, etc.) or internal? Is the root of our problems in our physical systems for living or in the choices we make and the world view and assumptions that underlie them? In Transition we

> "It's a good thing to avoid definitions, they only confuse things."
>
> Dr David Fleming, in a presentation to the Transition Network conference 2009

have taken a whole-systems approach, seeing that these two dimensions of human existence cannot be separated. Put simply, we shape our physical world in response to what we value and believe, and our values and beliefs are in turn shaped by the world around us.

In the environmental movement, the idea that the work we are doing might affect us on an inner level is often seen as something we don't have time for, something 'fluffy' that would distract from the real work of getting on with saving the Earth. Transition takes a different approach. I am always amazed when I meet climate scientists whose knowledge about climate change makes no difference to how they live their daily lives. There is a professional ability to compartmentalise different aspects of life that can't be entirely healthy. For most of us, encountering the reality of climate change and peak oil, or experiencing at first hand the impacts of the recession, are insights and impacts that affect us directly.

When I first found out about peak oil, the effect on my life was not a purely intellectual one. It kept me awake at night; it affected how I saw the future for my family; it was an almost physical sensation of discomfort and distress. Climate change, with its profoundly unsettling prognosis for the future of life on Earth, is also not a purely academic subject. The idea that people change by encountering distressing information, digesting it intellectually, and deciding, based on the balance of evidence, that they should insulate the loft and start growing potatoes, is not how things happen. Transition acknowledges that we are also emotional creatures.

Transition cannot be just about material change, such as putting up solar panels and planting trees.

Doing Transition, whether in our own lives or as a community process, can be exhilarating, stressful, terrifying, life-affirming, enraging . . . all human emotion comes into play. Being one of the people suggesting there is another way to go, trying to remind a community of its potential genius, is wonderful, but it can also leave you feeling that you are carrying the hope of the place on your shoulders.

Transition gives people the tools and the support they need to be effective. Many Transition initiatives have 'Heart and Soul' groups, working to support the wider process, offering support and counselling to those central to the process (see *Starting out* 14: Creating a space for inner Transition, page 140). This can be one-to-one support, facilitating processes such as Fishbowls or Appreciative Inquiry, conflict mediation or creating a space for safely exploring the distress and upset that peak oil and climate change can create.

Transition as . . . leading by practical example

Transition initiatives are about making change happen, rolling up sleeves and taking the first steps towards the relocalisation of communities, towards more resilience and happiness. There is huge power in starting things, in making practical projects a reality. It changes the atmosphere of a place, shows what is possible, invites engagement and starts to help people get a tangible sense of what a more sustainable world would feel like.

Transition as . . . an approach rooted in place and circumstance

Part of the beauty of the Transition approach is that it is very place-specific. For example, in Camden in London, there are eight separate Transition initiatives, each very different and rooted in the people and the culture of the place. In the film *In Transition 1.0*, MP for Tooting Sadiq Khan said:

> "I suspect that Transition Town Tooting will be different from a Transition town in Bristol, or even in East London, or even in West London, or in parts of Wandsworth,

and that uniqueness will give it its strength, because you can't impose upon Tooting a Transition town model from another part of the country, and that's why it takes time, and that's why you have to have patience."

As I visit different Transition initiatives around the country, I am constantly struck by how different they each are from each other. Transition is not a one-size-fits-all approach; people make it their own, embodying the 'open source' approach upon which the concept is founded. Transition is also culturally specific, being adapted into the culture of whichever place it happens to emerge from. So Transition in Brazil, emerging with a distinctly Brazilian flavour, will look very different from Transition in Edinburgh or in New Zealand, yet there will be enough in common for it to be distinctly Transition.

The concept of 'home' is alien to many people who have spent their lives on the move. Transition can offer a way to root in a place and to feel a part of it. Transition Barcelona's *caminatas* are guided walks around the city to visit people, projects, craftspeople and places that add to the place's resilience, offering a useful model for how to help people feel more at home and more connected to their place (you can read more about this on page 126). Observing this sense of ownership of the Transition concept in highly diverse communities around the world has been one of the most fascinating developments in the time since the whole thing began.

"If you look at the science that describes what is happening on Earth today and aren't pessimistic, you don't have the correct data. If you meet people in this unnamed movement and aren't optimistic, you haven't got a heart."
Paul Hawken[2]

Transition as . . . a tool for turning problems into solutions

There is a beautiful story in the classic Buddhist text Shantideva's *A Guide to the Bodhisattva's Way of Life*, written in AD 700. As an analogy to how the bodhisattva (someone who dedicates his or her life to the enlightenment of others) develops compassion, the story is told of mythical peacocks who live in a grove of trees which produce poisonous berries, toxic enough to finish off anyone unlucky enough to eat one. The peacocks, however, are able to eat these berries and turn them into beautiful, vibrant, colourful feathers. For Shantideva, the story shows that the bodhisattva uses the motivation caused by seeing the suffering of others to work for his or her benefit. In Transition, we take issues that feel poisonous, which are distressing and potentially catastrophic – peak oil, climate change, economic contraction – but we view them as possibilities, as opportunities. This ability to 'transmute' such issues is one of the key aspects of Transition.

Transition as . . . a cultural shift

When we started Transition in 2005-6, I imagined we were developing an environmental response, a sustainability-focused process. After five years of this fascinating international experiment, I now see it as a cultural process. It is about asking what the culture of your community would need to be like to be as resilient as possible in the face of great change. It goes beyond reducing energy and planting trees, and needs, ultimately, to seep into the culture of place: how a place thinks of itself, what it takes pride in. This is the depth of the change Transition initiatives are attempting to effect.

One could be mistaken for thinking that a Transitioned, powered-down future will require a complete overhaul of our cultural values, the wholesale replacement of our current approach with an entirely new set of values. However, as Tom Crompton, author of *Common Cause*,[3] explained to me, cultural values lie along a spectrum, from the 'intrinsic' (which, he argues, include "the value placed on a sense of community, affiliation to friends and family, and self-development"), to

An Open Space community
event facilitated by Transition
Stoke Newington, London.
*Photo: Transition Stoke
Newington*

the 'extrinsic' ("values that are contingent upon
the perceptions of others – they relate to envy of
'higher' social strata, admiration of material wealth,
or power"). These two act in opposition to each
other, but what matters is not somehow enabling
everyone to be intrinsic all the time – we show different values when at home with our families from
when out shopping or at work. What is important is
to achieve a healthy balance.

Studies show that concerns about social and
environmental issues tend to be linked to intrinsic
values rather than extrinsic ones. So what are the
factors around us that, from the considerable
research on the subject, can be shown to work
against society cultivating intrinsic values? According to Crompton, these include:

- public policy and the values it communicates
- commercial marketing/advertising
- participation in community and civic activism
- more television viewing
- cold and uncaring parenting
- certain educational pathways; for example, it
  has been shown that those studying law or economics tend to have enhanced extrinsic values.

Research also shows that when people adopt a
behaviour change due to an intrinsic motivation
they will pursue it for longer. Trying to motivate

> "People laugh when I say this, but I
> do try to practise it enough so that
> people take it seriously, that to the
> extent that we try to spend time roll-
> ing up our sleeves and working with
> others in our community, that we
> really find the people whose views are
> the most different from our own and
> really try to work it through: therein
> lies the real rocket fuel for making
> what we're talking about happen."
>
> Michael Shuman[4]

behaviour change through an extrinsic motivation
has been shown to not be effective in the long term
(for example, encouraging people to put up solar
panels because they're the 'must-have' consumer
durable for this month). Transition works because it
cultivates intrinsic values: feeling connected to
other people, working together, making positive
change happen around us where we live, and so on,

rather than appealing to extrinsic values. It is already showing that a cultural shift to more intrinsic values is a shift that can inspire sustained change.

Transition as . . . an economic process

The next section of this book proposes that Transition is headed towards a new culture of social entrepreneurship. After our communities and their economic futures have been so damaged by the irresponsibility of the banking industry and the vagaries of economic globalisation, perhaps there is a different way of doing things. As will be explored (see Tools for Transition No.19: Tools for plugging the leaks, page 257), at present our communities are like big leaky buckets – every leak represents a potential local livelihood or business. It is becoming increasingly clear that, as government budgets are cut, funding bodies reduce what is available, and as donors become more stretched, Transition initiatives need to be able to support themselves as well as the wider process of localisation.

Transition as . . . storyteller

A Transition initiative should shift the story the community tells about itself. At the moment, we are surrounded by stories of the unlimited power of technology to overcome any problems, of a world that will forever amaze itself with the brilliance of its own inventiveness; or by stories that tell of the rapid and disastrous unravelling of everything in an apocalyptic societal collapse. Transition tells a different story.

Why does storytelling matter? As Shaun Chamberlin puts it in *The Transition Timeline*, stories:

> "tell us what is important, and they shape our perceptions and thoughts. This is why we use fairy stories to educate our children, why advertisers pay such extraordinary sums to present their perspectives, and why politicians present both positive and negative visions and narratives to win our votes."

Members of Transition Town Kensal to Kilburn in London tend their 'community allotment' at Kilburn underground station. *Photo: Chris Wells*

What has fascinated me about observing Transition unfolding over the past four years in the town where I live has been how it has begun to change how the place talks about itself. As more people are getting involved, hear about what we are doing and come to visit, letters in the local paper start referring to the place as a 'Transition Town'. The new Mayor and the new MP discuss Transition in their inaugural speeches, the town council proudly declares itself a 'Transition Town Council', and district council officers, who may be suspicious about Transition, go to events outside the town to be met with "Oh you're from Totnes, *Transition Town* Totnes!" The story is changing the town; we underestimate the power of stories at our peril.

The philosophical underpinnings

Transition is based on a range of influences and ideas, which have shaped what it is now. By the time someone writes the next Transition book, there will be many more to add to this list. The following have been a particular inspiration.

- The study of addiction, through the work of people like Carlo DiClemente and his 'Stages of Change' model[5] (see *Starting out 9: Awareness raising*, page 124). This presents a very different understanding of how people change from the 'scare them to death, *then* they'll do something' approach so prevalent in the environmental movement.
- The 'wiki' approach to collaborative information building – the idea that concepts and information built jointly have a relevance, a depth and a sense of ownership far greater than the work of one individual.[6]
- The concept of the 'leaderless organization', as proposed in *The Starfish and the Spider: The unstoppable power of leaderless organizations* by Ori Brafman and Rod Beckstrom,[7] which suggests that self-ordering organisations are far more dynamic and effective than those with a rigid leadership structure.
- The science and the study of resilience (which has been explored in Chapter 4).
- Insights from how self-organisation works in natural systems, how they self-organise and regulate themselves on a range of scales.[8]
- Joanna Macy's work on 'despair and empowerment' and insights from ecopsychology.[9]
- Martin Seligman's concept of 'learned optimism' – the idea that optimism is a learnable skill.[10]
- The science of happiness,[11] the idea that happiness can be measured,[12] and the idea that Gross National Happiness would be a far more useful measure of national well-being than Gross Domestic Product.[13]
- An understanding of the power of the internet to enable ideas to spread virally.[14]
- Various models of organisational design, including Chaordic, the model that underpins Visa, where 'belonging' to an idea is made as simple as possible, with a simple purpose and a set of principles which, if you agree with them, means you are a part of the larger process,[15] and also Parecon,[16] The Natural Step[17] and the Viable Systems Model.[18]
- The design-led permaculture concept, which designs systems, from food production to social organisation, modelled on observations from how natural systems work.[19]

> "I think the real fizz and excitement in sustainability is to be found where lifestyles and business models are being radically transformed, [i.e.] The Transition Network and the collaborative consumption movement . . ."
> Ed Gillespie[20]

To use the analogy of music, many great innovations in music happen when someone thinks "What happens if I put this with that?" For example, the combining of drum breaks from James Brown records with Led Zeppelin records, leading to a whole new genre of music emerging.[21] Transition started as an attempt to see what would happen if permaculture principles[22] were applied to seeking responses to peak oil. In the time since then, it has also drawn in a range of other influences, all of which have made it much more robust and much more dynamic.

The principles of Transition

Transition is designed to be clear and concise enough for people to feel that there is a model that can be referred back to, but loose enough for people to make it their own wherever they are. So, here are the seven principles that underpin the Transition approach:

1. Positive visioning
Transition initiatives are based on creating clear and practical visions of a community to help it reduce or lose its dependence on fossil fuels. The primary focus is on practical possibilities and opportunities rather than on campaigning against current problems. Creating new stories is central to this visioning work. To quote from the old hymn,[23] "Who so beset him round with dismal stories, do but themselves confound".

2. Help people access good information and trust them to make good decisions

Transition initiatives dedicate themselves, through all their work, to raising awareness of peak oil and climate change, and of related issues such as unsustainable economic growth. In doing so, they aim to present this information in playful, articulate and accessible ways that help people feel change is a real possibility. Transition initiatives give people the best information available, when so much is deeply contradictory. The messages are non-directive, respecting each person's ability to respond how best they can.

3. Inclusion and openness

Successful Transition initiatives will need an unprecedented coming together of society. They dedicate themselves to openness and inclusion. This principle is based on the need to involve local business communities, community groups and local authorities. It stresses that, in the challenge of energy descent, there is no room for 'them and us' thinking.

4. Enable sharing and networking

Transition initiatives dedicate themselves to sharing their successes, failures, insights and connections across the Transition network, to widely build collective experience.

5. Build resilience

This stresses the fundamental importance of building resilience – the capacity of our businesses, communities and settlements to deal with shock. Transition initiatives help build resilience in many areas (food, economics, energy, etc.), locally and nationally, within a global/international perspective.

6. Inner *and* outer Transition

The challenges we face are caused not just by a mistake in our technologies but as a direct result of our world view and beliefs. Information about the state of our planet can generate fear and grief, which may underlie many people's denial. Psychological models can help us understand what is happening and avoid unconscious processes sabotaging change. Examples include addiction and behavioural change models. This principle also

> "Power is shifting from institutions that have always been run top-down, hoarding information at the top, telling us how to run our lives, to a new paradigm of power that is democratically distributed and shared by us all."
> Joe Trippi[24]

honours the fact that Transition thrives because it helps people do what they feel called to do.

7. Subsidiarity: self-organisation and decision-making at the appropriate level

This final principle stresses that Transition should not centralise or control decision-making, but allow everyone to be involved at the most appropriate, practical and effective level in a way that reflects the ability of natural systems to self-organise.

The 12 Steps

Many initiatives have found the '12 Steps of Transition' model useful. It first appeared in the free-to-download *Transition Primer*,[25] and then in *The Transition Handbook*. It emerged out of people visiting Totnes in Transition's early days and saying, "What are you doing, and how are you doing it?" We pulled together what felt like 12 steps, not to impose a system, but because people seemed to find them useful. This still seems the case, with many liking a step-by-step model that shows where to start and how to develop.

The need for this book was inspired partly by the experience of Transition Town Totnes (TTT), the first Transition initiative to complete its Energy Descent Action Plan (the last of the 12 Steps). Strictly speaking, TTT's work was over and everyone could reflect on a job well done. In reality it had only started, and discussions about further steps started to make the whole idea of 12 steps unravel rapidly. It soon became clear that some steps weren't so much steps as tools, so in the Transition Training they became known as the 12 Ingredients. You see, we really are making all this up as we go along but, for me, that's part of the beauty of the whole thing!

As many people still find them useful, the steps have been merged into the 'Ingredients of Transition' and the 'Tools for Transition' that follow, in Part Three of this book. Here is a list of the 12 Steps, and where to find out more information about them in the next section.

The 12 Steps of Transition[26]

1. Set up a steering group and design its demise from the outset (*Starting out* 1: Coming together as groups, page 92).
2. Awareness raising (*Starting out* 9: Awareness raising, page 124).
3. Lay the foundations (*Starting out* 11: Building partnerships, page 132).
4. Organise a Great Unleashing (Tools for Transition No.10: Unleashings, page 184).
5. Form working groups (*Starting out* 10: Forming working groups, page 128).
6. Use Open Space (Tools for Transition No.15: Community brainstorming tools, page 220).
7. Develop visible practical manifestations of the project (*Deepening* 2: Practical manifestations, page 146).
8. Facilitate the 'Great Reskilling' (*Deepening* 3: The 'Great Reskilling', page 152).
9. Build a bridge to local government (*Connecting* 2: Involving the council, page 204).
10. Honour the elders (*Connecting* 4: Oral histories, page 218).
11. Let it go where it wants to go . . . (not an ingredient or a tool, more an overall way of looking at it).
12. Create an Energy Descent Plan (*Building* 1: Energy Descent Action Plans, page 235).

If this approach works for you, that's great. The 12 Steps have certainly been effective in enabling the spread of Transition so far. However, the experience gained from this five-year experiment, and the ingenuity and dedication of many thousands of people, have led to a more holistic, useful and accurate model of Transition in practice. I hope you will find it useful.

Razia Ross (left) and Michelle Yang (right) of Transition Town Boroondara in Canada teaching the 12 Steps of Transition. *Photo: Peter Campbell*

Some of the qualities of Transition

Transition seems to have these key qualities:

- **Joyful:** if it's not fun and not adding to your life, something's not working . . .
- **Viral:** it spreads rapidly and to unexpected places.
- **Open source:** people shape and enact Transition, democratically and freely.
- **Self-organising:** it is not centrally controlled. People make it their own.
- **Hopeful and constructive:** it's not about campaigning *against* things, but working *for* a world that has embraced its limitations.
- **Iterative:** it learns from its successes and failures.
- **Clarifying:** it offers a clear explanation, based on the best available science, of where humanity finds itself.
- **Sensitive to place and scale:** Transition looks different wherever it goes.
- **Historic:** it tries to create a sense of this being a historic opportunity to do something extraordinary.

CHAPTER SEVEN

The story of four Transition initiatives told using ingredients and tools

By way of introducing the next section of this book, this chapter tells four stories, relating the unfolding of four different Transition initiatives and how they used the tools and the ingredients of Transition. The key point to note is that they all took very different paths, designing a process specific to their place and their community. They certainly didn't just slavishly work through the ingredients and tools in chronological order. The main point here is that there is no one right way of doing Transition and that creativity is central to this.

1. Transition Town Tooting [London, UK]

TRANSITION TOWN
TOOTING

Transition Town Tooting (another TTT) began when Lucy Neal picked up an early Transition Town Brixton leaflet, which she kept by her bed but didn't really 'get'. Then, on a visit to Totnes, she came to an evening event about education, and was touched principally by how people spoke. They were funny, practical and positive. She returned to London and set about looking for someone who might start a Transition group in her area, but one day realised, with shock, that she was looking for herself! She visited two 'elders' that she respected in this diverse community and asked how it sounded to them, and whether they thought it might work. She received a very positive response. She also realised at that stage that she couldn't do it alone, so she teamed up with her friend Hilary Jennings.

They focused on Tooting, as local people have affection for it and it seemed the natural SCALE (*Starting out* 5). One early decision was around BUILDING PARTNERSHIPS (*Starting out* 11): a decision was made to hold events only with other local groups. FORMING AN INITIATING GROUP (*Starting out* 4) emerged when Lucy was invited by local MP Sadiq Khan to a meeting in Parliament of local green activists, at which Lucy asked "Is anyone interested in starting TTT?", and the initial team members came forward.

The first steps in INVOLVING THE COUNCIL (*Connecting* 2) were a letter telling them TTT was starting, and a meeting with the town centre manager. At that time, an event at the South Bank brought together Transition activists from across London, who began FORMING NETWORKS (*Connecting* 3), which has since led to two cross-London meetings and the Transition London network.

TTT's foundations were (and are) RESPECTFUL COMMUNICATION (*Starting out* 3) and INCLUSION AND DIVERSITY (*Starting out* 2). These are particularly important in such a diverse community, recognising that people have much in common and much that is distinct. The group is constantly trying to be as inclusive as possible, though that isn't always easy. The group sees ARTS AND CREATIVITY (*Starting out* 8) as the way to inclusion and that CELEBRATING (*Deepening* 5) is one of the best ways to bring everyone together. As part of BECOMING THE MEDIA (Tools for Transition No.13), TTT produce short films, have an excellent website, use Twitter and Facebook, and produce a fortnightly email newsletter sent to over 600 people.

PAUSING FOR REFLECTION (*Connecting* 7) and getting EMOTIONAL SUPPORT TO AVOID BURNOUT (Tools for Transition No.9: Supporting each other) happens between the South London Transition initiatives who meet for mutual support. One of TTT's first events, the Earth Talk Walk, visited places of worship in Tooting to explore the care of the Earth in each tradition, including secular readings about how to speak of things like care for the Earth. VISIONING (*Starting out* 7) has run through TTT's work and has taken a range of forms. A TRANSITION TRAINING (Tools for Transition No.3) was held in March 2008, and TTT has yet to FORM A LEGAL ENTITY (Tools for Transition No.5), preferring to remain unincorporated. COMMUNITY BRAIN-STORMING TOOLS (Tools for Transition No.15) have been used sparingly at some events.

The members realised Tooting has no 'heart', being spread out along the A24 (10 million cars a year pass through Tooting), and that something that brought everyone together was essential. The idea emerged of the Trashcatchers' Carnival, intended to celebrate and include the whole community. FINANCING (Tools for Transition No.8) emerged through a grant for that specific project. ORAL HISTORIES (*Connecting* 4) were gathered about Tooting, and woven into the skirt of one of the carnival's key features, 'The Lady of Tooting'. The carnival set about ENGAGING YOUNG PEOPLE (*Connecting* 5), and local schools were involved from the start. It was a great example of THE ROLE OF STORYTELLING (*Connecting* 6), and also led to a lot of WORKING WITH LOCAL BUSINESSES (*Connecting* 3), who between them fed over 1,000 people for free at the carnival. The carnival was an extraordinary event (for more about it see page 119), giving the organisers a sense of the power of people making things together, what Lucy calls 'shared doing'. Framed around Transition and care for the Earth, it spoke to everyone, creating something benign but radical.

The carnival led to asking "HOW ARE WE DOING?" (*Deepening* 7) followed, a week later, by the UNLEASHING (Tools for Transition No.10) of TTT. A reflective autumn then explored what should happen next. One of the key PRACTICAL MANIFESTATIONS (*Deepening* 2) of TTT has been the annual Foodival

Children posing for a photo by the Green Man, one of the huge figures produced for the carnival. *Photo: Lucy Neal*

(see page 168), which brings people together around food. A 'Community Panel' was formed, of respected local people, who can be used as a sounding board for future projects. TTT is doing a lot of work around MEANINGFUL MAPS (Tools for Transition No.16), seeking to create a new map of Tooting.

TTT has emerged slowly, and FORMING WORKING GROUPS (*Starting out* 10) has been slow. There are now six: art and creativity, food, energy, arts, well-being and local economy. MOMENTUM (*Deepening* 9) is maintained through CELEBRATING (*Deepening* 5); they don't feel the need to 'perform on all fronts' all the time.

Future plans include TOOLS FOR PLUGGING THE LEAKS (Tools for Transition No.19) with a local currency, 'The Toot', and more work on the GREAT RESKILLING (*Deepening* 3). Rather than doing a huge piece of local design and reconceiving STRATEGIC LOCAL INFRASTRUCTURE (*Building* 4), TTT is working with the Wandsworth Environmental Forum. ENSURING LAND ACCESS (*Deepening* 10) happens through working with the local cemetery, the area's largest open green space. The long-term dream is lots more PRACTICAL MANIFESTATIONS (*Deepening* 2) and also for the council to pass a PEAK OIL RESOLUTION (Tools for Transition No.21), which presently feels a long way off!

See http://transitiontowntooting.blogspot.com

2. Transition Bristol, UK

Transition Bristol was one of the early starters, being just the fourth Transition initiative and the first Transition city. It sprang from a group of people who came together around the idea of doing an ENERGY DESCENT ACTION PLAN (*Building* 1). Many of them had an interest in and some experience of permaculture, so PERMA-CULTURE DESIGN (Tools for Transition No.1) provided a foundation for FORMING AN INITIATING GROUP (*Starting out* 4). They undertook TRANSITION TRAINING (Tools for Transition No.3) early on in their work and soon evolved into organising a whole series of AWARENESS RAISING (*Starting out* 9) themed talks and events. A lot of this involved members of the group STANDING UP TO SPEAK (Tools for Transition No.2).

People also then began setting up more local initiatives in neighbourhoods within Bristol, such as Transition Montpelier and Transition Easton. Transition Bristol facilitated a monthly meeting

bringing the neighbourhoods together, but after a lot of discussion around UNDERSTANDING SCALE (*Starting out* 5), it gradually became apparent that the majority of action and resilience-building needed to happen on the ground in local neighbourhoods. Over a period of several months, Transition Bristol came to the conclusion that the best way to support this was by acting more as an administrative group that represented and was accountable to each initiative, rather than as an overarching coordination hub. Coming to this conclusion inevitably involved a certain amount of CONFLICT (Tools for Transition No.11), as is normal when people are collectively working on facing significant challenges. What is important is that useful things arise from those conflicts and that helpful lessons are learnt as quickly as possible.

Consequently, nowadays Transition Bristol's work centres very much around a combination of supporting its emergent STRUCTURE (*Starting out* 12) and liaising at a city-wide scale. Its primary functions are to share stories of what's going on around Bristol via its monthly newsletter, to hold monthly 'sofa sessions' to let anyone come and meet / talk / share / be encouraged, and to BUILD

PARTNERSHIPS (*Starting out* 11) city-wide, particularly by INVOLVING THE COUNCIL (*Connecting* 2). This has involved participation in Bristol's Green Capital Momentum Group, which put pressure on the council to address peak oil as well as climate change, resulting in 2010 in the first UK city's peak oil report (see Tools for Transition No.21) – commissioned by and written with the support of the Council. Then, in 2011, the Bristol Food Strategy was published, with a good deal of input from Transition Bristol. All that said, Transition Bristol has been clear in setting boundaries with the council where needed. For example, at their first big event, they insisted on maintaining a strong sense of independence and declined the offer from the Leader of the Council to speak.

As this book goes to print, Transition Bristol is working on TOOLS FOR PLUGGING THE LEAKS (Tools for Transition No.19), and is looking to set up a city-wide local currency with support from Tudor Trust, partnering with the Bristol Credit Union and collaborating with the new economics foundation.

See www.transitionbristol.net

Bungay Community Bees: "a group of people striving to preserve pollinators and particularly the honey bee in our environment".

3. Sustainable Bungay, UK

The good ship **Sustainable Bungay (SB)** has been sailing for three years, and in terms of UNDERSTANDING SCALE (*Starting out* 5), its focus is the traditional market town of Bungay (population 5,000) and its surrounding villages. SB's core group comprises around 15-20 members; some active, some supportive. The age group ranges from 20 to 70. They meet formally once a month, and once socially for Green Drinks in the pub. Their strength lies in an ability to play to the different skills between them and perform different roles. They are all demonstrative and enjoy working as an ensemble, as well as on their own initiative, and RESPECTFUL COMMUNICATION (*Starting out* 3) follows naturally. Sharing practical and intellectual qualities and doing stuff together is the key attraction of Transition. HOW WE COMMUNICATE (*Deepening* 4) is based on the desire to showcase these activities with others, and from the beginning SB has been STANDING UP TO SPEAK (Tools for Transition No.2) with people in the community – from the Rotary Club to the local television cameras. Since FORMING AN INITIATING GROUP (*Starting out* 4), it has always been open to new members. Like all Transition groups, they are still mastering the art of RUNNING EFFECTIVE MEETINGS (Tools for Transition No.4) and are open about where they don't succeed, and change the format accordingly.

The group took an active part in a Bungay VISIONING (*Starting out* 7) day for the Town Plan in 2009 and have done a certain amount of MEASUREMENT (*Starting out* 6), such as their forthcoming Carbon Audit. However, they are less focused on workshop-type activities and more on AWARENESS RAISING (*Starting out* 9) and community gatherings. There is

a strong emphasis on ARTS AND CREATIVITY (*Starting out* 8) – the group including writers, singers, actors, artists, craftspeople and cooks – which comes in useful when COMMUNICATING WITH THE MEDIA (Tools for Transition No.6).

In 2010 the initiative set about FORMING WORKING GROUPS (*Starting out* 10) for projects, such as the Library Community Garden[1] and the biodiesel initiative.[2] They are also engaged in BUILDING PARTNERSHIPS (*Starting out* 11) with local organisations, from the social enterprise Bright Green to the Suffolk Wildlife Trust, and run film nights with Waveney Greenpeace. In terms of FINANCING THEIR INITIATIVE (Tools for Transition No.8), SB is largely self-funding, having received some funds to develop a Carbon Audit and donations for the community garden. Their innovative Bungay Community Bees[3] is run by subscription. No one gets paid, so the initiative is reliant on VOLUNTEERS AND VOLUNTEERING (Tools for Transition No.7).

Not HAVING AN OFFICE (*Deepening* 1), the group congregates around CELEBRATIONS (*Deepening* 5) – summer picnics, Christmas parties, birthday drinks, Green Drinks. SB's informal exchange system – bring-and-share meals, and plant, produce and

chickens swaps – is what really helps with SUPPORTING EACH OTHER (Tools for Transition No.9), the group having learnt that by communicating and working with each other and exchanging 'stuff', the responsibility for the larger initiative is shared. This also helps to sustain MOMENTUM (*Deepening* 9).

The group nearly did burn out in 2009. One of their greatest challenges arose when town councillors turned down SB's application to put on a Big Green Street Market around the same time as a stressful involvement occurred with a Community Consultation for the Town Plan and the planning for SB's UNLEASHING (Tools for Transition No.10). Several members had worked very hard on the project and the refusal was a big shock and very difficult to talk about, although with time they have learnt to CELEBRATE FAILURE (*Deepening* 6) and develop greater PERSONAL RESILIENCE (*Deepening* 11).

This shock helped to clarify for the group what they wanted to do next. They now hold occasional meetings to look at HOW THEY ARE DOING (*Deepening* 7) and have created a number of PRACTICAL MANIFESTATIONS (*Deepening* 2) within the town, including organising events everyone can attend, such as GREAT RESKILLING events (*Deepening* 3), sewing classes and the hugely popular Give and Take Days. The permaculture-designed community garden also acts as a Transition beacon, as do the LOCAL FOOD INITIATIVES (*Deepening* 8). Alongside 2008's Growing Local food conference, community beehives and seedling swaps, they are starting up a pig club[4] and an 'Abundance of Fruit'[5] project. This second phase began after May 2009's UNLEASHING (Tools for Transition No.10). Over 70 people came to hear Shaun Chamberlin speak about his book *The Transition Timeline*. SB's own Timeline was posted along one wall and the tables were organised according to the nine working parties / theme groups they wanted to create. The hall was decked with flowers and the tables loaded with home-cooked, low-carbon food. They had elderflower punch and beer from the local microbrewery, and were entertained by local musicians.

Sustainable Bungay regularly interacts with neighbouring initiatives to FORM NETWORKS OF

TRANSITION INITIATIVES (*Connecting* 1). Some of the group helped run the second Transition East Gathering and produce the 'Transition East 2009' document, which profiled 29 initiatives across the eastern region. In terms of BECOMING THE MEDIA (Tools for Transition No.13), one of the ways SB keeps in touch with everyone is through their lively community blog and quarterly printed and online newsletters. These also give value and meaning to what everyone is doing when PAUSING FOR REFLECTION (*Connecting* 7).

Regular blogging helps keep a record of their personal and cultural stories (THE ROLE OF STORY-TELLING (*Connecting* 6) and sparks the imagination of the town, documenting such things as making MEANINGFUL MAPS (Tools for Transition No.16) of local neighbourhood fruit trees, flower walks for Buzzing Bungay (BCB) and inviting schoolchildren to plant bulbs in the library garden. Other ways of ENGAGING YOUNG PEOPLE (*Connecting* 5) have been through the Bungay Car-Free Day and the local Cycle Strategy, and this summer SB are teaching classes on bees.

The initiative doesn't feel large or influential enough to start SCALING UP (*Building* 3), but is engaged in STRATEGIC THINKING (*Building* 7), evolving projects within a framework of the bigger picture. Future plans include setting up SOCIAL ENTERPRISES (*Building* 2) for their Bungay Community Kitchen, COMMUNITY SUPPORTED AGRICULTURE (Tools for Transition No.20: Community-supported farms, bakeries and breweries) and biodiesel projects.

Meanwhile they're communicating with local councillors, exploring the COMMUNITY OWNERSHIP OF ASSETS (*Building* 6), and with national government about their POLICIES FOR TRANSITION (*Daring to dream* 1) (Peter Aldous, the area's Conservative MP, came to the Unleashing). The group see themselves as a small Transition lifeboat, but, as Charlotte Du Cann of SB told me, "We're not afraid of big waves (or making them!)".

See www.sustainablebungay.com

4. PEDAL [Transition Town Portobello], Edinburgh, UK

Portobello Transition Town

PEDAL emerged partly in response to climate change and peak oil, but also inspired by the successes of Eigg and other communities that had taken back their land into community ownership, as well as by Portobello's own success in stopping a national chain superstore moving into the community – the community raised £23,000 to pay for an expert witness to show how, based on a traffic volume technicality, the superstore shouldn't be allowed.

Portobello is the right size or SCALE (*Starting out* 5) for people to identify with. It has been good at saying "no", and the superstore campaign was an indication of that. But how well would they do at

I'm part of
Fruitful Porty
pedal-porty.org.uk

Pedal
Portobello Transition Town

SOLAR PORTY

PEDAL are working with Glendevon Energy to offer reduced price solar hot water panels to local residents. These can provide you with up to 70% of your annual hot water, and so save money on your bills plus reduce carbon emissions.

Approximate prices for a standard solar thermal system fitted with AES panels are £3,155 for a one bedroom home, £3,245 for a two bedroom home and £3,525 for a three bedroom home.

*Please note these are guide prices only (ex VAT – at 5%) and are subject to survey. Actual costs may vary depending on roof space and access, current boiler system, and whether additional extras are required to fit your system.

If the following numbers of homes install systems, the following discounts will apply per order:

20 homes	30 homes	40 homes	50+ homes
£155	£220	£250	£315

Glendevon Energy is accredited under the Microgeneration Certification Scheme, which means your system will qualify for the Renewable Heat Incentives – government payments starting in 2011 to encourage renewable heat technologies.

This offer will be for a limited time – please call Charlotte Bickmore now to arrange a no-obligation survey on **0131 258 4483** or e-mail charlotte@pedal-porty.org.uk.

*Properties within a conservation area may need to apply for planning permission and may not be suitable due to planning regulations.

Pedal
Portobello Transition Town
Glendevon Energy

being 'for' something? In 2005 Eva Schonveld read Rob's permaculture article on what his students were doing in Kinsale[6] and PEDAL kicked off, aiming to create a positive vision – an ENERGY DESCENT ACTION PLAN (*Building* 1) – for the site that the superstore had been going to take over. It was an ambitious task, but the CORE TEAM (*Starting out* 4: Forming an initiating group) that formed around that challenge has remained steady and consistent since the early stages of the project.

Much time was spent putting in a Lottery Fund application, which was ultimately unsuccessful. By contrast, the AWARENESS RAISING (*Starting out* 9) was very successful, kicking off with an open space VISIONING (*Starting out* 7) meeting in 2005 – followed by a ceilidh with space for post-it notes feedback. This prompted them to FORM WORKING GROUPS (*Starting out* 10), and a food and waste group and a land reform group started, looking at ENSURING LAND ACCESS (*Deepening* 10), and PEDAL began work on the Energy Descent Action Plan. One member of the food and waste group was very keen to promote action on plastic bags, and came up with a 'PEDAL bags' scheme. Using a local grant, they made up an initial run of 2,000 hessian bags. This proved to be an immediate hit with the

locals, with much pointing and proud flourishing of the bags in the streets of Portobello.

In 2006, spurred on by the PEDAL bag successes, the team came up with a Car Free Day event, with the aim of making Portobello a 'better place'. They knocked themselves out raising the profile of the day locally, and there was a grand turnout of decorated bikes and local marketeers on the day.

Members of the food and waste group hit on the idea of a community orchard. And though it was initially hard to get local people involved in the planning stages, when the group got permission for the land and set a day for the planting, a broad range of local people came to help out. Fifty trees got planted, and the location of the orchard expanded Portobello's sense of place. A series of hugely enjoyable FUNDRAISING (Tools for Transition No.8: Financing your Transition initiative) and AWARENESS RAISING (*Starting out* 9) events – from salsa dancing classes accompanying the film showing of *The Power of Community: How Cuba survived peak oil* to CELEBRATING (*Deepening* 5) seasonal festivals in the orchard – have helped build MOMENTUM (*Deepening* 9).

It was early 2007, and Scottish politics played a big part in Transition in Scotland. The SNP needed the Green Party to get their budget through the Scottish Parliament. The Greens used their influence to establish the Climate Challenge Fund (CCF), aimed at promoting and expanding community action on climate change. Members of PEDAL had played a key part in getting that POLICY FOR TRANSITION (*Daring to dream* 1) to the national level as well as in setting up Transition Scotland Support to help enable a national NETWORK OF INITIATIVES (*Connecting* 1) to emerge in Scotland.

PEDAL applied successfully for CCF funding based on a detailed survey. It enabled them to get four full-time workers – a coordinator, two food workers (looking at reskilling, feasibility for a community farm, a plan for the orchard and a local growers' market) and an energy advisor (looking at solar hot water, 'warm tenements' and energy savers).

An energy project emerged, examining the possibility of a wind turbine for COMMUNITY RENEWABLE ENERGY (Tools for Transition No.18). As with many energy groups, it was composed mainly of men, who received a grant to undertake a feasibility study for a community turbine. This group went through a very steep learning curve (and all the money), discovering that, contrary to the advice they had received from the consultants to the project, neither the proposed location nor scale of turbine would create a viable energy supply. However, in the spirit of CELEBRATING FAILURE (*Deepening* 6), all was not lost, as they decided to combine their efforts with another community project in neighbouring Leith, to look at a much better site, situated between the two communities, and this project is now moving along very well. Additionally, an offshoot of these efforts became a local solar PV project.

Alongside all this money coming into PEDAL and the SCALING UP (*Building* 3) of the initiative, the nature of the overall project was changing. PEDAL took on an OFFICE (*Deepening* 1) on the high street, but later moved to one out of sight, enabling people to be out working on projects without giving the

Eva Schonveld of PEDAL's painted vision of a powered-down Portobello.

ironic impression that because the office was empty nothing was happening! They formed a proper board (as opposed to a 'steering group'), and meetings became much more businesslike. All in all, the impacts of PEDAL in the community have increased as their long-term work becomes evident in PRACTICAL MANIFESTATIONS (*Deepening* 2), but how to maintain the fun and positive effects of PEDAL on those involved is a key question, as is the question of how to expand the core team so that it is more INCLUSIVE AND DIVERSE (*Starting out* 2). Although the hub project (along with the accompanying pub) failed to get off the ground, despite five-figure sums of money being spent on it, PEDAL's LOCAL FOOD INITIATIVES (*Deepening* 8) have been very successful: the orchard is alive and well, there is a wonderful local organic market that involves WORKING WITH LOCAL BUSINESSES (*Connecting* 3), very popular GREAT RESKILLING courses (*Deepening* 3), and new GROWING SPACES are being sought (*Deepening* 10: Ensuring land access). Meanwhile, their long-term work on SECURING FUNDING to establish a large wind turbine continues (*Daring to dream* 3: Investing in Transition). Most crucially, in terms of HOW WE COMMUNICATE (*Deepening* 4) the community has shifted from seeing PEDAL's agenda as peripheral to seeing it as a positive and central feature of the social and physical landscape.

PEDAL has learnt that the value of large influxes of money needs to be weighed against the potential non-financial costs that can accompany formalising structures; that they have to be ready for failures as well as successes; that unpredictability and unintended consequences can both help and hinder an initiative. Meanwhile, PEDAL is receiving excellent FEEDBACK (*Deepening* 7: "How are we doing?"), is on its way to developing real and meaningful STRATEGIC LOCAL INFRASTRUCTURE (*Building* 4), and is a powerful motivator for sister initiatives across Scotland.

See www.petal-porty.org.uk

Thanks to Peter Lipman, Lucy Neal, Justin Kenrick, Ben Brangwyn, Eva Schonveld, Catrina Pickering, Ciaran Mundy, Angela Raffle, Charlotte Du Cann and Josiah Meldrum for their help with these stories.

"I do Transition because it's what needs to be done, and because it's the first positive, life-affirming process that I have found."
Judy Skog

"Transition provides me with the knowledge and contacts I need for the uncertain future ahead."
Russ Carrington

"Because it just makes sense."
Harriet Stewart-Jones

PART THREE:

How the Transition movement does what it does – Ingredients for success

Transition as cookery – making use of the ingredients and tools

So let's be clear, there is no right way to do Transition. As we have seen, every initiative does it differently, and that's part of the fun of the whole thing. Think of it like cooking. There are all kinds of amazing ingredients we can assemble in order to make, say, a cake, and the creation of every cook will be unique, reflecting his or her abilities and culture, and the local resources available.

At the same time, there are certain time-proven stages to successful cake baking. You can't just put the flour in a bowl, throw in some butter, put it in the oven and expect a cake to emerge. That wouldn't work at all. Similarly, with Transition there are distinct stages the process goes through, from meeting equally enthused people and deciding to give Transition a go ('Starting out'), to finding that

you are now becoming a viable, vibrant project ('Deepening'), then trying to broaden your engagement with the local community ('Connecting') and scaling up what you are doing in order to make localisation a reality on the ground ('Building'). Lastly, there is a visionary, speculative stage of looking forward to how things might be if this happened everywhere ('Daring to dream'). That's where things get *really* interesting.

These ingredients and tools are laid out in that sequence, but, beyond that, how you assemble them is up to you. You might read them all from start to finish, or just dip in at random. At the end of each ingredient are links to others that you might also find useful, so you can just bounce around the book. So, let's step into our Transition larder . . .

Image: Marina Vons-Gupta

Starting out

These first ingredients take you from Transition being just an idea or an aspiration to its being something that is under way with a good chance of success.

1. Coming together as groups

by Sophy Banks

The Transition Belsize group giving away trees. *Photo: James Piers Taylor*

How best to bring a group of people together, and lay foundations for their working together successfully?

One common mistake when forming a Transition group is to think that because everyone is committed to the core purpose that initially drew them together, there won't be any difficulty in working together. However, everyone has their own idea about how groups should be run, based on past experience and beliefs, and on their own strengths and abilities. This ingredient doesn't intend to specify one 'right' way that groups should structure themselves – each group will need to figure out its own way of working – but it offers some useful insights and strategies.

So, how can we create as many positive effects (the things we all love about being part of a project like Transition) as possible, and minimise what can be difficult (the things that turn a pleasure into a chore)? Investing time and energy at an early stage here can save a great deal more time and energy later on. The tasks involved in this may well take up most of the first few meetings, and appear on the agenda for the first six months or year, but this is time very well spent. Later phases of group life are covered in MOMENTUM (*Deepening* 9, page 172) and HEALTHY CONFLICT (Tools for Transition No.11, page 188).

The first thing to establish is what the *purpose* of the group is. This might include a mission statement, and then some secondary sentences about how you will carry this out.

Agreeing on the mission or aim of your group will help enormously in getting clarity about everything that follows – who joins the group, how you work together and where time should be spent, what are the priorities, and so on. Some groups bring their statement of purpose to every meeting so they are reminded continually of what they set out to do.

Below are some very different kinds of activities that groups may have as part of their purpose. You may want to spend some time thinking about how much these apply to your group as you start.

- Getting tasks done.
- Improving how the group works together.
- Building trust and safety and getting to know each other.
- Giving and getting support.
- Learning and sharing tools and skills.

You will also need to agree some basic ground rules, which describe how the group will work together. This also helps to reduce misunderstandings, and having it written down and available at group meetings keeps it in mind. Most groups update and add to these rules as new things arise. Agreements made at the start might include:

- When and where meetings take place.
- How meetings are run (agenda setting, facilitation/chair, managing the time, and so on – see RUNNING EFFECTIVE MEETINGS (Tools for Transition No.4, page 122).
- How decisions are made (consensus, majority vote, consent) and recorded.
- How you behave towards each other (respectful listening, arriving on time, supporting the group purpose, being willing to be challenged about

behaviour, appreciating each other's contribution and celebrating successes, maintaining confidentiality where appropriate).
- What kinds of things you will make time for in your meetings (planning, doing, reviewing tasks, learning, social time, feelings, visioning, reviewing and revising group agreements, giving each other feedback).
- Anything else that feels important to group members.

Agreements you might want to work out later in the group's life could include:

- Is the group open or closed? How and when can people join, and how and when do people leave? If new members keep joining, you will stay in the forming stage for a long time – fine if the purpose of the group is to welcome people to Transition, but hard if you want to get things done, or build deep levels of trust and support.
- How to deal with disagreements.
- How and when to review and change the group agreements.

The last thing to consider is who you need in the group. What skills are needed? Which voices aren't there that should be there?

From the outset, create clear structures and processes that help your group to work enjoyably and effectively – and take some time to get to know each other as people!

"Never doubt that a small group of thoughtful, committed citizens can change the world. Indeed, it is the only thing that ever has."
Margaret Mead

You might also enjoy . . .
INCLUSION AND DIVERSITY (*Starting out* 2, page 94), RESPECTFUL COMMUNICATION (*Starting out* 3, page 100), TRANSITION TRAINING (Tools for Transition No.3, page 112), RUNNING EFFECTIVE MEETINGS (Tools for Transition No.4, page 122), "HOW ARE WE DOING?" (*Deepening* 7, page 166), SUPPORTING EACH OTHER (Tools for Transition No.9, page 179), PERSONAL RESILIENCE (*Deepening* 11, page 181), HEALTHY CONFLICT (Tools for Transition No.11, page 188).

2. Inclusion and diversity

with input from Lucy Neal, Catrina Pickering and Danielle Cohen

Young people from Tooting pedal some of the local elders, in their own mobile living rooms, through the streets of Tooting as part of the 2010 Trashcatchers' Carnival. *Photo: Simon Maggs*

Ensuring that initiatives reflect the greatest range of voices and experiences is not easy, but is vital to their success.

Inclusion and diversity need to be embedded at the centre of Transition as a defining feature from the start; they cannot just be added in further down the line. It is helpful to distinguish between two forms of diversity. One concerns a level playing field of fairness and equal rights (e.g. access to housing, employment and health), and the other concerns what happens on that 'playing field' – a celebration of identity, distinct voices and cultural expression. The former concerns the rights of the individual and acknowledges that society has an inbuilt bias that

needs to be monitored and redressed. The latter concerns the richness of our cultural commons and draws on a dynamic exploration of renewal, exchange and transformation that benefits society as a whole. To be clear about the difference between the two[1] is to be able to embrace the celebratory aspects of difference along with the necessary measures to monitor inequality.

In Transition Town Tooting, the Tooting Earth Walk Talk visited the main houses of worship in the town to hear readings from texts and scriptures in addition to secular poems that draw people together around care of the Earth. The Qur'an, for example, urges humankind to be a good guardian of the Earth and not be wasteful, and in the Hindu religion Shakti and Shiva represent Earth and energy. Many key Tooting people who engaged with the day now form a Transition Town Tooting Community Panel, representing different professional and cultural backgrounds. Meanwhile, also in South London, Transition Town Brixton developed the Brixton Pound, which features activist Olive Morris and historian C. L. R. James (along with James Lovelock and Vincent Van Gogh), affirming the contribution made to Brixton history by African-Caribbean residents, many of whom have adopted the new currency.

Ethnic minority communities can be very resilient, having frequently overcome considerable adversity. That said, there is often a perception in environmental groups that some sectors of society are 'hard to reach'. It is worth considering this the other way around. Are environmental groups 'hard to reach'? Who is reaching out to whom? One study in 2005[2] found that 23 per cent of black and minority ethnic respondents were happy to engage with community voluntary projects, compared with only 9 per cent of white respondents.

Another myth is the idea that people on middle incomes tend to always be the people doing voluntary work, whereas in reality people on low incomes make a massive contribution to improving the lives of people in their communities through 'informal volunteering'. A survey in 2002 of household work practices in the UK[3] found that 6.8 per cent of exchanges in affluent suburbs are unpaid, as against 15.6 per cent in lower-income neighbourhoods. These exchanges might include, for example, transporting or escorting someone to hospital, keeping in touch with someone who has difficulty getting about, looking after a property or pet for someone who's away, babysitting or caring for children, cooking, cleaning, doing laundry or shopping, collecting pensions, writing letters and filling in forms, decorating and DIY.

When we start to look around our communities, it becomes apparent that there is an enormous amount already going on that Transition can support, collaborate with and learn from. As one interviewee of Danielle Cohen, who has done research into inclusion in Transition Stoke Newington,[4] said, "Transition should perhaps not be seeking to include others but should be seeking to be included by them."

It's important to consider how inclusive we're being in Transition activities. In Danielle Cohen's research on Inclusion in Transition Stoke Newington, she interviewed a woman who stated that, although she had done the Transition Training, she found it hard being the only person of colour in the group. "I didn't feel there were that many people like me."

Explaining Transition Town Tooting's 'Foodival' to a passer-by. *Photo: Simon Maggs*

Dancing at Fishponds: children from the Indian dance club at the Tooting Trashcatchers' Carnival. *Photo: Simon Maggs*

Some tips on making your initiative as diverse, equitable and inclusive as possible by Catrina Pickering of Transition Network

- **Be up-front in stating that you believe there is strength in diversity.** Be clear that you mean diversity in its widest sense, including ethnicity, disability, age, class, gender and sexual and religious orientation, and in a spirit that includes all national origins and a mix of combination of identities (everyone has that), as well as professional and non-professional status.

- **Listen, observe, be curious.** Seek to build common ground and common language around universal human delights and needs – love, food, family, engagement, connection. Speak to people and start with where they are right now, rather than insisting on your agenda. Be trustworthy. Be yourself. Ask what the barriers are to participation.

- **Use plain human language.** Avoid jargon.

- **Be aware that what you are doing might feel right for you but uninviting for others.** Different sectors of society meet each other in different ways. Be aware of alcohol and dress issues; cultural customs. Again, find common ground through forms of human engagement such as practical activities, food, the arts, creativity and celebration. Pay visits to local groups and projects in your area. How and where do they meet? Do they eat first, sing, pray? How do they make decisions? Challenge your own thinking.

- **Engage with young people.** They are familiar with the contemporary world's mixed cultural identities. They're often directly part of how society adapts and is renewed through the interplay of cultures, influences and the idea that one voice does not need to obliterate another. Work with schools in creative ways.

- **Look out for events and partnerships that can create connections,** participation and a sense of shared belonging to a place. The history of an area always holds keys to this through trade, history and – yes – sometimes exploitation, but the stories are there to be renewed and reconciled.

- **Learn to recognise power dynamics.** Focus on engaging in straightforward human ways to be collaborative and creative. Be open to questioning assumptions that arise. How do we feel about adapting or letting go of ways of thinking?

- **Consider diversity training with agencies that specialise in providing it.** It can give confidence and allow you to see where the opportunities rather than the problems lie. Transition Training is also looking at developing diversity training, so watch this space.[5]

But there were other aspects too which had to do with the meetings themselves. She found them inhibiting and what she termed "quite sit-downy". "I remember being in a meeting and there was someone just chatting complete s*** for 15 minutes . . . I often just found it really hard to talk." She expressed a sense of disappointment in Transition, which was challenging to hear.

The British Trust for Conservation Volunteers (BTCV) took a decision a few years ago to stop preaching to the converted and to actively work with those who, up to that point, they hadn't engaged with much. They intentionally sought to develop projects and initiatives in as inclusive a way as possible, by ensuring that those running the organisation asked themselves the following questions. This provides a great checklist for Transition core groups to keep referring back to:

- Do we really mean it? (That is, do we really mean to address this issue?)
- Do we know where we want to get to?
- Do we know why we're doing it?
- Does our leadership champion this?

Whether we are talking about Totnes, Manchester, Forres or Los Angeles, the hallmarks of diversity remain the same. Every community has a diversity of perspectives, skills, stories and experiences,

along with some power structures that are more dominant than others. Transition can begin to build alternative channels of community engagement that are open to everyone, regardless of differences, and should seek to acquire skills and tools to place diversity and inclusion at the centre of all its work.

Diversity can only come from a commitment to values of inclusion and respect throughout the organisation. Go out to people and listen, and build on the concerns and passions that fuel the people around you.

You might also enjoy . . .

RESPECTFUL COMMUNICATION (*Starting out* 3, page 100), ARTS AND CREATIVITY (*Starting out* 8, page 117), RUNNING EFFECTIVE MEETINGS (Tools for Transition No.4, page 122), AWARENESS RAISING (*Starting out* 9, page 124), BUILDING PARTNERSHIPS (*Starting out* 11, page 132), HOW WE COMMUNICATE (*Deepening* 4, page 155), CELEBRATING (*Deepening* 5, page 161), LOCAL FOOD INITIATIVES (*Deepening* 8, page 168), ORAL HISTORIES (*Connecting* 4, page 218), ENGAGING YOUNG PEOPLE (*Connecting* 5, page 223), THE ROLE OF STORYTELLING (*Connecting* 6, page 229).

Transition Llambed in Wales produced two posters to promote an event about diversity.

Tools for Transition No.1: Permaculture design

Students on a permaculture design course in York presenting their design project. They had been asked to redesign a back garden as a productive landscape, incorporating fruit trees and shrubs as well as vegetables.
Photo: Andy Goldring

Permaculture is a design 'glue' to stick together all the elements for a sustainable and resilient culture. The elements such a culture will depend on include local food production, energy generation, water management, meaningful employment, and so on. Permaculture helps assemble those things in the best way possible. It has been described as 'the art of maximising beneficial relationships'. I rather like that.

Permaculture began during the first oil shocks of the 1970s, as a primarily agricultural approach, a contraction of '**perma**nent agri**culture**'.[6] It was an approach for the design, implementation and maintenance of agricultural systems modelled on natural systems, particularly taking climax forests as the model. If forests can function for thousands of years in a way that is highly diverse and highly productive in terms of biomass, yet require no fertiliser, watering, weeding, and so on, then that might prove to be a better agricultural model than monoculture.

Since then, permaculture has evolved to be seen as a contraction of '**perma**nent' and '**culture**', as it goes beyond agriculture, arguing that food production is part of a wider culture of permanence. It is now perceived as a design system which draws from observations of how natural systems function and insights from systems thinking, applying them to how we design the world around us.

Let's say you want to design a landscape that includes a house, a pond and a vegetable garden.

You could position them purely for their aesthetics. They would do well enough, but, with planning, our three elements can do far more.

Let's say we put the pond on the south side of the house (using northern hemisphere bearing here), with the vegetable garden between them. Having the pond in front of the garden provides a heat sink, which means that the garden's temperature is now 1-2°C warmer than it would otherwise have been. The pond reflects winter sun into the house, reducing the need for lighting. Being right in front of the house, the garden demands less time, as there is no distance to travel to it. The silt from the pond can fertilise the garden, and watering becomes much easier. All of these benefits are possible because of the conscious design. Apply that approach to other challenges and you've got perma-culture. That's why, when we are rethinking our settlements with the Energy Descent Action Plan (see *Building* 1, page 235), permaculture design skills are so useful.

Permaculture is taught in many ways. The two-day introductory course gives a useful overview, which can be followed by the 72-hour Permaculture

> "Traditional agriculture was labour-intensive, industrial agriculture is energy-intensive, and permaculture-designed systems are information- and design-intensive."
> David Holmgren

Design Course. This is taught in various forms, from two-week intensives to evening classes over a year. A two-year diploma and a wide range of specialist training can then deepen the skills. There is an established network of permaculture teachers, local groups and also some excellent and well-established demonstration projects that are well worth a visit. In my experience, having at least one person in a Transition group who is steeped in permaculture can make a huge difference to the group. Try to encourage permaculture skills across your group and initiative. There are many overlaps between Transition and permaculture, and your initiative can be a part of deepening this relationship.

One application of permaculture design is the forest garden. What at first glance looks like a random jungle is actually a carefully designed assembly of edible and useful plants, layered to make best use of the space.

3. Respectful communication

Placards with a difference, at the launch of the Totnes Energy Descent Action Plan, May 2010.

Any group whose members can't listen to each other or maintain respectful communication will soon dissolve into rancour.

What is meant by respect? We all have our own concept of what it *isn't*; whether this is people we have encountered who are rude, brash and incapable of listening, or whether it is televised debates between politicians. We know respectful communication when we see it, and it draws a lot from civility. It is worth looking at civility in order to understand its healthy and unhealthy forms.

Unhealthy civility (defined as formality or excessive politeness) can uphold established power relationships, running counter to Transition's wish for a

vigorously sustainable culture. Civility can become confused with passivity. In some cultures, for example, it would be seen as uncivil for women to participate in civic and/or political life at all.

Virginia Sapiro has argued, about the historical advancement of women's rights,[7] that "There simply was no way for women to advance their interests through politics in a civil manner." As Ronald Reagan's son Michael put it, "After all, revolutions aren't made without ruffling feathers and revolutionaries aren't renowned for their etiquette."[8] Civility is, of course, easier to achieve when people are more likely to agree with each other and to understand each other. As Sapiro puts it, civility is "hard to achieve in any setting in which people have differences of status, history, culture or intent".

Some features of good listening
from the World Café
[http://theworldcafe.com]

- Listen to what the speaker is saying with the implicit assumption that he or she has something wise and important to say.

- Listen with a willingness to be influenced.

- Listen for where this person is coming from and appreciate that his or her perspective, regardless of how divergent from your own, is valid and represents a part of the larger picture, which none of us can see by ourselves.

- While you are speaking, it is good also to try to be clear and succinct, and not hog the space.

The local Mayor is presented with a bouquet of locally grown vegetables at her opening of the Transition North conference in Slaithwaite, Yorkshire.

Yet civility – or, in its healthier manifestation, respectful communication – is essential in a Transition initiative. One forceful, rude person can drive many more people away and can make progress impossible. Respectful communication is about being mindful. Mindful of trying to understand the views of your colleagues. Mindful of remaining open to persuasion; not attaching rigidly to the perceived rightness of your argument. Mindful of approaching others with courtesy and clarity.

Body language and active listening matter greatly. Nobody likes speaking to someone who clearly would rather not listen. Listening with folded arms, with wandering eyes and a mind that is clearly elsewhere, is not really listening. Sitting up, being attentive, maintaining eye contact and giving good feedback all introduce mutual respect and warmth when meeting and working with others.

Ultimately, this is pretty straightforward. There may be times politically when being uncivil is called for, but we all know how feeling respected *feels*. When

someone listens to us, we feel good, as opposed to the frustration that arises from being with someone rude and abrasive. If we know what feels good, it will benefit our Transition work hugely to always bear that in mind, and ensure that people we meet are left feeling the same way.

Value and cultivate qualities of compassion and respect throughout your initiative's work, promoting politeness and respectful communication in your meetings and all other areas of what you do.

You might also enjoy . . .
INCLUSION AND DIVERSITY (*Starting out* 2, page 94), HOW WE COMMUNICATE (*Deepening* 4, page 155), SUPPORTING EACH OTHER (Tools for Transition No.9, page 179), PAUSING FOR REFLECTION (*Connecting* 7, page 233).

4. Forming an initiating group

with input from Sophy Banks

An early meeting of the formative Transition Town Totnes initiating group, over a shared lunch.

Starting a Transition initiative can feel like an overwhelming task. How can this be made into a manageable process for one person or a group to kick off?

Once a group of people have come together and decided they want to start a Transition initiative, the best focus for that, that we have found so far, is the concept of the initiating group.

The work of the initiating group starts the core activities of Transition:
- Building partnerships
- Awareness raising
- Visioning
- Reskilling
- Practical activities
- Attending to the well-being of the group and the people in it.

Use the tips in COMING TOGETHER AS GROUPS (*Starting out* 1, page 92) as an aid to setting up this group to work well together from the outset.

Bring together people with enough diverse skills that they cover most of those above. People who know people and are well connected in the community are vital. Ask who's missing, and talk to them about whether Transition interests them. Check on the Transition Network website to see if there are other groups near you to connect with or for mutual support. Also on the site are events and projects that other groups have done, if you want inspiration.

A list of skills your initiating group might need
from the Transition Training materials

- **Facilitating meetings:** Agenda, facilitation, decision-making, communication skills.
- **Running talks:** Designing and facilitating processes – time for conversations, feedback, digestion.
- **Publicity:** Press releases and media, website, designing posters and flyers, blogs.
- **Managing information:** Email lists, website, 'to do' lists.
- **Event organising:** Booking rooms, DVDs, speakers, projector and screen, refreshments, facilitator, etc.
- **Organisational skills:** Finance, legal, insurance.

- **Public speaking:** At events and talks.
- **Networking:** Good connections with existing organisations and people in your community and wider.
- **Leadership:** Taking responsibility and following through. This may be many people or just a few.
- **Relationship and people skills:** Passion and commitment, humour, flexibility.
- **Sensitivity:** To both the community and the group.
- **Celebrating and appreciating:** The work of individuals and the group.

What if Transition doesn't really take off, in spite of the best efforts of your group? Don't be discouraged if it just doesn't seem to gain any meaningful traction – perhaps it's not the right time for your area, or the model and ideas don't suit the way your community likes to work. Find positive ways to use your energy in existing groups, or do the one project that inspires or interests you the most!

In *The Transition Handbook*, it was suggested that an initiating group would "design its demise from the outset", and some initiatives, such as Transition Forest Row, who used their Unleashing to tell everyone who had come that they were now handing the initiative over to whoever wanted to drive the process forwards, have put this into practice. For some it has worked really well – the initiating group's work ended at a launch, or an Open Space event (see page 220) at which new working groups were formed, and it then handed over running the Transition project to a new structure. For others the process is more gradual – as new groups form, new people join the group, and the initiators take a step back or move into a different role, perhaps finally

getting to do that practical project they wanted to do, or organising a specific working group.

An initiating group serves to kick the Transition process off, its members acting as the early pioneers who network and lay good foundations, until another group takes over the reins of what has become an established and wider-reaching Transition initiative.

You might also enjoy . . .

COMING TOGETHER AS GROUPS (*Starting out* 1, page 92), TRANSITION TRAINING (Tools for Transition No.3, page 112), VISIONING (*Starting out* 7, page 114), AWARENESS RAISING (*Starting out* 9, page 124), FORMING WORKING GROUPS (*Starting out* 10, page 128), BUILDING PARTNERSHIPS (*Starting out* 11, page 132), UNLEASHINGS (Tools for Transition No.10, page 184), FORMING NETWORKS OF TRANSITION INITIATIVES (*Connecting* 1, page 198).

Tools for Transition No.2: Standing up to speak

Steve Jenkins and Margaret Lyth of Transition City Lancaster addressing their initiative's Unleashing, April 2010.

The human brain is a fantastic thing. It is capable of incredible wonders, great poetry, mathematics and actually understanding how Sudoku works, yet it ceases to function when you stand up to speak in public. Surveys have shown that many people fear public speaking more than they fear death! It need not be like that, and it will help your initiative greatly if there are a number of people involved who feel confident in delivering talks about what the group is doing. Public speaking, like riding a bicycle, is a learnable skill. What follows is an attempt at a crash course in public speaking, although there is nothing like practice.

First, know your audience. You cannot expect to give exactly the same talk to wildly different audiences. Who are you speaking to? What makes them tick? What might engage and enthuse them, and what is guaranteed to turn them off? Then, you need to know your material. This doesn't mean you need to learn your whole speech by heart (although it might be useful to learn some bits of it), but you need to know what you're going to tell them, and have some kind of structure to what you are going to say. You need a beginning (what you're going to talk about, how long you will take, whether or not there will be time for questions, and so on), a middle (the main presentation) and an end (summarising your talk and an inspiring conclusion). There are a few ways you can be sure that you'll get it right:

- Write the main points out on to cards you can glance at as you give your talk.

- If appropriate, use PowerPoint slides to trigger you to talk on different subjects you feel comfortable with (but don't feel you have to use them; remember the art of fine storytelling – see *Connecting* 3, page 213 . . .)
- Write out your talk, and then summarise it into points that you can refer to as you speak.

Few things are duller than a talk read entirely from sheets of paper, interminable slide shows with endless incomprehensible graphs, or a standard talk given with no reference to the audience. Make it lively, relevant and entertaining. Begin by asking whether everyone can hear you, especially the people at the back. If using a microphone, establish the best place to hold it and keep mindful of holding it there, rather than flapping it about. Tell your own story, or stories of projects you have been involved with. Hearing someone talking honestly about his or her own experiences is worth a thousand slides, and really brings talks to life.

Don't pace up and down, and make sure you have regular eye contact with as many of the audience as possible. Use your hands but don't flap them about excessively. Keep an eye on the clock. Saying you are going to talk for 20 minutes and to still be there after 40 is very disrespectful of your audience. Most people have an attention span of 6-8 minutes: change the pace and change the medium to sustain their interest.

Remember that doom and gloom are not good tools for engaging people. You will lose your audience quickly. Also don't overwhelm people with too many graphs and statistics; use them judiciously and move on. What appeals to people, and what stays with them, is the emotion of what you are talking about. Why does Transition excite *you*? Tell your story; tell your initiative's story. Use positive language. Will you present Transition as being about disastrous and nightmarish scenarios of peak oil and climate catastrophe, or as about unleashing enterprise, creativity and community to seize the moment of this historic opportunity to rethink how our communities work? What you are trying to do is – with humour, compassion and kindness – to create, as George Marshall of Climate Outreach and

> "They may forget what you said, but they will never forget how you made them feel."
> Carl W. Buechner

Information Network (COIN) puts it, a new social norm, one in which Transition comes across as the most logical and the most satisfying thing to do in these times.

In the unlikely event that your first talk bombs, get back in the saddle and try again. Accept any invitation to speak; it is all good practice. In time, your confidence will grow, and when you take to the stage you will find that that space is *yours*, and that you are in command, that your two feet are planted firmly on the stage and that you feel at home. In time you can actually find that it is quite enjoyable! Finally, always be open to feedback. It may be uncomfortable, but it will help you to improve hugely. It is worth mentioning, though, that while a successful Transition initiative needs a small but diverse group of people able to speak in public, an interest in public speaking is not a prerequisite to engagement in Transition!

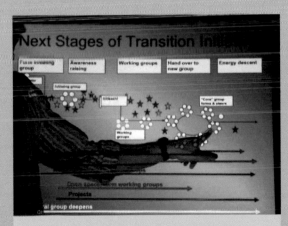

Transition trainer Nick Osborne outlining the Transition process. *Photo: Jan O'Highway*

5. Understanding scale

An early Transition Bristol event maps the neighbourhood initiatives popping up across the city.
Photo: Tulane Blyth

What is the most appropriate scale for your Transition initiative to work on?

In a rural market town with a distinct historical catchment, defining the scope of a Transition initiative is straightforward. There is often still a cultural memory of the reach of that catchment. In Totnes in Devon, for example, research I carried out[9] found that, for the majority of people surveyed, what 'local food' meant was food that was sourced within 30 miles, close to that of the town's historical market catchment. In large conurbations, such as San Francisco or London, this is more problematic.

There are around 40 Transition initiatives across London, from Transition Town Brixton to Transition

Finsbury Park. They concentrate on their neighbourhoods, building on people's sense of their part of the city. Since 2010, people have been discussing 'Transition London' as a city-wide network to support neighbourhood activities.[10] In Bristol, on the other hand, 'Transition Bristol' was set up to catalyse neighbourhood groups through a sense of being part of a bigger picture. While the neighbourhood groups have busied themselves with practical local projects, Transition Bristol has, among other things, worked with Bristol City Council to produce its 'Peak Oil Plan' (you can read more about Transition Bristol on page 82).

As with much of life, there are no absolute answers. Ultimately, the best scale for your initiative is that over which you feel you can have an influence. That

Transition and scale in London by Alexis Rowell, Transition Belsize

As a Londoner, one of the first questions I asked myself when I came across Transition was "Can it work in cities?" The key thing I've learnt from doing Transition in London is that it does, but not at the city level. It has to be a scale where people recognise each other in the street.

Totnes, for example, is a small town of 8,500 people. The London Borough of Camden, on the other hand, has 220,000 residents. Every day, 200,000 commuters come in to work. You can't create community on that sort of scale. So I went back to my neighbourhood, Belsize Park, to see if I could make Transition work there. Belsize ward is 8,400 people. Greater Belsize is about 16,000, about the same size as Lewes – another market town with a strong

Transition group. The one exception I have so far found to my rule is Brixton, which has a population of about 90,000 and a vibrant Transition initiative. It's the exception that proves the rule: it works because of an incredibly strong identity.

One founder of Transition Belsize left us after a while because his neighbourhood is some way away on the border of Camden and Barnet. His community, really, is his street. So he knocked on every door in his street, offered every resident a tomato plant and invited them round to watch the film *The Power of Community* (see Resources section). That's as much a manifestation of Transition as Totnes or Belsize or Brixton. But Transition London or Manchester or Bristol? I say no!

Transition Willesden celebrate their first meeting, in June 2011.
Photo: Jonathan Goldberg

How would Transition work on the scale of Los Angeles?
by Joanne Porouyow

Sensible people say it's impossible, but impossible things are happening every day. The Transition movement in Los Angeles is unfolding today via a series of neighbourhood initiatives. Our city hub supports seven active local initiatives that are holding regular meetings. On any given week, there are several Transition-type events offered within our local network. Our speaker's bureau maintains a brisk schedule, each week fielding several requests from other groups.

The local Transition initiatives have spawned time banks, community gardens, rainwater harvesting installations and a backyard food redistribution network. Our more colourful events have included bread-baking workshops, 100-mile meals, 'Repurposing Old Clothes' workshops and a Chicken Run Party, where participants built a coop together. Peel back the surface of any of these projects or events and you'll find far more than a cool, greener

thing to do. There is a conscious effort to create comprehensive solutions to the great challenges that humanity faces today, namely *peak oil, climate change and economic contraction, combined.* Back in 2005, when I was driving home from Santa Barbara, if you'd told me that within five years all these things would unfold, I'd have laughed through my pain and declared it was impossible.

Turning old clothes into new ones at Transition South Bay LA's 'Repurposing Event', September 2010. *Photo: Michael Vin Lee*

could just be your street, your block of housing, your school or village, or on a much larger scale. Permaculture co-founder Bill Mollison once said that you should situate your food garden "no further from the kitchen door than you could throw the kitchen sink". Similarly, with Transition, start with what feels manageable. If you get moving with that, you will no doubt inspire other people in neighbouring communities. They might start their own initiatives, creating a 'ripple effect' far more effective than if you had tried to do everything yourself!

Ultimately, the best scale to work on is the scale over which you feel you can have an influence. Single street? Perhaps not ambitious enough. Entire city? Possibly asking a bit much of yourselves. Choose somewhere in the middle that feels do-able and that feels like home.

You might also enjoy . . .

PERMACULTURE DESIGN (Tools for Transition No.1, page 98), TRANSITION TRAINING (Tools for Transition No.3, page 112), FORMING NETWORKS OF TRANSITION INITIATIVES (*Connecting* 1, page 198), ORAL HISTORIES (*Connecting* 4, page 218), PAUSING FOR REFLECTION (*Connecting* 7, page 233).

6. Measurement

Gathering data about the impact of your Transition initiative need not be an onerous process. *Photo: Dan Ball*

What is the best way of measuring the impact your Transition initiative is having, whether social, economic or environmental?

In the excited swirl of starting a Transition initiative, measuring progress isn't generally top of anyone's list of priorities. However, finding straightforward ways of gathering data is very useful from early on. Many books on sustainability auditing and measuring impact can be bewildering to all but the qualified accountant. Certainly, measuring the exact amount of carbon saved through the endeavours of the initiative is a big job, but there are various ways your group can start to gather data. Let's start from the easiest and go through to the most complicated. . .

Harvesting simple data from events and projects

Keep a spreadsheet of your events and the number of people who came. Record other easily measurable outputs from projects, such as the number of trees planted, students worked with in the local school, new allotments created, and so on. Simple feedback forms after any trainings or key events can check for satisfaction and degree of agreement with particular suggestions. Ask the different working groups to record data that emerges from their work. Also, although strictly speaking it isn't measurement, keep a photographic record of your Transition process. I take as many photos as possible of the Transition projects, events and initiatives I visit as possible – which have helped make this book what it is!

Using tools that gather data

Initiatives like Transition Streets (see Tools for Transition No.12, page 201), have great potential for gathering useful data for reductions in carbon emissions. Also, in Transition Horncastle, the group has worked with British Gas and the Energy Saving Trust's 'Green Streets' programme, which gives participating households Smart Meters and other support for energy reduction. One resident who took part stated that it has "revolutionised our lives". The project has also provided Transition Horncastle with data about what degree of energy use reduction is possible.

More detailed surveys

You may, if resources permit, decide to do an annual survey of the community to establish how opinions have changed, and what effect you are having. This level of research may be helped considerably with input from a local college or university. Sometimes you may be approached by students wanting to research your work, or you could approach teachers of sustainability courses,

or see if any students researching dissertations might want to do such a survey for you.

Designing a good questionnaire is an art. We have all been asked to fill in a 15-page questionnaire and not done so. There are a number of good guides to designing good surveys.[11] Far more reliable data is gained by door-to-door surveys than just stopping people in the street. Choose your sample carefully, trying to get as representative a spread as possible across the area. Someone with knowledge of statistics will need to process your data.

Other, less formal, tools

There are also tools for gathering useful data that are more about people's attitudes and behaviour. This approach is just as useful as the more quantitative ones just outlined. Semi-structured interviews, where a list of topics is explored through a series of open-ended questions, can be great for, for example, determining what those involved in a Transition initiative, or a particular project, would perceive as its being successful. You might also run some focus groups,[12] great for

Transition Ashtead conduct their bee survey at the Ashtead Village Day.
Photo: Kenn Jordan

Some tips for designing surveys

- **Make it as short as possible:** We all have busy lives and better things to do than trawl through endless questions.
- **Identify in advance what is essential to know:** Why are you doing the survey? What do you want to learn from it?
- **Use simple language:** Write in plain and accessible English. Avoid complex, lengthy or very abstractly worded questions.
- **Don't use leading questions:** Keep the tone as neutral as you can, so your impartiality and scientific method are respected.
- **Try it out first:** Pilot your survey on a few people first to iron out any glitches, any questions that don't make sense, etc.

Completed survey forms in Totnes, part of research conducted by Transition Town Totnes and the University of Plymouth, which fed useful information into the town's Energy Descent Action Plan.

brainstorming what people would see as indicators that a project had worked or failed. You can then return to these points at the end of the project.

Surveys and questionnaires can also be part of listening to your community. For example, Transition Helena, in Montana, USA, has done an attitudes survey as a precursor to any Transition awareness-raising activities. This involves a face-to-face interview with key community leaders to find out what they're already doing and to identify the concerns of the community. The results of this will underpin how Transition Helena formulate their activities.

As the effect of your projects grows, it will become increasingly important that you document it. Getting into the discipline from an early stage will stand you in good stead for later, as well as providing insights that will help increase your impact.

> "If you know before you look, you cannot see for knowing."
> Sir Terry Frost, RA

You might also enjoy . . .
INCLUSION AND DIVERSITY (*Starting* out 2, page 94), VOLUNTEERS AND VOLUNTEERING (Tools for Transition No.7, page 150), WORKING WITH LOCAL BUSINESSES (*Connecting* 3, page 213), ENERGY RESILIENCE ASSESSMENT (Tools for Transition No.14, page 216), MEANINGFUL MAPS (Tools for Transition No.16, page 226).

Resources
SurveyMonkey is a great tool for doing internet surveys: see www.surveymonkey.com.

Tools for Transition No.3: Transition Training

with input from Sophy Banks and Naresh Giangrande

Training for Transition – Minneapolis / St Paul, Minnesota, May 2010. *Photo: Shelby Tay*

Transition Training was developed by Transition Training and Consulting. It offers an immersion in the early stages of Transition, providing the basics for setting up, running and maintaining a Transition initiative. Trainings are run regularly in a number of countries, usually over two days,[13] and offer the following.

- **Experience Transition in action:** Every aspect of the training, from striving to make the training itself affordable to respect, inclusion and sharing of information, reflects the Transition process.
- **Focus on the early stages of Transition:** The training focuses on the first five 'steps' of Transition (now four 'ingredients' and one 'tool' – *Starting out* 4: Forming an initiating group; *Starting out* 9: Awareness raising; *Starting out* 11:

Building partnerships; Tools for Transition No.10: Unleashings and *Starting out* 10: Forming working groups), which address how to communicate Transition, the principles of resilience, how to set up an initiating group, and the importance of the inner aspects of Transition work.

- **Experience varied learning, participation and facilitation:** Transition Training offers participants first-hand experience of World Café, Open Space and other tools for running groups, presenting and ways to engage people.
- **Look into the inner aspects of Transition:** It covers the emotional aspects of Transition work, how to create a culture that supports change, and how to deepen our understanding of change, within ourselves and our initiatives.

- **Meeting others:** Transition Training gives you a sense of being part of a wider international cooperative, co-created movement, and a chance to ask questions, get feedback and be inspired by others' stories.

Other trainings have also been developed. These include Transition Talk Training, which aims to give people the tools and the confidence to give presentations about Transition, Energy Resilience Assessment Training (see also Tools for Transition No.14: Energy Resilience Assessment, page 216) and the Train the Trainers course, a four-day course for people who would like to be able to run training courses.

So how does doing Transition Training affect those who do it?[14] Valerie, from Transition Omagh, said:

> "I had no expectations of the gathering/ training, but it was brilliant, and totally surprising in many ways. For me the best thing is that it really affirmed what we had spent that last two years doing. As the facilitators went through the steps/ ingredients, I found myself thinking 'oh, we did that', 'yes, we did that' and 'we did that too!' It *really* strengthened our group to have members attend the training, and have a much fuller understanding of the process in action."

Jo Homan of Transition Finsbury Park said: "We heard lots of useful anecdotes about event organising and it was very reassuring [in terms of] the barriers we were already experiencing." Trish Knox of Transition Woodinville, USA, found that the Transition Training her group organised had some unexpected spin-off benefits:

> "One woman said that she is off of her antidepressants and now hopeful because she no longer feels alone. Another woman expressed gratitude for her dad, 90 years old, who taught her many of the skills on the list. "

As well as being a rich experience for those doing the training, it is also a powerful process for those leading it. One of the UK's Transition trainers, Nick Osborne, reflects from the trainer's perspective:

> "One of the things that stands out for me about the Transition Training is how it can take people on a journey. I have seen a number of people start the training in a fairly desolate place, feeling despair, depression and a real lack of positivity about the situation we find ourselves in. I have seen these people go on a journey and emerge looking forward to the next steps . . . and come to a much more positive place at the end of the weekend, feeling more connected, hopeful, motivated and inspired to take action. It is a very humbling thing to experience and be a part of people going through that kind of shift."

You can check the Transition Network's website for dates and venues of upcoming trainings to see if there is one near you, or you could organise one in your community. Some initiatives have successfully asked their local council or other local groups or businesses to fund the training, to make it available to the widest range of people.

See www.transitionnetwork.org/support/training.

A Transition Training at Kadoorie Farm and Botanic Garden in Hong Kong. *Photo: Sophy Banks*

7. Visioning

Visioning the future of Brixton: from a display prepared for the Unleashing of Transition Town Brixton.
Photo: Amelia Gregory

Not being able to imagine a lower-carbon world is a huge impediment to designing and realising it. How best to overcome this collective failure of the imagination?

Visioning helps distinguish Transition from most other environmental approaches. Rather than campaigning based on a grim portrayal of the future, Transition suggests we start by creating a positive vision of a future. It asks, "If you woke up in, say, 2030, and the transition had been successfully managed, what would it look, feel, smell and sound like? What would you have for breakfast? What would you see when walking down the street?" When I asked a senior planner for Totnes that

question, his response was revealing. "I suppose it would probably feel like going back to the way it was," he told me, before going on to paint a picture of the settlements of his childhood. Perhaps the Copenhagen climate negotiations in 2009 failed partly because few of those there on our behalf went with such a vision in their minds? Why fight for a low-carbon future if you can't even imagine it?

The first thing to consider about visioning is that context is critical. A completely open-ended visioning process is of little value: what matters is that it roots itself in a future world that has responded to climate change, has far less net energy than today, has moved beyond economic growth, and has adapted creatively and purposefully. The Totnes Energy Descent Action Plan (EDAP),[15] the

Transition in Action: 'Towards a resilient Taunton Deane' – from then to now   by Chrissie Godfrey

Workshops run by Taunton Transition Town with their local council, inviting them to create a vision for a post-oil Taunton Deane.
Photo: Chrissie Godfrey

In 2009, Taunton Transition Town (another TTT) ran an exemplary visioning exercise with their local borough council at the request of the council's strategic director. It brought together almost all the council's 375 employees, from senior management to plumbers, plus over half of the council's elected members, to create a vision for a post-oil Taunton Deane. They were asked to creatively get to grips with what the area needed to become resilient.

The resulting ideas were pulled together into 'Towards a Resilient Taunton Deane', a document whose story has kept the council buzzing ever since. The strategic director instantly created a Green Champions team to promote all things green across the organisation. The council joined the 10:10 campaign, and by November 2010 had achieved a saving of 9.87 per cent on its energy usage. Each department now has a Green Charter, and there are regular events to keep Transition alive for all staff.

Other spin-offs include:

- A planning officer and a car park attendant independently planting a new apple orchard on public land. They didn't even know each other before our workshops.
- Our being invited to address the Local Strategic Partnership (LSP) about peak oil and resilience, resulting in their giving TTT a grant to repeat the workshops in the community. We have now run seven, and after each one pulled together the visions and ideas into a printed and illustrated story to give back to the community, highlighting local priorities and intentions.
- After one workshop in the highly rural Neroche Parish, their new parish plan now has a strong 'green' element.
- In Wellington, the workshop helped the existing Transition group increase their membership and identify priorities. At least four other Transition-style groups are also emerging as a result.
- Local Transition members now work with the council's new climate change officer to recruit new volunteers to act as Home Energy Auditors. Ten of these, all trained to NVQ standards, provide free advice to householders on cutting their bills.

See www.tauntontransition.wordpress.com

Transition in Action: Visioning in Kingston

Local people taking part in the 'Our Kingston, Our Future' workshop, April 2009. *Photo: Artgym*

In April 2009, Transition Town Kingston (-upon-Thames) (TTK) did a community visioning process together with Artgym™, a community arts group. The project, 'Our Kingston, Our Future', brought together the under-25s with the over-50s to look at Kingston's past, present and future. It aimed to build understanding by bringing different generations together with film-makers, artists and designers. The resultant artworks were exhibited at Kingston Museum, alongside an exhibit about TTK. Visions generated through these and other visioning approaches form a strong base for Transition initiatives.

first such plan in the UK, begins by stating its assumptions, before setting out its vision of the Totnes of 2030.

One of the simplest visioning tools is to invite people to close their eyes and imagine themselves walking down the street in 2030 and stopping to look around. Ask them what they can see and hear. Invite them to record their impressions through drawing, painting or writing poetry, stories or perhaps small ads columns. Much popular media narrative is based on conflict, so creative exercises using, say, tabloid story methods which echo this, may work for some people.

Try to weave visioning into everything your Transition initiative does, asking: "If you were to wake up in 20 years' time, in a world that had successfully navigated the journey to a low-carbon, localised and more resilient community, how would it look, feel, smell and sound?"

You might also enjoy . . .

PERMACULTURE DESIGN (Tools for Transition No.1, page 98), ARTS AND CREATIVITY (*Starting out* 8, page 117), BACKCASTING (*Starting out* 13, page 138), ORAL HISTORIES (Connecting 4, page 218), COMMUNITY BRAINSTORM-ING TOOLS (Tools for Transition No.15, page 220).

8. Arts and creativity

with input from Lucy Neal

Transition Victoria (Canada)'s 'Shuffle Bus'. *Photo: Denise Dunn*

A Transition process without play and creativity would miss out on a vital way of reaching, touching and engaging people.

Transition revolves around our imaginations. We can bring a different reality closer by first imagining it. The arts are a brilliant way to build confidence in creating new stories to live by. Our initiatives start to come alive with possibilities – many surprising and unexpected.

By feeding people's imaginations, the arts create common ground between us, tapping into relationships, place and meaning. At a time when people can narrow their thinking and be fearful of change,

"The day is coming when a single carrot, freshly observed, will set off a revolution."
Paul Cézanne

the arts create pleasurable shared experiences and space to rehearse new ideas. They generate empathy and a sense of belonging. They build bridges across generations, cultures and different sectors of society. They can carry all that is resonant about a Transition initiative – lifting the spirits, while making space for loss.

> "History has remembered the kings and warriors, because they destroyed; Art has remembered the people, because they created."
>
> William Morris

The following are some ways in which the arts have been included in initiatives.

Creating fiction can help people imagine a future reality. Transition Town Tooting, together with other London Transition groups, created an 'Energy Descent Plan in Two Hours' show based on the idea of the fictional 'Transition Town Anywhere'. Members of the public were asked to improvise and pretend they were residents of the town. They rehearsed the '12 Steps' of Transition using interactive activities, film, large props and a three-minute Unleashing with cake, exploding confetti and the town's 'very recently elected mayor' (a member of the audience), and first performed the show at the LIFT Festival on London's South Bank in 2008. By the end the audience had created a huge book – the rudimentary Energy Descent Action Plan for 'Transition Town Anywhere'. The show was also performed at the 2009 Transition Network conference, and was a huge success.

Sometimes the arts raise awareness directly: Transition Town Shaftesbury was part of the 'Tipping Point' eco-circus, which used music, crafts and clowning to communicate climate change to a young audience.[16]

Above all the arts can be used for their collaborative potential and 'shared doing'. The act of creating something new with others makes a safe space that helps people feel better and happier.

Good design aids outreach. Often there will be a good designer in your team. If you don't have one, you could approach a local college that teaches

The 'Energy Descent Plan in Two Hours' show, from the 2009 Transition Network conference, Battersea Arts Centre.

> "Humans are capable of a unique trick, creating realities by first imagining them, by experiencing them in their minds . . . As soon as we sense the possibility of a more desirable world, we begin behaving differently, as though that world is starting to come into existence, as though, in our mind's eye, we are already there. The dream becomes an invisible force which pulls us forward. By this process it begins to come true. The act of imagining somehow makes it real . . . And what is possible in art becomes thinkable in life."
>
> Brian Eno

Transition in Action: The Trashcatchers' Carnival

Transition Town Tooting's Trashcatchers' Carnival looms into view. *Photo: Simon Maggs*

Traffic on Tooting High Street came to a stop when the Tooting Trashcatchers' Carnival came to town! In July 2010 over 800 participants from local schools, community groups and clubs took part in this unique carnival made almost entirely from household rubbish. Over 1 million plastic bottles and shopping bags, half a million crisp packets, half a tonne of renewable willow and half a tonne of other recycled materials were collected over a six-month period to create this extravaganza.

Organisers of the carnival were jubilant that it had gone so smoothly and according to plan. Lucy Neal, Co-Chair of Transition Town Tooting, speaking to ITV *London Tonight* news said: "Individually we may seem insignificant, but when we connect up in a community, we are very strong, we can make a huge difference. We are thrilled at how well it's come together

and amazed at the support we have received from the people of Tooting."

Some of the more amusing floats were the cycle-powered living rooms transporting some of the elders of the community. Sitting comfortably on her recycled armchair, Jaya Patel, born-and-bred Tooting resident, said: "The best bit about this carnival is that it's brought the whole community together from all sections, young and old, from all ethnic backgrounds." The South London Swimming Club had a cycle-powered float with swimmers, iceberg and sea made entirely out of plastic bags and bottles. The swimmers themselves came dressed as the colourful doors of their changing rooms at the Tooting Lido.

The Lady of Tooting, a six-metre-high animatronic creation, told the story of Tooting on her crinoline Victorian dress decorated with over 170 faces of the ladies of Tooting. Antonia Field-Smith, a Tooting resident, said: "It was great to see Tooting High Street without traffic and to be able to walk down the road without worrying about getting run over. I loved it, what a fantastic event."

Steven Cooper of the Metropolitan Police thought the carnival was a wonderful idea and one that he would like to see happen again the following year. The grand finale at Fishponds Playing Fields, with a shared picnic followed by dancing and music performed by local schoolchildren, was a fitting end to a spectacular day.

See www.trashcatchers.blogspot.com

"We are what we imagine . . . The greatest tragedy that can befall us is to go unimagined."

Navarre Scott Momaday

design, or try www.design21sdn.com, a collective of socially minded designers, who might be able to suggest someone to help you. Below is a selection of some Transition initiatives' posters to give you a flavour of how the visual arts could be used. There are many great posters, as well as other ways in which the visual arts are used. For example, Hebden Bridge Transition Town produced beautifully designed booklets called 'Making a Plan for a Sustainable Town', which were distributed free before their Unleashing.

Many Transition initiatives form their own arts group as a basis for the work of the organisation. Transition Town Totnes Arts Group (TTTAG) has a

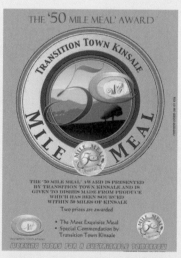

web page, and Transition Town Romsey's Arts group have secured some funding for supporting the role of the arts in their initiative. Transition Town Oswestry runs a project called Footfall, which includes art by local children that is then displayed in local empty shops.

Value the power of the arts and creativity to change our sense of what is possible in the world. Be big, bold and celebratory.

You might also enjoy . . .

VISIONING (*Starting out* 7, page 114), PRACTICAL MANIFESTATIONS (*Deepening* 2, page 146), THE 'GREAT RESKILLING' (*Deepening* 3, page 152), HOW WE COMMUNICATE (*Deepening* 4, page 155), CELEBRATING (*Deepening* 5, page 161), BECOMING THE MEDIA (Tools for Transition No.13, page 208), THE ROLE OF STORY-TELLING (*Connecting* 6, page 229).

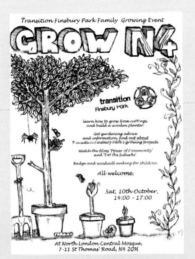

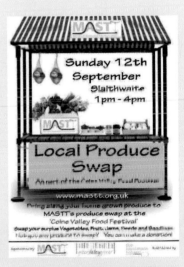

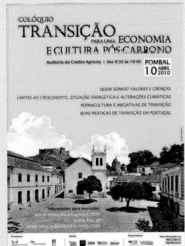

Tools for Transition No.4: Running effective meetings

Edible Landscapes London (part of Transition Finsbury Park) meeting in a greenhouse. *Photo: Deanna Harrison*

You will soon find that you are having meetings and need to get a lot done in little time. For most of us, even the mention of the word 'meeting' leads to a sinking feeling. One notable sustainability project that I followed for a while in the UK in the early 1990s folded after four years of innovative and productive work. I asked one of the founder members why. "I think we just met each other to death," she told me. It doesn't have to be like that.

Meetings need to balance having fun and feeling good about working together with getting things done. This is not always easy. Too often we assume it's a choice between one and the other. In fact, if we feel good about our meetings, we work together better and get more done. It is easy to see where many meetings go wrong . . . monotony is

one of our biggest enemies! All sitting round in a circle the entire time, week in week out . . . there are more creative ways to work as a group. Our meetings need to enable everyone present to participate (after all, why else would you come?), learn from each other and create a shared culture (or we might as well be working on our own!), welcome new people and get stuff done. They also need to be something that people look forward to.

There are a number of ways to make meetings far more productive and enjoyable.

'Go-rounds'

Transition groups often use these in two ways. First, at the beginning of a meeting we do a go-round of what has been happening in each person's group since the last meeting. We give each person 5-10 minutes, and avoid interrupting or getting into a discussion about what he or she has said. The person could also be asked to begin with 'how I am feeling right now', and then highlight what he or she would like on the agenda. In the group's early meetings, when the people are still getting to know each other, we also put in a 'throwaway question' for the end of each person's time. These can be things like 'the best meal I ever had', 'the most beautiful place I have ever been', or 'the greatest piece of music I ever heard'. There are of course many variations on this, but they enable the group to get to know each other a bit better, and to relax more with each other.

Open agendas

Although it can be useful to circulate an agenda in advance, it can help to start a meeting with a blank sheet of flip-chart paper and, during the go-round, write up what people want on the agenda. Once this list is complete, everyone goes through the list and labels each item between one and three, one being 'this must be discussed today', two being 'we'd like to talk about it today, but it can wait', and three being 'this could easily wait until next time'.

We assess how much time we have left in the meeting and allocate each item a strict time limit. It is a good idea to structure the meeting to ensure the last item is not contentious, to avoid arguments at closing time. It is important to keep the agenda visible to all, and to check with everyone that the item has been satisfactorily dealt with before it can be checked off the list.

Clear beginnings and endings

Make sure the meeting starts with something to mark its opening – perhaps a minute of silent reflection, or even just announcing that the meeting has begun. At the end, it is good to have something that formally closes the meeting, so there is a clear sense of closure, rather than just drifting off into the next thing. This kind of clear 'topping and tailing' can make a big difference.

Celebration!

Again, this is a key component of your meetings. One of the easiest and most satisfying ways of doing this is to eat together, perhaps at the end of your meeting.

Welcoming new people

Sometimes we encounter reports of people arriving at their first Transition event and not feeling welcomed. It is important to be mindful of welcoming and supporting newcomers, asking them about their interests and skills. Some constructive help can be given to newcomers in finding their role in the group.

> **Resources**
>
> Kaner, S., Lind, L., Toldi, C., Fisk, S. & Berger, D. (2007) *Facilitator's Guide to Participatory Decision-Making*. Jossey-Bass Business & Management.
>
> Seeds for Change has some great guides to running effective meetings and other useful tools: see www.seedsforchange.org.uk/free/resources#grp.

A meeting of the Transition Town Totnes Core Group.

9. Awareness raising

with input from Sophy Banks

Preparing to address the Unleashing of Transition Forest Row. *Photo: Mike Grenville*

What is the best way, in your community, to raise awareness about the issues underpinning Transition?

Awareness raising can cover a huge range of activities: anything that involves people understanding, learning or doing something new; visioning the future; working out how to change something in their lives; or talking to someone else about what they've done – all are part of the process of raising awareness about the need for Transition. Loud, outgoing events that make a big splash and get publicity will work in some places and for some people, while in others it may be more appropriate to take a quieter approach –

entering into conversations with existing groups and maybe supporting their work. For example, Transition Vancouver in Canada spent a year publicising and supporting the events of other groups before putting on any of their own.

One key to successful awareness raising is understanding the community you're part of. It can sometimes be the case that the people who are involved in Transition have moved to an area recently. If so, make sure you have good connections with people and groups who really know the place, listening to their advice before you start on visible activities. First impressions count, and treading on the toes of existing groups and relationships early on takes time and energy to put right later.

Awareness raising in different ways for different people

Understanding the process of change is a key tool in designing effective awareness-raising activities. A common mistake is to assume that once people have information that the existing system isn't working they will immediately take steps to make a change, that all they need to do is watch *The End of Suburbia* (see Resources section) and the next day they'll be lagging the loft and digging up the lawn. Experts in behaviour change tell us a different story – that people move through several stages between the first insight that something isn't right, and actually changing what they do. Addictions specialist Carlo DiClemente called this 'The Stages of Change',[17] suggesting that people at each of those stages have very different needs and need to be communicated with in different ways. So what do people at each of those stages need? These are described in the table below.

It is also important to note that different people learn in different ways. Some people learn and absorb

Transition Town High Wycombe introduce the public to their work and to Transition ideas.
Photo: Transition Town High Wycombe

How to customise your awareness raising

State of change	Key questions	Type of activities
Pre-contemplation (some awareness of the need to change but no immediate plans)	Is there a problem? What is it to do with me?	Films and talks about peak oil, climate change, consumerism, green solutions, wars, inequality. Time included to digest difficult information and share responses.
Contemplation (yes, I want to change, and will do something at some point)	What can I do? What are the answers?	Events that inspire, solutions. Eco-home or food garden tours. Hearing from people who have made a change. Space and time created for discussions and creative ideas – Open Space is great for this.
Preparation (next month, on the 17th, I'm doing to change)	I've decided what to do, I'm getting ready to make the change.	Information and resources – websites, leaflets, expert advice. Help with practicalities. Learning new skills. Support for new enterprises or projects.
Maintenance (avoiding relapse)	How do I keep going and integrate the change into my life? What's next?	Being with others in a change process to share difficulties and give encouragement. Acknowledging the challenges that arise. Celebrating and honouring successes.

Transition in Action: The Transition Barcelona Caminata   by Claudia French

A walkabout (*caminata*) in the neighbourhood of Poble Sec and Montjuïc hill, Barcelona, was organised by Barcelona-en-Transició (Barcelona in Transition), with the collaboration of local individuals, organisations and small businesses. After around four months of preparation and fieldwork, one Saturday in September 2010 we visited various places of interest related to the international Transition movement. We saw, for example, community allotments; local artisans, craftspeople and artists who use local material (wood, wool, leather, metal, etc.); as well as shops, cafés and food cooperatives that sell local, organic and/or loose (unpackaged) produce.

The *caminatas* we organise are opportunities for the people of the different neighbourhoods of Barcelona to get to know their area better, as well as getting to know the Transition movement and its aims. They are regular events, in which we aim to visit all the various neighbourhoods in Barcelona. We always finish the *caminatas* with a shared picnic, in which everyone brings local food and drinks to share, and we reflect on the event, answer questions, and generally have fun, while getting to know each other better. A piece of local joy, without the use of petrol . . . something to be celebrated!

Participants on Transition Barcelona's first *caminata*, September 2010.
Photo: Loudphoto/Barcelona-en-Transición

information mentally, through exposure to ideas, concepts and written or spoken information. Some respond more on an emotional level, through being engaged by what they care about; what they fear or hope for. For example, Rebecca Hosking's film *The Message in the Waves* had a visceral impact which led to her town, Modbury, banning plastic bags. Other people need to learn in a more physical way, by making something, building or planting something, through acting out scenarios . . . If you are able to create events that include something that will appeal to all these different learning types, you are far more likely to attain the depth of awareness you are looking for.

In terms of making your events as inclusive as possible, remember that different people are around at different times, and that some will not be able to access events at certain times or in certain places. Think about what is appropriate for people who are parents, children, elderly, workers, have English as a second language, have physical disabilities, or come from different cultures. Try also to think really creatively about the themes of the events you are holding, as different themes will attract very different audiences. Think of this as giving your initiative more 'edge', more surface area, a wider relevance to more people. In your Transition initiative you will have people who are passionate and skilled in the areas of food, building, the arts, crafts, politics, and so on: try to weave some of that into your awareness-raising programme.

Designing your events so that they invite participation of local politicians can be a very useful strategy for your initiative. Before the 2010 general election, many Transition initiatives, such as Transition Luton, held hustings events, inviting their local candidates to discuss issues relevant to Transition[18] (see *Daring to dream* 1, Policies for Transition, page 281). Transition Belsize in London developed the idea of inviting local politicians to sit in armchairs at the front during film screenings, and then asking them to give their thoughts afterwards.

Awareness raising needn't always be about speaking and telling people things – listening is also an important element. One woman in a small town in the US said that, as an incomer who had only lived in her town for 17 years(!) it wouldn't be appropriate for her to be organising events and talks; it would seem presumptuous and may switch people off. Her method of raising awareness was to include the phrase 'in the age of the end of cheap oil' in as many conversations as she could, and to get involved with lots of existing community activities. Her friend said you wouldn't believe how skilled she was at getting that phrase into all kinds of topics and with all kinds of people – who were now starting to use the phrase themselves. It is important also to design your awareness raising so that it makes sense to different people. Working in partnership with other organisations can help. This will also help to learn a bit about the strengths and skills in your community.

You may also find these suggestions useful:

- **Allow time for digestion:** Make space for people to talk and listen to each other after films or talks, as well as having question-and-answer sessions. Gather feedback and ideas, so people can see what others are thinking or feeling. Many groups hand out post-it notes and ask people to write ideas on them, to be collected at the end, or you might have a large sheet of paper on the wall that people can write on.

- **Give information but don't tell people what to do:** A key principle of Transition from early on was to give good information and then trust people to find their own response. Talking about your own reaction – how you felt or what you changed – is fine. Telling others they 'should', however, is almost always patronising and inappropriate, and is more likely to cause resistance than change.

It is also worth noting that over the life of your Transition initiative your approach to awareness raising will change. In the first two of the five stages set out in this book, 'starting out' and 'deepening', peak oil and climate change can prove forceful catalysers and offer a powerful lens through which to look at the resilience of the community. By the time you reach the fourth stage, 'building', you may find that most people in the community have made up their mind one way or another, and that continuing to press the point creates more division than engagement. Shifting the focus to raising awareness about economic resilience and setting up new enterprises and projects may prove far more productive.

Organise an ongoing programme of awareness raising, designed to appeal to your community in its themes, activities, style and language, and always give people time to digest information, to express or share feelings, and to come to their own decisions about what they can do.

You might also enjoy . . .

INCLUSION AND DIVERSITY (*Starting out* 2, page 94), RESPECTFUL COMMUNICATION (*Starting out* 3, page 100), PRACTICAL MANIFESTATIONS (*Deepening* 2, page 146), THE 'GREAT RESKILLING' (*Deepening* 3, page 152), HOW WE COMMUNICATE (*Deepening* 4, page 155), FORMING NETWORKS OF TRANSITION INITIATIVES (*Connecting* 1, page 198), THE ROLE OF STORYTELLING (*Connecting* 6, page 229).

10. Forming working groups

Forming into working groups as part of Transition Town Tooting's 'Energy Descent Plan in Two Hours', performed at the London's South Bank as part of 2008's LIFT Festival. *Photo: Mike Grenville*

How best to ensure that your Transition initiative is taking a rounded approach to building community resilience, rather than just focusing on, say, energy and food?

Transition works by harnessing the different passions of its participants. Unlike a single-issue campaigning organisation, there are many different ways into Transition, depending on your interest – hence the role of working groups. Such groups come into being in different ways. Sometimes the initiative tries to kick-start particular groups; for example, by running events about energy to initiate an energy group. Sometimes groups form spontaneously. Sometimes a Transition initiative 'adopts'

a group already active in the community, to support and build on its progress. Here are a few tips for how to maximise the success of a working group.

A group usually works best with a core of people who steer it and who meet regularly, but who are open to whoever else wants to come. Each group should continually ask itself "Who isn't here who should be here?", looking for new people with relevant skills, in addition to asking "What is a vision for a low-energy [insert name of community] in relation to this and what might a timetable for that look like?" By asking these questions, the group is assembling ideas and information that will enable them to put together their section of the Energy Descent Action Plan, as well as forming and developing practical projects.

Transition in Action: Which working groups to have?

There is no ideal mix of groups. Each group is determined by those involved. For example (to choose a few at random), Transition Town Lewes has the following: 10:10, Arts, Business, Currency, Energy, Food, Health, Heart and Soul, Schools, Textiles, Transport, Village Connections (linking the town to the surrounding villages), Waste and Water. Transition Town Berkhamsted has Energy, Food, Transport, Waste and Food groups, and Transition City Lancaster has Building and Design for Life, Energy, Food and Growing, Heart and Soul, Real Wealth and Livelihoods, Skills for Community Building, Transition Arts, Transition Education, Travel And Transport groups and the Transition City Lancaster Networking Group.

Each group should have access to the relevant section of the project's website and be able to use the logo in its publicity materials. Also, it is worth remembering that you cannot assume that everyone who offers to form and facilitate a group can do so effectively. Offering early training in running effective meetings (see Tools for Transition No.4, page 122) can make the difference between success and failure for some groups.

Actively initiate or facilitate the emergence of working groups on food, energy, education, and so on; whatever people see as important. See the role of the wider Transition initiative as being to support this.

You might also enjoy . . .
RESPECTFUL COMMUNICATION (*Starting out* 3, page 100), MEASUREMENT (*Starting out* 6, page 109), RUNNING EFFECTIVE MEETINGS (Tools for Transition No.4, page 122), COMMUNICATING WITH THE MEDIA (Tools for Transition No.6, page 136), HEALTHY CONFLICT (Tools for Transition No.11, page 188).

At Transition Cambridge's third birthday party, Martin Roach of TC's Food Group gives a seed-planting masterclass.
Photo: James Southwick

Tools for Transition No.5:
Forming a legal entity

with input from Patrick Andrews

Work-in-progress on designing Transition Network's legal structure, on a table outside a café in Bristol, summer 2008.

Many people switch off in conversations about legal structures. Yet the legal structure of a group affects its behaviour and how it is seen by others. Flexibility and informality is fine for a young initiative, but as you grow and take on more responsibilities you will need more structure and allocation of responsibility.

No single approach fits every Transition group. You have to decide what is right for you, depending on what you are doing or planning, what sources of funding you intend to apply to and how well the group can handle administration such as minute keeping and filing returns. You also need to consider how more formality will affect the group (for example, some people are unfamiliar with and suspicious of formal structures and may feel

excluded by too formal an approach). These are all important considerations, worth dedicating time to.

You may eventually need more than one entity. If you decide to set up a business, for example, you will have to create an independent organisation (probably a community interest company or a cooperative – see Appendix 1, page 293) to own it. The structure does not have to be permanent – you can change your legal form to match your circumstances. Doing so is time consuming and can be expensive, but there is no need to be trapped in an unsuitable structure.

To keep this section readable, the pros and cons of different legal forms are set out in Appendix 1. To simplify matters, we have ignored for-profit structures. Part A of Appendix 1 describes the five most suitable legal forms for Transition groups so as to best enable them to support the projects they have helped to catalyse. Part B describes structures for running a social enterprise (a business that aims to serve the community).

You must decide whether to apply to register as a charity. The aims of most Transition groups will qualify as charitable. Registering as a charity makes fundraising easier. However, the registration process is slow and can be tricky for those unfamiliar with the procedures. Once established, you must make sure you comply with charity law and the rules set out by the Charity Commission.

For many groups, the right initial choice will be to form a club (or 'unincorporated association', to give it its full legal name). This is easy to set up (a simple constitution must be drawn up and signed) and has minimal ongoing formality or administration. Provided the club's income is less than £5,000 per year, you don't have to register as a charity.

Clubs need a written constitution that is formally adopted by the group. Sample constitutions of Transition groups can be found online,[10] and you can copy one and adapt it for your needs. Some groups may be happy to remain a club; others may decide to become a limited company – a step up in complexity and administration, but the conversion from a club to a company is hardly more complicated than forming a new company.

If you want to run a business, such as a wind farm or a community-owned shop, you might opt for an industrial and provident society (the usual form for a cooperative), a legal form which has a long history and certain advantages when seeking to raise funds from many members of the community. Alternatively, you could choose a community interest company (CIC), a relatively new legal form specifically designed for social enterprises. See Appendix 1 for more information.

You should view choosing and forming a legal structure as an opportunity to clarify the group's vision and aims. The legal structure should not be chosen by a small clique and imposed on the group. It is far better to arrange for proper discussion about the options, to allow the parts of your group to have their say.

The legal structure can support your relationships with third parties. For example, you might invite the local council to be a 'member' of your legal entity (whether a club or a company). This lets them vote on many key decisions made by the group (including appointment of the committee or board) and will give them proper involvement. A more informal way of linking with your collaborators would be to invite individuals employed by the partner to become members of your group. This makes the committee more accountable and reduces the risk of a clique dominating the group and excluding others.

Choosing the right legal structure for your group doesn't need to be dull. The process can help clarify what the group is about and how it can organise itself. Learn from others who have been through the process. Keep formality to the minimum level possible. The key to long-term success, whatever structure you set up, is to retain flexibility and to ensure that those leading the group are accountable to its members and the community.

Another aspect of becoming a formal organisation is insurance. There are various types of insurance you will need to take out to protect your group. See Appendix 2 (page 296) for a brief overview of these.

Resources

For further reading on charities, see the UK Charity Commission website, www.charitycommission.gov.uk.

There are good sources of information about cooperatives at www.cooperatives-uk.coop.

The Financial Services Authority regulates industrial and provident societies: see www.fsa.gov.uk.

For further reading on community interest companies, see the CIC Regulator website, www.cicregulator.gov.uk.

Tools for Transition No.5: Forming a legal entity

II. Building partnerships

At the Brixton Pound launch event, every participating business had its details posted on the wall, showing the range of partnerships behind the scheme.

How best to ensure that your initiative doesn't imagine it can do without the support of, or partnerships with, other organisations – an approach that could leave it isolated and less effective than it could have been?

Transition initiatives were never intended to do all the work of decarbonising/relocalising their community on their own. Rather, they catalyse and support projects, trying to change how a place sees itself so that Transition becomes a community's way of thinking. Doing this requires skilful collaborative work and the building of strong local partnership.

It isn't just individual initiatives that can benefit from partnerships. In November 2009, a one-day conference was held in Slaithwaite in Yorkshire called 'Transition North', bringing together Transition groups from across the north of England.[20] The event was a partnership with the Co-operative Group and Co-operatives UK. It proved to be a dynamic coming together of organisations with many overlaps of philosophy and practice.

Within your community there will be many organisations that, though not obviously aligned with Transition, will overlap with some of what you do. Unexpected partnerships often lead to more interesting interactions and new contacts. Offer presentations to a wide range of local groups and

Transition and partnerships

In an interview on the Mid Wales Permaculture Network's website,[21] Dave Prescott of Transition Hay-on-Wye reflected on the partnerships his initiative had created. One, an alternative transport day, was co-created with Herefordshire and Powys councils, Sustrans and local business and environment groups. Transition Hay-on-Wye had also done work with the local Chamber of Commerce. Dave commented on the role of partnerships thus:

> "For me it boils down to the fact that as a group of six individuals there isn't a great deal we can do, but if we collaborate with existing groups and, over the longer term, encourage other existing groups to recognise that Transition is something they can be thinking about and acting on, then we have a chance of creating meaningful change."

Stalls from a range of local organisations at the Unleashing of Transition Whatcom, in Bellingham, Washington State, USA, April 2010.
Photo: Suzan Fiskin

Partnering organisations, however informal their link, must understand what they are doing. Misunderstandings can easily lead to fall-out, taking a lot of energy to resolve. Your initiative must do some skilful networking, because Transition needs to involve a far broader range of bodies than has been the case up to now.

Recognise the value of clear and mutually beneficial collaborations and partnerships, and seek them out.

tailor your talk, as best you can, to their interests. I once gave a talk to a local Women's Institute. Before my talk, they had been discussing how milk was too cheap and how that was affecting dairy farmers. It meant I was able to start by talking about localisation and globalisation, relating it to milk production as an example.

Key events can make such connections visible and bring in overlapping organisations in the community. For example, at the Unleashing of Transition Town Lewes, those attending entered the hall through another room, which included dozens of stalls – of local groups, food producers, businesses, and so on. Much the same thing happened at the launch of Transition Town Chepstow, with various local enterprises and organisations having stalls. Other groups have done the same.

You might also enjoy . . .

INCLUSION AND DIVERSITY (*Starting out* 2, page 94), HOW WE COMMUNICATE (*Deepening* 4, page 155), FINANCING YOUR TRANSITION INITIATIVE (Tools for Transition No.8, page 158), EDUCATION FOR TRANSITION (*Deepening* 12, page 192), ENERGY RESILIENCE ASSESSMENT (Tools for Transition No.14, page 216), SOCIAL ENTERPRISE/ENTREPRENEURSHIP (*Building* 2, page 239).

12. The evolving structure

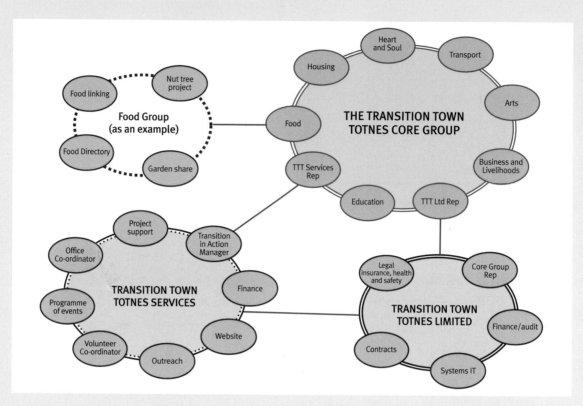

An attempt by Transition Town Totnes to map itself, showing how it functions as a 'Project Support Project'.

What might it look like if a Transition initiative were designed not to actually do a wide range of projects, but rather to support those that are doing them?

One thing that has been incorporated into Transition is the 'Project Support' concept, which originated with John Croft's 'Dragon Dreaming' model (see *Deepening* 5: Celebrating, page 161). This is the idea that the role of a Transition initiative isn't to do everything itself – to become a developer, a bank, an energy company, landowner, training organisation, and so on. Rather, its work is to catalyse, inspire and support the efforts to make things happen, helping the emergent projects on the ground, as well as to structure itself so that, as much as possible, it enables and supports the

people developing those projects. This is an important distinction.

See your Transition initiative's role as creating the infrastructure projects need as they emerge, offering a common sense of purpose, administrative support, publicity and fundraising.

You might also enjoy . . .

'TRANSITION TOWERS' – HAVING AN OFFICE, OR NOT? (*Deepening* 1, page 144), VOLUNTEERS AND VOLUNTEERING (Tools for Transition No.7, page 150), FINANCING YOUR TRANSITION INITIATIVE (Tools for Transition No.8, page 158).

Transition in Action: How Transition Town Totnes uses the 'Project Support' concept

After much consideration and design, Transition Town Totnes came up with an organisational model with the following elements:

Core Group: Meets monthly and is the main body that decides direction, priorities and day-to-day issues. Plans events.

Trustees Group: Also meets monthly, but is instead responsible for the support services of the organisation – for fundraising, financial management, recruiting and supervising employees, ensuring that the organisation's activities are in keeping with its Memorandum and Articles. It is where 'the buck stops'.

This leaves the projects, through the core group, to set direction, while ensuring they are practically supported. There is good interaction between the two bodies, and each is always represented at the other's meetings.

TRANSITION TOWN
TOTNES

Models of Transition: fennel, quilt or fungus?

How best to visualise the structure of Transition groups? Joanne Porouyow of Transition Los Angeles suggests the 'umbelliferae' model, like the flowers of a fennel plant. Its bright yellow flowers first catch the eye. The bees are buzzing and the pollen is dripping, so you don't notice at first the strong structure keeping the flowers supported, fed and connected. While the flowers are the entry into Transition, the structure behind them provides support and service.

David McLeod of Transition Whatcom suggested a 'crazy quilt', where small, irregular pieces are stitched into a practical and attractive whole. The last model, proposed by Scott McKeown of Transition Sebastopol, is of Transition as mycelium, a fine fungus that runs through undisturbed soils in networks. Scott suggests seeing the core team as a mycelium network that feeds and supports projects and groups from below. The offer then becomes not to be part of 'our' umbrella, but rather to link to a larger network created to build community resilience.

The flowers of a fennel plant: a model for Transition?

Tools for Transition No.6: Communicating with the media

A selection of Transition-related press cuttings from the author's archive.

It is vital from an early stage to get your local media on your side. This can be done in a few different ways.

Writing press releases

Press releases are a fact of life. Journalists are very busy, so make their lives simpler by offering fascinating stories with a memorable angle in a format that is easy for them to include with minimal editing. Consider the angle, the nub of the story. Follow up press releases with a phone call to check the paper has received it and intends to use it. Teen Ross, a reporter who commented on this ingredient in its draft form, said it is better to send a press release via email, and to include it in the body of the email rather than as an attachment. Make sure your initiative has a clear process for issuing press releases, that someone checks them to ensure consistency and accuracy, and that everyone is clear how this process works.

Tips for press releases:

- Deadlines: how far ahead do you need to plan to ensure your press release reaches the paper on time?
- Identify your contact at the paper. In the early days of Transition Town Totnes, I met the senior reporter on the local paper and introduced myself and the project to him. We have had a very good relationship with the paper ever since.
- Remember to clearly include the organisation's contact details and any further information.

- Compile a database of media contacts, as well as a list of all their deadlines.

A good structuring formula is 'AIDA':
A   Get the reader's **Attention** with a good headline, sub-headline and first sentence.
I   Give the **Information**.
D   Give the **Details** (when, where, contact info . . .).
A   Inspire the reader to **Action** (with an enticing last sentence).

Follow a press release with a phone call to see if they have everything they need.

Good images

Providing the local media with eye-catching images, chosen to suit the medium and to best get your message across, is very useful. Hopefully, someone in your initiative will be handy with a camera. These days, images should be in digital form: attach the image as a high-resolution .jpg file when you submit your press release. Make sure it is well composed, and try to imagine it reproduced in the high contrast format of a newspaper. With photos (and with TV interviews), make sure that the people on view are standing in front of something appropriate that creates the right impression.

Radio or TV interviews

Doing radio or TV interviews requires different skills from writing press releases. It can certainly be more nerve-racking! The most important thing is to speak clearly and calmly, and to have thought in advance about the key information you want to get across in the time allocated to you – it is a good idea to know beforehand how much time you will have and to adapt your messages to fit. In TV interviews, editors will probably go through and look for one or two 'soundbites', so practise speaking in short punchy sentences, and decide on the core messages you want to get across. Get a friend to film you. This can be uncomfortable, but very useful! (See also Tools for Transition No.2: Standing up to speak, page 104.)

Include quotes

Teen Ross suggests that editors like press releases that include quotes, because it gives the story an air of authority. For example: "'As fossil fuels such as oil become scarcer, prices rise, causing hardship for householders,' explained John Brown from Transition Auchenshoogle. 'This means that it makes a lot of sense to produce food closer to home.' . . ."

The Mayor of Lewes is interviewed by the local media at the launch of the Lewes Pound.
Photo: Mike Grenville

13. Backcasting

A timeline visioning workshop in December 2010 in Koganei, Japan, invites participants to tell the story of their town's transition. *Photo: Paul Shepherd*

Creating a vision of a desired future is one thing, but how to identify the steps to actually get there?

Backcasting is straightforward and follows naturally from visioning (see *Starting out 7*, page 114). I'm sure it has been around for a while, but I first heard of it in *The Natural Step for Communities: How cities and towns can change to sustainable practices* by Sarah James and Torbjorn Lahti (see Resources section). They recommend visioning a desirable future and then working backwards.

For example, if by 2018, 50 per cent of new buildings in a community are to be built to Passivhaus standard, using 80 per cent local materials (see page 64), backcasting identifies what new infrastructure, what training and what skills would need to be in place by when. It allows you to be more strategic and to identify the most skilful early interventions and the new enterprises required. If, for example, construction-grade hemp is to be a key part of that, backcasting allows you to consider:

- When would the infrastructure for processing locally grown hemp need to be in place?
- When it would it be necessary to begin training local builders in using hemp?
- When would the first trials on local farmland need to begin?
  . . . and so on.

When Transition Town Totnes was creating its Energy Descent Action Plan (EDAP), backcasting played a key role. In the first round of workshops, people identified their key assumptions about the kind of future they were anticipating. Then they looked at future scenarios, and what they felt to be most likely, concluding with a visioning exercise, inviting people to imagine the scenarios they had created. After this was done, the backcasting began, in two stages. First, workshop participants were invited to backcast in groups, moving around between the tables to share ideas, identifying what felt like the crucial stages in the journey towards the vision of the future that they had created. They also made use of 'The Transition Timeline' – a long laminated board showing a line running from 2009 to 2030, on to which people were invited to post future events or stories written on post-it notes (see photo below). Second, the team creating the EDAP then pulled together the material created in the workshops and used it as the foundation for a more detailed narrative; a more thorough timeline for Transition.[22] Backcasting proved to be a dynamic and highly creative process, involving a great mixture of serious thought and silly, but fun, imaginative flights of fancy.

One exercise that is a good way of bringing backcasting to life is the 2030 School Reunion exercise, which was first done at the launch of the process that led to the creation of TTT's EDAP.[23] Here four actors play different characters who all attended the local secondary school in 2010. The audience divides into four groups, each with cards that tell a different aspect of the story of what happened in the character's life in the intervening years. The audience share what they know about the character, and then, after discussion in the four groups, the actors role-play a school reunion, with the characters meeting each other and catching up on their lives. If done well, with good actors, it can be a surprisingly engaging and moving exercise.

Backcasting helps us to identify the structures and institutions we need in place in order for Transition to become a reality: where should we start and, indeed, what we have already done that might also be useful.

You might also enjoy . . .
ARTS AND CREATIVITY (*Starting out* 8, page 117), PRACTICAL MANIFESTATIONS (*Deepening* 2, page 146), COMMUNITY BRAINSTORMING TOOLS (Tools for Transition No.15, page 220), MEANINGFUL MAPS (Tools for Transition No.16, page 226), THE ROLE OF STORY-TELLING (*Connecting* 6, page 229).

Backcasting using the 'Transition Timeline' developed by Transition Town Totnes, at the launch of its EDAP creation process.

14. Creating a space for inner Transition

by Hilary Prentice

Transition is both an inner process and an outer one. The place where the two meet is undulating and fascinating.

Might it be that if Transition can find ways to bring together and integrate the inner and the outer dimensions of the change, it may turn out to be markedly more effective?

Does change start on the outside and work in, or start on the inside and work out? From the very beginning of the Transition movement, people from both perspectives have, literally, sat round the same table and worked together. Both perspectives are true: the outer creates the inner, *and* the inner creates the outer. What's more, some would argue,

in coming together we will be working to heal divisions and 'splits' that may well be at the root of the mess we are in.

The inner perspective is seen as drawing inspiration from, and weaving together, three distinct strands. First, the insights from the field of psychology and psychotherapy in the West, which seek to understand the roots of human destructiveness and dysfunction and to enable the healing of the wounded, and wounding, human psyche. To this has recently been added the insights of ecopsychology,[24] which argue that our relationship to the Earth, and to what is happening to it, has a

> "In the end this is about a change of heart. If that does not happen alongside the windmills, I'm not sure there's really any point."
>
> (Overheard at a Transition meeting)

significant bearing on our psychology. The second strand involves insights from teachings and writings about the transformation of consciousness, often drawn from Eastern traditions. The third major strand comes from the many peoples who still remember, and practise, Earth-centred wisdom, and who have not forgotten how to live sustainably on the Earth. All over the world indigenous peoples are coming together as they find the lands on which they live under environmental assault – from oil spills in Nigeria, Louisiana and Ecuador to climate change, deforestation and other forms of pollution. As well as campaigning for their rights and lands, frequently there is a clear call from these peoples to the rest of the world to 'wake up'.

In terms of the experience of inner Transition work on the ground, this has involved regular meetings around themes and events with speakers, and people have also begun to offer workshops locally, at which participants are welcome to share and explore feelings and questions on subjects including grief, fear and anger. Much of this stems from the work of eco-philosopher Joanna Macy[25] and rainforest activist John Seed,[26] who have developed easily learnt and powerful workshop forms to do this. This is where Transition connects with the

Spirituality and Transition

Groups exploring the area of spirituality and Transition are often called 'Heart and Soul groups'. Other similar groups have called themselves 'Well-being', perhaps feeling that the words 'heart' and 'soul' might be contentious, while the Transition Presteigne has called itself 'Spirit of Transition'. These decisions seem to reflect one of the challenges of bringing 'inner work' to the Transition table: that there are hotly contested views, and strong feelings, around spirituality in particular. It seems clear that a great deal of damage and wounding has gone on in the world in the name of organised religions, and of spirituality in general, and so some people are very wary indeed about the whole issue. From this point of view, allowing any spiritual presence within your movement could be seen as asking for trouble.

However, it is equally true that for many others, the qualities that this transition calls forth – a move from materialism to values such as community, care, love and creativity; from arrogance and inequality to compassion – are the very stuff that spirituality was always meant to be about in the first place. For many people, spirituality can be explicit as well as implicit, and their spiritual life is central to their personal resilience. If we are to be inclusive, it is perhaps necessary both that no one in any sense 'pushes' his or her spiritual approach, but, equally, that this whole area of human experience is not unwelcome. In the spirit of openness, tolerance, tact and kindness, appropriate discrimination and appropriate trust, a more vibrant, broader and richer movement is then possible.

wide range of practices, activities and tools from the areas of personal development, psychological, spiritual and philosophical traditions, some of which are mentioned in other ingredients in this book.

One specific project has been the 'Mentoring' scheme, by which experienced people such as counsellors, not centrally involved in Transition, have offered free confidential ongoing support to busy activists (you can read more about this in Tools for Transition No.9: Supporting each other, page 179). At one point Transition Town Totnes's Heart and Soul group facilitated the setting up of small support groups around Transition, called Home Groups. As one person involved in a Home Group in Totnes said: "Home Group was a place where we could share our feelings, exchange ideas and feel supported in a world where it's easy to feel isolated . . . friendships forged there still flourish." 'Heart and Soul-ers' have also helped to facilitate large and small local events, helped shape national conferences and organised a big workshop around conflict resolution, and 'inner Transition' has been woven into Transition Trainings that now take place all over the world.

The evolution of the 'inner Transition' approach in Portland, Oregon, is not dissimilar. Their Heart and Soul group have monthly meetings, share and support each other, have hosted big speakers/ events, run workshops as part of conferences, and are committed to clear ground rules for their meetings, designed to really support deep sharing and listening, to create safety and to take owner- ship of our feelings rather than projecting them on to others. As David, one of the group's coordina- tors, put it, "I see us as a group who meet to share, talk and support each other in our shared interests around H&S material. We have a quiet but steady presence within Transition here in Portland." No doubt other groups round the world are taking both similar and different routes, according to local conditions.

However, it should be acknowledged that, probably because there has been division in Western culture between inner and outer, and therefore inner- and

outer-focused people, there has been on occasion some confusion about what a group such as Heart and Soul can contribute to Transition. Clearly it would be a mistake for those working more on inner Transition to imagine that we are in any way more 'sorted' than anyone else, to push particular psychological or spiritual angles, or to believe anyone should take part in what we offer if they do not want to. But, equally, when some more practically focused people have found themselves willing to take part in an unfamiliar exercise, such as a process workshop at a conference, I have heard the 'penny drop' quite loudly about inner Transition, as people have found it helpful, moving, profound and supportive.

A group focusing on the inner aspects of Transition can bring a great deal to your Transition project, and the role it can serve in terms of supporting the wider Transition process should not be under- estimated.

You might also enjoy . . .

INCLUSION AND DIVERSITY (*Starting out* 2, page 94), RUNNING EFFECTIVE MEETINGS (Tools for Transition No.4, page 122), AWARENESS RAISING (*Starting out* 9, page 124), HOW WE COMMUNICATE (*Deepening* 4, page 155), CELEBRATING (*Deepening* 5, page 161), CELEBRATE FAILURE (*Deepening* 6, page 164), SUPPORTING EACH OTHER (Tools for Transition No.9, page 179), HEALTHY CONFLICT (Tools for Transition No.11, page 188), STREET-BY-STREET BEHAVIOUR CHANGE (Tools for Transition No.12, page 201), THE ROLE OF STORYTELLING (*Connecting* 6, page 229).

Resources

A useful website is www.greatturningtimes.org, which covers thinking, resources and events in Ecopsychology.

Some of the tools that Heart and Soul groups find especially useful were developed by Joanna Macy: see www.joannamacy.net.

Deepening

Your Transition initiative will build momentum and practical projects will start to emerge. You may have to design for the sustaining of the organisation and the deepening of its work, broadening its engagement across the community and being more efficient and effective. This set of ingredients and tools relates to what seem to be key elements of this stage. They explore the need to consider the sustainability of your initiative, for practical 'outer' Transition work, and also its 'inner' aspects.

1. 'Transition Towers' – having an office, or not?

Sustainable Bungay's 'office' is the kitchen table. *Photo: Charlotte Du Cann*

Would your initiative benefit from having a dedicated workspace?

Some of the longest-established Transition initiatives have an office space, but most don't. The principal obstacles are rental cost and staff (heat, light, paper, teabags, and so on also matter, but are relatively minor). It is a commitment not to be taken on lightly.

In drafting this ingredient, I asked via a post on Transition Culture[1] for people's views. Transition Town Kingston said they don't want or need an office. They hold their events in local venues and their meetings in members' homes, and stay in regular contact via email and Twitter.

This idea of remaining light and nimble was picked up on by Bart Anderson at Transition Palo Alto in the US. He argued that for groups such as his, meeting in people's homes is an advantage, and that Transition should do what corporations are increasingly thinking – encouraging more people to work from home – to create less bureaucracy. Palo Alto wants to postpone having an office for as long as possible.

Trawsnewid Llandrindod Transition has taken a similar decision, holding their meetings in local cafés. Transition San Fernando Valley in the US has a 'market circle', which invites people to meet at the regular local farmers' market. If three or more people turn up, that's a meeting. If not, they do their shopping and go home. Transition Los Angeles report that they do not need office space; rather, they make sure their website has a clear chain of meeting opportunities on its calendar. For some initiatives, however, an office becomes essential to its growth, and funding needs to be found.

Transition Town Totnes's office space, once described by the *Sunday Telegraph* as a "rickety set of rooms", also includes a meeting room, which is used by most of the working groups and for some smaller events. The office is open for people to drop in at certain times. It does, however, need one very busy paid part-time worker to sustain it. It is partly funded by ensuring that funding bids include a percentage for 'central services' (although not all funders will allow this) and also by supporters who donate monthly. It also enables many volunteers to 'hot desk'.

Finding affordable office space can be difficult, but a local Hub[a] (if you have one) can offer affordable space and networking with other local initiatives. The Empty Shops Network[3] encourages people to make temporary and creative use of empty shops, which could be a great opportunity for engaging people visibly.

A kitchen table or the corner of a local café can be all a Transition initiative needs, but if you do decide you need something more formal, make it serve many functions, such as for working, holding meetings, having social events, or hosting a café, a library or a drop-in centre for advice on energy-efficiency and other aspects of Transition.

You might also enjoy . . .
BUILDING PARTNERSHIPS (*Starting out* 11, page 132), VOLUNTEERS AND VOLUNTEERING (Tools for Transition No.7, page 150), FINANCING YOUR TRANSITION INITIATIVE (Tools for Transition No.8, page 158).

The office of Transition Town Lewes.

2. Practical manifestations

An event in Stoke Newington celebrates the projects under way in the area. *Photo: Transition Stoke Newington*

If nothing visible happens early on in your Transition initiative, it will become a talking shop, and people will start to drift away.

Your initiative must, from quite an early stage, roll up its sleeves and start making things happen. A Transition initiative with dirt under its fingernails will gain credibility, and the sight of things changing is a great way of attracting new people. These early projects should be engaging, uncontroversial and photogenic. Good promotion will increase interest and involvement. They could take such forms as:

- Productive tree plantings in urban spaces.
- Growing food in unexpected places, as brilliantly modelled in the work of Incredible Edible Todmorden.[4]
- Community gardens, such as Transition Newton Abbot's – converting a piece of waste ground owned by the council into a food-growing space.[5]
- Draught-busting workshops, such as those held by Transition Belsize,[6] and increasingly in other London Transition initiatives (see box on page 148).
- Urban gardens, such as Transition Town Brixton's[7] – involving community members in making a food garden.
- Acquiring land for a community allotment, as Transition Town Forres in Scotland did – they leased land around the town to create a new community allotment as one of their first

Transition in Action: Transition Malvern Hills' 'Gasketeers'

The Malvern Gasketeers. And a lamp.
Photo: Nathan Burlton

Malvern is home to some of the UK's most beautiful gas lamps, said to have been C. S. Lewis's inspiration for the lamp in *The Lion, the Witch and the Wardrobe*. However, today the 104 lamps are poorly maintained, produce little light, and each costs the council £130 for gas and £450 for maintenance, but they are listed and are central to the area's heritage.

Enter the Transition Malvern Hills Lighting Group, known as the 'Gasketeers', who, bringing together local and international expertise, have developed ways to refurbish the lamps (using local subcontractors) – improving their light output and preserving their unique character while significantly reducing their gas consumption, maintenance cost and light pollution. Installing timer controls, new electronic ignitions, more efficient burners and reflectors has reduced gas use by an average of 84 per cent, and maintenance requirements to just one visit per year – the lamps now costing just

£20 for gas and £50 for maintenance per year. They are ten times brighter than before, and create no light pollution at all. They will also last 100 years, compared with 30 years for conventional sodium lamps. The Gasketeers have even begun exploring how the lamps could be run on biomethane, improving on the carbon footprint of electric streetlights.

They calculated that if they were a professional consultancy, their work would be valued above £20,000, but they offered it free to the councils and the community. They found that the most effective way to achieve success with such projects was to research and demonstrate feasibility, and obtain the support of the town and parish councils. All repairs are done by Lynn Jones, the UK's first female gas lamp technician, who does her maintenance rounds with everything she needs (including her ladder) on a bicycle trailer. C. S. Lewis would have approved, I imagine.

Lynn Jones heads out to service the new gas lamps of Malvern with her bike and trailer.
Photo: Transition Malvern Hills

Transition in Action: Draught-busting workshops
by Sarah Nicholl of Transition Belsize

Draught-proofing a front door as part of Transition Belsize's 'Draught-busters' initiative.
Photo: Sarah Nicholl

Draught-busting workshops are hands-on, fun and practical, encouraging people to reduce their heating bills, learn useful skills and have fun, by learning how to draught-proof wooden-framed sash and casement windows and doors. The workshops started life as 'Draught Busting Saturdays', created by Sue Sheehan and Hyde Farm Climate Action Network. In November 2009 we learnt how to draught-bust, and the next week began delivering our own workshops. Camden Council was then piloting the Home Energy Efficiency Pro-gramme in the Belsize area of Camden, which offered residents free home-energy-saving advice and products, but no specific draught-proofing advice.

When the scheme ended, the council asked if we'd like to work with them to deliver ten workshops to Camden residents. We proposed that participating householders receive £20 of materials each (enough for roughly two windows and a door), the host would receive £50's worth and, as facilita-tors, we'd be paid for running the workshops – a win-win for everyone.

We began in July 2010 and, amazingly, there was a huge demand even though it was the hottest July in years! We also began to realise that for various reasons some people were not able to fit the products themselves, so we devised a 'tailor-made draught-proofing service' which is now finding its feet, and we have draught-busted local schools and several local homes. We are developing all this as a social enterprise, which will include a donation of any payments received to Transition Belsize, salaries for those carrying out the installation work and a continuation of skill-sharing, energy saving and community participation, connection and collaboration.

We have delivered workshops to Transition / low-carbon groups across North London, who now offer workshops/demos to local residents. The Transition Belsize Draught Busting team are just regular folk, but we've been bitten by the draught-busting bug; it is heart-warming to see people enabled to get on with it themselves.

activities (see *Deepening* 10: Ensuring land access, page 174).

There are hundreds of projects you could undertake. When putting on a public event to showcase what you have done, think about ways to make sure that they have high visibility. Invite the media, make it a celebration, and document it with photos or, ideally, a short film. Designing these practical manifestations is a great way to link with local businesses and other organisations.

For example, the Transition Town Totnes Nut Tree Project[8] is supported by various local businesses, including a local solicitor, who pays for one tree for every new will signed up at his office. It is a simple scheme and has in three years planted over 200 nut and fruit trees, some of which are already bearing nuts. It is creating an important infrastructure in an unthreatening way. John Croft, a community-led change specialist, recommends that members of the project group ask each other whether, if the project doesn't come off, they would be personally happy to cover any losses. The result, seen in many initiatives that have come through his Gaia Founda-

tion of Western Australia, is a greater determination for the project to succeed. It's an approach you might consider if proposed projects feel a bit 'stuck'.

From an early stage, get visible projects going, making them playful and unthreatening, and ensuring they are well publicised and sited where they will be seen, so as to prompt people to consider a low-energy future optimistically.

You might also enjoy . . .
MEASUREMENT (*Starting out* 6, page 109), AWARENESS RAISING (*Starting out* 9, page 124), BUILDING PARTNERSHIPS (*Starting out* 11, page 132), COMMUNICATING WITH THE MEDIA (*Tools for Transition* No.6, page 136), VOLUNTEERS AND VOLUNTEERING (*Tools for Transition* No.7, page 150), THE 'GREAT RESKILLING' (*Deepening* 3, page 152), EDUCATION FOR TRANSITION (*Deepening* 12, page 192), ORAL HISTORIES (*Connecting* 4, page 218), COMMUNITY OWNERSHIP OF ASSETS (*Building* 6, page 264).

Planting walnut trees in Totnes with Paul Hussell of Wills Probate, a local solicitor's firm which funds one new tree for every new will it sets up. *Photo: © Totnes Times*

Tools for Transition No.7:
Volunteers and volunteering

Volunteers planting up Transition Bath's circular vegetable garden at Hedgemead Park, a prominent spot in central Bath. *Photo: Iva Carrdus*

As your initiative evolves, the likelihood is that the vast majority of the work will be undertaken by volunteers, although, in time, some projects may be held by paid staff. While often a lot of thought is given to supervising paid staff, those volunteering are often less supported. At some point, you may feel the need to create more formal volunteering opportunities, reaching beyond the committed types of volunteers (those who facilitate projects and working groups and put on events) to those who have a certain amount of time each week to offer to community volunteering. For those who are already involved, ensuring good **RESPECTFUL COMMUNICATION** (*Starting out* 3, page 100), **RUNNING EFFECTIVE MEETINGS** (Tools for Transition No.4, page 122), asking **"HOW ARE WE DOING?"** (*Deepening* 7, page 166), **PERSONAL**

RESILIENCE (*Deepening* 11, page 181) and **PAUSING FOR REFLECTION** (*Connecting* 7, page 233) should be sufficient. However, for those invited to participate as more formal volunteers, some additional support might be helpful.

- **Recruitment:** Why would anyone want to volunteer for your initiative? What are you offering them? Your recruitment materials, whether flyers, adverts or emails, need to be clear about how people can get involved, which roles you are seeking to fill, what hours are expected, the skills required, and so on. Make sure people get a pleasant welcome.

- **Induction:** This is vital. Anyone volunteering for your initiative would probably appreciate learning what the initiative does and its general history. Offer a 'who's who', outlining the essential procedures and policies, and be clear about what is expected of them. Make them feel at home and appreciated.

■ **Training and development:** If people are going to give up their time to support the initiative, they may appreciate some training and development opportunities. When they start, find out what they would like to learn and see if you can help. It can benefit the initiative, especially when talking with funders, to be able to show what volunteers have gained as well as given.

■ **Leadership and communication:** Volunteers need to know who they can go to for advice and support. They must be able to communicate easily with whoever is supporting them. If they are working on their own, give them plenty of contact details. Volunteers should feel they are part of a keen team.

■ **Innovate:** Make sure you don't just use volunteers for doing the 'grunt work', but that you design something meaningful and varied for them to be involved in. It may be that some

volunteers work remotely (such as the team of volunteer translators who produced the many different language versions of the film *In Transition 1.0*), and they will need supporting in a different way. Many people who volunteer do so around very busy lives. Try to ensure that arrangements for meetings should put their needs first, whenever possible.

■ **Celebrate!** Try to make sure volunteers feel valued and happy and that they know they are helping to move the project forward. Appreciation is vital and only courteous. Organise events that bring volunteers together to see what they are all doing, and to enable the initiative to show its appreciation.

Transition Town Totnes has a volunteer who offers to help and support people who come forward to offer their time. She is a first contact, who talks with people about what they hope to get out of their volunteering, what skills they can bring, and knows which parts of the initiative need volunteers and what kind of work is involved. Her role is to match people to jobs – a key role many other initiatives may find useful.

The 350 Home and Garden Challenge, May 2011. Volunteers about to transform a water-wasting public library lawn in Petaluma, California, into a beautiful food garden as one of over 1,700 similar activities across the US in one weekend. *Photo: Trathen Heckman*

3. The 'Great Reskilling'

In February 2011, Portugal's Transição em Telheiras ran a course in creating a 'home garden', focusing on how urban apartment dwellers might grow food inside their homes. They all went home with a 'home garden' containing garlic, lettuce, tomato and parsley plants. *Photo: Filipe Matos*

A more resilient community will require us to be adept in a wide range of skills – skills that until recently were everyday but are now greatly undervalued (food growing, repairing things, natural building, maintaining renewable energy systems). How best to address this collective loss of practical skills?

Since the 1960s we have gradually lost skills that were once commonplace. Most people who grew up during the 1940s and 1950s learned, almost automatically, how to garden, repair things, look after small livestock, and generally make do with little. One person I interviewed who was a teenager in the early 1960s told me he was the generation for whom gardening became "something you did when your dad caught you", a punishment. Two generations have passed, during which the handing on of these skills has continued to decline. As a result, many people lack basic skills, which leaves them and their communities much less adaptable.

Some Transition initiatives, such as Transition Town Worthing, have a dedicated Reskilling Group.[9] Many others support this. For example, Transition Worcester,[10] Transition Town Stoke Newington[11] and

Deepening

> "We learn something by doing it. There is no other way."
>
> John Holt

Transition West Kirby[12] have run courses on bicycle maintenance, and others, such as Transition Town Tooting, have run days, in association with the Energy Saving Trust, to train people to conduct basic energy audits of homes and workplaces.[13] Some Transition initiatives, such as Sustainable North East Seattle,[14] have scaled this up, and Transition Putney have run a whole series of reskilling workshops.[15] So did Transition Town Kapiti in New Zealand, whose 'Winter Skills Series' offered training in skills such as worm farming, Earthship building, brewing and composting. Transition Ann Arbor in the US ran a whole Reskilling Festival, featuring a wide range of skills and skilled people to learn them from,[16] and Transition Santa Cruz in the US held a 'Reskilling Expo'.[17]

Yet in Transition we need to think bigger (hence the 'Great' in 'Great Reskilling'), such is the scale of change necessary and the absence of the skills required. For example, retraining the construction

Participants on Transition Cambridge's 'Grow Your Own' training. *Photo: Transition Cambridge*

industry to produce Passivhaus buildings using mostly local materials, and training a new generation of farmers familiar with agroforestry, growing for local markets and relying less on fossil fuels, means we urgently need to attend to the scope of this work. There are promising signs of this. The School of Artisan Food in Nottinghamshire[18] is training a new generation of cheesemakers, bakers and other dwindling food producers. The Centre for Contemporary Agriculture near Norwich[19] is seeking

Introducing a new generation to natural building at the Belsize Eco Fair. *Photo: Sarah Nicholl*

Dunbar Transition Village's food preservation demos at the Dunbar Harvest Festival, Canada. *Photo: Shelby Tay*

to train a generation of new farmers. The Centre for Alternative Technology in Wales[20] has for many years run practical courses in renewables, building and food, which have gained a very good reputation.

In disadvantaged communities, the loss of skills is often closely linked to other deleterious impacts of the move to a post-industrial society, such as a loss of roots, a blurring of values and a feeling of being left behind by the fast-running currents of 'progress'. Disadvantaged communities often have more skills simply because they've had to be more resourceful and resilient. They can't simply buy in skills to help them through life in the way that wealthier communities can. Gehan McLeod of the GalGael Trust in Glasgow gave a presentation to Transition Scotland's 'Diverse Routes to Belonging' conference in November 2010 on her organisation's work in the former ship-building area of Govan, where more young men die each year from violence than in the Gaza Strip. The Trust sees the role of reskilling not as about helping people, but rather creating environments in which people can help themselves. She argues that a keystone of resilience is people reclaiming their right to be responsible – the key role of reskilling in very disadvantaged communities. She quoted George McLeod, a priest from Govan who rebuilt the church on the Isle of Iona, who said that "only demanding common task builds community".

This needs to run throughout our education system at all levels, and throughout our lives. Whatever Transition initiatives can do to enable and support this reskilling work in their communities is vital. Working with local colleges to run reskilling evening classes, working in schools, involving local universities, working with organisations who support retraining and reskilling of the long-term unemployed, can all be very effective.

Be bold and make it fun. I taught practical permaculture for many years and can't remember anyone saying "I really wish you hadn't taught me gardening . . . I was doing all right until then. It ruined my life."

Make reskilling a core part of your work, in the form of events, practical projects or courses run independently or with local educational institutions.

You might also enjoy . . .
AWARENESS RAISING (*Starting out* 9, page 124), BUILDING PARTNERSHIPS (*Starting out* 11, page 132), WORKING WITH LOCAL BUSINESSES (*Connecting* 3, page 213), ORAL HISTORIES (*Connecting* 4, page 218).

Learning to forage for wild foods on Hampstead Heath. *Photo: Transition Belsize*

4. How we communicate

Members of Future Proof Kilkenny, Ireland, Vered Zur (left) and Councillor Malcolm Noonan (right), present a copy of *The Transition Handbook* to local Mayor Pat Crotty (centre) at the launch of their Spring 2009 events. *Photo: Future Proof Kilkenny*

To many, green campaigners can appear fanatical, naive, uninformed, smug, judgemental, patronising or extreme. So what is the most skilful way to get the message across?

When I lived in Ireland in the late 1990s and was involved in developing one of Ireland's first eco-village developments, we held a public meeting in the village hall in the run-up to submitting our first planning application. We were inspired, enthusiastic and naive, and were convinced that because we thought it a fantastically exciting project, so would everybody else. We compiled our drawings, slides and maps and our reasons why it was such a great idea and set off for the hall. Once the event was under way, we found ourselves in front of a hall filled with local people with their arms crossed, suspicious looks on their faces.

I had been involved with environmental projects for years, but had never encountered the perception of 'greener' options as being an inherent criticism of how things are presently done. When we talked about how we were going to build green, low-energy houses, back came the tight-lipped question, "What's wrong with my house?" When we talked about mixed, diverse land use and sustainable food production, the question came back, "What's wrong

Transition in Action: Transition Stroud's Potato Day

Philip Booth and Norah Kennedy (aka Maris Piper), one of the authors of the Potato Day recipe book. *Photo: Philip Booth*

In February 2011, Transition Stroud celebrated National Potato Day with its own event in celebration of our nobbly national icon. They set up shop in the local shopping precinct, rather than at the local farmers' market, which introduced Transition Stroud to a whole new audience. It proved to be a bold and highly beneficial step out of the comfort zone. A grand total of 4,700 seed potatoes of 20

different varieties were sold during a manic day that needed 20 volunteers to keep up with demand. The group also produced a book called *Pan-fried, Peeled and Proud: Potatoes from Stroud*, written by the aptly named Maris Piper and Desiree de Romano (not, I am told, their real names), which was available on the day. Several local restaurants also did interesting things with potatoes for the day in support of the event. The rare and unusual varieties attracted great interest, especially the 'Salad Blue', which produces blue mashed potato![21]

Transition Stroud's stand in the local shopping precinct celebrating Potato Day. *Photo: Dave Cockcroft*

with my farm?" That experience greatly shaped my thinking. The film we showed, featuring an Australian ecovillage with people doing Tai Chi in the sunset and an old man bellydancing, which we thought was great when we watched it with each other, probably didn't help much either.

Over subsequent years I rapidly developed a sense of what people like, and what turns them off. I also learnt that, within the environmental movement,

there can be a lack of awareness of what turns other people off: we can be so convinced of our rightness that we don't think we need to pay any attention to *how* the message is communicated. The fact that it is communicated is enough. The ultimate example of that was the, to me, deeply mistaken film produced by climate campaign group 10:10, *No Pressure*, which showed people who didn't believe in climate change being blown up.[22] A visual in-joke that when viewed by people outside the circle of those who conceived it, became a very unpleasant, bewildering and, unfortunately, self-defeating piece of work.

How we come across can depend on the time and place. I often think of doing Transition skilfully being the ability to change hats depending on who you are meeting. I present Transition very differently to a council, to a group of businessmen or to community activists. With each there is language that engages, and language that leads to the listeners switching off. Talk of communities having fun, of community-building, of the psychology of change, tends to leave councillors cold. Talking to businesspeople about economic contraction, showing graphs of peak oil and waxing lyrical about planting nut trees, will rapidly lead to their glazing over. They want to hear about opportunities, about how to get things done with little time available to make it happen. They want, often, to know about the bottom line. Speak to people in their own language, appeal to their passions and about what fires them up.

When you get invited to speak somewhere, do your homework first. Who are you speaking to? Why have they invited you? What attracts them to hearing about Transition? Dress appropriately . . . you wouldn't wear a suit to speak to the local school, but you may well to address the council. I always like the idea of confounding what people expect of you. If people imagine a Transition speaker to turn up in a kaftan and sandals, wear a suit. If they imagine you'll turn up in a suit, dress more casually (but probably best not a kaftan). You'll find it makes a big difference.

Be mindful of the language you and your group use in talks, printed materials and events, avoiding divisive 'them and us'-style messaging, however subtle. Work actively to avoid perceptions of being 'hippy' or excessively rooted in alternative culture; rather, ensure that the project remains as accessible to as wide a range of people as possible.

Beautiful promotional materials, such as this poster, can be vital for deepening engagement.

You might also enjoy . . .

RESPECTFUL COMMUNICATION (*Starting out* 3, page 100), BUILDING PARTNERSHIPS (*Starting out* 11, page 132), COMMUNICATING WITH THE MEDIA (*Tools for Transition No.6*, page 136), 'TRANSITION TOWERS' – HAVING AN OFFICE, OR NOT? (*Deepening* 1, page 144), PRACTICAL MANIFESTATIONS (*Deepening* 2, page 146), EDUCATION FOR TRANSITION (*Deepening* 12, page 192), INVOLVING THE COUNCIL (*Connecting* 2, page 204), BECOMING THE MEDIA (*Tools for Transition No.13*, page 208).

Resources

There is an excellent talk by Barrett Brown on how the insights of Spiral Dynamics can inform how we communicate sustainability to a wide range of different people: see http://tinyurl.com/68wr4n4.

Tools for Transition No.8:
Financing your Transition initiative

This adopt-a-fruit-tree programme helped pay for insurance at the new community garden being built by Transition Los Angeles. *Photo: Christine Tope*

Initially, a Transition initiative can thrive on small donations and income from running events, but increased funding from whatever source will greatly influence what is possible. Transition Haddenham raised modest funds through selling Transition books at its events, which they invested in an apple press which they now rent out. They should recoup 75 per cent of their investment in the first year. Transition Denman Island, in British Columbia, ran an all-day 'Transition Expo' event, where 34 different groups from across the island met. The group raised funds by serving refreshments. Some initiatives raise money through members giving talks to other organisations. Blake Poland from Transition Oakville in Ontario has raised over $1,000 for his initiative in this way.

Two schools of thought have emerged regarding funding. Joanne Poyourow of Transition Los Angeles promotes 'resilient non-profits',[23] arguing that Transition initiatives need to be 'peak-proof' and resilient to economic contraction. She argues, "It is absurd, in this post-peak day and age, to set up a non-profit organisation with the expectation that it will run on society's cash surplus (i.e. donations and grants)." We are in effect, she suggests, nearing 'peak grants'. Her model is to remain nimble and light, holding as little in the way of money as possible, operating without paid employees, without premises, without incorporating as a legal entity and, where possible, without 'stuff' (i.e. the usual clutter that fills offices). This is the model adopted by quite a few Transition groups.

Transition in Action: Transition Lewes's Glyndebourne Fundraiser! by Adrienne Campbell

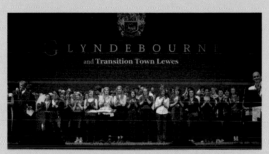

Transition Town Lewes's fundraiser at Glyndebourne. *Photo: Chris Smedley*

In the autumn of 2010, Transition Town Lewes (TTL) was offered a wonderful opportunity: to hold a fundraising event at the world-famous opera house Glyndebourne, in the countryside near Lewes. Gus Christie, the owner, knew about TTL – he came to the Richard Heinberg talk for local landowners, he'd been at all our launches, we'd supported his application for a wind turbine, and he also knew Oliver Dudok van Heel from TTL.

Over the summer, Gus, Oliver and a small team pulled together some great local musicians. By the autumn, they had lined up a bagpipe group; a special choir of over 100 people, conducted by John Hancorn; The Baroque Collective and the world's best recorder player, Piers Adams; The God of Hellfire, Arthur Brown; and international opera stars Paul Austin Kelly, Liz Brice, Thomasin Trezise and Riccardo Simonetti, performing together; Glyndebourne's Youth choir and The Galliard Ensemble, one of Britain's leading chamber ensembles. We've got amazing talent here in Lewes, though quite a few of them depend on international travel – for now.

There was the usual scramble to make the publicity (thanks to Chris Smedley of TTL, who runs a design company, Hudoq), and, when nobody had booked with a month to go, more publicity. But in the end the event was virtually sold out, with 1,100 tickets going for £20 or £10 concessions, with under-12s free. In the lead-up, we could have been better organised, especially at communicating what Transition was about to people who were just there to support the choir. We didn't model it well, failing to organise buses, bike routes and car shares.

Gus Christie himself wove together the performances with a wonderful story about the history and all our characters and escapades, including Tom Paine, the Lewes Bonfire Council, Harveys Brewery and of course the Lewes Pound. After costs, we raised a net of £8,000 – which pays for our two part-time workers to run the office and newsletter, and for OVESCO, our energy company, to pay for legal fees and marketing of a share issue in 2011 for what we believe is Britain's first community-owned solar power station.

Looking around the auditorium at one point I was deeply moved by the 'magic' – that more-than-the-sum-of-the-parts effect that I come across quite a lot in Transition, a powerful shared experience that will live long in memories. The last song of the evening involved the choir and the audience singing the song that was created at the launch of the Lewes Pound – a great cheer for Transition, Lewes and all that we have to be glad about.

Funding applications tips   from Fiona Ward of Transition Consulting

- **Work out what you need funding for:** Collect ideas for projects, decide on evaluation criteria to help you decide which projects are most important to you, assess and prioritise with your core group, and then create a one- or two-page summary of the project, which you can refer to in any funding bids.
- **Identify potential funders:** A good match makes a bid worth your while, otherwise you are wasting everyone's time. You can get good advice (in the UK) from your local Council for Voluntary Services (CVS) (see resources, below; many other countries have similar government-funded bodies that support voluntary groups and can provide funding advice); your local council might issue funding updates, which can save you a lot of legwork; have a look at Funding Central, the free funding database (see below; again, in the UK only) created by government for the third sector; ask any rich contacts you might have!
- **Create applications:** When filling out the applications, give the funding body only what it asks for, and ensure you relate the bid and your answers to its needs and objectives, not the other way round. You need to also keep track of any conditions it might have, such as reporting back (if you are successful).

While this approach may appeal to some initiatives, for others, seeking funding is important. There is a role for explicitly raising funding to support your work. Local philanthropists can support Transition initiatives. In Totnes, one local supporter donated nearly £5,000, which funded a member to submit funding applications that generated over £90,000-worth of grant funding – a fine example of using a relatively small donation to unlock a much greater resource.

Applying for grants takes time and a varying amount of effort depending on the funder. Establishing a record with small grants first can help with larger applications, as can providing hard data about the impact of your work. Try to design into each funding bid a percentage that goes back to supporting the initiative's core costs (not all funders will allow it). Often funding is linked to specific projects. For example, New Forest Transition raised £14,604 from the New Forest National Park Authority's Sustainable Development Fund to promote local produce and develop a local food strategy. This enabled them to engage over 2,500 individuals and 50 businesses. The larger the potential award, the more time is usually needed to apply for it.

Project-specific grants will only get you so far, and core funding is notoriously hard to find. I would argue that Transition initiatives need to become more entrepreneurial, seeing what they are doing as offering a number of possibilities for generating income. For example, Transition Town Totnes has identified a three-year process of becoming independent of grant funding, through setting up social enterprises, building a membership who pay an annual amount, coordinating 'Transition Tours' of groups visiting the town to find out about Transition, and other income-generating activities.

Resources

Find out about your local CVS office from NAVCA: see www.navca.org.uk.

Funding Central: www.fundingcentral.org.uk.

5. Celebrating

Transition Town Kingston celebrate their Unleashing with a cake decorated with a chocolate-and-marzipan allotment, made by Maria Bushra, Libby Wells, Jonny Helm and Tara K. *Photo: Jonny Helm*

Being in such a fevered rush to create a powered-down world can mean that we never pause to celebrate our achievements, even the seemingly minor ones. This can lead to the whole process starting to lose its spark, and end up feeling burdensome and exhausting.

Those of us active in Transition, and in community sustainability initiatives, tend to be very poor at celebrating what we have achieved. We often feel such a need to act that we rarely pause to take it all in. John Croft, a community-led change specialist, has developed an approach to community development called 'Dragon Dreaming'. Based on his observation of hundreds of projects, this model argues that successful ones have four stages:

- **Dreaming or visioning:** The initial stage of asking "What would happen if . . . ?", "What would this sort of project look like?", "Does this sound like a good idea?", "Can you imagine our town with a . . . ?" and so on; a bold look into the future.
- **Planning:** Here the project moves from ideas to practicality. Questions might include "How do we make this happen?", "Who's going to design it?", "How many people in the team?", "What skills are we missing, or which do we have?", and "How might we finance it?"
- **Doing:** By this stage you have signed your

contracts, employed your workers, installed the phone lines and your baby has come to life. The theory is now practice. With time it becomes so familiar that you forget it was a theory not so long ago.

■ **Celebrating and evaluating:** At this stage the emphasis is on celebrating the success of the project and looking at the failures and difficulties before starting the cycle again. Questions might include "Has the project reached your expectations?", "Which phases of the project went well?", "Which phases were difficult?" and "Was the project fun?"

Celebrating can make a big difference to the success of Transition initiatives and can take different forms. It might be as simple as people from your initiative going out for lunch together, or sharing a meal one evening. It can take the form of bigger events to celebrate key points in the evolution of your initiative, such as an Unleashing, or an anniversary of your first event.

These things can be celebrated in a variety of ways: singing, dancing, making things . . . a wide range of possibilities for celebrating where you have come from, what you have done, and where you are going. One of the most fascinating things I see when I visit Transition celebratory events is the role that food, in particular cakes, plays in celebrations.

When they held their Unleashing, Transition Town Brixton produced the most extraordinary cake – huge, and beautifully decorated with the name of every Transition initiative that existed at the time painted on to the icing with food colouring. It was topped with a giant sparkler, forming a beautiful and tasty centrepiece to the celebrations. Transition Town Kingston's 'Big Launch' was graced by an exquisitely decorated cake with a chocolate-and-marzipan allotment, complete with a tiny table and chairs. Transition Town Totnes's first birthday party featured three amazing cakes, each complete with a marzipan Totnes Pound. At the Unleashing of

Join us for the first **Transition Brunswick Picnic** in Warr Park (cnr Albion & De Carle Street), Sunday the 30th of January at 3:00pm.

This is a great opportunity to meet up with other locals, **get inspired, share some ideas and exchange stories**.

Special guest Tammy from Moreland Council ("Zero Waste Week Challenge") will give a short talk on **easy ways to reduce your landfill waste**.

Come along, bring some friends and fruit, cake or biscuits to share and join us for afternoon tea.

We Look forward to seeing you there!

Warr Park
Corner Albion &
De Carle Streets
Brunswick

transitionbrunswick.wordpress.com

Transition Brunswick celebrated with a 'Picnic in the Park' in late January 2011. A brave time of year to hold a picnic!

Transition Bro Ddyfi in Wales, guests were treated to not one cake but nine, all in a row, with a story of the town's Transition running above the cakes, a kind of 'edible Transition Timeline'.[24]

Transition Kensal to Kilburn organised the Kilburn Big Lunch street party. Transition Lampeter's lantern festival was a great celebratory event with lanterns made by local children. Transition Leytonstone held a Winter Faiths festival, a celebration of food, faiths and sustainability.

People can make and bring cakes and sweets from whichever part of the world they come from, from Banbury cakes in Oxfordshire to Middle Eastern baclava or Brazilian Brigadeiros. The love and creativity that people pour into a landmark celebratory cake or other celebratory foods at key moments in their Transition initiative feel to me to be an important and symbolic part of the event.

Transition Town Lewes's launch of the Lewes Pound featured a mouth-watering and eye-catching spread of local food from a local restaurant, and those attending the Unleashing of Transition Town Tooting were fed by a local Indian restaurant. The message here is that it's important to celebrate the small as much as the big, to celebrate often, and that pausing to celebrate is very healthy for the initiative and all those involved in it. We are social creatures, and social occasions help to strengthen our initiatives.

If this is to feel, as Richard Heinberg puts it, "more like a party than a protest march", we all need to grab a bottle, dress up and be thankful, to celebrate and celebrate often, celebrate small and large things, and mark anniversaries.

You might also enjoy . . .

ARTS AND CREATIVITY (*Starting out* 8, page 117), AWARENESS RAISING (*Starting out* 9, page 124), FINANCING YOUR TRANSITION INITIATIVE (*Tools for Transition No.8*, page 158), CELEBRATE FAILURE (*Deepening* 6, page 164), UNLEASHINGS (*Tools for Transition No.10*, page 184), THE ROLE OF STORY-TELLING (*Connecting* 6, page 229), PAUSING FOR REFLECTION (*Connecting* 7, page 233).

Transition Town Totnes's first birthday cake; note the marzipan Totnes Pounds . . .

6. Celebrate failure

Cuban permaculture activist Roberto Perez being interviewed outside a site in Totnes which Transition Town Totnes had hoped was about to be gifted to the community for a food-growing project. It wasn't.

Are we really to imagine that everything we attempt will work fantastically well, or might there be something to be learned from accepting that part of taking risks and being adventurous is that some things will fail, and that's OK?

H. L. Mencken once famously said "There is always an easy solution to every human problem – neat, plausible and wrong." For much of what a Transition initiative does there are no easy solutions. There is often no way of knowing whether a project will succeed. We live in a risk-averse culture, nervous about experimenting and looking ridiculous. However, it is only through experiment that we

learn and develop new models. If Transition initiatives never talk about their failures, they will not learn from them.

One example of this was Transition Oxford. After about 18 months of meeting and awareness raising, the Core Group decided to put the initiative into what they hoped was 'temporary hibernation'. However, rather than that being the end of story, each member of the group shared with Transition Culture their thoughts about why things hadn't worked out. Among their observations were the following.[25]

- A perception that their Core Group was closed to new members, leading to their becoming a bit ossified.

- The Core Group found itself looking to the wider group to say what they wanted to take the initiative on, and the wider group looked to the Core Group for leadership.
- Not enough was done to work with existing groups.
- There was not enough in place to support those carrying the initiative, nor were those people good at asking for support.
- Some members of the Core Group felt overawed by their companions. As one put it, "I felt I'd landed by accident in a group of experts."
- Little time was given to assessing how the project was doing.
- For some, Core Group meetings were not enjoyable. In spite of enthusiasm for Transition, enthusiasm for meetings began to ebb away.

These are valuable lessons for other initiatives, and we hope Transition Oxford might yet revive. The main point is that it is important to value projects that fail as much as those that succeed. What Transition does is provide a creative spark, a pulse, an invitation for people to get the transition to a low-carbon world under way where they live. Everyone involved in Transition needs to know that people will be applauded for taking risks, even when they go wrong.

Celebrate your initiative's failures as much as its successes, seeing your work as research that will be valuable to subsequent initiatives. Use Transition Network to share the stories of things that didn't work out as you had hoped.

You might also enjoy . . .
BUILDING PARTNERSHIPS (*Starting out* 11, page 132), VOLUNTEERS AND VOLUNTEERING (Tools for Transition No.7, page 150), PERSONAL RESILIENCE (*Deepening* 11, page 181), HEALTHY CONFLICT (Tools for Transition No.11, page 188).

Deepening

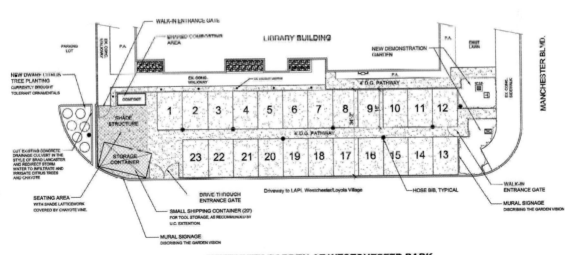

COMMUNITY GARDEN AT WESTCHESTER PARK
23 individual garden plots, each 10' x 15'
plus demonstration garden

Not To Scale

A community garden that never happened. The Transition group in the Westchester area of Los Angeles tried for over 18 months to get approval from Parks departments and various levels of City administration. Ultimately, they had to move to another site with different stakeholders. *Image: John Tikotsky*

7. "How are we doing?"

One useful technique for evaluating how far the project has come is to draw out its history as a long, colourful sequence.

Those involved in all projects need to reflect on their progress, be honest about their shortcomings and listen to constructive criticism. If they can't do these things, they will begin to lose connection with reality.

In the swirl of keeping your initiative moving forward and doing exciting things, it is easy to stop asking if the process is moving in the right direction, in a healthy way. Stopping regularly to ask "How are we doing?" is an essential safety check. This can take place on a range of scales. Adding five minutes at the end of each meeting to discuss how effective it was and how it could have been better run can be very useful.

For a more in-depth process, you could plan an internal day for assessing how and where things are going. A more public reflection can also be good. For example, you might hold a 'How Are We Doing?' evening, which invites the community to say how they were finding the process. You might begin with each of the working groups giving a three-minute report on what they were doing, and on projects that were under way, followed by an 'Appreciate Enquiry' that asks "What is going well?", "What could we do differently?" and "What concerns do we have?"

Transition in Action: Taunton Transition Town's annual 'mull' by Chrissie Godfrey

Taunton Transition Town reflecting on their journey so far, using paper, pens and a lot of playfulness. *Photo: Vicky Briggs*

We started quite slowly, a bit unsure about what we were doing, whether it mattered if we couldn't draw, what it was going to be OK to include. But pretty soon, the process moved from being quite contemplative to very playful. One person's doodle would jog someone else's memory. Snatches of "do you remember" conversations sprang up, sometimes with much laughter, sometimes moments of mourning. We noticed where we had overcome difficulties, where we had lost our way, and where the unexpected had made unimaginable things possible. It became both celebration and surprise. We had done so much more than it had felt like at the time.

Hooked by now, we did it again in January 2011, looking back at 2010. This time, we relished how there were simply no blank spaces at all, but a jostling array of colour and energy. With our previous 'mull' stuck up on the wall to remind us of our journey, this time we noticed how people were drawing lines that linked different events, that we had started to work a bit more strategically, setting up longer-term projects rather than one-off events. We saw that Transition in our own lives figured just as heavily as the 'out-there stuff': lots of chickens, allotments and bikes! We also saw the fragility of what happens when one group member suffers temporary burnout; when another gets a full-time job.

This 'mulling' seems to do more than just record what happened. The very experience of making it has a vividness to it; a palpable energy of group life that gives us permission to 'draw it like it is', and helps us celebrate ourselves and each other in this extraordinary experiment we call Transition.

Put time aside regularly to evaluate how your initiative is doing, through either internal or public events, which offer the opportunity for honest appraisal of your work. Make sure the ideas generated and the information gleaned are made widely available and acted upon.

You might also enjoy . . .

MEASUREMENT (*Starting out* 6, page 109), RUNNING EFFECTIVE MEETINGS (Tools for Transition No.4, page 122), PRACTICAL MANIFESTATIONS (*Deepening 2*, page 146), CELEBRATING (*Deepening* 5, page 161), CELEBRATE FAILURE (*Deepening* 6, page 164), HEALTHY CONFLICT (Tools for Transition No.11, page 188).

8. Local food initiatives

Transition Kensal to Kilburn created this community allotment on the platform of Kilburn underground station in London, working closely with London Underground. This garden was entered for the 'London in Bloom' competition. *Photo: Chris Wells*

It is only in the past 50 years that we have perfected the art of the completely useless and unproductive urban landscape, at the same time as we have become nearly completely dependent on long, and highly oil-dependent, supply chains. Yet within this vulnerability is a huge opportunity for rethinking how we feed ourselves.

Food is often where Transition initiatives start, and it offers a great way of finding common ground, given that everyone interacts with food on a daily basis! Here is a taster (pardon the pun) of some of the varied projects under way. Some start by planting productive trees in urban spaces. Transition Town Finsbury Park planted fruit trees around their local station,[26] and Taunton Transition Town developed their 'Tasty Borough' scheme with the local council, planting traditional apple varieties around the town (leading to a dreadful pun on their website about wanting to 'put Taunton Deane at the core of the apple country'). Transition City Lancaster's urban tree-growing project is called 'Fruity Corners'.[27]

Transition Town Tooting's annual Foodival is a great way of reaching people and bridging cultural divides. Growers from across the area bring their surplus produce, which is cooked by local cooks in different ethnic styles.[28] One of the intentions of the Foodival is to create new traditions, which was apparent at the 2010 event when two people were overheard having a conversation: "Has this happened before?" The reply was, "Oh they do it every year", in spite of its being only in its third year!

Some Transition initiatives, such as Tunbridge Wells,[29] Bramcote and Wollaton, Ashtead[30] and Forest Row,[31] are creating community allotments, where people for whom a whole plot feels daunting get together and share one. One of the earliest incarnations of this idea was in Transition Canterbury, where they also keep a very informative blog about what they are learning and how it is progressing.[32]

Other Transition communities, such as Wandsworth in London,[33] Louth[34] and Ashburton,[35] have set up community gardens, where people learn to grow food together and support each other. Inspired by the Fife Diet,[36] some places are experimenting with eating a seasonal and local diet. Transition groups in North Cornwall[37] and in the New Forest[38] are exploring the practicalities of eating a more local diet, and what this can teach us about food relocalisation. Some places are setting up their own community-supported farms, for example, Matlock,[39] Stroud and Kippax (near Leeds). Here the

Transition in Action: Garden-share schemes

Transitions Stirling, Cambridge,[40] Bristol,[41] Stratford,[42] Clitheroe,[43] Totnes[44] and Falmouth[45] have begun 'garden-share' schemes, which link committed, enthusiastic growers with local garden owners who are happy to share their space and see their gardens being used more productively. The benefits for the garden owners include a share of the produce, the pleasure of seeing a lovely developing veggie plot, and the sense of community in being part of a sharing initiative.[46] I asked Lou Brown of Transition Town Totnes, the first Transition garden-share scheme, for her thoughts after three years of running the Totnes scheme:

Garden share schemes match garden owners with would-be gardeners. *Photo: Lou Brown*

"All I can say is that the experience has been profoundly positive and there have honestly been no drawbacks. All the gardeners and the many garden owners have worked and shared their spaces with respect and commitment. Sure, there have been a couple of gardeners who haven't put in the work and have been disappointed, but inexperience and lack of time has been the worst of it – and

these cases are astonishingly rare! The idea is a very basic one, and humans are so good at cooperating and working together beautifully as long as everyone knows what to expect. People don't tend to take advantage of each other when they are working together on this kind of project – it's about sharing, community, and a bit of hard work. I find that seeing how people cooperate like this and how happy it makes them to do so really inspires me to believe in our potential for community living."

Transition in Action: PEDAL [Portobello Transition Town]'s local organic market   by Eva Schonveld

PEDAL's local, organic market runs on the first Saturday of every month. It began with a Climate Challenge Fund (CCF) grant, but is now self-sustaining, managed by a paid market manager and a small team of local volunteers. In 2009, with some money from the CCF, we did a door-to-door survey to see which of our projects would be most likely to get local support, and included several questions on local food. These projects all came out with very high ratings, with people keen on the idea of growing courses, a community farm and a local market. On the strength of this, PEDAL got money for a food worker (and two other workers looking at local energy saving and generation), one of whose duties was to get the market started.

Setting up Portobello Organic Market took much longer than we had anticipated. Finding the right site and applying for three licences took almost all of one half-worker's time. It was close to the wire, but the first market opened on a gloriously sunny day on 4 September 2009, and most of Portobello turned up, or so it seemed. The market has gone from strength to strength, even proving the importance of local food during the heavy snows in December, when no one could get to the supermarket, but the market was there with bread, fruit, veg, lamb joints and cakes!

We were worried about the effect on local traders, and so were they. We were also worried about our relationship with them if things went too well for us! So we ran this as a pilot. The feedback was that the market either benefited their trade or did not affect it, so fears evaporated. We even have one of the shops from the high street selling at the market. We are looking forward to selling the produce of the community orchard and farm, and may bring in other community growing projects and other new producers, but that's for the future!

PEDAL's new organic market has been a great success. *Photos: PEDAL*

community owns shares in the farm and is involved in what it grows. Transition Town Kinsale set up a Community Supported Agriculture scheme (CSA) with a local farmer to produce potatoes and oats for its members[47] (you can read more about CSAs in Tools for Transition No.20, page 267).

Transition Town Dorchester are creating a 2-acre community farm on land made available by the Duchy of Cornwall for a peppercorn rent.[48] Many places produce a local food directory to help people source local produce: Forest Row, Glastonbury, South Kerrier in Cornwall[49] and High Wycombe[50] have done so, and Transition Cheltenham is going for an online rather than a printed version.[51] Local food directories are a great means of connecting with local producers, processors and consumers in a very accessible way.

There are many food projects a Transition initiative can start, from garden shares to community-supported farms. Local food projects that involve local schools, other local organisations, councils, church groups or whoever else feels like a useful ally offer much potential for boosting new Transition initiatives.

You might also enjoy . . .

MEASUREMENT (*Starting out* 6, page 109), RUNNING EFFECTIVE MEETINGS (Tools for Transition No.4, page 122), FORMING A LEGAL ENTITY (Tools for Transition No.5, page 130), VOLUNTEERS AND VOLUNTEERING (Tools for Transition No.7, page 150), FINANCING YOUR TRANSITION INITIATIVE (Tools for Transition No.8, page 158), ENSURING LAND ACCESS (*Deepening* 10, page 174), EDUCATION FOR TRANSITION (*Deepening* 12, page 192), STREET-BY-STREET BEHAVIOUR CHANGE (Tools for Transition No.12, page 201), TOOLS FOR PLUGGING THE LEAKS (Tools for Transition No.19, page 257), COMMUNITY-SUPPORTED FARMS, BAKERIES AND BREWERIES (Tools for Transition No.20, page 267), STRATEGIC THINKING (*Building* 7, page 272).

"The pleasure of eating should be an extensive pleasure, not that of the mere gourmet. People who know the garden in which their vegetables have grown and know that the garden is healthy will remember the beauty of the growing plants, perhaps in the dewy first light of morning when gardens are at their best. Such a memory involves itself with the food and is one of the pleasures of eating."

Wendell Berry, 'The Pleasures of Eating'

9. Momentum

Marsden and Slaithwaite Transition Towns (MASTT) keep moving forward by presenting the possibility of a community-owned and -managed shop, November 2009. The project was successful (see page 242) and has, in turn, led to a number of new projects.

How best to sustain the momentum of your Transition initiative over the longer term?

In any Transition initiative, indeed in any community project, there will be moments when energy and enthusiasm dwindle. Boredom can set in. While it is possible that your initiative has come to the end of its useful life, it probably hasn't. This ingredient suggests a few ideas for giving it new momentum.

It may be that in all your earnest attempts to make things happen, you have stopped building into your project the space for members of your initiative to

meet informally. Designing such events which have no agenda other than getting to know one another can be very productive. These events can even be better than more formal methods at getting people involved in practical projects.

Initiatives can get stuck because they don't plan for succession. Who are the next generation, the people who will be coordinating the initiative in two years' time? A failure to plan for succession can lead to a sense that "we have to do everything or this whole thing will fall apart", and to burnout among those holding central functions. Succession rarely happens by accident. People need to be invited in, told "we need help with this", and asked to take responsibility for an aspect of the work. People coming into the initiative and who want responsibility might shadow someone for a while, who gives them some support while they're learning the ropes.

Another reason for loss of momentum can be a feeling that the project is shared between fewer and fewer people. If the same faces present all public events, it can give the impression that a small, closed and constant group of people runs the entire thing and has little need for others. Giving as many people as possible the opportunity to present events, or having multiple presenters, can offer good public-speaking practice and attract more people.

Sometimes, a perceived drop in energy can be due to unaddressed problems between members of the group: anger, disappointment, frustration, and so on. A lot of the group's energy is then used to suppress feelings. Creating space for meetings which focus solely on "How are we doing?" (see *Deepening 7*, page 166) can create a constructive outlet for that. Providing mentoring and support to those at the heart of the initiative (perhaps through a 'Heart and Soul' group – see *Starting out 14*, page 140) can help to enable healthy responses to this problem.

Energy can also run low because money is short. It may be time to look hard at what the group is doing and to say that unless some funding can be found to support particular aspects of the work, those aspects will have to be dropped. This can lead to useful strategic thinking about doing better by doing less – which can be helped by ensuring that the things you concentrate on are what most excite people. Build on the passions in the group.

Finally, momentum can flag because there is a perception that the project has turned into a 'talking shop', with little practical work taking place. Some well-designed and high-profile practical initiatives can be a huge boost to morale, as well as acting as a great way of engaging new members. All projects will ebb and flow, with some areas more active than others, so what feels like a loss of momentum may just be the initiative's energy finding a different outlet or expression.

This is where the principle of 'let it go where it wants to go' comes in. Transition is at its best when it emerges naturally and shapes itself.

Momentum can be supported through seeking new members, promoting new involvement, a range of events, and a sense that the initiative is moving upwards and onwards. Momentum won't be constant, as different parts of the initiative will ebb and flow over time.

You might also enjoy . . .
FINANCING YOUR TRANSITION INITIATIVE (Tools for Transition No.8, page 158), CELEBRATING (*Deepening 5*, page 161), CELEBRATE FAILURE (*Deepening 6*, page 164), PERSONAL RESILIENCE (*Deepening 11*, page 181), UNLEASHINGS (Tools for Transition No.10, page 184), HEALTHY CONFLICT (Tools for Transition No.11, page 188), FORMING NETWORKS OF TRANSITION INITIATIVES (*Connecting 1*, page 198), PAUSING FOR REFLECTION (*Connecting 7*, page 233), SCALING UP (*Building 3*, page 234).

10. Ensuring land access

Mark, who organises 'Stand Up Dorchester', a popular local comedy night in the town, hands a cheque for over £1,000 to Jenny Shackleford of Transition Town Dorchester (TTD) in support of 'Under Lanche Community Farm', a TTD initiative on land leased from the Duchy of Cornwall. *Photo: Transition Town Dorchester*

How will you actually get your hands on land for whatever land-based projects or enterprises your Transition initiative has decided to pursue?

Localising the production of food, fibre, fuel, and so on will mean obtaining access to land. Our towns and cities could be a network of intensive market gardens, productive fruit and nut-bearing trees, fish- and vegetable-producing hydroponics systems set up on areas of hard standing, productive ponds and new allotments. Such a tapestry of land uses would greatly increase the biodiversity and food security of the community.

An aerial photograph of any town or city shows plenty of unused (or underused) pockets of land in or around it, but there are a number of reasons why that land may be hard to gain access to. The owner may be holding on to it in the hope of getting planning permission for development at some point. Ownership may be contested. It may be owned by the local authority, which has no use for it. It may be contaminated by its industrial past. Perhaps nobody knows whose it is! To own or lease land or property, your Transition initiative will need a constitution and to be a legally recognised entity (see Tools for Transition No.5, page 130, and Appendix 1, page 293); under UK law, there are only four organisational models that can do this, as follows.

- A company limited by guarantee
- Industrial and provident societies
- Community interest companies
- Charitable incorporated organisations.

If your Transition initiative is an unincorporated association or a trust, it cannot exist as a legal person separate from the people who run it, and therefore cannot own or rent land in its own name. This can be overcome by one person doing so on behalf of the group, though he or she would have sole legal liabilities for the purchase or lease.

So how do you actually acquire land? Rachel Roddam in Transition Derwent found that getting involved in the community in a range of groups helped her find land. This has proved a great way of starting Transition and of removing any fear of making land available to Transition groups. She is a member of her local Hall and Recreation Ground committees; they had ignored the Transition initiative on particular projects, but now, with a fresh committee, the Transition group gets a much fairer hearing. This has opened the door to various potential local food projects.

Unusual land access has been secured by the 'Food from the Sky' initiative[52] in Crouch End, London. They have been working with their local Budgens supermarket to increase its stocking of local produce (it now stocks 1,500 products from within 100 miles of the shop), and have started a food garden on the shop's roof. Legal and insurance concerns meant that getting access proved complex, but now the garden is providing produce for the shop and local people, and is attracting many volunteers, including pupils from the local school.

On the Isles of Scilly, Transition Scilly wanted to create a community orchard. They approached the Duchy of Cornwall, which owns most of the land on the islands, to ask for a plot. The Duchy wasn't keen on letting land to Transition Scilly as an unincorporated organisation, being much happier with leasing land either to individuals or business-es. One of the group's members, who is already a farmer on the islands and leases land from the Duchy, added the site to the portfolio of land he

rents. Two-thirds of an acre was identified by a sympathetic and supportive land steward. The orchard was planted at a community tree planting day (pictured below) in March 2010 and is now growing nicely.[53] Some local authorities actively encourage communities to develop community orchards on council land. Chichester District Council, for example, has developed its own guidance notes on this,[54] and offers support and simple agreements for any local groups wanting to set up such projects.

Planting the Scilly community orchard (above). The following June (below) the trees are established and growing nicely in their new home.
Photos: Jonathan Smith

Transition in Action: New allotments in Forres
by Carin Schwartz

Allotment holders at the entrance to the Transition Town Forres community garden.
Photo: Carin Schwartz

In April 2009, Transition Town Forres was invited to negotiate a lease with Moray Council for 1.45 acres of horticultural land. The negotiation succeeded, as we agreed to have a community garden rather than allotments (meaning the council could give us a longer lease but with less security of tenure). Had we operated allotments they would have been bound by the Scottish Allotments Act of 1892 and would not easily have been able to end the lease.

After much discussion, and inspired by permaculture design, it was decided to have round 'pods', each 250m², rather than traditional rectangular plots. Each one is shared between four to six people. After two growing seasons:

- We currently have 90 people growing food.
- People who didn't know how to grow food are learning from each other.
- Illness or absence has been 'covered' by fellow pod holders, so we have very few neglected pods or pod slices.

- Many new friendships have been created and even the most quiet or reserved gardener interacts at least with people in his or her own pod.
- Each pod has found different solutions to how it operates. Some grow produce in individual slices while others work together.
- Every pod is inspiring.
- Only 14 people have left in two years, 20 per cent of those who began. Some local authorities see up to 50 per cent of allotmenteers leave in the first couple of years.[55]
- We have 26 chickens, two beehives and eight wormeries.

Bringing this about has been an amazing community process. We have people from all parts of the local community involved. Many have gradually taken on more roles and, by and large, I would say it works well. After much negotiation, we recently extended the lease to 30 years, and we hope to turn a large shed into a community environmental education centre.

The Forres allotments aren't rectangular like traditional allotments, but are arranged in round 'pods'.
Photo: Carin Schwartz

Transition in Action: Engaging landowners in Transition

'Estates In Transition': In June 2007 landowners from across south-west England came together to reimagine their land use policies in the light of peak oil and climate change.

Another route to accessing land is to draw local landowners into the Transition process. In June 2007, Transition Town Totnes and the Dartington Hall Trust (owners of around 1,000 acres of land on the edge of Totnes) co-presented a one-day event called 'Estates in Transition'. This brought together landowners and estate managers from across the south-west to hear from speakers such as Chris

Skrebowski and Jeremy Leggett the effects peak oil and climate change would probably have on land-management decisions. Much of the day was run as World Café sessions, exploring what land management might look like if based on an understanding of peak oil and climate change.

The local Sharpham Estate attended and has since become very involved in local Transition. Dartington has conducted a land use review process, looking at how to use its land beyond 2014 when the current tenant farmer's lease expires. Transition Town Totnes is represented in this process. Attracting local landowners and inviting them to be part of this process is an excellent way of gaining their participation. Landowners do tend to be conservative, so working with an organisation they respect often helps greatly. It's possible that far fewer landowners would have come to 'Estates in Transition' if it hadn't been hosted by Dartington, a respected local landowner, and been chaired by the local head of the Country Landowners' Association.

The old saying "If you don't ask you don't get" is well illustrated in the story of the North Queensferry Transition Initiative in Scotland and their quest for a community forest garden site. They talked with Fife Council, who invited them to look at maps of the land they own and identify any sites they were interested in. Luckily, the site they identified is owned by a part of the council that has a very supportive allotments officer, who is taking the group's designs[56] to the planning department. He actively encourages models of community gardens

as opposed to traditional allotments, because it simplifies things for the council, which needs only one contract with one organisation rather than multiple leases to individuals.

In Narberth in Wales, ten years of trying to get the local council to provide new allotment land had been unproductive, leaving many in the community associating the word 'allotment' with feelings of intense frustration. In 2008 a new approach was taken. A new group approached a landowner who

Transition in Action: Transition Town Dorchester's Community Farm

The Transition Town Dorchester group, inspired by the book *Local Food* by Tamzin Pinkerton and myself,[57] decided to start a community farm. Using Google Earth, they identified five bits of land in the area. With the help of the local town council they looked into who owned the sites, and found that four were owned by the Duchy of Cornwall. They called the Duchy office and had a very productive conversation with an intrigued official, who told them, "Put together a proposal, send it to me and I'll see what we can do." The group created their proposal, which they described as "all very official and professional", and sent it in.

They met with the Duchy official and found that the site they preferred wasn't available, but that three others were. They negotiated a five-years' tenancy (£200 per year for a 2-acre site), while the Duchy paid for fencing the site, installing paths and providing topsoil. The site was designed as a mixture of vegetable plot, polytunnel, orchard, poultry area and wild area. When the agreement was signed, a public meeting was held, and now the project, 'Under Lanche Community Farm',[58] is well under way, with a local comedy night donating over £1,000. Membership is open to anyone. Time from initial idea to securing the lease of the site? Eight months.

was keen to support them. They leased a 3-acre site for ten years at a reasonable rent, and ploughed and divided it into plots. The allotments have been well subscribed and there are now plans for a community orchard on the site. The group found input from local Transition groups and the Federation of City Farms and Community Gardens (see resources, below) to be very helpful. Getting support where it's available can make a big difference.

Access to land can be secured in a range of imaginative ways. Work with landowners. Seek land that is currently unused and can be used for free. Raise funds to buy land into community ownership. Invite landowners to see opening up access as being both in their and the community's interest.

You might also enjoy . . .

PERMACULTURE DESIGN (Tools for Transition No.1, page 98), STANDING UP TO SPEAK (Tools for Transition No.2, page 104), RUNNING EFFECTIVE MEETINGS (Tools for Transition No.4, page 122), FORMING A LEGAL ENTITY (Tools for Transition No.5, page 130), BUILDING PARTNERSHIPS (*Starting out* 11, page 132), VOLUNTEERS AND VOLUNTEERING (Tools for Transition No.7, page 150), FINANCING YOUR TRANSITION INITIATIVE (Tools for Transition No.8, page 158), LOCAL FOOD INITIATIVES (*Deepening* 8, page 168), EDUCATION FOR TRANSITION (*Deepening* 12, page 192), INVOLVING THE COUNCIL (*Connecting* 2, page 204), COMMUNITY OWNERSHIP OF ASSETS (*Building* 6, page 264).

Resources

The Community Council of Devon has some excellent guides to the legalities of taking on land for community projects: see http://tinyurl.com/5st5gba.

Federation of City Farms and Community Gardens: www.farmgarden.org.uk.

Tools for Transition No.9: Supporting each other

by Sophy Banks

Taking time out at a Training the Trainer course. *Photo. Sophy Banks*

There are two main areas of support that will greatly strengthen and enhance Transition work. The first is about learning from each other – as individuals and as projects. This might be a form of peer mentoring or support, where people who are in similar roles, or who each have experience that is beneficial to the others, meet or speak regularly and each have perhaps an hour to spend on their work and well-being. Some Transition projects have found it very useful to be in touch with other projects, both to network and to share learning and questions. For individuals supporting each other, the co-counselling movement has short trainings that address key issues around listening skills, boundaries, confidentiality, and so on, which help to make peer support a success.

The second area of support is around the wide range of feelings that come up during the Transition process. One of our strongest and most pervasive cultural figures is the hero who works alone, feels nothing, but keeps going despite attack, danger and death surrounding him (or, more rarely, her). This is perhaps the most unhelpful figure to have in mind when doing Transition work. Many organisations have cultures that require people to conform to this myth – asking for long hours, to prioritise work over home life, to give value only to things that produce hard outcomes, i.e. planning, doing, evaluating.

Transition asks us to engage with powerful information – from peak oil to climate change; from social justice issues to the despoiling of our environment.

It is natural that we feel things as we learn more. Some suggest that Transition invites us to meet our deepest fears for the future, and our greatest longing. Feelings are a natural part of human response to what is happening, and when they can flow they energise and connect us. Unexpressed, they can be damaging – leaking into meetings as inappropriate anger or tension, sapping energy, and even leading to depression or burnout.

Some of us feel uncomfortable in this territory, and it's important that it's always OK to opt out. If you are in a position of responsibility in a Transition group, it might be interesting to check how you feel about including some of your feelings in what you talk about, especially where you feel vulnerable, and to see what effect this has on others and the group culture. Talking about feelings, especially where we are vulnerable, almost always helps to build trust and a sense of connectedness in groups.

Resources

Co-counselling International (UK):
www.co-counselling.org.uk.

Transition in Action: Transition Town Totnes's mentoring scheme by Rosemary Bell

The Mentoring/Support project forms one of the more tangible outputs of Transition Town Totnes's Heart and Soul group's work. It started in December 2007 to provide regular, reflective one-to-one support for activists at the heart of TTT. It is staffed by professional counsellors and psychotherapists, who give their services as part of their commitment to the Transition process. Three years after they started, they surveyed those making use of the scheme to get a sense of how it was working. Here are some samples from the feedback they received:

- "It gives me an ability to find meaning and depth in my work that makes it even more powerful."
- "It provides the opportunity to talk through all aspects of life/work with someone who has knowledge, compassion, experience and appreciation of the challenges that exist."
- "It helps me in problem-solving, new

strategies for dealing with things."

- "It gives me support in recognising that there are limits to what I can do, that it's not all my responsibility, that if some things don't get done then that's fine, but what I do, I mostly do well."
- "The confidentiality and the trust to explore difficult feelings/relationships within the movement . . . a chance for the person being mentored to be appreciated, celebrated and valued for the work they are doing; the sense I was able to be part of a resourcing stream."
- Two respondents said they would like more activists to take up the offer of mentoring, "and for there to be a positive culture around this work which encourages people to take it up".

11. Personal resilience

with input from Sophy Banks

Giving our energy to making Transition happen can be both energising and tiring; taking time out can make a huge difference.

People who are drawn to Transition care deeply about the world around them, their children, their communities and about the future of life on this planet, but all too often give more of their time, energy and skills than is sustainable.

When engaged with Transition, what is the best way to stay balanced in what we give and receive, protect space and time for rest, and find sources of nourishment that restore our reserves? Alongside social and community resilience, the more personally resilient we are, the more we are able to face, and respond to, the challenges of our times. If resilience refers to 'bouncebackability', then someone with a resilient body, heart and mind will be able to feel whatever feelings arise in response to challenges and stressful situations, and 'bounce back', returning to a normal state of well-being.
The less personally resilient we are, the more

> My candle burns at both ends;
> It will not last the night; But ah,
> my foes, and oh, my friends –
> It gives a lovely light!
>
> Edna St Vincent Millay

challenges overwhelms us and we find ourselves struggling with physical exhaustion, losing sleep, isolation or inability to cope with relationships, mental stress or loss of meaning, to name but a few. As our resilience diminishes, the pathway back to healthy functioning takes longer, and in extreme cases of burnout it can take months or even years for a person to fully recharge.

Some simple factors that are known to increase levels of resilience on a personal level include the following.

- Having basic needs met; being financially resourced.
- Eating a healthy diet and taking regular exercise; spending time in nature.
- Feeling seen and appreciated for what we offer
- Feeling connected – to a partner, family, friends, colleagues and the community, and knowing that people will treat us with respect and care.
- Feeling able to effect change and make a difference.

These may feel familiar to those involved in Transition.

Training for personal resilience

Jo Hardy, a facilitator who works with Transition groups, argues that the basic principles for personal resilience are that we learn best by a combination of receiving information that helps us understand more deeply challenges and solutions, self- and group reflection, listening to and hearing each other's experience and sharing our own stories and experiences. She suggests that workshops designed to build personal resilience might include some or all of the following.

- A group brainstorm around what personal resilience feels like when we have a good degree of it and what it feels like as it diminishes.
- A talk around the idea of resources and a sharing and exploration of the 'resources' we personally have and can employ.
- An exploration of what works and what doesn't work so well in our working relationships, i.e. where we struggle around issues such as unclear boundaries and learning to name areas of difficulty before they escalate too far.

- An understanding of the physiology of stress and what happens to us when stress overwhelms our capacity to re-source ourselves.[59]
- The basic techniques of Mindfulness Based Stress Reduction* and how these can significantly contribute to increased personal resilience if we are struggling.

We learn by repetition, so to be more effective such workshops need to be followed up by ongoing practice and sharing groups, and/or individuals engaging the support they need to further develop resources.

* Mindfulness Based Stress Reduction is finding increasingly wide application in organisations including the National Health Service, schools and businesses as a way of reducing stress, increasing health and well-being and even managing chronic pain. Developed by Jon Kabat-Zinn, the idea is to increase awareness of what is happening in your own mind, body and heart so you naturally have more of a sense of what is going on. As we give more attention to the feedback from our bodies, hearts and minds we more easily respond by attending to what is needed – rest, exercise, food, company, having a change of scene or pace, whatever is called for. The repeated act of noticing our behaviour in stressful situations also increases our ability to choose our response and not get caught in habitual stressful reactions, some of which may be old patterns learnt long ago and no longer useful or relevant. See www.mbsr.co.uk.

Deepening

The Transition process itself helps with many of these – working together to achieve positive and practical outcomes; making friends and building a sense of local community – these all support the personal resilience of those involved. And yet, many people involved will have felt, or known someone who felt, overstretched, stressed or exhausted partly by their involvement.

Two key features of any resilient system, as described in *The Transition Handbook*, are feedback loops and tight coupling, i.e. that 'the system' is open to feedback and is conscious of and listens to the feedback sooner rather than later. Applying this to ourselves, there are always signs that we are going beyond our natural coping capacity. These will be different for different people, but common ones include:

- feeling tired
- losing sleep
- being unable to switch off
- feeling overwhelmed by new requests for responses to challenges
- being irritable or snappy with people we are close to
- feeling depressed, hopeless or overwhelmed by sadness in ways that seem disproportionate to what's happening
- feeling isolated or cutting off from friends or colleagues
- feeling guilty or resentful, that we are doing too much or not enough.

It's common in our culture to override these warning signs, and we can often be praised as being heroic in keeping going in spite of them. In this we repeat the pattern of our wider culture: ignoring the warning signs of climate change, environmental degradation and exhaustion of resources and speeding up in response, rather than slowing and changing what we do.

The things that best restore, nourish and replenish your energy will be specific to you. Spending time discovering what really works for you is time well invested. The list might include fun activities, or doing things or being with people that are nothing to do with Transition! Time spent in nature, listening to

music or being creative, or turning off the constant flow of emails and switching off from 'mental' activities, give the rational left brain a rest and nourish feelings of connection and flow. Physical exercise helps the brain as well as the rest of the body. For some, it's time alone that is most restorative.

It is really important that people who are most active in Transition visibly attend to their own well-being, putting boundaries around work and taking time to look after themselves. Talking about avoiding burnout is meaningless if you are working flat out without resting yourself, and those most active in a project have the most influence on setting the culture of what's valued.

Each of us is responsible for our own well-being. Ensure a balance of activity and rest, be aware of the early symptoms of burnout and don't shy away from seeking support sooner rather than later.

You might also enjoy . . .

COMING TOGETHER AS GROUPS (*Starting out* 1, page 92), RESPECTFUL COMMUNICATION (*Starting out* 3, page 100), ARTS AND CREATIVITY (*Starting out* 8, page 117), CREATING A SPACE FOR INNER TRANSITION (*Starting out* 14, page 140), CELEBRATING (*Deepening* 5, page 161), SUPPORTING EACH OTHER (Tools for Transition No.9, page 179).

Tools for Transition No.10: Unleashings

Ben Brangwyn of Transition Network and Duncan Law of Transition Town Brixton cut the celebratory cake at the Brixton Unleashing. *Photo: Amelia Gregory*

An Unleashing is a celebration of place, history and the potential of a low-carbon, post-oil future. It is envisioned as the event that future generations will commemorate with a blue plaque in celebration of the day when the community's transition began in earnest. How to do an Unleashing is work in progress, and every community that has one does it differently, which is as it should be.

The question is often asked, "When is the best time to hold an Unleashing?" The best time, I think, is when your awareness-raising work seems to be starting to influence a significant number of people, when you feel some sense of a 'buzz' coming back to you. At the time of writing, there have been twelve Unleashing events in the UK, five in the US that I know of, and one in Brazil.

The Transition Langport Unleashing team, with guest speaker Michael Eavis, organiser of the Glastonbury Festival. *Photo: Cara Naden*

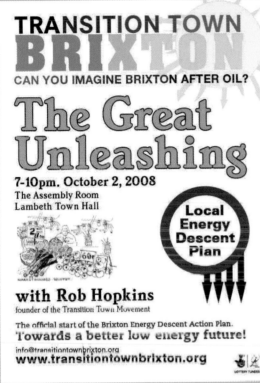

Image: EcoLabs

Transition Town Totnes held the first, in September 2006, after nine months of awareness-raising work. It featured an introduction from the local mayor, two talks, and lots of getting people talking together and visioning (but no cake).[60] The next one was Transition Penwith in Cornwall, who found that Richard Heinberg was able to give a talk in their area. They decided, having done very little previous awareness-raising work, to make that their Unleashing. Next was Lewes, whose Unleashing was a huge event that packed out the town hall, featuring stalls from many local groups and organisations. This was a big community celebration.[61]

The next two were Transition Town Brixton and Transition Norwich.[62] The Brixton Unleashing was the first to feature an impressive cake, as well as lots of community visioning and inspiring talks. Transition Norwich's also featured lots of Open Space discussions (see Tools for Transition No.15: Community brainstorming tools, page 220) and bringing people together to discuss the future.[63] Transition Chep-

stow's featured local ales, a raffle and a man in polar exploration gear.[64] Transition Narberth's event brought together local campaigners on a wild, wet and windy night, leading to a local headline 'Storm heralds great success for Transition Narberth's Unleashing'.

Transition Langport took a different tack, opting for a daytime rather than an evening event. Their Unleashing ran from 10 till 4, and featured a wide range of stalls and events, workshops and food.[65] Over 250 people turned up for Transition Town Kingston's Unleashing, which featured an amazing cake (a marzipan allotment!), short talks, Open Space sessions, the premiere of a film about TTK[66] and music and dancing into the early hours.[67] Transition City Lancaster's Unleashing was in two halves: a first half of talks and then a second half of celebration, including the cutting of a celebratory ribbon that encircled the whole audience.[68]

One of my favourite Unleashings was that of Transition Malvern Hills. It was held in the largest theatre in the town and featured three choirs, many speakers, films and music. Transition Town Tooting held their Unleashing off the back of their Trashcatchers' Carnival, and the evening featured local ethnic cuisine, an amazing cake, storytelling and streamers.[69] Sustainable Bungay also held an Unleashing,[70] which sounded like an inspirational event.

The first US Unleashing, run by the Sandpoint Transition Initiative, filled the 500-capacity local Parida Theater for a mixture of talks, music and networking.[71] The whole thing was streamed live

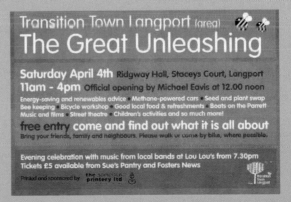

Transition in Action: Unleashing the first Transition favela by May East of Transition Brasil

Signing the letter to Transition Network.
Photo: May East

It was a sizzling Saturday morning in December 2010 when members of the low-income Brasilândia community of 247,000 people in São Paulo gathered for the official Unleashing of 'Transixion' Brasilândia. The first part of the morning celebrated a remarkable chain of achievements. In only eight months, 85 community members had gone through the Transition Training, with many of them studying the Portuguese Primer. This, combined with their inherited resourcefulness, their *mutirão* (collective action) spirit and emerging social entrepreneurial skills, has generated seven working groups and many actions on the ground:

- The Public Space Regeneration group has adopted seven abandoned places and turned them into community gardens.
- The Brasilândia Filmes group has worked with many local youngsters, who have been filming all Transition activities. At the Unleashing, they held the world premiere of their documentary, rescuing the oral tradition of the guardians of the memory of the region.
- The Social Enterprise and Local Business group has learnt how to run Exchange Fairs and has offered a lively 'Exchange Market'. They are also opening a community bakery and a sewing business.
- Other working groups include Fair for Sustainable Health (promoting the well-being of community members), Food Security (offering wild harvesting and urban growing workshops) and Zero Waste (preparing to launch an amazing initiative from Estonia, for cleaning and eradicating waste in the neighbourhood . . . !).
- The Water and Preservation group involved local children in cleaning a local stream, including traditional songs and rituals to baptise/reconsecrate the sweet running waters. The same group planted the 228 native trees, and their intention is to reforest 19 acres of the Cantareira Forest over the next two years. The group is now launching a citywide campaign, 'The Forest Invades the City'. The campaign will be punctuated by a series of awareness-raising events promoting the concept of *florestania* (forest citizenship) and agroforestry activities creating ecological corridors to connect the mother forest with the urbanised lanes.

In the second event of the morning, members of the working groups shared their common vision for the next 20 years, the result of a recent backcasting exercise (see *Starting out* 13, page 138). This was witnessed by a wider circle of attendees. João Leitão from Transition Pombal in

Portugal connected via Skype and shared ideas on how Brazil and Portugal could further exchange experiences and collaborate, and later on Rob Hopkins came online. With an eager audience and faulty equipment we could hear and see Rob but Rob could only see but not hear us!

One of the highlights was when Japa, a young local rapper, sang the Transition Rap.[72] Rob, unable to listen, danced in sync on the other side of the screen. The crowd was amazed and amused! Other traditional acts came to animate the party, sharing their songs and visions for a resilient and healthy Brasilândia.

The Unleashing ended in high spirits, with all signing a letter to Transition Network. This was a memorable morning, a joyful, empowered and unique opportunity for regeneration of these people's loved Brasilândia – land of Brazil.

Mayor Heller addresses Sandpoint Transition Initiative's Great Unleashing, 14 November 2008. *Photo: Suzan Fiskin*

online, and was followed the next day by a big community Open Space day. The Great Unleashing of Transition Whatcom was a huge event,[73] with bands, speakers and stalls on an amazing scale. Transition Bloomington's Unleashing took the form of a large Open Space event, and they are seeing it as being Part 1, with Part 2 to take place a year later. Transition Carrboro-Chapel Hill's Unleashing attracted 150 people and led to the formation of a mighty 21 working groups! Transition Laguna Beach's 'Great Unleashing Party'[74] attracted over 500 people to a celebration with food, music and dancing, which built on a year and a half of awareness-raising work.[75]

An Unleashing should feel dynamic, colourful and celebratory, and balance the informative with the entertaining; the factual with the inspirational. A liberating note: some people don't like the word 'Unleashing'. If you don't, call it what you like! What matters is that you create an event that will be commemorated in 15 years' time . . .

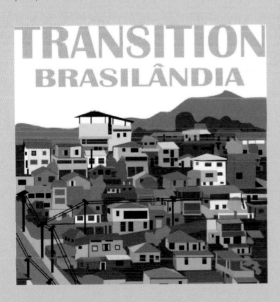

TRANSITION BRASILÂNDIA

Tools for Transition No.11: Healthy conflict

by Charlotte Du Cann, Adrienne Campbell, Sophy Banks, Sarah Nicholl and Jo Hardy

Conflict within groups can end up feeling as raw and as entrenched as this. However, it doesn't have to be like that . . .

Sooner or later all initiatives will encounter conflict. Conflict is a normal and natural stage in the evolution of any group or partnership. Left unaddressed, conflict can escalate, take a lot of the group's time and energy and make it unattractive to newcomers. However, creative tension and challenge, where there is an ethos of respectful communication and tools to help people come to good decisions, are good agents for change. Practice in these things will help us forge strong and flexible relationships that can deal with the very real challenges that lie ahead.

There are many things groups can do to avoid unnecessary conflict. These include spending time getting to know each other, creating clear roles and agreements, and taking time for reflecting together

on how you work as a group. All these will help to prevent misunderstanding, build trust, and address any issues early on. These are covered in the ingredients listed on page 191.

Conflict is a huge topic, so what is included here are just a few ideas and pointers based on the experience of some community and Transition groups.

Because of the threat – real or perceived – and the strong emotions that arise with this, it can be difficult to find a steady grounded place once a conflict is happening. So anticipation is invaluable – understanding why and how conflict arises and practising some skills for dealing with it – even inviting someone with these skills to be part of your group or making a connection with him or her. Even

A Conflict 101

from Helpguide.org[76]

- **A conflict is more than just a disagreement.** It is a situation in which one or both parties perceive a threat (whether or not the threat is real).
- **Conflicts continue to fester when ignored.** Because conflicts involve perceived threats to our well-being and survival, they stay with us until we face and resolve them.
- **We respond to conflicts based on our perceptions of the situation**, not necessarily on an objective review of the facts. Our perceptions are influenced by our life experiences, culture, values and beliefs.
- **Conflicts trigger strong emotions.** If you aren't comfortable with your emotions or not able to manage them in times of stress, you won't be able to resolve conflict successfully.
- **Conflicts are an opportunity for growth.** When you're able to resolve conflict in a relationship, it builds trust. You can feel secure, knowing that your relationship can survive challenges and disagreements.

strange, but it helps everyone in the meeting to step back and look at what's happening rather than just being caught in the feeling. Working on a group's ability to have and recover from these times of tension is a good start to learning to include conflict in the normal and healthy working of the group.

In the second stage of conflict things get more heated, and perhaps more personal. Now it's difficult to find a way through, but people are still talking and there is still some goodwill present. This is a key stage to catch, because finding a solution here will save enormous amounts of time and energy if the conflict escalates. The following strategies will help at this stage.

- Step back from the discussion or argument and recognise that 'we have a problem'.
- Don't let it escalate through, for example, gossip, or inflammatory or reactionary emails – talking in person or on the phone is much less likely to cause any further misunderstanding or hurt.
- Take a positive approach to finding a resolution, where discussion is courteous and non-confrontational, and the focus is on issues rather than on individuals.

Usually when conflict arises in a group it's a group issue – even if it seems to be focused around one person. Though it is often tempting to scapegoat that person, listen carefully to what he or she is saying – this may provide important information about the group, and that person may become your most useful ally in resolving the conflict.

if your group never has any conflict, the insight or skills you gain may be useful in all your work and personal relationships.

We could identify three stages of conflict. In the first, the disagreements or challenges may cause ripples to the smooth flow of the group's discussion, but these are contained without much difficulty. It can be helpful if someone acknowledges that there was a moment of tension or charge, or that the discussion is starting to feel more heated. Naming dynamics as they come up in meetings can feel

Sometimes, however, a group will encounter someone who makes group life very difficult. Use this as a challenge to the whole group to set and assert boundaries, expressing the group will clearly. Name the behaviour that is difficult rather than labelling the person, and explain how this works against the group's purpose or needs. If possible, ensure that the person has support – a friend or someone from the group – during the meetings, and possibly outside the group. Be creative in finding solutions, which might include finding a specific role for the person outside the group,

Transition in Action:
Conflict resolution in Lancaster   by Chris Hart

An initial attempt to set up a Transition City Lancaster (TCL) in 2006-7 failed because of poor group dynamics and disagreement as to how the group should be run. For any new group that picked up the baton of Transition in Lancaster it was clear that internal group relationships had to be at the centre of the process. In fact, this is what did happen, and most of the new steering group were members of a pre-existing deep ecology group. This was perhaps not surprising, because deep ecology recognises the importance of seeing ourselves as part of a larger web.

Unlike the first incarnation of TCL, the second attempt used a more centralised approach with a closed steering group that took primary responsibility for leadership and direction. This in itself was somewhat contentious, but it has been the way TCL has evolved, indeed very successfully and dynamically, maintaining a mindfulness about ensuring space for new people to come in via regular public meetings.

During the two-and-a-half years the initial steering group has existed, we have met most Wednesday evenings to plan, organise and develop the group. We prioritised making this as convivial a space as possible. In particular, we often started with a shared meal and wine, and a short time of silence. To help us along we had chocolate and biscuits and always finished with cheery stories. We consider all these aspects to be very important.

I think what is remarkable about TCL is that it has been so dynamic, and a huge amount of this has to be down to the way the members of the steering group worked among them-selves. We were all quite outspoken and we far from agreed on many issues. These included the group structure and constitu-tion, the centralising or dispersement of powers and decision-making powers within TCL, the autonomy or otherwise of the special interest groups, and the priority of events – all items of considerable contention and not unanimously agreed on. Instead, we tended to continue to thrash them out and evolve as time went on.

Even this was not always satisfactory, and unfortunately we did lose a few people along the way, particularly through difficult situa-tions that arose to do with the autonomy of special interest groups. It is probably worth bearing in mind that conflicts will always emerge and it is in addressing those that the work is done. Perhaps it is best to recognise this and always try to be humble and compas-sionate in the process, while also sometimes having to make difficult decisions.

Looking back from the vantage point of three years on, I think overall we are delighted with the way things have worked out. Each of the ten or so special interest groups are going from strength to strength and it is a while since any major issues of communication arose. We are now faced, though, with the next step, which is how do we develop from the strong base we have created and what happens if we need to start employing people to deliver, lead and administer ambitious projects.

perhaps somewhere else in the Transition project where he or she can make a real contribution.

If your group finds itself in conflict, make an assessment about whether you have the skills and experience to handle it. Conflict nearly always feels edgy, so don't underestimate yourselves – but do bring in an outside facilitator or other support if needed. Having a neutral person facilitating is a big help to reaching solutions.

In the third stage it's difficult to get people to meet or speak without acrimony. By now the group is usually facing some kind of split or collapse – whether one person is leaving, or two groups are in opposition. While it's possible to reconcile from this stage, it takes a serious commitment on both sides, and further time and energy. The situation will probably need skilled facilitation or mediation to negotiate a resolution between the two parties. It's still worth putting time and effort into making a respectful separation, and making at least some agreements, for example about how each side will speak about the other in the community.

In some cases of conflict, Transition groups have fizzled out, only to be reborn, while some have folded and in some the issue has been resolved. Some Transition initiatives, such as Bristol, Crewkerne, Brighton, Penwith, Lancaster and Lewes, have spoken about their troubles. Some initiatives have sought professional help and used outside facilitator and mediation services (see resources, right). Sometimes outside intervention has not helped, or has even exacerbated the difficulties, and initiatives have collapsed or faltered in spite of them. In the case of Transition Lancaster (see box, left), conflict transformed the initiative.

> "Speak when you are angry and you will make the best speech you will ever regret."
> Ambrose Bierce

Ingredients that you may find useful in dealing with conflict

Coming together as groups (*Starting out* 1, page 92), Inclusion and diversity (*Starting out* 2, page 94), Respectful communication (*Starting out* 3, page 100), Forming an initiating group (*Starting out* 4, page 102), Running effective meetings (Tools for Transition No.4, page 122), Momentum (*Deepening* 9, page 172), Supporting each other (Tools for Transition No.9, page 179), Personal resilience (*Deepening* 11, page 181).

Resources

Conflict Resolution Network (Australian): www.crnhq.org/pages.php?pID=10205.

There are many organisations and practices designed to increase skills or resolve conflict. To find these, look for trainings, resources or organisations that focus on topics such as conflict resolution, mediation (a method used for resolving conflict, sometimes used in place of courts), facilitation, peacemaking, and working with and managing emotions, particularly anger, and restorative justice.

Cooperatives UK publishes a series of five downloadable booklets called 'From Conflict to Cooperation': http://tinyurl.com/6krc9fr.

Decision Lab, for advice on Formal Consensus Decision-making: www.decisionlab.org.uk.

Seeds for Change also has many useful free leaflets on good practices: www.seedsforchange.org.uk.

12. Education for Transition

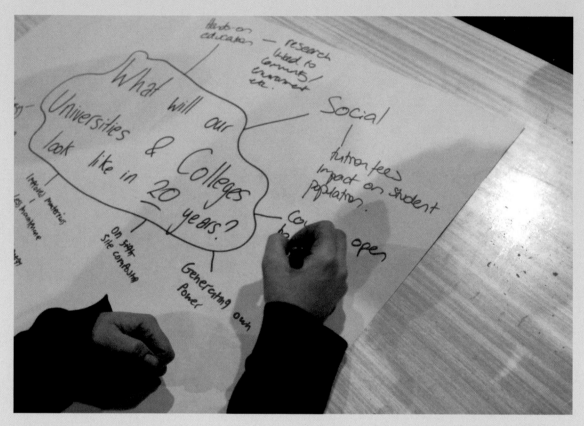

Making notes about what a resilient university would be like in practice, at a Transition Edinburgh University meeting. *Photo: Transition Edinburgh University*

How can education, at all levels, best contribute to the Transition process, building resilient individuals, resilient communities and resilient learning institutions?

The future that young people and those in further education are currently being educated for is not the future that is, in reality, approaching. The failure of government, and of much of the education system, to put resilience and sustainability at the centre of their planning and teaching means that a whole generation is being prepared for business as usual while deep down most young people, and

their teachers, know that the reality will be very different. This is a woeful neglect of duty.

Education, at all levels, will have to reappraise what it does and how it does it in the same way that all other aspects of society will: a process that will be simultaneously challenging and exciting. Transition can help by provoking public debate; shifting government thinking and influencing the remodelling of teacher training, especially as it moves from higher education to schools, so that teachers are equipped with deep understanding of the skills for resilience; supporting schools and universities to make their own transitions and creating a presence that educators can interact with.

"Sustainability is about the terms and conditions of human survival, and yet we still educate at all levels as if no such crisis existed."

David Orr

Transition schools

Schools are so constrained today in terms of the need to continually improve exam results that there can be a sense that there is no space for anything else in the school timetable. There is good evidence, however, that spending regular time doing physical work, growing plants and working outdoors can improve overall academic performance[77] and leads to better results and behaviour.

Adopting a Transition approach could also pave the way for schools and colleges to become Transition learning centres, opening up their facilities to the community once the teaching day is over, as well as being home to working market gardens and orchards, which could lead to students setting up their own enterprises to retail or value-add the produce. What would also help enormously would be a GCSE in Transition (or perhaps in 'Practical Sustainability') which could then in turn lead to an A-level where students can choose a mixture of practical skills as well as the necessary expertise to turn them into viable businesses.

A look at UK schools in 2011 (for non-UK readers I apologise for being so UK-specific in this ingredient) shows many pioneering developments. Some are doing interesting things in terms of food growing (having their own allotment or even, in some cases, market gardens or farms), healthy eating (using local, fresh and organic food in their kitchens and teaching students how to cook healthy meals), energy-efficiency (there are some great low-carbon

school buildings, and some have impressive renewable energy installations) and social enterprise (teaching kids how to set up their own businesses in school). However, there isn't, as yet, a 'Transition school' that pulls all of that together in one seamless whole and thereby provides an overarching purpose for the learning activities. A 'Transition school' could, potentially with the support of its local initiatives, do some or all of the following:

- Have a clear understanding of the impact of peak oil and climate change on the future world for which it is preparing its pupils; speak openly and often about that future and its challenges and opportunities; use that insight and vision to govern and shape its curriculum choices and, crucially, both its teaching and its learning methodologies.
- Focus on developing resilience as a key concept and skill for all, with self-knowledge, empathy, flexibility, adaptability, collaboration, communication and engagement as some of the key components.
- Empower students to take a full and active part in the leadership and organisation of its school and community.
- Regularly assess and address the temperature of the school community's health, well-being and happiness.
- Help birth the local economy of the future (see *Building 4*: Strategic local infrastructure, page 252). The school would become an integral part of the local economy, identifying the need for new sustainable businesses and developing as a centre of training in a range of skills, as well as the skills required for running a successful business.
- Deepen participation by placing students and parents right at the heart of this work, enabling them to realise their ideas and their wishes for the school.
- Make space for inner Transition. As the school, along with the community, enters times of uncertainty, staff and students will need the inner tools to support and nurture each other. Schools will need to create an ethos that is enabling in its structures and its relationships, so personal resilience can develop throughout.

Transition in Action: Transition Newent's garden at Newent Community School   by Tish Rickard

Members of Transition Newent working with local ELBS students. *Photo: Tish Rickard*

In early 2008, science teachers Des Marshall and Jane Price decided to run a new GCSE science course, ELBS (Environmental and Land Based Science), which offered a practical, hands-on approach to growing food. The teachers needed to create a working garden ready for year 11 ELBS students by September.

Transition Newent (TN) Food Group saw this as a great opportunity, and the gardeners, smallholders and growers in the group were keen to offer physical help and plenty of expertise. We visited the school in May, and Jane and Des welcomed our suggestions and offers of help. This included a polytunnel, which fruit grower Euan Keenan offered to install, free of charge, through his work with a local company, Haygrove. By July the polytunnel was up, providing a superb classroom and growing space. During August, Jane Price arranged working parties with students, teachers and TN Food Group. These were fun occasions with a healthy mix of young and old, expert and novice, clearing the site around the polytunnel and creating raised beds. TN Food Group continues to contribute with working parties, community activities and talks, and the ELBS course grows year on year.

Jane Price expressed "a huge thanks to Transition Newent. It's an amazing group. They've been so supportive." Of all school subjects that year, ELBS received the highest approval rating from students. Student Jamie summed it up: " . . . understanding how plants grow. I love it. It's excellent." A member of Transition Newent told me that, as a result of this project, "the students' grades all went up and the Biology department was accordingly given the money to take on a technician to organise the growing. This really is delivering the goods."

Transition colleges and adult education

The area where the most innovation is happening around the 'Great Reskilling' is in colleges and adult education. Here education can be more vocational, teaching people in detail how to become solar panel installers, market gardeners or woodsmen (or -women), plus many more vital skills that we will need a lot more of. Colleges such as Bicton College[78] offer a wide range of courses in many of these subjects. In 2000 I set up a course at Kinsale Further Education College in Ireland, with the intention of creating the course I always wished I had been able to do myself. It has now grown to include modules in permaculture design, sustainable woodland management, natural building, organic production principles and food production, natural nutrition, craft, community leadership and conflict resolution.[79] People seeking to learn practical skills for Transition will more likely be drawn into further education colleges than into universities, and many very high-quality trainings now exist. There are many opportunities for Transition initiatives to engage with such colleges. Transition initiatives can also set up and run their own evening classes through their local adult education college.

Transition universities

Lastly, what might Transition look like at the university level? As with schools and colleges, there are many universities that run courses which look at different aspects of sustainability, but only one that I am aware of contains a course that is explicitly built around Transition. In 2011, Schumacher College, together with University of Plymouth, new economics foundation and Transition Network, developed an MSc called Economics in Transition,[80] which includes an approved module called 'Creating a Transition Initiative'.

In addition, representatives of a number of universities have been meeting regularly, for example at the Universities Leading the Transition conference in Winchester in February 2011. The idea of universities *of* Transition (those weaving Transition into what they teach and how they teach it) and universities *in* Transition (changes to the institution and how it practically functions) is proving a useful focus. Transition is a harder thing to do in a university, with a transient population, than it is in a settled community, but one might imagine a Transition university as:

- having courses with both practical and academic components
- offering students allotment spaces, with training and support to allow them to grow some food to offset the costs of their education[81]
- supporting students in reducing their carbon footprints and also helping them minimise indebtedness through good money management
- promoting the concepts of localisation and resilience, both within the university and beyond
- raising awareness about these issues with the

staff, the students and everyone who comes into contact with the institution
- seeing the institution as a key driver for the decarbonisation and relocalisation of the surrounding community: university as farm, as market garden, as power station, and so on . . .

The student organisation People & Planet is one of the most useful organisations to work with that is promoting practical sustainability initiatives in universities. It already has active groups at around 100 universities, and has been very engaged with Transition in that context.

Where possible, work with local schools and universities to support them in their journeys towards embedding Transition in their activities and becoming a powerful force in the Transition of the wider community.

You might also enjoy . . .

TRANSITION TRAINING (Tools for Transition No.3, page 112), AWARENESS RAISING (*Starting out* 9, page 124), CREATING A SPACE FOR INNER TRANSITION (*Starting out* 14, page 140), THE 'GREAT RESKILLING' (*Deepening* 3, page 152), STREET-BY-STREET BEHAVIOUR CHANGE (Tools for Transition No.12, page 201), ENGAGING YOUNG PEOPLE (*Connecting* 5, page 223), SOCIAL ENTERPRISE AND ENTREPRENEURSHIP (*Building* 2, page 239), STRATEGIC LOCAL INFRA-STRUCTURE (*Building* 4, page 252), COMMUNITY-SUPPORTED FARMS, BAKERIES AND BREWERIES (Tools for Transition No.20, page 267).

Resources

Eco-Schools initiative: www.eco-schools.org.uk.

People & Planet: www.peopleandplanet.org. Its Going Greener campaign: www.peopleandplanet.org/goinggreener.

Here's a great film People & Planet made about Transition universities: http://tinyurl.com/3ptp6r2.

Transition in Action:
Transition Edinburgh University by Ric Lander

Transition Edinburgh University's logo, made up of hundreds of small pictures of their activities.
Image: Transition Edinburgh University

Inspired by Transition, a small group of students and staff decided to do what we could as a community to see a low-carbon transition take place. We asked, "What do we want our university community to look like?"

Some things seemed just right: world-leading teaching and research in environmental issues, thriving student community groups, campuses powered by locally generated heat and power, to name a few. But we saw other things too, though. A student and staff mainstream hooked on consumerism and high-carbon exploits, an academic culture driven by internationalisation and globalisation, and many disconnected students and staff with no links to their peers.

So Transition Edinburgh University set its mission to inspire big changes by putting practical action on climate change centre stage at Edinburgh University. Our Food Working Group began bringing local veg and organic everything straight to students and staff. We've been reusing the unwanted possessions of freshers by passing them on to next year's students. And, with help from the Scottish government, we ran a two-year project cutting energy usage in student homes, helping people choose local, flying-free holidays, and raising awareness with campus Go Green Weeks, photography exhibitions and courses like Carbon Conversations.[82]

We are not a department, a committee, a coalition or an umbrella group. What we are is a space where things happen; some ambitious, some just fun. We move forward as part of other groups and others as a part of us.

And we've taken our ideas beyond Edinburgh. As part of the People & Planet network we have helped hundreds of fellow groups start projects at their universities and colleges, many of them running the Going Greener campaign, which we have helped develop and spread. We have also worked with staff unions and the National Union of Students, who are making great strides as well. Informal and informal networks have all proved key.

We are a community of interest, not of place. In engaging such a community, we are overcoming the challenge of a dispersed and transient population. Yet the value of this work remains – after all, it is in such spaces that people work, grow and, often, find meaning.

See www.transitionedinburghuni.org.uk.

Connecting

It is often said that the scale of a proper response to peak oil and climate change would be akin to the preparations for the Second World War. Every aspect of our lives needs to turn on a sixpence, in a coordinated and effective way. The ingredients in this section explore how Transition initiatives can play a part in that process, and take Transition to a wider audience . . .

1. Forming networks of Transition initiatives

TRANSITION
LONDON

CROUCH END

TUFNELL PARK

STOKE NEWINGTON

LEYTONSTONE

BELSIZE

FINSBURY PARK

HIGHBURY

KENSAL & KILBURN

KENTISH TOWN

HACKNEY

EALING

PRIMROSE HILL

BETHNAL GREEN

WESTCOMBE

PECKHAM

HEATHROW

NEW CROSS

BRIXTON

WANDSWORTH

STREATHAM

BROCKLEY & LEWISHAM

WIMBLEDON

TOOTING

CRYSTAL PALACE

KINGSTON

find your local transition initiative at
HTTP://LONDON-TRANSITION.ORG.UK

A promotional leaflet produced by London's Transition groups, showing all the London initiatives as of June 2011.

Might there be something to be gained for Transition initiatives, rather than working on their own, networking with other local groups to share ideas and support each other?

As Transition initiatives spread and their effect increases, regional networks have emerged. They usually do some or all of the following.

- Share what works and what doesn't.
- Nurture emergent Transition groups.
- Facilitate communication and sharing of resources between these local groups.
- Create a body that can interact with the local authority and other bodies on different issues.

- Identify good speakers and other resources.
- Help newly forming initiatives learn what has already been done and where they can find support.

Some of these networks hold regular events and send out regular communications, while others are less formal and come together just to present occasional events. London has many Transition initiatives that have formed at the neighbourhood scale across the city, so it was inevitable that a network emerged to support their efforts. Transition London was initiated by the emerging Transition Town Stoke Newington group, who saw it as a good way to tap into the expertise across the various Transition groups in London. Transition London helps group members to feel part of a bigger movement, and enables the sharing of ideas, successes, failures, events, and so on. They run a simple website,[1] which offers links to all the London initiatives, and ran a city-wide gathering in April 2010. They produce two regular email mailing lists: the first, 'ltn-news', is a monthly summary of newsworthy events "which might plausibly be interesting enough to travel across town for". The second, 'ltn-talk', is a more focused sharing of resources for those involved in the core groups of different initiatives.

NETTAN is the North East Transition Town Activist Network,[2] and supports Transition initiatives across the north-east of England. It began in 2008, and now links 20 Transition initiatives. It enables groups to connect with each other – to offer support, especially to new and emerging groups, and to share information about events.

The South East Transition Initiatives network (SETI)[3] was formed by Mike Grenville (Transition Forest Row) and Adrienne Campbell (Transition Town Lewes), initially as a way to get funding to allow them to better support the many Transition initiatives emerging in the south-east. Their funding bid was unsuccessful, but an active network has appeared. They have created a website and an occasional newsletter, and at the time of writing have held three regional gatherings, the most recent in Brighton in 2010.[4] The group also interfaces with regional bodies when the need arises. The

network defines its role by stating that it "does not try to be a Transition initiative, but rather a catalyst and supporter of initiatives in specific places".

The genesis of Transition Support Scotland[5] is a little different. At the time it was formed there were 20 embryonic Transition initiatives across Scotland. A successful funding proposal was put to the Scottish Assembly. Until early 2011, Transition Support Scotland held annual national gatherings, produced a monthly newsletter, ran an interactive website and provided advice and support for initiatives. It also provided a very useful networking service. In early 2011 it lost its core funding and produced an excellent report reflecting on the lessons from its activities,[6] and it is hoped now that a more informal Scottish network will pick up some of its activities.

Sometimes, networks just come together for one-off events. Transition North was the name of a one-day conference in Slaithwaite in Yorkshire on 6 November 2009, which brought together Transitioners from across the north of England. The event was presented in partnership with the Cooperative Group and Cooperatives UK, and was a galvanising day for Transition in the area.[7]

Transition Somerset was formed by members of Transition Glastonbury as a way of showing Transition growth in the county. In March 2008 a one-day conference was held, which led to the formation of

Participants from Transition initiatives across the south-east meet in Brighton in 2010.
Photo: Mike Grenville

Transition initiatives from across the north-west US come together for the 'Transition Cascadia Regional Summit'. *Photo: Shelby Tay*

Connecting

local groups. Another event was held in May 2009, with talks by Jeremy Leggett, Shaun Chamberlin and Rebecca Hosking. A Google group was set up to allow the different groups to communicate.

When Somerset County Council (SCC) passed its Transition resolution in July 2008 (see *Daring to dream* 1: Policies for Transition, page 281), the need became clear for one body to speak on behalf of the county's initiatives. Transition Somerset met various council members to help shape how a Somerset council in Transition might look. This worked well, as the council found it much easier to work with one representative group than dozens of individual ones. Transition Somerset also organised a day of Transition Training for the council in April 2009. This role, however, raised concerns about accountability. Who are these representatives? Should they be elected? Transition Somerset exists now as a Google group, and has been active in lobbying SCC into formally renouncing their Transition status in the light of their downgrading, in February 2011, of their climate change work[8] (see page 283).

Transition East[9] is an informal network for Transition initiatives in Bedfordshire, Cambridgeshire, Norfolk, Suffolk and Essex. At the time of writing they have held two regional gatherings. For the 2009 event, they produced an exemplary document: 'Transition in the East: Co-operation, Collaboration, Support and Influence'.[10] This illustrated what each of the groups had done and appraised very honestly the challenges each faced. Transition networks in Cornwall,[11] North Cornwall,[12] Suffolk and North Somerset[13] mostly function as email lists.

North American regional networks are starting to emerge. In September 2010, the first regional gathering was held in Seattle for Transition initiatives across the north-west US, under the banner of the 'Transition Cascadia Regional Summit'. Groups represented included Village Vancouver (Vancouver, British Columbia), Transition Whatcom County (Bellingham and surrounds), Methow Valley Community Preparedness Committee, Transition Port Gardener (Everett, Washington), Sustainable NE Seattle, Transition Whidbey, Bainbridge Island, Vashon Island, Transition Seattle, Transition Olympia, Port Townsend, Sandpoint Transition Initiative, Transition PDX (Portland, Oregon), Salem, Eugene and Transition Reno.[14]

Regional networks work best when they emerge naturally when initiatives feel the need to join forces. Modern internet resources make this relatively easy, allowing the network to do what it feels useful and possible. For Charlotte Du Cann of Transition Suffolk, networks are important because they "help to break everyone out of small-town thinking (and thinking it is only your initiative that experiences challenges!)". However, Bart Anderson, of Transition Palo Alto in the US, argues for networks to have a different role. Rather than being groups of strong local initiatives, he sees that in some places they can support new Transition initiatives. His community initiative is vibrant, but in surrounding settlements people feel more isolated. Networks can help support their work and give it a context.

The emergence of these networks marks an important step for Transition in an area. Realising the value of collective action can be a huge boost to morale, as well as saving a huge amount of wheel-reinventing.

Create wider networks that allow the sharing of local experience, representation at a wider political level, more visibility and the hosting of larger, more effective events. There is no need to rush towards wider networks, but when the need arises, support them to

You might also enjoy . . .

FORMING AN INITIATING GROUP (*Starting out* 4, page 102), UNDERSTANDING SCALE (*Starting out* 5, page 106), COMMUNICATING WITH THE MEDIA (Tools for Transition No.6, page 136), CELEBRATING (*Deepening* 5, page 161), BECOMING THE MEDIA (Tools for Transition No.13, page 208), MEANINGFUL MAPS (Tools for Transition No.16, page 226), STRATEGIC LOCAL INFRASTRUCTURE (*Building* 4, page 252).

Tools for Transition No.12:
Street-by-street behaviour change

A meeting of one of Totnes's 'Transition Streets' groups gets under way. *Photo: Lou Brown*

Transition Streets (previously also known as Transition Together)[15] is a model that emerged from Transition Town Totnes as a way of enabling Transition at a street by street level. It works like this: a group of five to ten households get together, ideally in the same street, meet regularly (weekly, fortnightly, whatever works . . .) and self-teach through a workbook of seven sessions.

These are:

- **Getting started** (meeting each other and agreeing how to run the sessions).
- **Spend less on energy** (learning how to measure energy and how to use less of it).
- **Spend less on water** (looking at all the ways we use water and how to conserve it).
- **Spend less, eat well** (looking at food, how to avoid waste and eat a lower-carbon diet).
- **Wasting away** (avoiding waste; recycling and composting).
- **Getting around** (reducing dependency on the car).
- **Wrapping up** (next steps and evaluation of the programme).

Transition Streets gathers useful data in every session, allowing participants to measure their progress. It provides a 'before and after' snapshot of how participation has led to real savings in each household. In June 2011 this project was recognised with a prestigious Ashden Award for its success with behaviour change. (If you'd like to start your own version of Transition Streets, please contact Fiona Ward via www.transitionstreets.org.uk.)

Transition in Action: The measurable results from Transition Streets in Totnes   by Fiona Ward

Data gathered from Transition Streets groups in Totnes shows the kind of result that is possible. Participating in a group led to average carbon savings of 1.2 tonnes per household, and financial savings of around £570 per household. At the time of writing, there are over 60 groups in the town (480+ households). So far, this project has led to total carbon savings of 576 tonnes, with total financial savings of £273,600.

Participants give feedback at the end of the programme, most of whom value the new relationships with neighbours above carbon and money savings! We also see significant positive changes occur in awareness and knowledge, with the largest improvements shown in such areas as:

- "I understand how these two issues [peak oil and climate change] affect me, my family, my local community, and the planet."
- "I know what practical, effective actions I can take to reduce the potential impacts on me/others."
- "I'm aware there are simple, easy things I can do to reduce household costs – and I know how to do them."
- "I feel connected to, and a part of, my local community."

Ten other Transition initiatives have also been running Transition Streets pilots, adapting the Transition Streets materials (which are very place-specific) to their own situations. For example, Transition Leicester produced 'Footpaths', adapting the Totnes materials to focus more purely on carbon reduction. Transition Town Taunton (TTT) have been running Transition Streets with 30 householders. As Chrissie Godfrey of TTT said:

"People enjoy the social aspect of this as much as the practical stuff . . . it means they can share ideas and motivate each other. But our groups are telling us that this kind of initiative needs to go into local schools and businesses too, so we are happy to hear from people who might like to set up a group in those settings."

There are other approaches similar to Transition Streets that have been very effective. Transition Norwich started a less formal approach called 'Transition Circles',[16] in which small groups of people meet to talk about making lifestyle changes starting with individual actions, which they have found to be a key element of urban Transition. The groups have since broadened their focus to look at larger practical initiatives, such as wholefood-buying co-ops.

Another similar model is Carbon Conversations,[17] developed by Cambridge Carbon Footprint. This is a much more formal process, which takes place over six meetings held with a trained volunteer facilitator.

Six to eight people meet in a process that aims to 'engage people emotionally as well as practically'. The sessions are rooted in the psychology of change, and examine why people fail to respond. This has been very successful in getting people to reduce their household's carbon emissions, and a number of Transition initiatives are also experimenting with this approach. Another approach worth mentioning is Eco Cell, which is more in-depth and intensive than Carbon Conversations and was developed by Christian Ecology Link, with a Christian-based perspective.[18]

Transition in Action: The evolution of Transition Streets by Adrian Porter

Transition Streets is one of many projects that aim to support the area of Totnes and District to reduce its carbon footprint. The project evolved from working just with self-managing groups, to be a three-stage project supported by a grant of £625,000 from the Department of Energy and Climate Change (DECC) 'Low Carbon Communities Challenge', one of 20 projects selected nationally. Transition Streets encourages and supports people to form groups in order to make 'effective, practical, money-saving and energy saving changes with a group of neighbours, friends or family'. This is the 'behaviour change' element.

The second stage then focuses on energy-efficiency, through training one member of each group so that he or she can assess home energy-efficiency and domestic renewable energy options for the rest of the group.

Stage three gives participants the chance of a Transition Streets grant towards the installation of solar photovoltaic (PV) panels. Two levels of grant are available: a standard grant of £2,500 and a higher grant of £3,500 for those qualifying as low-income applicants (having less than £250 disposable household income per month). The low-income partici-pants also have access to a low-interest loan partially subsidised by South Hams District Council. To be eligible for the PV grant, properties must meet a minimum level of energy-efficiency.

We estimate that around 35 per cent of the Transition Streets participants are low-income households, and we have now installed 141 domestic solar PV systems (the grant period ended in June 2011). This project also funded the installation of a PV array on the roof of Totnes Civic Hall in partnership with Totnes Town Council, with 14kWp (kilowatt peak) of energy-generating capacity, or around 13,000kWh of electricity per year.

Totnes Civic Hall shows off its PV roof.
Photo: Lou Brown

2. Involving the council

Transition Town High Wycombe (TTHW) launches its Energy-Saving Kits for Loan in partnership with Wycombe District Council, August 2010. Left to right: Lesley Clarke, Leader of the District Council; Mark Brown, Chair of TTHW; Lesley Stoner, the council's Environment Officer. *Photo: Wycombe District Council*

To deepen your effectiveness, developing a good relationship with your local authority will be vital, but how to do that most effectively?

If your Transition initiative decides to talk to the council to interest it in your work, what is the best way to make sure that the conversation goes well? How can you prevent it going badly?

Alexis Rowell was a Camden councillor for four years and one of the founders of Transition Belsize. In his book *Communities, Councils and a Low-carbon Future*[19] he sets out his advice for Transition initiatives wanting to approach their local council. First, he suggests, councillors are only human, and spend much of their time being berated about different problems, so they love people who bring solutions rather than problems. Consider what your initiative can do that helps councillors solve a problem they are facing.

Second, make them feel a part of the process. Invite them to events, such as film screenings, as guests of honour, and invite them to comment after the film. You could invite them as 'Keynote Listeners' to your events (as Transition Network did with Ed Miliband in 2009 when he was Secretary of State for Energy and Climate Change – see page 281). Make

Four tips for community groups wanting to approach their local authorities

from the Community Development Foundation[20]

- Be persistent, polite and ready to work with others.
- You need patience and networking skills to find the right person who is interested and supportive of your work.
- You must have something to offer. For example, how can your group help the council meet its targets?
- Often the council is already dealing with other third-sector groups. You may have more influence as part of a coalition.

sure they know of your events. Even if they can't attend, they should get a sense of the buzz you are generating, at second hand at least. You might invite them to Open Space events (see Tools for Transition No 15: Community brainstorming tools, page 220). Offer them first refusal on dates when planning the event, to ensure they can attend.

Third, think about why you are going to see them. What are you asking for? Don't go too early: as Alexis warns, make sure you get all your organisational 'birthing pains' out of the way first. It works better if the 'buzz' around your work reaches them first, or if you have a practical project under your belt first, to show that you aren't just another 'talking shop'. Make sure you have a clear ask; don't turn up empty-handed (or -headed).

Michael Dunwell of Transition Forest of Dean has worked with his local council on establishing Transition thinking at council level. He told me that experience impressed on him the importance of Transition Training (see Tools for Transition No.3,

page 112). He cited two reasons why the training really comes into its own when engaging local councils.

First, "the training itself strengthens and supports commitment and feeds the desire to see a healthy community". Without this it would be hard for

Some 'dos and don'ts' on giving a presentation to your local council by Alexis Rowell

- **Do** dress the part. Wear a tie, or wear something smart; have a haircut if needed.
- **Do** tailor your presentation to your audience. If you are addressing the financial directors, tell them how Transition can save them money. If you are talking to the disaster-planning officers, tell them how Transition can help build resilience, and so on.
- **Do** practise what you are going to say, and ensure your co-presenters know who is doing what.
- **Do** try to get one or two sympathetic councillors on board before your presentation.
- **Do** offer your services as experts in consultation processes, as did Stroud (see page 207).
- **Do** try to not come across as unfocused and woolly . . .
- **Don't** take your family, friends, dog, etc. along with you.
- **Don't** spend the first ten minutes showing them peak oil graphs and pictures of stranded polar bears.
- **Don't** slag them off, presenting them with a list of 'the council doesn't do this, and it doesn't do that . . .', and so on.

Connecting

Transition in Action: The Monteveglio Transition Resolution

Members of the Transition Town Monteveglio group with local councillors and the Mayor (wearing the sash). *Photo: Gabriele Baldazzi*

One of the most amazing resolutions passed by a local authority happened in Monteveglio, Italy, in 2009. Among other things, it committed the authority to:

> "Strategic partnership with the Association Monteveglio Città di Transizione [Transition Town Monteveglio] with whom this administration shares a view of the future [the depletion of energy resources and the significance of a limit to economic development], methods [bottom-up community participation], objectives [to make our community more resilient, i.e. better prepared to face a low-energy future] and the optimistic approach [although the times are hard, changes to come will include great opportunities to improve the whole community's quality of life]."

I asked Cristiano Bottone of Transition Town Monteveglio (TTM) how the resolution came about. He said that it began with his giving talks about peak oil and Transition, which were well attended by local councillors. This led to the forming of TTM, who organised talks and other events and hosted a Transition Training by Naresh Giangrande and Sophy Banks, who developed the Transition Training sessions. Local elections were pending, so some within TTM decided to put themselves forward for election. Others preferred to continue with the Transition initiative. The candidates used Transition approaches such as World Café (see page 220) to generate ideas for their electoral platforms. They were all elected, enabling TTM and the council to work closely together despite recent public spending cuts. Cristiano offered three tips for approaching local authorities:

- **When communicating with institutions, talk to the people, not their roles:** Speak to the parent, the citizen, the carer, rather than the title on the door of the office.
- **Create the conditions for change (no.1): create a 'new way':** When done well, Transition can create a new social and political space that politicians notice, and which gives them and local people new room for expression.
- **Create the conditions for change (no.2): move beyond competition:** Transition helps reduce competitiveness in local politics and promotes active, involved cooperation.

MONTEVEGLIO
CITTÀ DI TRANSIZIONE

people with little previous experience of local government to withstand exposure to it.

Second, it brings you into contact with people who have worked with government, which encourages you to seek their help. He concluded, "I have found that the impenetrable jargon of local government makes you doubt your own ability to think or speak, so be sure that you can express to yourself what it is you believe in. Only utter what you know you can understand and don't try to out-jargon the others. It really is important that the Transition message speaks a different language."

Transition Stroud works closely with Stroud District Council. At the IDeA (the Improvement and Development Agency for Local Government) conference in June 2009, Simon Allen and Cllr Fi Macmillan told how that relationship emerged.[21] Transition Stroud became involved with the council's Local Strategic Partnership (LSP), which held a series of 'Inquiries'. At the Inquiry about food, Transition Stroud realised there were "no specialists on food supply in the district and we know as much as anyone". After much research, they produced the report for the food Inquiry, along the lines of 'Can Stroud Feed Itself?' (see page 272). The report was accepted as evidence to the LSP on food policy. The council later said that this strengthened the relationship between Transition Stroud, the LSP and the council. Transition Stroud offer the following tips for other Transition initiatives:

- Don't worry if your Transition group looks 'home-knitted' (which is in contradiction to Alexis Rowell's advice above!) – we've got energy, commitment and great ideas.
- Work on what you want to achieve, not what sets you apart.
- Look for people in your Transition groups who welcome collaboration.
- Build that relationship; take risks and learn to trust each other.
- Careful communication, review and reflection build that trust.
- It won't initially be easy; relationships need work.
- It won't happen overnight; be patient.

Derrick Anderson, CEO of Lambeth Council, says at the launch of the Brixton Pound that he wants it to become "the currency of choice for Brixton".

- Internal concerns have to be managed.
- Outcomes might change, so just work on a shared agenda.

When your initiative feels ready and has sufficient momentum, approach whoever seems the most sympathetic person in the council. Explore ways of collaborating, how you can help, and how your initiative can feed into council policy-making and activities. Where your group has relevant expertise, offer to help draft policy.

You might also enjoy . . .

RESPECTFUL COMMUNICATION (*Starting out* 3, page 100), AWARENESS RAISING (*Starting out* 9, page 124), VOLUNTEERS AND VOLUNTEERING (Tools for Transition No.7, page 150), HOW WE COMMUNICATE (*Deepening* 4, page 155), FINANCING YOUR TRANSITION INITIATIVE (Tools for Transition No.8, page 158), ENSURING LAND ACCESS (*Deepening* 10, page 174), ENERGY RESILIENCE ASSESSMENT (Tools for Transition No.14, page 216), SOCIAL ENTERPRISE AND ENTREPRENEURSHIP (Building 2, page 239), COMMUNITY RENEWABLE ENERGY COMPANIES (Tools for Transition No.18, page 246).

Connecting

Tools for Transition No.13: Becoming the media

At the 2011 Transition Network conference, the 'social reporting' project invited attendees to interview each other about their projects and insights. These were then posted online. *Photo: Mike Grenville*

A wide range of media can help a Transition initiative communicate, both internally and externally, what it does. Here are some of the options.

Films

Making, editing and posting your films online has never been easier. Transition Town Tooting made short films in the run-up to their Trashcatchers' Carnival, showing how the workshops were progressing and capturing people's expectation.[22] Transition Finsbury Park in London ran an event called 'Welcome to Finsbury Park',[23] inviting people to "submit videos of places that matter", lasting less than a minute. As more regional gatherings take place, more are being filmed and made available. For example, the film of the Transition South East gathering in March 2010 offered a great record of the day,[24] as did the film of the 2009 Transition Scotland gathering.[25] *In Transition 1.0*,[26] a Transition Network documentary, gathered much of the footage initiatives had taken and edited them into a film. Making short punchy films of your events gets it out to lots of people.

Photos

Many Transition initiatives gather their photos in online galleries, as a record of their activities and in case anyone else wants to use them (these galleries have been very useful in preparing this book!), often using sites like Flickr and Picasa. Some good examples are the libraries set up by Transition Stroud[27] and Transition Langport.[28]

Twitter

Twitter is a useful social networking tool, and a good way of keeping people informed about developments and events. It is like writing haikus, given that you have only 140 characters, but is an increasingly useful way to share things among those interested in your initiative. It is easy to register and get started. When I last looked, there were over 160 Transition initiatives with their own Twitter accounts, which they use for sharing news, making announcements and networking with other initiatives. Transition Network's Twitter account is 'transitiontowns'.

Blogging

Blogs are a great way to communicate stories, news and thinking – one of the best options for 'becoming the media'. Getting set up is easy, with sites such as wordpress.com offering a free service. Some Transition initiatives, such as Transition Alnwick[29] and the Ealing Transition Community Garden,[30] blog regularly. Some very good bloggers have emerged through Transition initiatives, such as Joanne Porouyow in Transition Los Angeles,[31] Transition Norwich's Charlotte du Cann and Transition Town Kingston's Shaun Chamberlin. At the time of writing, Transition

Transition in Action: The Norwich Bloggers
by Charlotte Du Cann

In October 2009 Transition Norwich (TN) launched 'This Low Carbon Life' – 'an experiment in community blogging', its aim being to collate the personal stories and experiences of people-in-Transition that would not be covered by the events-based objective reporting of the TN news blog and monthly bulletin. It also acts as a daily creative record of the initiative.[12]

At the time of writing, the Transition Norwich blog has twelve bloggers, six of whom write regular three-day slots in a rota system. We also run theme weeks and photo-blogs approximately twice a month in which everyone can take part (Sundays are also free days). Topics have included flying, waste, climate change, food patterns, inner resilience, reskilling, the 7 Deadly Resistances, spring gardens and autumn woods. We look at every aspect of Transition, from keeping allotments to zero waste. Our styles and outlooks are very different, and the posts are a mixture of the serious, funny, beautiful, hard-hitting, philosophic, practical and cosmic. Most of the photography is original and tries to capture our own experiences of trying to downshift. We deliberately have no censorship or rules about content or length. So long as it's within the frame of Transition and carbon reduction, everyone writes what they like. This is *creative diversity* at work, which is unusual in an era when most communications focus on brand marketing and promotion – saying what things should be, rather than how they really are. 'This Low Carbon Life' is pure editorial. It's about what Transition looks like, feels like and tastes like, through our own personal experience.

Three of us keep an editorial eye on the page, checking for typos and problematic picture alignment. Otherwise it's very much run by consensus.

See www.transitionnorwich.blogspot.com

Transition in Action: Transition Cambridge's e-newsletters   by Anna McIvor

In Cambridge we've been writing a weekly e-newsletter since August 2008[33] (I calculate we must have done more than 100 issues – we should have celebrated number 100 but it passed us by!). It's a lot of work, shared between three people who take turns to write it (it takes two to four hours each week). Currently we have 1,400 subscribers, and it receives a lot of praise.

We feel it's a big part of what we do – its main function is to communicate our activities and all the other sustainability-related activities in and around Cambridge. But it also supports cultural change, as each week people feel part of a wider movement with the same agenda (and, judging by the increasing number of events that we advertise, that culture is getting stronger). We know that a lot of people read it but don't actually come to things very often, but they nevertheless feel very connected with what we are doing.

Network is launching the 'social reporting' project to encourage Transitioners to blog, film, tweet and generally record their experience of being in Transition, and tell our story.[34]

Websites and newsletters

A website is a brilliant communications tool for any community organisation, as it allows you to publish your information and events freely and allows anyone to keep up to date with your activities. Newsletters are invaluable too. Your website links should go on all your posters, and you should enable people to subscribe to your newsletter online as well as to your events.

In Transition Network's 2010 web survey, newsletters were the single most important communications tool for initiatives – a well-timed newsletter (Thursday or Friday lunchtimes are popular) gets straight to people's attention. Many initiatives put out regular newsletters: some good examples include Transition Town Exmouth[35] and Transition Town Berkhamsted.[36] It's a good idea to archive previous newsletters for reference.

Planning and designing your website makes a difference to how useful it is, but this does not need to be a big deal; all you really need at the beginning is to publish news and events. Really – keep it that simple. There are some great Transition websites. New Forest Transition's 'New Forest Food' website[37] was voted the 'Best Healthy Lifestyle website' in the Hantsweb awards 2010, and other examples of good, clear, accessible websites are Transitions Hebden Bridge,[38] Lewes[39] and Finsbury Park.[40] Make sure your site has links to Transition Network's site.

You do not need sub-groups and forums and multi-user ding dongs; not yet, we promise. You just need to get used to publishing news regularly and sending out regular newsletters. All the free online services (see http://tinyurl.com/3z9lp7z) have great site-building tools for you to click and choose from – there's no need for hours of angst designing fiddly pages, because:
- a) you can change the templates as you need, from thousands available
- b) the most important thing is content, not precision layout of pages.

Tools for Transition No.13: Becoming the media

Recording a presentation at the Northwest Transition Summit, Seattle, Washington, September 2010.
Photo: Shelby Tay

Transition in Action: Moffat Online   by Jane Gray

Moffat Online, launched in May 2009, is the community networking site for Let's Live Local,[41] the Transition initiative for Moffat, in Dumfries and Galloway, Scotland. We wanted to see how far *structured* social networking could create community within an area. Early feedback was encouraging and we got members from all age groups and sectors of the Moffat community, as well as some ex-Moffatonians who missed their former home.

We freely offer Moffat Online support to help promote the work, the events and the membership of a range of local voluntary groups, many of whom operate with no external funding. We host an extensive events listing, local versions of Freeshare and a Car Boot facility, and a range of other groups which encourage sustainable activities. We frequently send round information about local sustainability initiatives and grants from which people might benefit. Our next development is to create local business pages to encourage local trade.

I think my favourite 'success' was sending out a plea for one of our members who needed a repair to a Wurlitzer jukebox – we got an offer of help from another member within a few hours!

It's taken a huge amount of unpaid time and effort to get to the current level of activity, and we know we're only starting to scratch the surface of what we can do with the site. It's a real privilege to be able to offer this service and we're delighted at how people have taken to it.

See www.moffatonline.co.uk

Transition in Action: Transition newspapers

Transition Lancaster's awareness raising took the form of a newspaper, the *Lancaster Transition Times*, which was to be distributed to 20,000 homes before their Unleashing. Unfortunately, the distribution company failed to do so and few newspapers reached their audience. Other groups have produced similar publications, such as Transition Town Worthing's *Post-Carbon Gazette*. Transition Town Haslemere has a monthly column in the local *Herald* newspaper. Belfast Area Transition, in Waldo County in the US, produced the *Belfast Area Transition Times*, which was written as a newspaper from 2021, filled with stories from a Transitioned future.

Caroline Jackson and Samagita Misha of Transition Lancaster with copies of the *Lancaster Transition Times*. Photo: Samagita Misha

Beware of embarking on a mega-web project early on – it is tempting to think that the website has to do everything, but it doesn't! This is the classic technology trap – we think we're doing something important but we're actually spending time over-complicating our lives in front of the computer when we could be in our neighbourhoods building real relationships. You can get to the rocket science later, when you know what you need and have people in place to manage the technical and editorial work.

Websites should be light and flexible, not big burly cumbersome beasts that scare everyone, including the beleaguered techie who volunteered early on and then found him- or herself struggling to deliver something far too complicated that no one really understands. Your site must be understandable and usable by more than one person, preferably not a techie too.

Transition Network offers very simple 'Community Microsites'[42] for initiatives starting out on the Transition process. These are simple 'websites in a box', and make it easy for people to add their own news and events and resources to a site they can call their own. They are deliberately simple and you may grow out of them, but that's the point: once you know you need something more sophisticated, you'll be more confident about what you need!

Facebook and other social media

Facebook, Twitter and Ning (and YouTube and Flickr for videos and photos) have exploded in popularity in the last few years. Since their foundation they have gone from strength to strength, collecting millions of users, making them an important part of many people's internet practices. Being social networks, they mimic group processes online, enabling people to set up groups, follow their friends, serendipitously find new friends, and other things that might happen in a group social setting.

Transition initiatives have used these networks to grow their memberships, coordinate events, connect with other initiatives, share ideas, and so on. They use social networks along with other media including mailing lists, their own websites, YouTube and Flickr. They are very powerful tools, and great fun if you like that sort of thing (though many don't). Give them a try. It can't hurt![43]

If your initiative doesn't have the skills to use the media you feel would be useful, it might be a good idea to find someone helpful who does.

3. Working with local businesses

with input from Fiona Ward and Graham Truscott

'Quids In', the commemorative beer brewed by Harvey's Brewery to celebrate the launch of the Lewes Pound.

Connecting

Localisation without the engagement of the local business community will prove impossible. But what is the best way to engage them?

Successfully working with local businesses is very important for Transition initiatives. Yet it may not come naturally, and we are likely to need to learn a new language, new concepts, and a new way of connecting. This ingredient provides a few examples of Transition initiatives working with their local businesses. Early in the life of Transition Town Totnes, workshops were run with local businesses using the NISP (National Industrial Symbiosis Programme) model, which brings together local businesses in a workshop to look at how best they can match their outputs with another's needs. Happily, they were from the same industrial estate, and the kinds of connections made included a business with lots of cardboard boxes to dispose of working with a local removal firm who need cardboard boxes. This was very productive.

Local currencies can be a great way of drawing in local businesses. Transition Town Lewes's Lewes Pound features on the back of the note a list of the key local businesses that support and endorse the pound. The launch of the Lewes Pound was attended by many local tradespeople. The local brewery, Harveys, one of the businesses named on the notes, brewed a commemorative beer called 'Quids In' to celebrate the launch. (I had a bottle and I have to say it was very tasty.)

Five tips for engaging local businesses in Transition
by Fiona Ward of Transition Training and Consulting

- **Be credible:** You need to speak their language, look professional, and understand basic business concepts such as revenue, profit margins, fixed/variable costs, etc.
- **Be open-minded:** Don't criticise their business decisions. Present facts, not opinions. Accept their assumptions and gain trust and credibility before introducing new ideas.
- **Be realistic:** Realise that the bottom line is key, even in environmentally minded businesses – if they're not at least breaking even they will not be around to do their work more sustainably. Also, small businesses have very little time or money to do anything other than survive. Even if they want to do the 'right' thing, they may not have the time to be actively involved.
- **'Sell' the benefits:** Be very clear about the benefits to the business of whatever it is you want to do with them – be they financial, environmental or social.
- **Tell stories:** Case studies of other credible, local/well-known businesses are very powerful, so long as the people you are presenting these to can relate to the size or type of business. Try to work first of all with a small number of friendly but influential local businesses, create good success stories with quantifiable benefits, and they will then attract others.

Transition in Action: Engaging the New Forest's food business community

The New Forest Local Food Summit.
Photo: New Forest National Park Authority

In April 2009, New Forest Transition (NFT) launched the New Forest Food Challenge,[44] funded by the National Park Authority.

Although an NFT initiative, it was deliberately branded without much reference to the organisation, and was set up to support local food businesses. After a year's imaginative promotion of local food across the area (which included creating a local food Google Map[45]), they held a 'Local Food Summit' in September 2010, which brought together 70 people who represented over 30 local businesses, as well as members of the district council, the National Park Authority and the local MP. All who attended signalled a commitment to helping. The next step is to create a local food strategy for the New Forest, with the network of local food businesses already formed.

Transition in Action: Transition Chepstow's Plastic Bag Free initiative by Janet Rawlings

Transition Chepstow's first project was the Plastic Bag Free Chepstow initiative, which replaced plastic bags with a cloth one that featured a design by a local artist.

Local businesses promised to reduce the number of plastic bags they handed out and received My Chepstow Bags as a substitute. We followed up the bag give-away with a prize draw in the local paper to encourage people to remember to take their bags with them when they went shopping. The Free Press was running a 'Shop Local' series, and we joined in by offering a fortnightly prize (£10 gift voucher in a local shop) for people photographed shopping local with their My Chepstow Bag.

Graham Eele shows off his Chepstow Bag.
Photo: Janet Rawlings

On a smaller scale, in 2010 Transition Cambridge ran a story-writing competition sponsored by local businesses. They also advertise a new Transition-related business in each of their newsletters and, like the New Forest, are creating a Google Map of local food businesses.[46]

Another good strategy is to form a Business and Livelihoods working group within your initiative, which creates a forum for local businesspeople and acts as an incubator for ideas and projects.

Offer services that support local businesses and that better connect them to the local economy, acknowledging the vital role they will have to play in the Transition process. Forming a Business and Livelihoods working group will be key to this.

You might also enjoy . . .
BUILDING PARTNERSHIPS (*Starting out* 11, page 132), PRACTICAL MANIFESTATIONS (*Deepening* 2, page 146), HOW WE COMMUNICATE (*Deepening* 4, page 155), FINANCING YOUR TRANSITION INITIATIVE (Tools for Transition No.8, page 158), LOCAL FOOD INITIATIVES (*Deepening* 8, page 168), EDUCATION FOR TRANSITION (*Deepening* 12, page 192), SOCIAL ENTERPRISE AND ENTREPRENEURSHIP (*Building* 2, page 239), TOOLS FOR PLUGGING THE LEAKS (Tools for Transition No.19, page 257), COMMUNITY-SUPPORTED FARMS, BAKERIES AND BREWERIES (Tools for Transition No.20, page 267), INVESTING IN TRANSITION (*Daring to Dream* 3, page 287).

Resources
Transition Training and Consulting: www.ttandc.org.uk.

Connecting

Tools for Transition No.14:
Energy Resilience Assessment

with input from Fiona Ward

An Energy Resilience Assessment is a great way for a business to establish where its vulnerabilities to volatile oil prices lie.

Energy Resilience Assessment (ERA) is a tool developed by Transition Training and Consulting (TT&C). It argues that in a time of rising, volatile energy prices, a business that relies on fossil fuels is highly vulnerable – and this is particularly the case with liquid fossil fuels. A report in 2010 by Lloyds and Chatham House[47] on the combined effects of peak oil and climate change on business viability concluded:

"energy security is now inseparable from the transition to a low-carbon economy and businesses plans should prepare for this new reality. Security of supply and emissions reduction objectives should be addressed equally, as prioritising one over the other will increase the risk of stranded investments or requirements for expensive retrofitting."

In other words, climate change and peak oil present key vulnerabilities and risks for any business over the next five to ten years. But where might a business or an organisation start to identify where vulnerabilities might lie, and how might a Transition initiative work with local businesses?

An ERA examines the use of fossil fuels for transport and power, where raw materials in the supply chain are vulnerable to the oil price (e.g. plastics and other petroleum-based products), and how customers' behaviour may change when energy costs rise. It identifies where a business is most exposed to rising or fluctuating energy prices, quantifies this risk and highlights mitigation strategies. This analysis and information are needed to assess the assumptions that underpin any business model and strategic plan. An ERA can make a clear, hard business case for less energy use and shifting the focus of a business closer to the local economy.

An ERA carried out by TT&C for a National Trust property estimated the effect of rising oil prices on visit revenues, given that 94 per cent of visitors drove private cars on an average round trip of 66 miles to visit the property. To offset this potential drop in visitor income, the following on-site opportunities were identified, as follows.

- The property should become a food producer.
- The National Trust could train local people in a range of skills.
- The property could produce building materials for its own buildings and for local builders.

ERA analyses can be surprising. An assessment undertaken for a printing business might have assumed that running presses for 24 hours a day, an energy-intensive practice, was the main vulnerability. In fact, the work revealed that a key vulnerability was that all but one of the staff lived at least seven miles from the business because of high local house prices. The lack of affordable housing increased the oil vulnerability of the business (and the town). As a result, the firm began an apprenticeship scheme for local young people, to bring more of them into the business.

Developing resilience in today's businesses and organisations
by Graham Truscott, Transition Training and Consulting [www.ttandc.org.uk]

Few existing businesses or organisations (large or small), even if they are aware of peak oil and energy-security concerns, have yet considered the profound implications of the decline of the fossil-fuel era. Fewer still have yet explored the specific impacts on them – their activities, turnover, profits and employees.

At first sight, the Energy Resilience Assessment (ERA) is a risk-management tool: it turns a spotlight on, and quantifies, areas of specific vulnerability in a critical part of a business to the external energy-related shocks likely to hit that business. In practice, because the ERA explores a measurable risk (dependence on cheap oil), which also underlies every other current business activity, it will raise questions about the 'sustainability' of what the business does

and how it does it. The ERA suggests possible mitigation strategies in the specific area it measures, but the implications can be significant and wider for the organisation concerned.

From inside a business, used to doing things a certain way – or indeed to constant change – it can be difficult to see what should be done differently, or better, in light of resource constraint and climate change – or how to respond positively to the big global issues. The ERA number-crunching and analysis inevitably draws attention to aspects of an organisation and unspoken assumptions that may not have been considered previously.

In the brave new world of energy descent, new ways of thinking about business, new areas of business or organisation, and new ways of doing business, are critical and necessary.

4. Oral histories

Transition Town Totnes's Hal Gilmore shows visitors from Taiwan around Totnes on a 'Transition Tour', illustrating the tour with images from the town's past. *Photo: TEIA*

It is often said that there is nothing new under the sun . . . What can we learn from our elders about more frugal and resilient ways of doing things that might help us to design the future?

Oral histories give substance to understanding how the place we live in functioned before cheap oil changed it profoundly, dismantling its resilience to a point where little remains. These histories populate the vague past with real characters and stories. They change the way you look at the place where you live. They help a more localised economy feel tangible. However, they are not about nostalgia – our aim here is not to romanticise some

'golden age'. The future cannot be like the past, but it needs to learn from it if Transition is to succeed.

I love doing oral history interviews. Here are a few tips:

- The first few people you interview may well be people you know, neighbours or acquaintances. They will probably be able to point out other people to talk to, or your local museum may be able to suggest some.
- Make sure your subject is happy to be interviewed and recorded, and for you to print excerpts.
- I usually start by asking for a potted ten-minute history of the person's life so far. I then return to the period I want to focus on (usually the

1940s-50s) and explore his or her experience of food, energy, housing, employment, community and so on.

- Record the interview digitally for transcription.
- Interview one person at a time to avoid 'reminiscing' conversations between your subjects.
- Send interviewees the transcript of the interview so they can check details.

"My dad and George Heath were both in the amateur operatic society and would be singing in the same Gilbert and Sullivan show, so they would sing little bits to each other [in George's shop], and then George would say 'Oh no, tomatoes, we got no tomatoes, but let's go get some then' . . . and then we all went over. That's what we did. We all went over to the greenhouses at the nursery and picked tomatoes, and they sang songs to each other wandering up and down and talked about this and that."

Andy Langford, from the Totnes oral history interviews

The shop-display style favoured by this butcher's shop in Dartmouth, Devon, may not find favour with twenty-first-century Health and Safety officials!
Photo: Totnes Image Bank and Rural Archive

You might also want to gather old songs and folklore. I tend to stay with practicalities. Where was food grown? How did people manage with less energy than today? What kind of work did people do? Were they happy? How did they entertain each other? What did frugal living look like in practice?

For Transition Town Totnes's Energy Descent Action Plan, 14 people were interviewed. The article produced from their interviews opens the plan, setting out the history of the town in which the EDAP has its roots.[48] Tales of urban market gardens, life with no need for a car, more seasonal diets and a town more related to its farmland offer a fascinating glimpse into the past, which can do much to inform our future plans. You can see a film about Totnes oral histories at http://youtu.be/pyhAvIXy6vg.

PLAN-it Environmental Education in Cornwall ran a programme called 'Traditions to Transition'. Pupils from Cape Cornwall School discussed life before cheap energy with their elders, contacted via Age Concern. The result was a fascinating bringing together of the generations that would be easy to replicate elsewhere.

Bring elders and local storytellers into schools. Create events and meeting places where young and old people can tell their stories, formally or informally. Use artists and musicians to create evenings of storytelling and song about the local community.

You might also enjoy . . .
INCLUSION AND DIVERSITY (*Starting out* 2, page 94),
ARTS AND CREATIVITY (*Starting out* 8, page 117),
AWARENESS RAISING (*Starting out* 9, page 124),
BUILDING PARTNERSHIPS (*Starting out* 11, page 132).

Connecting

Tools for Transition No.15: Community brainstorming tools

Open Space sessions at the 2009 Transition Network conference, Battersea Arts Centre, London.

Belief in external experts and our dependence on their telling us what to do next has become commonplace. However, much of what we need is around us. We need ways to unlock the knowledge and ideas of our community. Two approaches often used by Transition groups are World Café and Open Space. The following information will help you run sessions using them.

Open Space Technology[49]

This is for groups from 10 to 1,000 people who need to explore a major issue. Its originator, Harrison Owen, bases it on four guidelines:

- Whoever comes are the right people.
- Whatever happens is the only thing that could have happened.
- When it starts is the right time.
- When it's over, it's over.

And one 'law', 'The Law of Motion and Responsibility':

> "If, during the course of the gathering, any person finds themselves in a situation where they are neither learning nor contributing, they are invited to use their feet and go to some more productive place."

Here is a step-by-step guide to running an Open Space event:

- You'll need a room large enough for those attending to be able to sit in a circle (or, in the

An Open Space session that took place in Tsuru City at the all-Japan Transition meeting, August 2010. *Photo: Paul Shepherd*

At an Open Space event in Totnes.

case of large numbers, in concentric circles), a wall you can stick things on to, and places (rooms, tables, corners) for conversations.

- An overarching question must appear in publicity and invitations for the event.
- Sit participants in a circle. In the centre is a pile of sheets of A4 paper and pens. On the wall is an empty timetable, with the timings of the different sessions on one axis, and the various breakout spaces on the other.
- Explain the guidelines and process of Open Space, and say that the only rule for proposing a question (other than its having some relevance to the overarching question) is that you host that discussion and take legible notes.
- Anyone with a question writes it on a sheet of paper and sticks it to the timetable in one of the time slots. If there are more questions than available time slots, the leader or participants can consolidate relevant ones. Once your timetable/agenda is complete, allow people a few minutes to look at it and work out what discussion sessions they want to go to. Then announce the start of the first session.
- In theory, the rest of the day will now organise itself!
- At the end of each session, let people know it is finished, collect the note-filled sheets, and put them on the wall in the area called the 'Marketplace'.
- It can be very useful to have a 'Newsroom' –

someone who is scribing the notes from the sessions. He or she can then give people leaving the event a printed account of what was discussed, post the notes online or send them to participants the following day.

- Leave 30-40 minutes or so at the end for a go-round to reflect on the process rather than issues raised.
- The notes generated can be typed up and circulated to everyone who attended. No specific consensus is reached as such; it is rather a harvesting of ideas from which future activities will emerge.

Open Space is great for gathering ideas that lead to practical projects. Meeting others who share your passion helps turn ideas into action.

Those who have ideas bring them to an Open Space looking for collaborators. Open Space makes private ideas public and helps kick-start explorations around their feasibility, which then attracts others.

World Café

This has been summarised as being about 'awakening and engaging collective intelligence through conversations about questions that matter'. It differs from Open Space in that it is more directed and explores specific issues. It rests on the ancient truth that food and drink prompt thought and conversation.

So here's how to run a World Café session:

- Plan the event well, frame the question(s), and decide who should be there and how you will invite them, where and when it will be, and what results you want.
- Create a hospitable space with round tables set out café-style, with room at each for about five people, with sheets of paper, marker pens, flowers, perhaps a candle, and food and drink.
- The questions (either one overarching one or a number that explore different aspects of an issue) should be clear, thought-provoking and relevant to those attending.
- Encourage everyone to contribute by moving people around frequently. Every 15 minutes, ring a bell to show it is time to go to another table. Over a few hours, participants meet most, if not all, the people in the room. Each time people move, they bring threads of the previous conversation they were in to a new group of people. Each table has a host, who records the points on the sheet of paper. Each time the groups change, the new session begins with the host sharing what was previously discussed at that table, and the new people briefly share what happened at the tables they were on previously.

- At the end, draw the event together through sharing what came out of the discussions. You might pin up all the written-on sheets of paper for all to see, or each host could summarise the main points on his or her table. This could then be followed by a more general 'go-round' for sharing reflections on the process and what deeper questions were raised. This summarising process can be continued by typing up the sheets and emailing them to everyone a few days later as 'minutes' of the discussion. These can form a very useful basis for future events.

Ambience, good food, conversation, lots of mingling and ideas – World Café and Open Space. Begin!

Resources

One very powerful tool is 'The Art of Hosting': www.artofhosting.org/home.

The World Café: www.theworldcafe.com.

There is a great clip from the Powerdown Show showing World Café in practice at www.youtube.com/watch?v=Su_w9gYrtuk.

The self-organised timetable for Open Space sessions at the 2009 Transition Network conference.

5. Engaging young people

Transition South Bay LA Repurposing Event, September 2010. Workshop participants brought their sewing machines and old T-shirts for hands-on learning about how to create useful tote bags (to replace single-use plastic bags) out of old T-shirts. *Photo: Michael Vin Lee*

If young people fail to see a role for themselves, Transition will lose the engagement of a crucial part of the community.

Transition is about designing a more localised and resilient future for everyone. Today's young people will be starting families and building livelihoods in that world, so they should be a central part of Transition. What follows are different approaches for particular age groups.

A first impression may be that peak oil and climate change aren't issues that concern teenagers greatly.

As a 17-year-old girl at my local sixth form college told me, "I don't think years into the future . . . only three months ahead . . . learn to drive, go to college, learn to drive go to college." A 21-year-old who commented on Transition Culture said:

> ". . . there is still a very natural inclination to cling to the oil-driven lifestyle. Our generation grew up with it; it's all we ever knew. If you don't go and read through history books, you'll think that oil is a necessary part of human life."

He, however, began a Transition initiative in his community. Transition initiatives have been using a range of ways to engage and involve young people. For Joanne Porouyow at Transition Los Angeles, it is not a case of organising events for young people. Rather, "We have simply folded the young people right in as full participants in whatever the Transition groups are doing." In practice, this includes:

- Encouraging parents to bring children to events and meetings.
- Getting young people to run events. For example, Transition Mar Vista, in Los Angeles, offered a workshop called 'Repurposing old clothes', run by the 16-year-old granddaughter of a member of the group. Transition Los Angeles' 'Cluck Trek', a visit to several families who keep chickens, was led by the children of several chicken-owning families.

Young people can easily use blogs and Facebook to write about being involved with Transition. During the research for this book, Gerri Smyth pointed out her granddaughter's website, 'My Chickens', which she has set up to document her experiences of keeping chickens.[50] Blogging for kids is very easy and can offer a fresh perspective on Transition, as can running workshops to teach them how to make their own short videos, another interesting resource.

Transition Belsize in London are setting up 'Transition Kids NW3', which will offer workshops and activities decided by the kids. Initial ideas include foraging workshops, wildlife survival skills, cob building and dawn bird spotting. Also in London, Transition Finsbury Park is working with the local primary school. They found that the best time to try to engage parents and children is immediately at the end of school, especially for hands-on events. They set up an after-school food-growing club, which became so popular that Jo Homan, the organiser, said kids could come to the group only if they brought their parents. After-school Transition events were also run by Transition Tynedale. Some

Transition in Action: The Oil Memorial

Michael Dunwell of Transition Forest of Dean stands next to the Oil Memorial, made by students at the local community college.
Photo: Tish Rickard

One of my favourite examples comes from Transition Newent, in the Forest of Dean. Students from the local community college made the 'Oil Memorial', a project featured in Transition Network's wiki-film *In Transition 1.0*. A tower was built from blue plastic barrels. The children brought in many items made from oil, which were fixed to the tower. The project emerged from the desire to, as Michael Dunwell of Transition Forest of Dean put it, "get people to understand all the things oil does for us. I asked the children 'What's plastic made of?', and they replied 'plastic'." Looking back, Michael said, "It's just fun, getting people involved in making something with a message . . . just to celebrate the incredible achievements that oil has brought for us, then to turn it into a memorial to say goodbye to it."

Drawing from the workshop for kids at the 'Diverse Routes to Belonging' conference in Edinburgh, 2010.

of the kids run an organic vegetable stall in the school grounds, sourcing produce from a local Mencap college.

At Transition Scotland Support's 'Diverse Routes to Belonging' conference in Edinburgh in November 2010, participants could bring their children, who enjoyed a parallel programme of activities organised by Sussex-based Moving Sounds. The kids organised and presented the morning's warm-up activity, and then prepared a performance for that evening. At the Transition North conference in 2009, local teenagers Ruby, Hayley, Eugene, Paddy, Adrian and Linda, through the Two Valleys Radio, interviewed delegates and then edited a voxpop piece, which was presented to everyone at the end of the day.[51]

Transition Ottawa in Canada worked with media studies students at the local university, who were set a project to make short films (under five minutes) to convey a powerful and practical message in order to inspire their fellow students to live more simply. They were given six topics to choose from: food, water, energy, transport, waste and simple living. Members of Transition Ottawa were available for questions, and the resultant films were then shown at Transition Ottawa events.[52] And even the youngest people can be involved in Transition! Transition Town Letchworth (TTL) run 'Transition Tots', which meets once a month. Parents of children up to the age of three get together to

discuss the 'trials and tribulations of sustainable parenting' and to work on TTL projects.[53]

Anyone working with young people in the UK will need to be checked by the Criminal Records Bureau and follow the child protection policies of institutions they work with (similar rules probably apply elsewhere). You should also be aware that there are laws regarding the publication of photos of children: if these are not taken at a public event, or are in any way related to commercial gain, you will need the permission of the children's parents/guardians.

Involve local schools and youth clubs, and use the media they use: Facebook, YouTube, Twitter, and so on. Try to ensure that young people are represented in your group's core group.

You might also enjoy . . .

RESPECTFUL COMMUNICATION (*Starting out* 3, page 100), VISIONING (*Starting out* 7, page 114), ARTS AND CREATIVITY (*Starting out* 8, page 117), RUNNING EFFECTIVE MEETINGS (Tools for Transition No.4, page 122), THE EVOLVING STRUCTURE (*Starting out* 12, page 134), BACKCASTING (*Starting out* 13, page 138), EDUCATION FOR TRANSITION (Deepening 12, page 192), MEANINGFUL MAPS (Tools for Transition No.16, page 226).

Connecting

Tools for Transition No.16:
Meaningful maps

The 'Mappa Sustainability', created by Transition Hereford for their 'Small Steps, Big Difference' event, October 2010.

In the autumn of 2010, Transition Hereford created the 'Mappa Sustainability', modelled on the thirteenth-century Mappa Mundi. This modern version, naturally, shows Hereford in pride of place, and has been a centrepiece of many of the group's activities. It is an imaginative way of documenting what is happening and, as Rob Garner of the group told me, it "helps people to see they are not working on their own".

When Transition Hereford and New Leaf (an organisation set up to bridge sustainability groups and the local council) were planning 'H.Energy week' (H =Hereford), they decided they wanted a physical map on which individuals and organisations could register existing initiatives and future commitments.

The Mappa Sustainability was first exhibited in a city-centre church, before being paraded through the streets to a big launch called 'Small Steps, Big Difference'. It then went to other venues, before being a centrepiece for 2011's H.Energy week. People were invited to attach stickers showing what they are doing, what else is happening where they live, and their visions. Rob told me it had been a great success: "In my view it increases a sense of togetherness, community involvement and success."

Many Transition initiatives use electronic maps, in particular Google Maps, in their work. For example:

- Transition Los Angeles has created a Google Map of 'Transition in LA', which maps individual

Transition in Action: Community Resilience Mapping in Port Phillip by Chloe Farmer

The Community Resilience Mapping project sprouted from Transition Town Port Phillip, Australia, in April 2010. Our vision is to explore, through creative mapping, different themes central to resilience, and to uncover, develop and strengthen connections in our local bayside community (south of Melbourne).

We chose to begin with handmade maps as a direct approach to engaging with the community. We've been taking maps to local community events and inviting people to map themselves, their connections, projects, resources and examples of emerging resilience. The maps attract interest, stimulate stories and facilitate the sharing of insights, knowledge, skills and resources. They become living, evolving tools. Community Resilience Mapping is a rewarding process and a powerful creative pathway to invite community interaction and participation, and to stimulate awareness and collective vision.

Food is a great place to start. The Food Resilience maps, which have had a few incarnations, depict farmers' markets, community gardens and redistribution and educational programmes, among other networks. The Eco Connections Map was seeded by project groups involved in the local council sustainability programme, and is growing at the Port Phillip Eco Centre. We're continuing to explore community connections in the arts, public space, water, culture and 'heart and soul', and will be hosting creative mapping workshops and exploring online mapping in the future.

participants, initiatives and projects across the city as a public map, offering a very accessible way in for newcomers.

- Transition Town Stoke Newington's 'Hackney Harvest' project and Sustainable Haringey's 'Urban Harvest' projects both use Google Maps to map street fruit trees in the area.
- Sustainable Frome created the 'Frome Apple Tree Map', showing all the town's apple trees. They also use Google Maps to map potential sites for future wind farms and other Transition infrastructure.
- Transition Cambridge have done much the same; theirs includes the intriguing entry, to a walnut-lover like myself, that there are "two walnut trees near the boathouse at Fen Ditton". I'm on my way . . .
- Taunton Transition Town went a step beyond fruit trees with their Google Map project, the 'Wild Food Free Food Map', which mapped the wide range of forageable wild food in the area. They combined this electronic mapping with more old-fashioned mapping exercises. At their 'Abundant Taunton' event, they invited people to plot fruit and nut trees, and other wild food, on physical maps, which were subsequently uploaded to the Google Maps.
- One of the most cutting-edge uses of maps is being developed by Geofutures in Bath, in association with Somerset Community Food. The 'Foodmapper'[54] website invites people to become community researchers, mapping all the land in the area being used by the community to grow food. It has huge potential as part of more detailed analyses of potential local food security.

On the other hand, sometimes physical mapping can be better . . .

Transition in Action: Making maps with people

Mapping with people at the Transition Network conference, Cirencester, 2008.

Maps can also be made with people. At large Transition events, mapping is often used for a quick insight into those attending. By asking people to stand in different places, you can get instant and useful insights. For example:

- **Geographical:** "North is this end of the room, south is the other end, arrange your-selves in relation to each other in terms of how far you have travelled to be here."
- **Attitudinal:** "If this end of the room is 'passionately agree' and that end is 'massively disagree', arrange yourselves in relation to the following question . . ."
- **Age:** "Youngest this end, oldest that end."
- **Stage in the Transition process:** "If you think your Transition initiative has just started, go to this side. If you think it is very advanced, go to that side."

. . . and so on. When each question has been asked and the group has mapped itself, have two people with radio microphones move among the group asking people at different places for their stories. This exercise has become a key feature of Transition Network conferences, and for events that explore attitudes towards particular questions. However, be aware of the needs of your audience when doing this – this is an activity that can be more challenging for people with mobility issues or who are partially sighted.

- At a Transition Los Angeles event, a large printed map of the city was displayed, and people were asked to put themselves on the map. Joanne Porouyow of Transition Los Angeles said this "gave people a sense of how much of the area was represented at the session".
- Making your own maps is worthwhile. Transition Finsbury Park in London ran their 'Places that Matter' project, which invited people to make short films about what they loved about the area. They held an event where people made their own 'imaginative maps', which "made explicit the different ways people view the same place". People worked in groups and created their own maps of the places that matter most to them, weaving in their visions for the future of the place.

Maps can, of course, be used to do more than show what exists. They can also be a powerful way to explore the future. Sustaining Dunbar's 2025 Map and Action Plan (MAP) project uses maps to encourage people to set out how they would like the community to become more resilient.

Resources

Green Map is a very useful emerging resource: www.greenmap.org.

Open Street Map – an open-source map of the world: www.openstreetmap.org.

Tom Chance has been developing sustainability maps – check out this emerging version for London: http://tomchance.dev.openstreetmap.org/london.html.

6. The role of storytelling

David Heath, whose father George ran, until 1980, a big commercial market garden in the centre of Totnes – now a car park – shows a group of people around the site of the former garden.

The stories the media tell us and that we tell each other about the future are usually not actually very helpful as we move forward, giving us unrealistic expectations and no sense of the challenges and the opportunities ahead.

Every culture and every generation tells stories about itself. Our dominant cultural stories speak of the ability of technology and human inventiveness to overcome challenge, and of perpetual economic growth, unfettered by living on a finite planet. In these less certain times, we need better and more appropriate stories.

As Shaun Chamberlin points out in *The Transition Timeline*,[55] Transition is a story that presents a collective view of energy descent as an opportunity, not a crisis. Storytelling is used in many ways in Transition, often in a literal and traditional way. In 2010 Steph Bradley of Transition Network spent six months walking around England visiting Transition initiatives, telling and gathering stories. While walking she kept a blog, chronicling her journey.[56] A gifted storyteller, the tale she now tells in workshops of her travels and of what different initiatives around England are doing is very inspiring.

Some initiatives use storytelling to reach young people. Transition Tales is a programme developed

As part of Transition Town Tooting's 'Transition in 2 Hours' performance, John, who moved to Battersea from Jamaica in the 1950s, tells the story of his arrival and his early experiences of living in London.
Photo: Mike Grenville

by Transition Town Totnes for all Year 7 students at the local secondary school. Over three sessions, students first learn about peak oil and climate change, then about storytelling, and are then invited to be TV newsreaders of the future, their 'broadcasts' being filmed and edited.

Much of what Transition initiatives do is akin to storytelling – creating projects that people talk about, and that indicate a possible future. For example, stories of towns creating their own currencies, setting up their own energy companies or growing food in unexpected places have a resonance far beyond the community where they occur.

Stories need not always be about the future; they can be used to bring the past to life too. One Transition Town Totnes event brought David Heath, son of George Heath, who had, until 1980, run an extensive market garden in the centre of Totnes, back to where the garden had been (it is now a car park). David was invited to talk about how it ran and what happened where.

Weave storytelling, in its widest sense, through your Transition initiative, making films, raps, newspaper articles and small ads from the newspapers of the future, cartoons, animations, etc.

"Those who do not have power over the story that dominates their lives, the power to retell it, rethink it, deconstruct it, joke about it, and change it as times change, truly are powerless, because they cannot think new thoughts."
Salman Rushdie

You might also enjoy . . .
STANDING UP TO SPEAK (Tools for Transition No.2, page 104), UNLEASHINGS (Tools for Transition No.10, page 184), BECOMING THE MEDIA (Tools for Transition No.13, page 208).

Tools for Transition No.17:
Speaking up for Transition

Local dignitaries talk of what Transition means to them and what they are doing to support it, at the Unleashing of Transition Malvern Hills, May 2010.

In May 2010 at 'People Make Transition Happen', the Unleashing of Transition Malvern Hills, in a section called 'Endorsing Transition' 11 people from organisations in and around Malvern had a minute each to say "what Transition means to me". What was so impressive was that they were the local Member of Parliament, the head of the local police force, the principal of the local college, the headmistress of the local secondary school, the head of the local council, and so on. This was for me the highlight of an extraordinary evening,[57] a powerful sign of respect for the initiative and of the relationships it has forged.

A few months later, an event called 'Small Steps, Big Difference' (organised by Transition Hereford, who had seen the idea at the Malvern event) took

this idea to another level. The plan was to give the idea of 10:10:10 a physical form, with three lots of ten people (the event took place just a few days after the 10:10:10 day of international action on climate change).

The first group represented leaders from the county council, the primary care trust, the local bishop, a representative of a major local landowner and some political parties. The second group represented local sustainability organisations, including a local sustainable housing group, cycling organisations, groups promoting renewable energy and local food, and social enterprises such as a cycle-powered taxi company and a hydrogen car company. The third group, who appeared near the end of the event, comprised members of local community

Local leaders at Transition Hereford's 'Small Steps, Big Difference' event, October 2010, offer their 'Transition Endorsements'.

groups – mostly Transition initiatives across Herefordshire, but also carbon reduction action groups and local environmental groups. People each had 45 seconds to speak, and were asked to cover what they are already doing, what Transition means to them, and their aims for the next year.

It was impressive and moving to see at both events the strong expression of the relationships between Transition activists and influential local figures. The effect also works the other way, in that those offering the endorsements get to experience the buzz of a Transition event, and to feel a sense of the wider process at work. All the 'endorsers' I spoke to after the event found it a very powerful thing to be part of.

Although you wouldn't want to overuse this tool, for big events, such as an Unleashing, it could form a key element. (You might also want to use an alternative word to 'endorsements', which has unfortunate connotations of product placement and shameless advertising!)

How we organised our 'Transition Endorsements'

by Will Tooby

When planning Transition Malvern Hill's Unleashing, I approached some members of the Local Strategic Partnership who I thought would commit to making a public endorsement at the event. The invite also went out to our then prospective MP, Harriett Baldwin, who said "yes" in the run-up to the general election. My brief to them all was to state where they stood with regard to Transition issues and what they are doing in their own organisations or constituencies about climate change. On the evening, I was really touched by these endorsements, which added a real power and kudos to the event, and which have led to many good subsequent outcomes.

7. Pausing for reflection

Sometimes it is important just to take time out to reflect on whether your Transition work is still nourishing you and those around you – and to make some changes if not . . .

This is a very short, very simple ingredient.

By this stage in doing Transition, you will hopefully be starting to see real change happening around you, and you will be engaged in helping to make it happen. This is really just a reminder to manage your time, to not take on too much and to take time out for yourself and for your friends and family. Keep the people closest to you right where they are. Stop and reflect on how your life is going, and whether or not your work with Transition is helping you to do what you want to do. Reflect quietly, and speak with those closest to you. Reflect honestly on how you are balancing your personal and Transition lives. Get independent support if you feel it would help.

You might also enjoy . . .

VISIONING (*Starting out* 7, page 114), ARTS AND CREATIVITY (*Starting out* 8, page 117), VOLUNTEERS AND VOLUNTEERING (Tools for Transition No.7, page 150). SUPPORTING EACH OTHER (Tools for Transition No.9, page 179), "HOW ARE WE DOING?" (*Deepening* 7, page 166), PERSONAL RESILIENCE (*Deepening* 11, page 181).

Building

Transition groups aim ultimately to catalyse the localisation of their local economy. They strive to move from running small community projects to thinking and acting much bigger. New skills and ways of thinking will lead Transition initiatives to become social enterprises, such as becoming developers, banks, energy companies, and so on. This approach often challenges those traditionally involved in community environmental issues, but is vital for big results. The ingredients in this section explore aspects of this step up.

1. Energy Descent Action Plans

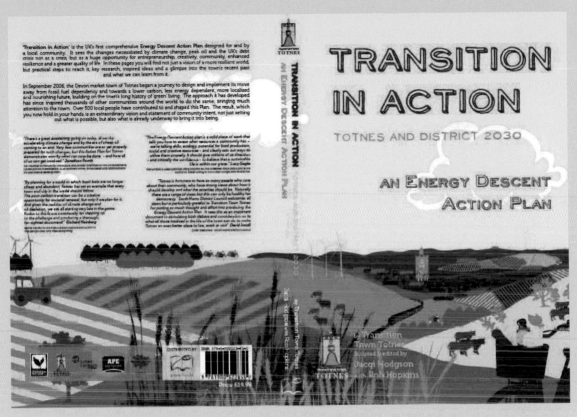

The cover of the Totnes Energy Descent Action Plan (published April 2010).

Our leaders, when designing for our future, assume there will always be cheap energy, economic growth, growth in car use, and so on – all of which are highly questionable assumptions. Surely we can do better than that?

Energy Descent Action Plans (EDAPs) are an emerging and dynamic ingredient of Transition. There are excellent peak oil plans and climate change strategies being developed around the world, but an EDAP emerges from a community, and is as much about storytelling and visioning as planning.

An EDAP is a community Plan B, a drawing-together of the visioning and backcasting work done up to

that point, focusing on how Transition could happen. It pulls together initiatives and puts them in the wider context of planning for the relocalisation of the settlement. But what is it? Is it a step-by-step plan with stated outcomes? A vision document? A story of how a powered-down future would be? Or a rewriting of council policies, showing how enlightened leadership would promote Transition?

Nobody yet knows for sure, but we have some experience to go on. The first one, the Kinsale Energy Descent Action Plan,[1] was a student project based on the question "What would it look like if . . .?" Although much celebrated, it was based on very little community consultation and was largely a student initiative. It did, however, contain the seed of what many saw as an important concept.

Transition Forest Row's 'pre-EDAP' set out a vision for a post-carbon community, told as a story.

What would a Transition initiative need to start creating an EDAP?

You will need:
- A dedicated group of people, involving and representing the views of as many other organisations in the community as possible (the local council, schools, other environmental groups, community groups, and so on)
- Funds – EDAPS cost money.
- Strong Transition working groups who pull together.
- Plenty of early awareness raising.
- Good web facilities to enable discussion of ideas, joint editing of drafts, promotion of events, etc.

The EDAP of Transition Sunshine Coast (Australia) was also coordinated by students, on a 'Time for an Oil Change' course. The final plan, though, had a far wider political effect. It led to Transition featuring in the council's climate change and peak oil strategy and in its draft Energy Transition Plan, and to the council's vision being "to build a low-carbon, low-oil, resilient future for the Sunshine Coast".

In 2009, Transition Forest Row (TFR) produced 'Forest Row in Transition: A community work in progress',[2] a short 'pre-EDAP', which offered a brief vision of a powered-down future Forest Row. Their budget didn't allow in-depth research, and they didn't feel they had enough members of the community on board, so they decided on a light-weight narrative, combining graphic design, humour and some information. Mike Grenville of TFR told me that it raised local credibility and awareness, but would have been better with some market research pre- and post-publication to assess its effect. It is still a source of inspiration, referred back to regularly.

The most substantial EDAP so far is 'Transition in Action: An Energy Descent Action Plan'[3] produced by Transition Town Totnes in June 2010. This emerged from community visioning workshops and other activities, and offered a credible vision of Totnes in 2030. It began with an oral history of Totnes in the 1950s and explained the role of storytelling, before presenting a detailed timeline for the decarbonisation and localisation of food, energy, housing, education and much more. It also contained two detailed pieces of research, 'Can Totnes and District Feed Itself?' and an energy budget for the area. Reviewing the Totnes EDAP in *i4* magazine, Michelle Colussi wrote:

> "In short, as impressive a document as 'Transition in Action' is, it falls short of being an Energy Descent Action Plan. Instead, it seems to be more of a vision – a remarkably explicit, exciting and community-based vision that tells us exactly what is to come about, but not how or by whom. Ultimately, the document acts like more of an Energy Descent Invitation than a Plan. It entices other communities to have a go at the process for themselves."

Be mindful of other past or present community planning processes in your community. *Another*

Transition in Action:
Transition Town Worthing's EDAP   by Steve Last

Transition Town Worthing (TTW) began its journey towards its EDAP in 2010. The process started from asking people their views on what the future might look like during awareness-raising events. TTW are expecting that the EDAP will be published in 2012. The process looks a bit like this:

Step 1: Creation of a Transition Timeline for Worthing. This fold-out board on to which people added post-it notes was showcased at every opportunity for over a year, asking people to add a note to a year between 2011 and 2031.

Step 2: Visualising a positive future. TTW has run sessions which have taken the audience on a guided visualisation to a future where the transition to a low-carbon economy has happened. This, along with exercises from Joanna Macy called 'Meet the Descendants', has proved a very powerful tool to create visions of what the possible future might be like.

Step 3: Oral histories. We've had great enthusiasm among members for 'heritage' issues; we wanted to gain valuable insight into how Worthing operated before cheap fossil fuels.

Step 4: Views from 2030 in the *Post Carbon Gazette*. TTW's monthly newsletter has featured numerous articles based on food, transport, reskilling and energy, written from the viewpoint of someone in a successful decarbonised future.

Step 5: Setting up a Transition Tales group. We wanted to provide a creative outlet for people to express their ideas. This now includes agony-aunt columns, cartoons, poems and news stories. This includes a writing competition for schools.

Step 6: Collecting data. A few TTW members are keen on local statistics . . . Good!

Step 7: Running several EDAP events, including films, a launch evening and an EDAP World Café to carry out some backcasting with the timeline, with local councillors and business leaders invited.

Step 8: Writing funding bids. We'd like to publish the EDAP and distribute as widely as possible. We need some funding to make this happen.

community group starting *another* community planning process can lead to people rolling their eyes, and it may be best to work with the process(es) already under way. An EDAP, if just a document, has little value. It needs to have a central role in inspiring, raising awareness, organising the initiative and determining its progress.

What might an EDAP process look like in a city? In London, Transition Town Brixton has run a big Open Space day, and has started drawing together the visions that have been generated at other events, including their Unleashing. The question they face is what a city EDAP looks like, and whether they should develop a template that other urban groups

Transition in Action: Dunbar 2025 –Local Resilience Action Plan by Philip Revell

Sustaining Dunbar's Dunbar 2025 project has two strands:

- A home energy advice service.
- Developing an action plan for the changes the local economy will require to move to a zero-carbon future.

An ambitious two-year programme of community engagement involved awareness-raising events, workshops, roadshows and interviews with hundreds of local residents. Further research created a picture of local resources and their flows, and showed that most people do want to make changes for a more localised future, but face many barriers to doing so. We have worked hard to dovetail our proposals with those of the local authority. Most importantly, we try to hold a shared vision of what a vibrant and resilient low-carbon community could look like, and create the necessary support and infrastructure.

See http://ourlocality.org/2025

can use. Can areas of a city power down, or can only the whole city do so? Should the council take a lead and Transition initiatives support their work? (The Bristol Peak Oil Report – see Tools for Transition No.21: Peak oil resolutions, page 278 – is an example of such an approach). Would the results justify the effort?

These are all unknowns, to be tested. Some form of EDAP feels, indeed vital, whatever the result. Integral to successful EDAPs should be ensuring that everyone's voices are heard in the process. Creative consultation events, perhaps using the arts, can gather ideas and feed back in an informed way that can start to create a real buzz around a different way of looking at the future.

Oh, and by the way, you can call them whatever you like! Some people prefer 'Community Resilience Plan' or a 'Community Futures Plan' . . . although 'Community Resilience Action Plan' hasn't really caught on, perhaps for obvious reasons . . .

Design a creative, engaging and research-based community process to form a powerful, practical story of the future. Start with a vision of a lower-energy future, and then backcast, telling how it was achieved, year by year, setting out the vital first steps and the catalyst projects needed to get the ball rolling.

You might also enjoy . . .

PERMACULTURE DESIGN (Tools for Transition No.1, page 98), UNDERSTANDING SCALE (*Starting out* 5, page 106), MEASUREMENT (*Starting out* 6, page 109), ARTS AND CREATIVITY (*Starting out* 8, page 117), FORMING WORKING GROUPS (*Starting out* 10, page 128), HOW WE COMMUNICATE (*Deepening* 4, page 155), MOMENTUM (*Deepening* 9, page 172), ORAL HISTORIES (*Connecting* 4, page 218), MEANINGFUL MAPS (Tools for Transition No.16, page 226).

2. Social enterprise and entrepreneurship

Preparing vegetable boxes at Growing Communities, a local food social enterprise in Hackney.

Visioning a powered-down local economy is one thing, but how do we bring it into reality in such a way that it supports the wider transition of the community and can thrive independent of external funding?

Transition is about creating a new, economically viable local infrastructure that creates livelihoods, skills and resilience. These projects need to be economically viable, and one vehicle for this is social enterprise. This is gaining a lot of traction and interest, sometimes in the context of the government's 'Big Society' agenda. The idea of this ingredient is, first, that Transition initiatives might better meet their aims by stimulating and supporting

social enterprises and entrepreneurs locally and, second, that in the pursuit of initiatives becoming financially viable, social enterprise has a key role to play – possibly through the initiative setting itself up as an enterprise offering services, selling training in its projects, etc., through to getting an ongoing donation or revenue cut from enterprises it has helped support or that have emerged from the initiative's work.

But what does social enterprise actually mean? The first thing to note is that it is not a new idea. The Cooperative movement in the 1860s created viable businesses to strengthen local economies and create meaningful employment and local ownership. Futurebuilders, who support third-sector organisations, define social enterprise as follows.

"Social enterprise is a business or service with primarily social objectives whose surpluses are principally reinvested for that purpose in the community, rather than being driven by the need to maximise profit for shareholders and owners."

Futurebuilders[4]

In essence, social enterprises strive to be financially viable, with explicit social aims and an ownership model that increases social participation. Often they stem from one visionary, bold individual; an entrepreneur. I asked Nick Temple, formerly of the School for Social Entrepreneurs,[5] what qualities seemed typical. He told me that being a social entrepreneur is as much an attitude as a specific business model. In essence it is about approaching social and environmental problems entrepreneurially. His advice:

- **Just get on and do stuff:** The best thing is to get started and learn from your own and other people's experience. Pilot things, measure what

Transition in Action: The REconomy project
by Fiona Ward

Fiona Ward introduces REconomy at its launch event in Totnes, January 2011.

The project is working with ten Transition initiatives during 2011 to help them to define, then strengthen, the skills they need to:
- engage their existing local businesses and organisations in discussions about Transition issues, the implications and the potential solutions
- stimulate the start-up of new social enterprises that can take advantage of the low-carbon and relocalised markets, and shape a more sustainable and equitable local economy.

The REconomy project aims to help Transition initiatives to engage local businesses and organisations, and stimulate new social enterprises in order to strengthen their local economy and increase community resilience. This is phase one of what we hope will be an ongoing programme by Transition Training and Consulting – the part of the Transition Network that engages with business and organisations, including social enterprise. This project has been kindly funded by the Roddick Foundation.

We also aim to pilot a means to estimate the economic potential of a local Transition economy, including its land/energy assets, skills and other resources, and then explore how this can be used to best effect to engage all the relevant players in a coordinated, and prioritised, set of activities to deliver this economic potential.

**For more information see
www.transitionnetwork.org/projects/reconomy**

Transition in Action: From the ground up by Stephanie Hofielen

From the Ground Up (FGU), a working group of Transition Town Kingston, is a volunteer-run, not-for-profit, organic fresh-fruit-and-vegetable box scheme. We operate within the Transition Town Kingston umbrella but are autonomous in the pursuit of our objectives. The scheme was launched in March 2010 as a buying group for eight families in response to the high expense and inaccessibility of organic food. The group was very clear in its goal of sourcing organic fruit and vegetables at affordable prices while supporting sustainable food systems. The principles underpinning FGU are as follows:

- All fresh food is sourced from ethical certified organic suppliers (Soil Association certified in the UK).
- Food is priced at near trade (wholesale) prices, with only a minimal charge to cover FGU costs – not to make a profit.
- FGU provides a marketplace for local producers of organic or natural food products.
- Food miles are minimised by offering food that is seasonal for our geography and 'local when possible', with preference given to UK suppliers (other countries we source from are near-European: Spain, France and Italy).
- We work with suppliers that ensure farmers are using sustainable practices and getting a fair price for their product.
- We engender a community spirit by having set locations for meeting, working and collection of orders.

What started as a vision and a shared passion for safe, good food, now boasts:

- close to 300 names on its mailing list
- two active collection venues, offering customers flexibility in pick-up times and location, with more planned for the near future
- an engaged management team
- enthusiastic volunteers who perform a wide range of activities, as well as sorting and packing customer orders.

FGU has recently expanded its offerings to include organic bread from one of London's few organic bakeries and organic cheese from Somerset. Feedback from our customers has so far been very good.

For more information see www.ttkingston.org/groups-and-projects/ground-up

Volunteers preparing From the Ground Up's weekly vegetable boxes. *Photos: Dan Ball*

Building

Transition in Action: Growing the Green Valley Grocer   by Jon Walker

The opening of the Green Valley Grocer in Slaithwaite. *Photo: Jon Walker*

In 2009, the small greengrocer in Slaithwaite went out of business. We had early warning of this, and an idea emerged of the community itself taking over and running the shop – but only if there was significant support from local people. It had to be their shop, set up with their money, doing what they wanted it to do. We set up a website and used email to spread the news. We held a public meeting on 8 May, where it became clear that there was good support, so we got to work getting everything in place to launch a community share issue to raise the necessary capital. We also created a partnership with another start-up cooperative – The Handmade Bakery (see page 268) – to share the premises and thereby reduce our costs and massively strengthen the retail offer simultaneously.

At the second meeting, on 29 May, we launched the cooperative and the share issue. That evening we set a target of raising £15,000 in ten days. If we didn't reach the target, we would call it a day, give people their money back, and go back to the day job. But we did reach it, and so we agreed to press on. Work began on the shop, and we were ready to open in just ten days. Amazingly, the cost of it all was under £10,000, mainly because everyone worked for free.

The local Mayor opened the shop on a beautiful sunny Saturday (see picture). It's going really well, the numbers of customers and members are increasing, sales are way above initial expectations, and (remarkably) the local Co-operative store reports that trade has improved since we've been open – despite our success. It looks as if people who used to travel to shop are now staying here as it's so much more enjoyable. The bakery has been an essential part of this.

We continue to make every effort to source local food: actively looking for and encouraging local growers, and buying everything that anyone in the area has to spare, from allotments, gardens, window boxes and pots outside their front door. Last summer we issued the Green Valley Grocer Garlic Challenge: the only garlic on the market came from China. We bought lots of garlic cloves to grow and sold them at cost to our customers. This year we should have mostly local garlic.

In spring 2011 a bunch of Marsden and Slaithwaite Transition Town people set up a growing co-op called Edibles, mainly to supply us. Our vision is of clusters of cooperatives all working together for everyone's mutual benefit and building a more resilient, local food network.

happens, don't wait for permission; just get started on a scale that feels achievable.

- **Mission before everything else:** Why are you doing this? What is the big idea? Being clear about your purpose enables you to check against it when you are planning your enterprise . . . everything else flows from this.
- **Measurement:** The whole reason for creating a social enterprise, as opposed to a more conventional business model, is to benefit society. Measuring your influence is vital for funding, investment, credibility, etc. Methods exist for measuring results, so don't reinvent the wheel.
- **The Person is the Organisation:** Social entrepreneurs often have a certain 'something'. They have often got to where they are through being naturally gifted at building trusted relationships and leading by example.

How could your Transition initiative foster a culture of localised social enterprise? Firstly, inspire people with good examples of existing social enterprises, arrange visits, and bring in inspiring speakers. Training from local entrepreneurs would provide a worthwhile course, perhaps over a few evenings. There are organisations who offer start-up resources to help catalyst projects become investment ready (see right). The skills and support are available.

Understand from an early stage the need for social entrepreneurship. Design and support initiatives, providing training and events, and link with existing entrepreneurship support providers.

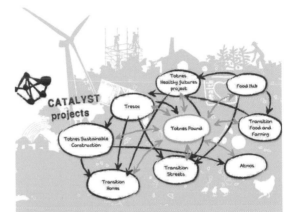

CATALYST projects

Transition Town Totnes has identified a number of social enterprises as 'catalyst projects' and sees them as integral to the economic regeneration of the town. *Image: Emilio Mula*

Resources

The following organisations can offer support:

Black Training Enterprise Group: www.bteg.co.uk.

Carbon Leapfrog: www.carbonleapfrog.org.

Community Builders Programme: www.communitybuildersfund.org.uk.

Co-operative Enterprise Hub: www.co-operative.coop/enterprisehub.

Co-operatives UK: www.uk.coop.

Local United can offer excellent case studies of successful social enterprises, and has produced 8 excellent 'Diffusion Packs' – nuts-and-bolts guides to setting up a variety of social enterprises, from local energy companies to food hubs: http://tinyurl.com/6yz5v74.

National Energy Foundation for energy projects: www.nef.org.uk.

Regional Social Enterprise bodies, e.g. Social Enterprise London: www.sel.org.uk.

School for Social Entrepreneurs: www.sse.org.uk.

Social Enterprise Ambassadors: www.socialenterpriseambassadors.org.uk.

Social Enterprise Coalition: www.socialenterprise.org.uk.

UnLtd: www.unltd.org.uk.

You might also enjoy . . .

MEASUREMENT (*Starting out* 6, page 109), BUILDING PARTNERSHIPS (*Starting out* 11, page 132), ENSURING LAND ACCESS (*Deepening* 10, page 174), EDUCATION FOR TRANSITION (*Deepening* 12, page 192), ENERGY RESILIENCE ASSESSMENT (Tools for Transition No.14, page 216), COMMUNITY OWNERSHIP OF ASSETS (*Building* 6, page 264), COMMUNITY-SUPPORTED FARMS, BAKERIES AND BREWERIES (Tools for Transition No.20, page 267), INVESTING IN TRANSITION (*Daring to dream* 3, page 287).

Building

3. Scaling up

with Patrick Andrews

The Village, an eco-village development in Cloughjordan in Ireland, has successfully scaled itself up from a small group of people to a vibrant, large-scale project. *Photo: Davie Philip*

How to successfully manage the evolution from a small and informal community group to one capable of delivering big projects and setting up new social enterprises?

To be really effective as a Transition group, we must be prepared, at the appropriate time, to increase the size of our organisations through bringing in more people or by linking to other groups so we can achieve more. This inevitably adds complexity to the running of the group.

Many of those involved in Transition, perhaps inspired by E. F. Schumacher's 1973 classic book *Small is Beautiful*, believe that small is the optimal size for organisations. Advantages to staying small include convenience, humanity and manageability. But, as Schumacher acknowledged, sometimes you also need large organisations. The successful initiatives, he suggested, are able to make one large organisation feel like a group of small ones.

Organising a large group requires different skills from running a small one. For example, a small organisation may be able to rely solely on volunteers, meet in pubs and make decisions quickly. With scale, you may need office space, staff, and to be far more formal and thorough. We shouldn't be scared of getting bigger, but there are traps for the unwary that can be avoided.

The people issues can be particularly challenging. Sometimes the people who initially led the smaller group cannot run a larger one. This can be uncomfortable for all involved. As a group grows, there's a tendency for those with the loudest voices to dominate. A hierarchy appears, tending to push power and information upwards and out of the hands of those doing the work, which is where it should be. A more suitable model for a Transition group is a network, which distributes information and power rather than concentrating it.

When developing a structure, start by listing the group's functions. For example, you might decide that the group must do the following:
- Operations (doing the work)
- Coordination and communication
- Strategy
- Dispute resolution.

Different individuals or teams can take on these roles. The trick then is to balance them so no individual or team dominates. Developing a structure for a growing organisation is not easy, but nor need it be left to experts. People have been organising themselves into communities for millennia, and we need to rediscover the faith in ourselves to handle these important tasks. We can learn from nature and from organisations that have trodden this route.

One inspiring example of a healthy, large organisation is the Mondragon federation of cooperatives, based in the Basque region of Spain.[6] Started in the 1940s, this now has over 85,000 people. It is the largest business in the region and competes globally in various fields of business. None of the individual cooperatives exceeds 500 people – they grow by adding new cooperatives, not by making existing ones bigger. They have created an ecology of interlinked businesses with their own university and bank but with minimal hierarchy and no external owners.

The Village, a new and growing eco-village in Ireland,[7] is applying the Viable Systems Model,[8] a tool for understanding the viability of an organisation, developed by cybernetics guru Stafford Beer.

I asked founder member Davie Philip what lessons the project learnt as it scaled up from a small group to an entity with 40 houses under construction.

"Our biggest challenge in scaling up our ideas was to find a structure that allowed decisions to be made in a coordinated way by the doers and drivers of the project. For an idea that is as large and ambitious as the eco-village, and which is member-driven, it was important to put in place an organisational structure that would manage the complexity of the project while allowing autonomy and decision-making at every level and within every working group."

When the time is right, evolve your initiative to take the steps your organisation needs to be most effective as the world around it changes. Hold to your purpose and values – these will help the group retain its identity and effectiveness amid great change.

You might also enjoy . . .

FORMING A LEGAL ENTITY (Tools for Transition No.5, page 130), FORMING NETWORKS OF TRANSITION INITIATIVES (*Connecting* 1, page 198), INVOLVING THE COUNCIL (*Connecting* 2, page 204), WORKING WITH LOCAL BUSINESSES (*Connecting* 3, page 213).

Resources

Hock, D. (1999) *The Birth of the Chaordic Age.* Berrett-Koehler Publishers.

Turnbull, S. (2002) *A New Way to Govern: Organisations and society after Enron.* new economics foundation pocketbook (available for free download at: http://tinyurl.com/66y5mcl).

Wheatley, M. & Kellner-Rogers, M. (1996) *A Simpler Way.* Berrett-Koehler Publishers.

Building

Tools for Transition No.18: Community renewable energy companies

with input from Dan McCallum

Awaiting the beginning of the evening event where the Lewes community power station shares were launched. *Photo: Mike Grenville*

One of the main pieces of infrastructure that a resilient community needs is control of its energy generation to the maximum possible extent. In terms of the 'Plugging the leaks' analogy (see Tools for Transition No.19, page 257), every time we pay our energy bills, millions of pounds pour out of our communities that could have stayed there creating jobs and a locally owned energy infrastructure. How possible is it that a community could own and manage significant local energy generation? A few years ago, the answer would have been "not very", but now many successful projects are emerging. Their experience leads to the following suggestions, which apply whichever renewable energy technology is being contemplated.

- **Form a group:** A project like this will need a focused team, strong leadership and good, clear group processes. It will need to be honest about the skills it has, and happy to bring in skills it needs. Go as a group to visit and learn from successful projects. Establish quickly how much time people have.
- **Build community support:** If this is to be a community initiative, it needs the community. Organise some fun, interactive events about the possibility of a community energy company. Is anyone interested? Is there support? What resources are there? What has already been attempted, and what lessons can be learnt?
- **Establish feasibility:** Do this soon to prevent time and effort being wasted, preferably by

Transition in Action: Transition Linlithgow's Solar Bulk Buying Scheme   by Alan Brown

Installing solar panels as part of Transition Linlithgow's solar scheme. *Photo: Transition Linlithgow*

In 2010 Transition Linlithgow (TL) began an ambitious bulk-buying project for solar thermal heating systems (STH). The project involved selecting a manufacturer and installer, and negotiating a discount to encourage participation. When selecting the hardware we looked at all aspects of manufacturing and the environment (green manufacturing processes with minimum waste) and local manufacture (no large carbon footprint due to shipping from somewhere in the world to Scotland). Other key criteria are performance, lifespan (guarantees) and an ethical business approach.

Initial interest and awareness for the project was raised through an exhibition organised by TL. Using a demonstration unit as well as promotional literature, people could leave their names for future contact. We linked the bulk-purchasing project to home energy audits, and whenever someone was interested in renewable technology we investigated the suitability of the house with an in-depth audit. Issues like boiler type, hot-water cylinder (whether a dual coil is already installed), roof design, etc. all play a part in the final advice provided. We created a multipurpose contract 'to fit all'. A contract with pre-set prices allows for variations, with up-front pricing for extra design features. Householders can choose between a complete installed STH system (choice of three sizes) or a DIY kit, for the budding DIYers who wanted to save even more money.

As the project has grown, we have experienced a lot of interest from neighbouring community initiatives for assistance with their possible bulk-buying projects. Some wanted to hitch on the existing project with us, while others sought advice on how to embark on a bulk-buying project or wanted training from us in order to train their own staff in how to do it.

The success and positive experience of the STH bulk-buying project have led us to embark on other bulk-buying schemes, such as photovoltaic panels systems, ground source heat pumps and possibly micro CHP (combined heat and power). We are creating a social enterprise, which can apply potential income generation towards a sustainable group by giving back to the community. So far three new jobs have been created between the manufacturer and installer, with the potential to create many more in the years ahead.

For more information see
http://transitionlinlithgow.org.uk

raising money for an independent feasibility study. An assessment should examine resources (how much potential energy there is), the forms of possible energy generation, the site location and ownership, environmental constraints such as noise, grid connection, delivery access (the lorries for wind turbine blades can be 40m long), infrastructure costs and planning permission.

- **Design the project:** Your business plan should evaluate all costs, including project development, planning consent, advice, grid connection, financing, and so on. Select your organisational model (most tend to take the form of charities and companies limited by guarantee). Ensure that you have strong leadership and skills for project management and financial accountability.

- **Secure your site:** Without it, all else fails. If the community owns the site, there is no problem, but negotiations with a landowner need to be conducted carefully. The ideal outcome is a lease on the site for the lifetime of the project. You will need to secure wayleaves over the course of the whole access track, including any bits you might need in order to widen sections of track. Legal agreements should be in place before a planning application (if one is required). Planning consent rests with the land, not the developer: there are cases where landowners have developed sites for which community groups had planning permission.

- **Planning permission:** Talk to the planners early on to get their initial opinion of the project's feasibility. Do your environmental assessment work. Be clear about the planner's position; some assessments can happen only at certain times.

- **Financing the project:** You are seeking finance for the three key stages of your project: pre-development, planning and preparation, and post-planning and construction. Your business plan should show a mix of debt, grant and equity finance, and be able to show that the project is viable and offers a good rate of return for investors. Will funding be via a community share option or private investors? The 'holy grail' (or at least the first major step) is planning consent and options/leases. From that point, the scheme has commercial value and can usually be financed one way or another.*

Eco Dyfi, a community regeneration initiative in Wales, have documented their experiences with community renewables schemes such as Bro Dyfi Community Renewables' two wind turbines, and offer the following advice based on their experiences.

- Initial grant aid makes a big difference, as otherwise such projects are only marginally viable.
- People are unlikely to invest significantly before planning permission is obtained, so the early stages either need some form of funding or should be kept as cheap as possible.
- Groups need support in the early stages from financial, legal and community development experts.
- Working with communities can often take a long time.
- Successful projects usually rely on individuals with patience, enthusiasm and persistence.

Awel Aman Tawe[9] is another community-run charity in south Wales which has planning consent for two

---

* With regard to financing, Dan McCallum of Awel Aman Tawe told me: "The cheapest source of finance will be bank debt, and banks such as Co-op and Triodos have funded community wind schemes in Scotland, such as the 900kW turbines owned by Tyree and Westray Development Trusts. The banks will fund up to 80% of the capital costs. It is therefore important to ensure that every aspect of feasibility is well documented and professional ('bankable'), as bank finance will probably be needed to build the scheme. The banks lend on a 10- or 15-year term against the value of the planning consent, land agreements, Power Purchase Agreement, wind report, Turbine Supply Agreement and Balance of Plant contract. Tyree and Westray Directors had to sign over 60 contracts in order to reach financial closure with the bank. The degree of bank finance in these projects should not be offputting to community groups – it actually protects them. If the banks are not satisfied that a project can repay its loan following the Due Diligence process, they will simply not lend."

Transition in Action: Harveys Brewery in Lewes becomes a community-owned solar power station
by Chris Rowland

OVESCO (the Ouse Valley Energy Services Company Ltd) was established in 2007 to encourage energy-saving practices in domestic, business and public buildings, and to create local generation of non-polluting energy. In 2010 the company directors founded OVESCO Ltd to:

- help individuals reduce their energy bills and their carbon footprint
- contribute to local and national CO_2 reduction targets to generate electricity from green sources (solar, wind, etc.)
- make jobs by supporting local firms
- assist local people whose houses are not suited to existing forms of renewable generation to make their homes more energy efficient
- support Lewes District Council with programmes and events to reduce energy consumption and fuel poverty.

In 2011 it took on its most exciting and ambitious project to date. Harveys Brewery and OVESCO Ltd began working together to install a 98kW solar photovoltaic array on the roof of Harveys' main storage and distribution warehouse in Daveys Lane, Lewes. This ground-breaking installation is turning the building into one of the first solar power stations in the country, and continues to build on Harveys' reputation as an environmentally responsible company. The 544 photovoltaic (PV) panels will generate 93,000kWh of green electricity each year – enough to save more than 40 tonnes of CO_2 annually.

OVESCO has received planning permission for the installation and has raised the financing for the project through a community share launch.[10] A launch event was held in April 2011, which was attended by 300 people.[11] Within five weeks the target of £307,000 had been reached. Interest will be paid to shareholders via the solar PV feed-in tariffs, which are guaranteed by the government for 25 years. Money invested will be repaid in full at the end of the 25-year scheme, or earlier at the request of the investor and subject to conditions. While the investment is held, a dividend will be paid after the first year, which is expected to be around 4 per cent.

'Sunshine Ale', a special beer brewed by Lewes-based Harveys Brewery to commemorate the share launch for the solar system on its roof, April 2011. *Photo: Mike Grenville*

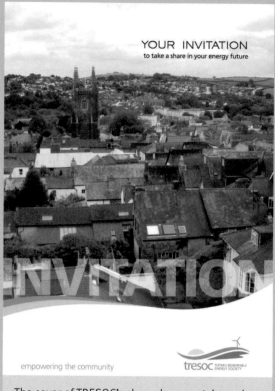

The cover of TRESOC's share document, issued late 2010.

found one, it then negotiated in confidence for over two years with wind developer partner Infinergy and the landowner, to secure agreement to develop a wind farm. At the time of writing, TRESOC is working with Infinergy to secure planning consent, and the parties will form a special purpose company to construct the wind farm when consent is obtained. The project will deliver two 2.3MW wind turbines on the edge of the town, capable of generating enough electricity for 2,500 homes.

The aims of TRESOC are:

- To develop the profitable supply of energy from renewable resources for the benefit of the community resident in Totnes and 15 surrounding parishes.
- To ensure democratic control of the renewable energy resources by the local community through extensive society membership.
- To ensure that the maximum value from the development of these resources shall stay in the local economy.
- To provide an opportunity for public-spirited people and organisations to contribute financially to the community with the expectation of a social dividend as well as a financial return.

TRESOC directors have invested personal capital, and a lot of their time, into the society to get it started. Following signature of the agreements to proceed with the Totnes Community Wind Farm, TRESOC was fortunate to obtain a short-term loan from the National Energy Foundation, now repaid, to support the costs associated with the launch of the share issue. Anyone living in Totnes and Environs was able to become a member of the society for an investment of between £20 and £20,000 worth of shares. The share offer was open for three months, and members can later increase their shareholding, if desired. Society membership stands at 378, with a further share issue planned for 2011.[12]

TRESOC is now actively engaged with local stakeholders and technology providers in developing a portfolio of renewable energy projects in wind, biomass, solar and hydro power.

turbines. They have held a detailed consultation exercise using a range of methods. The group, in common with most energy schemes, encountered opposition from some local people, which was difficult to deal with at times. The most effective awareness-raising method was encouraging local groups such as Old Age to go and visit wind farms. They then became the project's spokespeople in the community.

The Totnes Renewable Energy Society (TRESOC) is an Industrial and Provident Society that emerged from a Transition Town Totnes Open Space day on energy. A group got together at that event to work on community-owned renewable energy, leading to the establishment of TRESOC as an independent organisation in November 2007. The society then worked to identify a good wind site. Once it had

Transition in Action: Bath Community Energy

Bath Community Energy (BCE) grew out of Transition Bath, in particular a meeting of its energy group where people looked at each other and said "we could actually do something about this", and the ball started rolling. It is set up as an industrial and provident society, with the intention of installing renewable energy, wind, solar, biomass and hydro in a way that is locally owned, locally controlled, generates local income and provides local jobs. The project is established from the outset as an enterprise (as opposed to being dependent on grants), and as one that can deliver renewable energy at scale. Profits will be recycled back into the community.

One of the first things BCE did was to form a partnership with the local council. They also formed a partnership with Scottish and Southern Energy, who have offered them loan finance at very attractive terms in order to enable BCE's first steps to get under way. Their first projects are to do with solar photovoltaics (PV) and, at the time of going to press, they were in discussion with 30 local schools and had signed contracts with 10. The plan is to install 10 PV arrays on local schools during the 2011 summer holidays: BCE will pay for the panels and the schools will get free electricity. The reason for doing these solar installations first is to build a solid foundation and confidence in advance of a community share launch. The aim is then to raise £500,000 in shares from local people, who will be offered a 6-7-per-cent return each year on their investment, which is very attractive.

In the longer term, BCE is looking at three local potential wind sites and a hydro project, which, combined, will need around £11 million, but which it is hoped will generate around £350,000 for community projects. They will also develop renewable-heat and energy-efficiency projects. It is a great model, very much replicable in other Transition initiatives.

Resources

The following organisations and resources may be useful:

Community Energy Scotland: www.communityenergyscotland.org.uk.

Energy4All: www.energy4all.co.uk.

Hockerton Housing Project: www.sustainablehockerton.org/vilturbine.html.

Local United's Diffusion Pack on Community Wind Developments: http://tinyurl.com/6gwxccq.

Ynni'r Fro, supporting social enterprises in Wales to develop renewable energy schemes: www.energysavingtrust.org.uk/Wales/Ynni-r-Fro.

4. Strategic local infrastructure

The last working mill in Totnes before its closure. It is now the town's tourist information office.
Photo: Totnes Image Bank and Rural Archive

Much of the infrastructure a powered-down more localised economy will need doesn't exist. What will we need, and how best to start rebuilding it?

The picture above shows the last working mill to close in Totnes. It was in the centre of the town, was powered by the river that runs past it, and deliveries were made using a horse-drawn wagon. How's that for a low-carbon local food enterprise? Now it is the town's tourist information office, and a very good one at that, but clearly it is much easier to turn a flour mill into a tourist information office than it is to turn a tourist information office into a mill again.

"The pessimist sees difficulty in every opportunity. The optimist sees the opportunity in every difficulty."
Winston Churchill

Much of the infrastructure that would have supported a more local food economy, and generated much of the employment in our communities, has been dismantled or converted for other uses. The infrastructure most settlements have today has little resilience. We aren't able to grow much of our own food, turn our local timber into useful things, or process milk into cheese, apples into cider or fleece into clean, usable wool. We will need to put it back, but it won't look or work as it used to. It will be based on our best current knowledge and be managed for the community's benefit.

So what new businesses, buildings, livelihoods and infrastructure might a low-carbon community need? Here, in the table below, is a list to get your Transition initiative started. There are many opportunities for local economic development that need very little infrastructure as we currently understand the term.

New business opportunities in a more localised economy

Employment sector	Industry type	Opportunities for economic development	Infrastructure needed
Food production / land use	Organic farming	Farm workers, research and innovation, value adding and processing, retail, Community Supported Agriculture initiatives	Farm buildings, packing houses, farm machinery
	Organic food production	Training, freshwater aquaculture, organic gourmet mushroom production for food and medicines, intensive market gardening, food preservation	Glasshouses for aquaponic fish production, sealable buildings for mushroom cultivation, greenhouses, composting
	Urban agriculture	Coordination, land access provision, edible landscaping consultancy, online tools for linking growers and consumers, large potential for commercial production, plant nurseries and propagation	Greenhouses, tools, access/ deliveries by cycle, horse or electric vehicle, space for storage, packing and processing
	Forestry	Timber for construction and a variety of uses, sawdust for mushroom cultivation, charcoal, wood gasification, coppice products, saps, tannin, bark mulch, education, training, food crops, fibre	Mobile sawmills, wood gasification equipment, shredders, drying kilns, covered working space, timber storage space
	Agroforestry systems	Design consultancy, planting and ongoing management, selling of a wide range of produce, long-term enhanced timber value, courses, publications, research	Tree nursery beds, nut harvesting equipment, processing
	Textile production	Farming, processing, manufacturing	Factories with facilities for washing, scouring, retting, grading, spinning, weaving, dyeing and finishing
	Gleaning	Apple harvesting and pressing, hedgerow drinks and other products, education	

Building

New business opportunities in a more localised economy			
Employment sector	**Industry type**	**Opportunities for economic development**	**Infrastructure needed**
Food production / land use	Schools	Edible landscaping, teaching, Education for Sustainable Development, food-growing training, apprenticeships, bespoke Transition training programmes	Polytunnels, garden infrastructure, tools and equipment
Manufacturing and processing	Recycling	Salvaging building materials, processing and reclaiming materials (bricks, timber, etc.), making insulation from waste paper and glass bottles	A yard or industrial space with covered area, the various appropriate equipment for the relevant tasks
	Sustainable industry	Renewable energy technologies manufacturing and installing, technology systems	Workshops with specialist equipment, office space
	Repair	Extending the life of machinery, building for durability	Covered space for working on machinery, appropriate equipment
	Scavenging	Materials reuse, refurbishing, resale to low-income families	
Services	Healthcare	What a more localised and resilient healthcare system looks like is a bigger question than this book can cover. More localised health provision? Promotion of exercise and healthy eating? Herbal medicines where appropriate?	Glasshouses/polytunnels, laboratory, bottling
	Hospice / bereavement services	Hospice services, supporting families who keep relatives at home, green burials	
	Energy	Home insulation advice, energy monitoring, energy-efficient devices, investment coordinators, sale of energy to grid or decentralised energy systems, producing woodchip/pellets for boilers, Energy Resilience Analyses for businesses	
	Compost management	Collecting, managing, training, distribution, education, potential links to urban food production	
	Information Technology	Creation of effective software systems for energy management, carbon footprinting and much more	
	Financial investment	Credit unions, local currencies, mechanisms whereby people can invest with confidence into their community, Green Bonds, crowd funding	

New business opportunities in a more localised economy			
Employment sector	Industry type	Opportunities for economic development	Infrastructure needed
Government	Councils	Opportunity to organise efforts throughout region/parishes	
	Researchers	Opportunity to gather information from the many projects and enterprises under way	
Education and design	Educators	Wide range of opportunities for supporting the 'Great Reskilling', developing distance learning programmes, training for professionals	
	Sustainable designers	Landscape architects specialising in edible landscaping, zero-carbon buildings	
	The Arts	Art projects documenting Transition, installations, exhibitions, public art workshops, local recording studios, storytelling	
	Transition Consulting	Working with businesses on energy audits, resilience plans, a range of future-proofing strategies	
Personal / group support	Counselling	Personal 'Transition counselling', group support, community processes	
	Citizens Advice	Debt advice, housing advice, financial management skills, debt scheduling	
	Outplacement / redundancy support	Support, retraining, ongoing support and training	
Media	Print media	Local newspapers, small print run books on different aspects of Transition	
	Internet	Online retailing systems for local markets	
	Film media	Online TV channels documenting inspiring examples of Transition in action	
Construction	Reskilling	Retraining builders to use local materials and green building techniques, improving awareness around energy-efficiency in building, setting up local construction companies, rainwater harvesting systems, design and installation	Demonstration site where people can learn by doing, storage for natural building materials, a shop where people can buy them

Building

New business opportunities in a more localised economy			
Employment sector	Industry type	Opportunities for economic development	Infrastructure needed
Construction	Materials	Creating local natural building materials, clay plasters, timber, lime, straw, hemp, etc. Growing, processing, distribution, retail, etc., locally made wallpaper	Hemp-processing equipment, sawmill, limekilns and roller mixer, yard and covered space, equipment for processing, bagging and storing clay plasters
	Architects	Specialists in Passivhaus building, local materials, retrofit advice	Demonstration buildings as showcases
Transportation	Low-energy vehicle fleets	Marketing, maintaining, renting, chauffeuring	Garage space for repairs, recharging points
	Bicycles	Selling, servicing, maintenance training, rental	Bicycle workshop for repairs
	Rickshaws	Importing, servicing, taxi service, weddings, etc.	Garage space for repairs, fuel processing
	Biodiesel	Sourcing, processing, selling, training and advice	Simple equipment for processing biodiesel
	Biomethane / electric vehicles	Fleet management, sales, leasing, car clubs	

This presents many opportunities for new livelihoods. Someone who grew up in Totnes in the early 1960s told me:

" . . . all of the little back streets had some kinds of artisans or builder's yards or something going on in them. You didn't have to go very far out of the high street before you were in light industrial premises. All of the top of town, like Harris's ironmongers, they had their big ironmongery shop, but on the other side they had . . . an agricultural machinery shop. Can you believe it?! There was agricultural machinery sitting there which was for sale!"

This diversity of enterprises would give a far richer tapestry than that provided by our 'Clone Town' high streets, out-of-town arcades and business parks. A more resilient community will surely be a more nourishing, interesting place than many of our present towns.

Where elements of a more local economy exist, find ways, such as the community support model (as in CSAs – see page 267), to support them and increase their viability. Where they don't exist, your Transition initiative, social entrepreneurs, private businesses and local authority can work together to create them.

You might also enjoy . . .

BUILDING PARTNERSHIPS (*Starting out* 11, page 132), FINANCING YOUR TRANSITION INITIATIVE (Tools for Transition No.8, page 158), EDUCATION FOR TRANSITION (*Deepening* 12, page 192), INVOLVING THE COUNCIL (*Connecting* 2, page 204), WORKING WITH LOCAL BUSINESSES (*Connecting* 3, page 213), ORAL HISTORIES (*Connecting* 4, page 218), COMMUNITY RENEWABLE ENERGY COMPANIES (Tools for Transition No.18, page 246), COMMUNITY-SUPPORTED FARMS, BAKERIES AND BREWERIES (Tools for Transition No.20, page 267).

Tools for Transition No.19: Tools for plugging the leaks

with input from Molly Scott Cato and Peter North

Unveiling the Brixton Pound notes at the scheme's launch.

The new economics foundation (nef) coined the concept of the 'leaky bucket'. Our local economy is like a bucket full of holes. Money flows in from salaries, grants, pensions and other sources, but much pours out again each time we pay a distant utility company, shop in a supermarket or chain store, invest in foreign banks or favour imported goods over local ones. Our money's potential to generate economic activity and create employment at the local level is lost. However, as nef points out, every outflow of money is a potential enterprise opportunity. If Transition is to revitalise local economies, we need to develop strategies and models that support and strengthen them. But what is so important about local businesses? As nef puts it:

"Local enterprises are more likely to employ local people, provide services to improve the local quality of life, spend money locally and so circulate wealth in the community, promote community cohesion and, by reducing transportation of goods from across communities, are likely to have a smaller environmental footprint."

Another reason is the 'multiplier effect': supporting local businesses puts life into the local economy. Research[13] has shown that £10 spent with a local grower circulated two-and-a-half times locally, being worth £25 to the local economy. The same money spent in a supermarket left the community

Transition currencies (clockwise from top left). Various Totnes Pounds, Lewes Pounds, the 'Brixton Brick' (a prototype), the Brixton Pound, Stroud Pounds, the Tchi (from Chichester) and the Hawick Pound.

much quicker, with a local multiplier of just 1.4, being worth just £14. Transition initiatives look at encouraging the multiplier effect in a range of ways, described below.

Local currencies

As Peter North puts it in *Local Money*,[14] "local currency models are still in their infancy, more like Wright's biplane than a Boeing 747". Transition groups have experimented with local currencies, generating valuable experience and knowledge. These experiments have also learnt much from previous attempts at local currencies, such as Ithaca Hours and the currencies that emerged during the economic collapse in Argentina.[15] The idea is straightforward. A printed currency that can only be spent in a given community can circulate only locally. It cannot leak away. The first Transition local currency experiment, the Totnes Pound, was a limited issue of 300 £1 notes, accepted in 18 local shops. The second issue was made available at a 5-per-cent discount, so that 95p sterling bought one Totnes Pound, creating a 5-per-cent subsidy for supporting local businesses. The current issue of the Totnes Pound is a straight one-for-one exchange, accepted in over 80 businesses.

This inspired other places to develop more sophisticated schemes. The Lewes Pound was initially issued just as £1 notes, generating an unprecedented demand from currency collectors worldwide: three days after launching, the first printing had sold out and notes sold on eBay for up to £50! The Lewes Pound was expanded to include a £5, £10 and a £21 note (well, why not?), and I still consider them the most beautiful bank notes I have seen. Over 150 traders accept it and the scheme has a part-time project coordinator.

The London Borough of Brixton launched the Brixton Pound, an experiment for the area. The faces on the notes were chosen through a 'Vote for the Note' poll, and featured figures with historical links to the area. Lambeth Council funded the design and printing of the notes, and the council's CEO told the launch, "I want this to become the currency of choice for Brixton". The Stroud Pound was organised by the Stroud Pound Co-operative to ensure control by the community (other people can still use the currency, picking it up in change). It required a small charge every six months for the notes to retain their value, as an incentive for their circulation. The Hawick Pound in Scotland was a smaller scheme, issuing just a £1 note. As with all these schemes, it generated a lot of media coverage.

Transition in Action:
The Bristol Pound by Mark Burton

In Bristol we are working to launch a currency across the whole city region. Following an extensive design and consultation period, here is what the project looks like at the time of writing. Like the pioneering Transition currencies, the Bristol Pound will be fully backed by, and exchangeable with, sterling. But it will be different in three important ways:

First, and most exciting, is that Bristol Pounds will be used electronically, with mobile phones as the payment device. There will be notes of several denominations, as important symbols of community values and identity, but most face-to-face transactions will take place electronically. A shopper will send an SMS text containing payment information and the trader will receive a confirmation text to say the funds have been received. It's as simple as that! Both texts will contain security checks and the transaction will be as convenient as conventional card payments. Transactions will also be possible over the internet. Incorporating electronic payment systems gives a number of benefits:

- It makes the currency far more convenient and usable.
- Use of the currency can be easily monitored.
- Certain behaviours can be rewarded and incentives incorporated. In Bristol, users will be rewarded in proportion to how much they use Bristol Pounds.
- Crucially, it allows an income stream, meaning the currency can become financially sustainable. In Bristol a small transaction

fee will be deducted equivalent to established card payment fees.

Beyond these pilots it will be available to all communities setting up a local currency, and the platform will have flexibility, able to run different currency models and rules tailored to the needs of each particular community.

Second, the Bristol Pound is being developed with involvement from key institutions in Bristol. The accounts will be run by Bristol Credit Union – an established, well trusted and regulated local financial institution. This builds on current local financial expertise. Bristol City Council is working on ways it can accept and spend the currency. How the currency develops will be up to the people of Bristol.

Third, the currency will ultimately operate over a region with a population of more than a million people. This scale of operation includes a large and diverse business community, increasing the ways for the currency to circulate. It will also allow sufficient use of Bristol Pounds for the system to become financially sustainable.

We believe that we have the ingredients to achieve high participation levels for the currency in the short term. In the longer term, having an established local currency infrastructure provides the means to better adapt to changing global dynamics and to the changing needs of Bristol.

For more information see www.bristolpound.org

Peter North argues that local currencies appear to work well among 'green' and 'lifestyle' businesses, where alternative-minded customers accept them in their change. For Molly Scott Cato,[16] one of the originators of the Stroud Pound, "making people believe that change is possible is the first step towards change. Local currencies do that like nothing else." North notes that all Transition currencies so far focus on consumption; none has yet influenced local production of local goods for local consumption.

Transition currencies, he argues, need to start "moving from being a means of circulation between existing local businesses to tools for building greater local resilience by stimulating new local production". For Cato, while local currencies have not stimulated local production, they are "a fantastic educational tool because they demonstrate this weakness with local supply (and therefore lack of resilience) so clearly". For her, the next step is for local currencies to partner local food production.

Backing local currencies with something tangible, such as food, or Shann Turnbull's idea of energy-backed currencies, such as 'Kilowatt Dollars',[17] could help develop these currencies. Another important consideration is that so few people regularly use cash in their daily transactions. We increasingly favour cards and electronic transfers of money – forms of exchange that reduce a community's financial control. Transition Network and nef are developing an electronic currency system; at the time of writing being piloted in Bristol and Lambeth, London (see box on page 259).

Time banks

Time banks are an exchange system using time as the unit of exchange. With time banks, everyone's time is worth the same, whatever their work. People help each other and claim return favours when needed. Transactions can take place between individuals, organisations or agencies. Time banks have a good track record; they are straightforward and can be especially useful for disadvantaged communities.

LETS

Peter North describes LETS (Local Exchange Trading Systems) as being "really just a network of people who agree to share their skills with each other by means of a local currency that they have created and agree to use". Members list the skills they offer and the services they would like, and these are compiled into a directory. Members are then encouraged to trade with each other, with LETS units exchanging hands as cheques or electronically. One more recent experimental evolution of LETS is the Lewes SwopShop,[18] where members trade goods and services online.

Transition Chichester in early 2011 launched the Tchi, which is an interesting hybrid between a printed currency and a LETS scheme. The value of a Tchi is equal to an hour's work, and it can only be used by people who are members of the scheme. Then, as in a LETS scheme, members can trade with anyone else who offers services through the scheme's extensive directory. The notes are, at present, only in 1 Tchi denominations, and feature a picture of local hero William Morris and his quote "All that lives, lives not alone, nor for itself."[19]

Local procurement

One of the key ways to plug 'leaks' is by local procurement of goods and services. Hospitals and local authorities have large budgets and could have a major local economic impact. The UK public sector spends £1.8bn a year on meals, around 7 per cent of the entire UK catering market. EU legislation sees specifying local produce as 'anti-competitive'. However, there are ways around this. Many cases can be justified under broader environmental policies, such as designing into tenders clauses that specify:

- fresh ingredients (tends to promote locality, as distance and transport time reduce quality)
- demanding food in season
- favourable service criteria such as fresh food, minimal packaging and organic food.[20]

Tools for Transition No.19: Tools for plugging the leaks

Promoting the Brixton Pound at the Urban Green Fair in Brockwell Park, London.
Photo: Mary Linley

Transition initiatives could help their local schools or hospitals to procure locally. The Soil Association's 'Food for Life' programme[21] can be very helpful with this. As Kevin Morgan and Adrian Morley of Cardiff University point out,[22] procurement, if done well, is about stimulating demand for local produce and services. What is also needed is the developing of the supply to meet that demand. If done skilfully, good procurement can be vital to local economic regeneration.

Other approaches

Creating new financial institutions can be attractive to some initiatives. Credit unions are easier to set up than new community banks, for which UK regulations are onerous. Local banks (six municipal banks still exist in Scotland) or credit unions will help plug the economic leaks of your community. There is plenty of scope for new models once the principle of maximising the number of local transactions is established.

Peter North has speculated on how these various tools might hang together:

"We can see a LETS system or time bank being used for local production and exchange of things we can produce at home or in a local community – helping each other out; sharing food grown on allotments; renovating each other's houses. More complex goods would be produced by local businesses, perhaps using a local or regional scrip at a national level . . . or a business-to-business exchange. More local production could be developed using local currency loans, or through a local bank or financial vehicle. Special-purpose currencies could finance local food production and Community Supported Agriculture, and local power generation. Local bonds could finance a major renovation or our housing stock and a new green infrastructure to replace our out-of-date Victorian infrastructure."[23]

5. Appropriate technologies

Cob greenhouse, The Hollies Centre for Practical Sustainability, West Cork, Ireland. The cob walls absorb heat and radiate it out slowly, moderating the temperature in the greenhouse. They are also gorgeous.

When choosing the technologies to underpin Transition, how can we best avoid those that result in more dependency on distant supply chains and unnecessary levels of complexity?

The following email from Matt Dunwell at Ragman's Lane Farm in Gloucestershire[24] came shortly after the 'Great Freeze' of winter 2009-2010. It offers a powerful insight into the issue at the heart of this ingredient:

> "I have the exquisite pain of no heating at the farm, having installed a biomass system with a titanic budget, which has decided

to break just as we start our three-month residential permaculture course. It's very expensive kit but suppliers and installers are still feeling their way, and there are loads of teething problems. It will take a good few years of mugs like me to pioneer these systems before they are safe to be let loose on an unsuspecting public.

Hey ho. Now it has been bust for ten days – first they thought it was the electric motor on the flue [£400], now they think it's the circuit board that controls the whole boiler [£800] – and the pipework that is meant to be super-insulated to carry hot water to outlying buildings has frozen solid. We have finally got the boiler working, but are now faced with the task of thawing super-insulated pipes that have frozen whilst the ambient temperature slips to -15°C. Every now and again we tow another student on to the farm with a tractor that is running with no cooling system, as the antifreeze froze in the tractor engine and frayed the fan belt as it passed over the water pump, which makes me want to hit it with a broom. Meanwhile the entire shower block has frozen solid, promising all sorts of water sports when the terrifying halogen heaters that we have hired start making an impact.

How precarious it all is. I had the strange experience of passing the engineer for the boiler whilst I was servicing Reinhart's

Ceramic Stove, the only thing that is presently providing heat for the whole course. I dug a bucket of clay from the pond and mixed it with a bit of sharp sand. I had the chimney off, swept and replaced in about 20 minutes. He was standing over a box of capacitors, probes and electric spare parts, on the phone to the wholesaler in Lincoln, who was trying to source parts from Austria while the airports were closing down all around."

Creating a Transition infrastructure will require hard thinking about what technologies to use. As a principle, we might look first at locally made equipment or ensure at least that it can be repaired locally and parts are fairly easy to obtain. The image on the facing page shows a cob greenhouse, made using on-site subsoil mixed with straw and sculpted to produce walls that store heat from the sun. The glass is recycled and easily replaced. Its owners understand how it was built and how to repair it – a different proposition from a kit greenhouse from overseas, with complex heating and cooling systems and reliant on imported replacement parts.

As far as possible, keep it simple. Choose technologies that can be made or repaired locally, which you understand, and where you can see the supply chain for parts; ensuring that they bring social, economic and community benefits to the area.

This masonry stove is both beautiful and functional: a highly efficient way to heat a home using wood, and sculpted from local subsoil. William Morris would have approved.

You might also enjoy . . .

MEASUREMENT (*Starting out* 6, page 109), PRACTICAL MANIFESTATIONS (*Deepening* 2, page 146), ENERGY RESILIENCE ASSESSMENT (Tools for Transition No.14, page 216), SOCIAL ENTERPRISE AND ENTREPRENEURSHIP (*Building* 2, page 239), COMMUNITY RENEWABLE ENERGY COMPANIES (Tools for Transition No.18, page 246), STRATEGIC LOCAL INFRASTRUCTURE (*Building* 4, page 252).

Building

6. Community ownership of assets

Perhaps derelict sites such as this one might be better developed by the community itself rather than by large developers? The potential benefits are enormous.

Development, like money and energy, is usually something done *to* communities, rather than *by* or *with* them. How can we step outside of that by enabling communities to own their own assets, so that any development directly benefits them?

Development is a particularly large hole in our leaky bucket (see Tools for Transition No.19, page 257) and is something over which communities have very little control. It is a huge driver for social inequity, for taking money and value out of communities that could have been retained there. Communities taking charge of their own assets is a key tool for building greater social justice and empowerment.

"For hundreds of years the idea of community-owned assets has run like a golden thread through our social history. Generation after generation, people have called for a different way of doing things, where land and buildings would belong neither to private landowners nor to the state, but would be held instead in trust and controlled by local communities, to provide amenities and create prosperity for the common good."
Steve Wyler[25]

Localisation often depends on communities owning and developing their assets. While this is not always essential, it is usually very beneficial. For example, if your community wants a crèche, it doesn't need to own the building. I asked two experts in the field of community asset development, Sarah Neuff from Coin Street Community Builders[26] (a community-owned development on the South Bank in London) and Dave Chapman of Locality[27] (a national network of over 600 community-led organisations) why they felt communities should own their assets. Sarah's reasons were as follows.

■ If your community organisation has a freehold or long leasehold, it goes on the organisation's balance sheet as an asset. This puts you in a much stronger position to act as a business.
■ Any added value you can generate through ownership of that asset benefits the community and pays for services otherwise hard to fund.
■ Third, "the other reason why it's important is around control and independence, and that's both political and financial controls. If a community owns its assets, then the community itself can decide what's important within that community and it's not subject to the vagaries of say, changes in local government or changes in government funding even. All of those things mean that you can actually keep going regardless of the chaos around you, you can control your own situation, earn your own money and deliver your own balance of business in that way."

To these points, Dave added self-determination. This means that a community gains control of where it wants to go; where it sees its future economic direction. While other approaches tend to suck resources out of a community, this enables more money to cycle locally. It leads to redefining the idea of profit. He elaborated: "It means that you start to return profit – which is either job creation, local wealth in terms of social capital that might be gained through training, education, supported employment schemes or opportunities to access services that don't currently exist because public sector providers can't provide them – you get the opportunity to create that mix at a local level."

So why do we not see communities everywhere acquiring assets and developing them in their long-term interests? According to Sarah, the main reason is because it isn't easy. I asked her what she sees as being the key things a Transition initiative needs to succeed in such a project. First, she suggested, they need a strong community spirit. They need good leadership, a strong vision, and to be tenacious, as they will be in for the long haul. Sarah reminded me: "Coin Street bought the land 26-odd years ago, and that was after a seven-year campaign, and we're still developing – we still have two undeveloped sites." They also need to check feasibility rigorously if they are not to waste a lot of time, money, energy and goodwill. The group must have the skills to run a business. Scrutinise your organisation, and bring in new people if possible.

For Dave, legal structures and organisational form are essential. There must be access to people who understand bureaucracy, finance and business planning. The ideal projects, he suggests, are "a mix of people, plan and passion". For Sarah it similarly boils down to "actually understanding what it is you actually want to do, being imagina tive about what the opportunities are in your local area and creating something which is strong, positive and everybody can get behind. This is actually the first step."

Almost since it began, Transition Town Totnes has, with the Totnes Development Trust, been trying to buy an 8-acre site in the centre of town, next to the train station. At the moment, thousands of people's initial impression of Totnes when they arrive in the town is of a decrepit ex-milk-processing plant. The project that emerged is called 'The Atmos Project' (named after Isambard Kingdom Brunel's experimental 'atmospheric railway', which was piloted there but never took off because of technical problems). The intention is to bring the site into community ownership and develop it so that it catalyses a green/Transition local economy. It would offer low-carbon work units, a School for Food Entrepreneurship, a restaurant/venue space, a microbrewery, affordable low-carbon housing and a 'hub' for emerging businesses and edible landscaping. It has been a long, involved and testing process.

Dave, one of the key movers behind Atmos, explained why the community should acquire that asset.

Building

"To start with, owning a chunk of real-estate land – that in itself is quite significant. It's a context changer, because all of a sudden you're taken as credible in certain circles. It has the tendency to open up doors for discussions that you weren't previously engaged in, which starts to enable you to position a community and the stuff that goes on within a community in a completely different way. You can then think about things you can do within those buildings that you weren't doing before . . . it generates added value in so many areas."

Transition initiatives may benefit from learning how to bring land and property assets into community ownership. This is a big step, but an essential one. It is a complex field, requiring far more space than is available here, so I have included (see right) a list of organisations/resources who can support and guide communities wanting to know more.

Dave Chapman exploring the derelict Dairy Crest site in Totnes, which, it is hoped, will become home to the Atmos project.

Steadily increase community ownership of assets through mechanisms such as development trusts, community bonds and shares. Bring land and property into community ownership for development, Community Supported Agriculture or renewable energy projects.

You might also enjoy . . .

INCLUSION AND DIVERSITY (*Starting out* 2, page 94), PERMACULTURE DESIGN (Tools for Transition No.1, page 98), FORMING A LEGAL ENTITY (Tools for Transition No.5, page 130), BUILDING PARTNERSHIPS (*Starting out* 11, page 132), THE EVOLVING STRUCTURE (*Starting out* 12, page 134), HOW WE COMMUNICATE (*Deepening* 4, page 155), INVOLVING THE COUNCIL (*Connecting* 2, page 204).

Resources

Coin Street Community Builders: supports the community acquisition of assets, from the early stage through to detailed implementation. http://tinyurl.com/6g7p2vd, 020 7021 1600.

Community Land Trusts network: best for projects with a housing focus. http://tinyurl.com/6jjc363.

Ethical Property Foundation: useful advice on managed workspace. www.ethicalproperty.org.uk.

Hart, L. (2005) *To Have and to Hold: The DTA guide to asset development for community and social enterprises*. Development Trusts Association. Available from http://tinyurl.com/5wtytem.

Locality: a network for community-led organisations: http://locality.org.uk.

Plunkett Foundation: specialises in rural village assets; communities wanting to take over their local shops or pubs. http://tinyurl.com/deo9yw.

Social Investment Business: supports social enterprises, charities and community organisations, and runs the Communitybuilders fund. www.thesocialinvestmentbusiness.org.

Tools for Transition No.20: Community-supported farms, bakeries and breweries

CSAs or subscription-based businesses don't always need to be big . . . here is a small pig club, run by six families as members in Totnes. The author's shoes appear to be of particular interest. *Photo. Totnes Times*

Community Supported Agriculture (CSA) emerged in the US in the 1980s and has more recently begun to be picked up in the UK, where there are now over 100 schemes. They are farms where local people become involved in the running of the farm through buying shares or becoming members, making decisions and even helping with the growing and harvesting of the produce. It ensures a secure market for farmers, who feel supported by those around them. The consumer has fresh local food, the opportunity to learn new skills, and a say in where his or her food comes from. It is a fundamental way to build local food resilience.

Stroud Community Agriculture (SCA) was set up in 2001 by four local residents who wanted to support a struggling local farmer. A public meeting generated a lot of interest. Seed funding was raised through pledges at that meeting, with new members paying in advance for their produce. In 2002, an industrial and provident society was set up for the project. The first farm eventually failed, but a second site was found. SCA now has 200 members (the maximum desirable number agreed by the members) and manages 50 acres of land producing beef, lamb, pork and vegetables. Another CSA project has also begun in the area. Members of SCA pay £2 a month to be members, and £33 a month for their shares, reduced if they attend work days and help with the food production. Produce can be collected from the farm or from two drop-offs in town.

Jade Bashford of the Soil Association, an expert on CSAs who spoke at the first meeting of the Stroud

Four key principles for Community Supported Agriculture projects, from *Local Food: How to make it happen in your community*[28]

by Tamzin Pinkerton & Rob Hopkins

- **Shared risk:** Food production risks such as climate and varying demand are shared between farmers and consumers.

- **Transparency:** Shared risk brings shared responsibility, trust and transparency. Members can be very involved in the running of the farm. As production is visible, some CSAs feel no need for expensive organic certification.

- **Community benefits:** Such schemes tend to benefit local economies. Low overheads mean farmers can often charge less than supermarkets, while often providing better food.

- **Building resilience:** CSA schemes have strong potential to build community food resilience, creating sustainable local food production for the local economy.

CSA group, has five main suggestions for beginning a CSA scheme:

- Start by finding out what everyone needs and wants, including farmers, community groups, landowners and those trying to start the project.
- Be clear about what you want to achieve.
- Think 'outside the box' about how to work together to achieve everyone's needs.
- Make sure the money adds up; do a proper budget and business plan.
- Go and visit other projects, learn from their successes and failures, and read as many case studies as you can . . .

The Handmade Bakery in Slaithwaite, Yorkshire, is a fascinating example of a community-supported bakery, and also of people with enthusiasm but no great reserves of capital getting new businesses under way. Begun by Dan and Johanna McTiernan, it is "an artisan bakery in West Yorkshire producing traditionally crafted, slowly fermented bread with no hidden additives". Inspired by the Real Bread Campaign started by Andrew Whitley, their aim is to:

> "offer a viable local alternative to industrially manufactured bread by bringing back traditional skills and community-scale produce. And, most importantly, give people a say in where their food comes from and how it's made."[29]

They started small, first baking from their oven at home. They began building a base of subscribers, who paid for two loaves of bread a week, which were collected from a local pub. They observed that most bakers get up at 3am – something that, with

Dan and Johanna McTiernan of The Handmade Bakery showing off some of their delicious bread.
Photo: The Handmade Bakery

Transition in Action: The tale of Topsham Ales

Topsham Ales shareholders proudly displaying their share certificates *Photo: Mark Hodgson*

Transition Topsham's initial efforts included reviving the Wassail tradition (which hadn't taken place in the town since 1936), an Apple Day and planting a new community orchard. The idea also emerged of creating a community brewery, linking the group's aims of localisation, community ownership and social enterprise. A project group heard of an opportunity to buy brewing equipment at half price, and was offered space at the back of the Globe Hotel. They formed Topsham Ales Cooperative, needing to raise £35,000 to get started. Members were invited to each invest a minimum of £500 in exchange for one vote and an annual dividend (to be agreed by the members), or to become 'Friends of Topsham Ales' for a small fee and receive regular updates on the project's progress.

Within two months and with little marketing other than word of mouth, 56 members had bought all the shares, with a waiting list of more. Much of the work to get the brewery established was done by volunteers, but some professional work was paid for with shares.

At the time of writing, Topsham Ales have three beers available: River ('deep gold'), Mild Winter! ('dark, chocolatey, hoppy') and The Mythe ('bright, dry and refreshing'). They are keen that their beers be a celebration of Topsham, researching local history when designing the names of the beers. I asked Mark Hodgson, one of the founders, for his tips for others wanting to create a similar project.

- **Involve the community as much and as early as you can:** Generate enthusiasm, show it is possible, keep it moving and keep people informed.
- **Create a good business plan:** Send it round the group for comments, get expert help, try to get the business model right, always overestimate and plan for the unexpected (for example, they planned for the first three months of operation not to produce any drinkable beer!)
- **Be different and exciting!:** Be proud of saying it will be local, community-owned and cooperative . . .

Topsham Ales models localisation in practice. Its spent yeast goes to a local baker, its spent hops are enjoyed by local pigs, local deliveries are by bicycle and trailer, and it is increasingly sourcing hops from a grower in East Devon.

See www.topsham-ales.co.uk

Tools for Transition No.20: Community-supported farms, bakeries and breweries

Transition in Action: Sustaining Dunbar's community bakery   by Philip Revell

Coming soon: the Dunbar community bakery!
Photo: Philip Revell

In early 2008 we became aware that the only bakery in town was going to close due to retirement of the family who owned and ran it. Unbeknown to us, they had been trying for a couple of years to sell the business as a going concern but, having failed to do so, were now looking to sell their whole property, a large high-street tenement block with a double shop front, two large flats, the bakehouse and the backlands area, as a property development opportunity – offers over £900,000.

We managed to raise some funds to employ a consultant to help us carry out a feasibility study and to draw up a business plan for setting up a bakery in alternative high street premises. Unfortunately, before we could finish this, these premises were sold. We were then offered a short lease on the existing bakehouse, completed the business plan on this basis, set up as a community-owned cooperative and launched a share issue to raise as much of the working capital needed as possible. The share issue proved very successful, not only in bringing in funds but in attracting a whole new group of people to become involved, excited by a different way of starting a business and regenerating our struggling high street. Many of these people had no particular interest in peak oil or climate change but did share a passion for our community and developing our local economy – and they brought a huge range of business expertise on to the cooperative's newly formed management committee.

As it turned out, the old bakehouse needed much more investment to satisfy current environmental health standards than we had originally estimated, and a short lease could not be justified. There followed a frustrating search for another suitable property, which only ended with the signing of a long lease on a former newsagent's shop in the autumn of 2010. A local firm of architects was appointed and detailed conversion plans drawn up. As I write, we are expecting our planning permission and building warrant to come through. Then it will be a question of appointing a building contractor, purchasing equipment and recruiting staff – not to mention raising the remainder of the finance.

Starting a business by committee is never going to be easy. But, we now have a business owned by over 250 local people who have invested more than £36,000 to date, and soon the smell of bread being baked will once again be wafting down Dunbar High Street.

See www.dunbarcommunitybakery.org.uk

a small child, they were understandably keen to avoid. They also observed that most people make toast in the morning, which can be done with staler bread. The time when people want fresh bread is lunchtime.

They wanted to expand, but had no premises or big oven. Ingeniously, they approached a local pizzeria, whose oven was used only during the evenings, and arranged to use it in the mornings. Two days a week they baked bread for their subscribers. Every Saturday morning the pizzeria became an impromptu bakery where people could drop in.

Their next opportunity came when their local grocer's shop became a customer co-op (see page 242) and so, after six months, the Handmade Bakery left the pizzeria for its own premises in the back of the shop. It is an ideal partnership for both businesses. They now bake 1,200 loaves a week, mostly sold within 7 miles of the bakery, and employ nine part-time staff. Thirty per cent of what they sell is sold through the shop. The rest retail through other outlets and directly to subscribers. Subscribers receive a discount and can collect it when it is convenient for them. They know they won't find their choice has sold out, and they are emailed options for what they would like the following week.

Dan told me that for him, the CSA/subscription-based approach is best at the earlier stage of the business. When they started, 100 per cent of their business came from subscribers; it is now more like 10 per cent. The advantages, he told me, are that you build instant customer loyalty, create many champions in the community, and much of the risk of starting a new business disappears. Amazingly, many of the initial subscribers signed up without tasting the bread!

When I spoke to Dan, he told me that the business had grown so well that they plan to use the same model to finance a move to larger premises. The bakery runs courses in breadmaking and how to start your own bakery, which are very popular. To have a larger space for baking, training and community events, they need to raise £20,000. The idea is to invite investment as three-year rolling

loans offering 7 per cent interest (a very attractive borrowing rate), but with the interest paid in bread.

I spoke to Mick Marston, the Soil Association's Community Supported Agriculture expert for the north of England. He told me that while the subscription model is experimental, it is a great way for new businesses to look at finance. Having been involved in supporting many such operations, he is unable to see a disadvantage.

New businesses must either risk their owners' own capital, or approach a local bank. Subscription means your customers fund the difficult start-up period. He told me the approach has been used by beekeepers and cheesemakers, and is being looked at for woodlands. It can be a great way of using the networks and goodwill generated by your Transition initiative to start new food enterprises and food infrastructures.

The Handmade Bakery's former premises at the Green Valley Grocer. *Photo: The Handmade Bakery*

Resources

Hackney's Growing Communities have a great model for community social enterprises and have developed training for groups keen on their approach: see www.growingcommunities.org

7. Strategic thinking

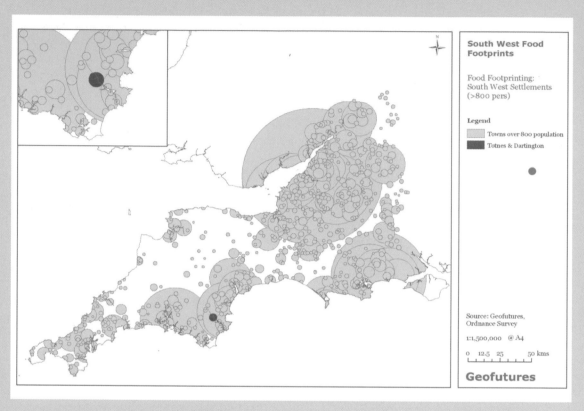

A food footprint map of the south-west of England, showing the food footprints of all the settlements of over 800 people. *Image: Geofutures (contains Ordnance Survey data © copyright Crown copyright and database right 2010)*

What kind of information about your local area – its soils, its energy generation, the levels of food production it might realistically attain, and so on – do you need to gather in order to underpin your work?

While in Transition we may not always have all the answers, it is vital that in our work we try to at least ask the right questions. As has already been discussed, a low-carbon, more localised economy will not come about by accident; it is a collective design project. It demands that we think strategically, because nobody else, none of the statutory bodies who you would imagine would be doing this

work, appear to be actually doing it. Several Transition initiatives are starting to do some very interesting work looking strategically at the practicalities and the possibilities of an intentional localisation process.

In 2008, Transition Stroud produced a document called 'Food Availability in Stroud District: Considered in the context of climate change and peak oil' for their Local Strategic Partnership Think Tank on Global Change.[30] It looked at the land around Stroud and to what extent it would be able to feed the local population (110,000 people). Using DEFRA data for the area and its current patterns of land use, and assuming a more seasonal, less wasteful diet in the future, they concluded:

"In terms of food self-sufficiency, much more work is needed to assess both food requirements of the population and the food production capacity of the farms. However, in broad terms it is likely that the district could be self-sufficient in meat and dairy products [although it may not produce enough cereals for animal feed], and it probably has the capacity to produce much more fruit and vegetables. However, the district is unlikely to be able to produce enough basic carbohydrate [cereals for bread, potatoes, etc.] or sugars to meet people's basic needs. This is only a preliminary analysis and further work is planned."

As part of creating its Energy Descent Action Plan, Transition Town Totnes undertook two detailed studies, 'Totnes and District Renewable Energy Budget'[31] and 'Can Totnes and District Feed Itself?'[32] The former was based on data from a report done a couple of years previously, which was reworked and updated. 'Can Totnes and District Feed Itself?' was a detailed piece of work, carried out with Mark Thurstain Goodwin of GIS mapping consultancy Geofutures and Simon Fairlie, Editor of *The Land* magazine. Part of it included looking at the context in which Totnes sits, and the pressures on whatever it might grow, which generated the map on the facing page, showing that although it may see itself as a market town with a distinctive rural hinterland, it falls within both the food footprints of Plymouth to the west and Torbay to the east. The conclusions of the study were that Totnes and District could feed itself, but that it would not be able to do that as well as heat all local homes with wood fuel, and it also noted that producing vegetables is the easy part; that the greater challenges lie in producing grains, fats and sugars.

East Anglia Food Link (EAFL) and Transition Norwich did a similar study as part of Transition Norwich's 'Resilience Plan' for the city.[33] Their conclusion was that Norwich could feed itself, and that all it required was food grown within 6 miles of the city centre (due in part to their ability to grow cereals,

which produce high levels of calories on relatively little ground). They argued that the principal obstacles to this happening are the lack of storage and processing facilities, which prevent locally grown food from feeding local people. They also argued that a revival in market gardening would be a key part of any strategy. Their study was based on DEFRA's land use data, and it assumed a simpler, more seasonal diet, which would be lower in meat and dairy products.

What is fascinating about the Norwich project is that it led to the identification of several key projects that would kick-start the food relocalisation process, which were then worked into a successful Local Food Fund bid (see box overleaf). I asked Tully Wakeman, who coordinated the Norwich research, why such a study is important. He told me:

"It is important to have a sense of the whole food picture for a settlement such as Norwich. A trap a lot of NGOs fall into is overthinking about vegetables. The tendency for people to equate renewable energy just with electricity rather than the range of different ways we use energy is even truer when we look at food. Only one-tenth of what we consume, in calorific terms, comes from fruit and vegetables, yet that is often the main focus for community NGOs looking at food security. Yet where is the other 90 per cent going to come from? Growing vegetables in gardens, allotments, community gardens, and so on offer a degree of food security and can happen relatively rapidly. However, the other 90 per cent requires the rebuilding of the infrastructure required for growing, processing, cleaning, storing, milling and distributing grains and cereals, and that takes longer and requires more planning."

I also asked Mark Thurstain-Goodwin of Geofutures for his thoughts as to why this kind of work matters.

Building

"This is vital for key strategic decision-making," he told me. "It enables us to look at relocalisation efforts not in isolation, but to really get a sense of how different settlements overlap with each other." But is this something that community groups can do on their own? Mark is doubtful. "There is some of the key data that you can get access to, and this can be useful, but it can also be misleading. What you really need is a data geek, and there aren't that many people around who understand this stuff. Much of the data is held by local authorities, and so doing this work in partnership with them would be the ideal. While a lot of decision-makers can see the point of this, none are yet undertaking it. For

Transition in Action: Transition Norwich's Local Food projects   by Tully Wakeman

Transition Norwich's CSA group planting a new hedge in their CSA field. *Photo: Jeremy Bartlett*

Transition Norwich Food Group has combined with East Anglia Food Link to secure £137,000 of funding from the Local Food Fund to create several schemes with food resilience in mind:

- Two market garden schemes: a 4-acre field on a local farm, 6 miles from Norwich city centre, and a 2-acre site on the playing field of Hewett School in Norwich. Both sites are supported by the same full-time employee, and 2011 was their first full growing season. A formal Co-operative Board of Trustees has been set up, drawn from members of Transition Norwich, and 100 'subscribers' (who each buy into the scheme by ordering a vegetable box). The produce from the school site will provide vegetables to the school kitchen, with the rest sold to people in the neighbourhood. Part of the funding has already purchased a tractor for use on both sites.

- A Norwich flour mill: installed in a city-centre location to mill locally grown wheat, this electric mill can mill 1 tonne of grain a day. A good baking and distribution system already exists in Norwich, with a well-known independent wholefood wholesaler and retailer on board to sell the newly branded 'Norwich Loaf' that will be created.

- An oats and beans project: This involves brokering with other local small farmers to grow beans and oats for local consumption, with a shift away from other cash crops that are otherwise sold on the open market.

Transition Norwich also supports an existing 'Grown Our Own' project – a community allotment scheme where members are able to rent small land strips and use shared tools, seeds and facilities, with expert advice from the scheme coordinator.

We see all these projects, which can be easily replicated, as part of creating exemplars of infrastructure for a more resilient Norwich.

Transition in Action: Economic blueprints
by Fiona Ward

This work, part of the REconomy project (www.transitionnetwork.org/projects/reconomy), aims to assess the local resources and explore the vulnerabilities and opportunities of three districts with Transition initiatives in their midst, in the light of climate change, peak oil and wider economic uncertainty.

In each place, we will identify and quantify a number of economic opportunities that exist in a new type of local, Transition economy, and then help existing businesses and social entrepreneurs to act on them. We will produce and begin to implement an integrated 'economic blueprint', working with key local organisations such as local authorities and Chambers of Commerce.

The work will generally focus on energy security, local food production, retrofit of homes and some goods or services important to the local economy. With our project partners, we will consolidate and analyse existing data and knowledge about each district, with additional data collection activity initiated as required.

A working group of local strategic bodies will take responsibility for taking forward the most viable ideas. Benefits will include identification of the most viable economic opportunities, a better understanding of the area's vulnerabilities, stronger partnerships between local organisations and a better-coordinated and better-informed response to the challenges facing each district.

this kind of work to really accelerate and gain traction it needs to be low cost, and that needs initial investment."

A project proposed by Transition Training and Consulting, which would have worked with Forest of Dean District Council to do a resilience analysis for the area, and which would have developed many of the tools discussed above, has so far failed to proceed due to insufficient funding. It is hoped that awareness of this vital aspect of Transition will grow and that the much-needed tools will be developed.

This kind of strategic overview thinking is specialist work, and your initiative is likely to need some help with this. Seek the support and engagement of local universities/specialists, or seek funding to resource it. Only take this work on at a depth you feel you can manage.

The data generated by this kind of research is hugely useful to relocalisation efforts, providing an underpinning to stimulate social enterprise and create key strategic local infrastructure.

You might also enjoy . . .

PERMACULTURE DESIGN (Tools for Transition No.1, page 98), MEASUREMENT (Starting out 6, page 109), VISIONING (Starting out 7, page 114), BUILDING PARTNERSHIPS (Starting out 11, page 132), PRACTICAL MANIFESTATIONS (Deepening 2, page 146), LOCAL FOOD INITIATIVES (Deepening 8, page 168), ENSURING LAND ACCESS (Deepening 10, page 174), EDUCATION FOR TRANSITION (Deepening 12, page 192), FORMING NETWORKS OF TRANSITION INITIATIVES (Connecting 1, page 198), INVOLVING THE COUNCIL (Connecting 2, page 204), ORAL HISTORIES (Connecting 4, page 218).

Building

<u>MOTION IN THE NAME OF COUNCILLOR BULL – FORTHCOMING IMPACT OF PEAK OIL</u>

D by Councillor Bull, seconded by Councillor Chapman:-

ouncil acknowledges the forthcoming impact of peak oil. The Council therefore needs to respond, and help the citizens it serves respond, to the likelihood of shri
a way which will nevertheless maintains the City's prosperity. It acknowledges that actions taken to adapt to and mitigate against climate change also help u
d peak oil.

do this by:

developing an understanding of the impact of peak oil on the local economy and the local community
encouraging a move across the city towards sustainable transport, cycling and walking throughout the city
pursuing a rigorous energy efficiency and conservation programme through its carbon management plan, the work towards EMAS accreditation and on leading o
awareness across all sectors to reduce dependency on oil based energy in the city
supporting research and production within the city which helps develop local effective alternative energy supplies and energy saving products in order to encoura
from oil based fuels and also in order to create local 'green collar jobs'
co-ordinating policy and action on reducing our city's carbon dependency and in response to the need to mitigate and adapt to climate change and peak oil.

is way Nottingham City Council will not only be helping the city to rise to the challenge of peak oil but also encourage the city to grasp the opportunities which peak

er discussion the motion was put to the vote and was carried and the Council RESOLVED that this Council acknowledges the forthcoming impact
uncil therefore needs to respond, and help the citizens it serves respond, to the likelihood of shrinking oil supply but in a way which will neverthe
e City's prosperity. It acknowledges that actions taken to adapt to and mitigate against climate change also help us adapt issues around peak oil.

will do this by:

- developing an understanding of the impact of peak oil on the local economy and the local community
- encouraging a move across the city towards sustainable transport, cycling and walking throughout the city
- pursuing a rigorous energy efficiency and conservation programme through its carbon management plan, the work towards EMAS accreditati
  on raising energy awareness across all sectors to reduce dependency on oil based energy in the city
- supporting research and production within the city which helps develop local effective alternative energy supplies and energy saving pr
  encourage a move away from oil based fuels and also in order to create local 'green collar jobs'
- co-ordinating policy and action on reducing our city's carbon dependency and in response to the need to mitigate and adapt to climate chang

this way Nottingham City Council will not only be helping the city to rise to the challenge of peak oil but also encourage the city to grasp the o

The peak oil resolution passed by Nottingham County Council in December 2008.

Getting your local council to officially recognise peak oil as a challenge can be a key step in moving towards resilience – for both the council as an organisation and you as a community – and to the council's engagement with the Transition process. Local and regional authorities aren't yet planning strategically for peak oil, and it is not a concern reflected in their policymaking. They may not even understand it. Without a clear statement of concern about the issue, any further steps or actions on the issue will not have a foundation. This is an approach much more established in the US, where the first peak oil resolutions began to emerge in 2006.[34] US towns and cities that have passed peak oil resolutions include Berkeley,[35] Chapel Hill,[36] Cleveland,[37] Bloomington[38] and Nevada City.[39] For some, this has been followed by the setting up of a Peak Oil Task Force, and the creation of some kind of Peak Oil Plan. Of these, my favourites are those for San Buenaventura in California[40] and Portland, Oregon.[41] From the US experience, one can observe that peak oil resolutions provide a very dynamic first step in the active engagement of a local authority.

Post Carbon Institute's Daniel Lerch identifies two goals that a peak oil resolution can achieve:

- Raising awareness, among both the council staff and the wider public.
- 'Getting the ball rolling', in that it gives legitimacy to the issue and sends an important signal of support to those already working with it, enabling them to work on it more confidently.[42]

The first (and, to the best of my knowledge, the only so far) UK council to pass a peak oil resolution was Nottingham City Council. Cllr Katrina Bull, Portfolio Holder for Environment and Climate Change, had met with people from Transition Nottingham and had discussed peak oil with Graham Chapman, the council's Deputy Leader, who then asked for a paper on its implications for the council. Cllr Bull asked Transition Nottingham what might help with their work, and the idea of a peak oil resolution was born. At that stage no one else in the council was familiar with the idea of peak oil, so she had to do quite a lot of explaining to her fellow councillors!

The text of the resolution was written by Cllr Bull and was seconded by Cllr Chapman. It was put forward at a full council meeting in December 2008, and preceded by a screening of a part of the film *A Crude Awakening* (see Resources section). This led to a good discussion about the implications of peak oil for the city, and its current levels of oil dependency. The resolution, which went on to be passed unanimously, read as follows.

"This Council acknowledges the forthcoming impact of peak oil. The Council therefore needs to respond, and help the citizens it serves respond, to the likelihood of shrinking oil supply but in a way which will nevertheless maintain the City's prosperity. It acknowledges that actions taken to adapt to and mitigate against climate change also help us adapt to issues around peak oil. It will do this by:

- developing an understanding of the impact of peak oil on the local economy and the local community
- encouraging a move across the city towards sustainable transport, cycling and walking throughout the city
- pursuing a rigorous energy-efficiency and conservation programme through its carbon management plan, the work towards EMAS accreditation [the EU Eco Management and Audit Scheme] and leading on raising energy awareness across all sectors to reduce dependency on oil-based energy in the city
- supporting research and production within the city which helps develop local effective alternative energy supplies and energy-saving products in order to encourage a move away from oil-based fuels and also in order to create local 'green collar jobs'
- coordinating policy and action on reducing our city's carbon dependency and in response to the need to mitigate and adapt to climate change and peak oil.

In this way Nottingham City Council will not only be helping the city to rise to the challenge of peak oil but also encourage the city to grasp the opportunities which peak oil offers."

I talked to Cllr Bull about the impact the resolution has had since it was unanimously passed. She described it as having been "crucial" in the council's work around energy-efficiency and in boosting awareness of energy issues in general. She said that she had talked about climate change in the council for ages, but had struggled to really engage her fellow councillors. However, peak oil and the issues around increasing price volatility helped hugely. "Everyone is convinced," she told me.

One of the key outcomes of this has been the council's Energy Strategy, which is built around the challenge of energy security as well as climate change. The council's waste strategy now has anaerobic digestion at its heart, and its Transport Strategy focuses on a big increase in public transport and a new fleet of electric buses. "None of this would have been possible", she told me, "had it not been for the peak oil resolution."

Bristol City Council, although it doesn't have a peak oil resolution, has made great strides in this area.

Tools for Transition No.21: Peak oil resolutions

In 2008 Daniel Lerch gave a presentation to the council about peak oil and local authorities, following an invitation by the Green Capital Momentum Group (GCMG), a cross-sector body set up to try to steer the city towards being a 'green' city. Transition Bristol had already done significant work in raising the profile of peak oil at the GCMG, the council and across the city. Following Daniel's talk, a Peak Oil Task Force was set up, with representatives from the council, GCMG, Transition Bristol and others, and it was decided that the best first step would be to commission a peak oil report, which it did. The report, 'Building a Positive Future for Bristol after Peak Oil', was written by Simone Osborn of Transition Bristol, and was accepted by the council, the Bristol Partnership and the GCMG group. Its main recommendations are set out in the box below.

In February 2010 the council adopted the Bristol Climate Change and Energy Security Framework, which states:

"That the Cabinet resolve that:
- improving the energy efficiency of the city and securing affordable low-carbon energy supplies are key priorities for the city council
- the Peak Oil Report be welcomed, endorsed and used to inform the development of council services, strategies and plans.

That the Cabinet adopt for consultation the draft Climate Change and Energy Security Framework for Bristol set out in this paper, including:
- A commitment to partnership working to achieve the opportunities presented by a transition to a low-carbon, resilient city.
- Carbon dioxide emission, energy and resilience targets for Bristol's road

Six Options for Action: from the Bristol City Council peak oil report

- **Acknowledgement:** Publicly acknowledge peak oil as a threat. Pass a resolution to take actions now to lessen the impacts which peak oil would cause.
- **Leadership:** Set up a cross-sector team, with a budget, to take the work forward. This could be owned by the Bristol Partnership, with oversight on team selection and monitoring of progress by the Green Capital Momentum Group.
- **Engaged communities:** Emphasise the role which communities have to play in Bristol's future. Support community engagement activities and provide education and assistance on building resilience and reducing reliance on public services.

- **Focus on accessibility:** Drive actions and policies which reduce the need to travel for essential services and needs. Support cycling and walking and development of a sustainable and effective public transport system.
- **Food security:** Drive actions and policies which improve food security by supporting local food growing and production. Develop sustainable agricultural practices.
- **A robust economy:** Support and develop a local business environment which can thrive in a low-carbon, low-waste economy. Ensure that jobs and opportunities are available across the city to avoid creating conditions for social breakdown.

Simone Osborn presenting the Bristol peak oil report. *Photo: Fredrik Hjerling*

the GCMG released a follow-up report called 'Who Feeds Bristol?',[44] which has its roots in the recommendations of the peak oil report; the issues it raised about the implications for food security being one of its findings that created the most ripples. Both the GCMG and Bristol City Council are also actively involved in the new economics foundation / Transition Network's Bristol currency project (see Tools for Transition No.19, Tools for plugging the leaks, page 257) and it is also adding weight to the council's transport and health policymaking.

One interesting observation Simone made revolved around the tension between national and local policymaking. In creating its Local Plan, Bristol City Council declined to include any reference to peak oil, despite the existence of the Bristol peak oil report and despite direct requests from key partners to include peak oil issues within the Core Strategy of the Bristol Development Framework. The justification for omitting peak oil was because there was no national policy that required or justified its inclusion. The UK government's official position is still, at the time of writing, that:

> "... with sufficient investment, the Government does not believe that global oil production will peak between now and 2020 and consequently we do not have any contingency plans specific to a peak in oil production."[45]

It is clear, however, that peak oil resolutions and the creation of peak oil taskforces can have a galvanising effect on a local authority, and lobbying for one can be a very useful initiative for a Transition initiative to undertake. Lobby your local council to pass a peak oil resolution. Numerous examples now exist, and they can be a great boost to those within the council working to build awareness. Explore with them the possibility of a Transition Training for Local Authorities being run for key staff. Once the resolution is passed, heap great praise on the authority, and explore with it ways in which your Transition initiative can help with the next steps – a good example of which is Bristol City Council's peak oil report.

transport, business/public sector and homes with clear accountabilities and monitoring.

- 20 strategic activities to progress towards those targets.
- 40 specific actions for 2010/11.
- Integration of climate change and energy issues into the work and processes of the council to enable delivery of the targets, including the creation of a high level group integrating economic development, digital infrastructure and services and green capital activity.
- That the Cabinet agree to consult on the draft Framework and to further develop and refine the Framework with partners in the city and with the Department of Communities and Local Government.[43]

I asked Simone what impact the report has had since its publication. The council's climate change and energy security policy was greatly helped by the inclusion of peak oil in the policy. In spring 2011

Daring to dream

The old saying 'Think global, act local' is still relevant. The ingredients and tools included in the sections so far in this book, if implemented, will create a groundswell for change; a catalyst for communities across the world to see an energy-constrained future as the motivator for creative change, rather than as a disaster. But without Transition thinking being embraced by national government and business, and becoming central to the national infrastructure, it will remain marginal. The ingredients in this section imagine the stepping up of Transition thinking to the national stage – imagining what it might look like if every settlement had vibrant Transition initiatives setting up food networks, energy companies, growing food everywhere and catalysing a new culture of social enterprise . . .

1. Policies for Transition

with input from Peter Lipman

The then Secretary of State for Energy and Climate Change, now Labour Party leader Ed Miliband, attends the 2009 Transition Network conference at Battersea Arts Centre as a 'Keynote Listener'.

How might it look if government policy, at both the local and the national level, were underpinned by the desire to enable resilience and localisation, and seeks to support and accelerate Transition and remove any obstacles in its path?

How would things look if local and national government began to shift its focus towards enabling the rapid building of resilience and localisation nationally – drawing from, enabling and supporting Transition initiatives on the ground? Here we start to enter the realm of the speculative, but already some good thinking is going on as to what this might look like.

One example is Holyrood 350, set up in Scotland to try to push the Scottish government "to take immediate action to stop accelerating climate change by radically reducing our carbon emissions and so setting a global example for other countries to follow". They have identified and proposed four key areas of action that they see as central to a government-led push towards taking climate change seriously:

- Pricing carbon out of the economy.
- Shifting from an energy-obese to an energy-healthy society.
- Establishing a 'New Green Deal'.
- Rapidly relocalising the economy.

What might happen if local authorities actively got

behind their local Transition initiatives and supported their work? We have already looked at the Monteveglio resolution in Italy (see *Connecting* 2, Involving the council, page 206), and peak oil resolutions have already been explored in Tools for Transition No.21 (page 276), but some local authorities have also passed resolutions in support of their local Transition groups. The best known is that passed by Somerset County Council in July 2008. While not committing the council to any financial support of initiatives, it stated that the council:

- Acknowledges the work done by communities in Somerset on Transition Towns and that the independence of the Transition movement is key to its grassroots appeal.
- As demonstrated in its Climate Change Strategy, fully endorses the Transition Town movement and subscribes to the principles and ethos of the organisation's goals to reduce dependence on fuel oil and create more sustainable communities.
- Commits to providing support and assistance to all towns in Somerset that wish to join this initiative to help them achieve the goals they set for themselves as local communities, as demonstrated under the 'Community Initiatives' section of the Climate Change Strategy.
- Therefore, requests the Scrutiny and Executive Committees to consider through the council's strategic planning process; allocating funds to assist in achieving the outcomes of the Transition Towns Movement in Somerset and requiring all directorates to engage with and provide support for Transition Initiatives in Somerset.
- Through the work outlined above, seeks to become the first Transition Authority in the UK.
- Agrees to undertake a review of its budgets and services to achieve a reduction in dependence on fuel oil and produce an energy descent action plan in line with the principles of the Transition initiative.

This took everyone by surprise. It was drafted and passed with no consultation with either the Transition initiatives on the ground in Somerset or Transition Network. We were all amazed and delighted. While clearly an exciting and ground-breaking

> "If you want to catch a glimpse of the kinds of places outside the political mainstream where the new politics might be incubated, take a look at the Transition movement . . . [it] is engaging people in a way that conventional politics is failing to do. It generates emotions that have not been seen in political life for a long time: enthusiasm, idealism and passionate commitment."
> Madeline Bunting[1]

development, it resulted in a lot of head-scratching.[2] Subsequently, as a way of exploring how the resolution might work in practice, a document, 'A Transition Audit of Somerset County Council'[3] was written by Dan Hurring for the council in 2009, which audited existing activities and how they overlapped with Transition.

However, soon after it was published, there was an election, and the administration changed, becoming a Conservative-led council. This brought with it a considerable change of attitude and organisational priorities. In February 2011, the council moved from having a commitment on climate change, as stated in its 2008 Climate Change Strategy, to:

> "providing leadership to prepare the county for the effects of climate change and to reduce emissions of greenhouse gases, as well as engaging local communities, key stakeholders, government agencies and the business community to deal with the challenges presented by climate change"

. . . to their 'Medium Term Financial Plan', which states that:

"some services will be stopped completely, e.g. climate change work, work on renewable energy, natural environment policy and delivery".

Justified by the cuts sweeping through local authorities, the council's climate change officer was made redundant, and the Sustainable Development team abolished. This short-sighted demoting of climate change, and insistence on seeing it as a stand-alone issue rather than one that cuts across all activities, represents a huge missed opportunity and is hugely disappointing after such a promising start. There are many local authorities, however, who are still showing leadership and vision around climate change, such as Kirklees, and the potential for visionary authorities to engage creatively with their local Transition groups is enormous.

On the national scale, some tools already exist which could prove very useful to Transition, such as the **Sustainable Communities Act**. Passed in 2007, it establishes the right for local people and councils to submit proposals for government action. It requires government to 'try to reach agreement' and to implement those agreements. It is based on a core philosophy that local people are the experts on their own problems and the solutions to them.

You and your councils can use the Act to submit proposals for government action to promote and protect truly sustainable communities. So you can put forward *any* proposal, so long as it meets the following two criteria:

1. It requires *central government* action, e.g. to change the planning rules so that local people have the final say over whether a new supermarket opens.
2. You can show argument and evidence that it would promote at least one element of the Act's four-part definition for 'local sustainability':
   - **local economies,** e.g. promoting local shops, Post Offices, local businesses and local jobs
   - **environmental protection,** e.g. promoting local renewable energy, protecting green spaces

   - **social inclusion,** e.g. protecting local public services and alleviating fuel poverty
   - **democratic involvement,** e.g. promoting local people participating in decision-making and democracy.

Transition initiatives can submit their proposal via the government's 'Barrier Busting' website.[4]

The **Localism Act** is less clearly beneficial overall, but on the positive side it will introduce Community Rights to Buy, Bid and Build (in the light of the huge unmet demand for allotments, one might add a Right to Dig to this . . .).

One government-led strategy that has proved very successful in Scotland has been the Climate Challenge Fund, set up by the Scottish government to support community initiatives around carbon reduction. The fund, of £27 million, has led to 360 substantial projects in 260 communities, and has proved a considerable kick-start for community initiatives. In England and Wales one can only speculate as to the impact such a scheme would have, and the potential of what it would unlock. It is important to state, at this point, that government support for Transition, and for localisation/decarbonisation projects in general, needs to be founded on a Transition analysis of peak oil, climate change and economic fragility: solutions designed to address just one of these can often have undesirable side effects. For example, the UK government's Green Deal, which is built around Tesco and B&Q being among the key deliverers of energy-efficiency products and advice, could have a disastrous impact on smaller traders and local businesses unable to compete.

Another strategy that national government could implement is Tradeable Energy Quotas, developed by Dr David Fleming with support from Shaun Chamberlin. This is a national carbon-rationing system which would allocate a carbon allowance to everyone in the UK, to be gradually contracted annually. It is simple and easily implementable, and introduces a much fairer system than what we have at present, which is, in effect, rationing, whereby the poorer struggle disproportionately with rising oil prices. There are also alternative models such as Cap and Share, which seek to create a similar kind of government-led intentional and gradual reduction in carbon emissions.

Might it be, as some are now suggesting, that what is needed now is a 'Transition Enabling Act' – a piece of radical legislation designed to urgently accelerate the localisation, decarbonisation and resilience-building process across all sectors, in the same way that legislation passed just before the onset of war is designed to enable a rapid re-gearing and refocusing of society? The discussion as to what such an Act might look like is already under way, and it is hoped that this book will stimulate these discussions. The UK government was able, between 1936, when the Food (Defence Plans) Department was set up, and 1939, to completely refocus and rethink the UK's food system to that it was able – just – to support the nation. We need that kind of legislation at both the local and the national level.

If the transition we have discussed in this book is to take place at the scale it needs to, it will need the support of meaningful, well-thought-out and visionary legislation. This is not about the 'greening' of society – its gradually becoming more 'environmentally friendly' – it is about a shift in focus, enabling resilience at all levels and fast-tracking the creation of a more appropriate and, where possible, localised economy.

You might also enjoy . . .
VISIONING (*Starting out* 7, page 114), FORMING NETWORKS OF TRANSITION INITIATIVES (*Connecting* 1, page 198), STRATEGIC THINKING (*Building* 7, page 272).

Some thoughts on running a Transition hustings

One good way to engage local political candidates around election time is to run a hustings event, as indeed many Transition groups did before the 2010 General Election. A good hustings event needs good chairing and clarity about the ground rules, and should be engaging and clarifying rather than riotous and antagonistic. One option is to run a traditional-style hustings event, where audience members are either invited to stand up and ask questions, or questions are written upon arrival and sorted and chosen by the event's chairperson.

Another approach, and one perhaps more in keeping with the Transition ethos, could be run as follows. Start the evening with a ten-minute presentation about Transition, drawing together the work that the group has done

thus far, showcasing projects under way and the larger idea of economic localisation and resilience. Then invite each candidate to speak for three minutes, particularly in relation to the themes covered in the talk. Then invite each candidate to sit at a different table and, as in World Café or Open Space (see Tools for Transition No.15, page 220), to move between tables and to discuss their issues and questions with each candidate. Then, to wrap the event up, each candidate is invited to give a three-minute reflection on the process and any closing thoughts.

Transition Network has produced a guide for initiatives wishing to hold a hustings event, which you can download at http://tinyurl.com/3nwqqwn.

2. A learning network

by Naresh Giangrande

Transition Network was set up in July 2007 to inspire, encourage, support, network and train Transition initiatives. *Photo: Chris Croome*

If Transition initiatives work in isolation from each other, doing brilliant innovative things but not sharing what they learn, we miss the possibility for a rapid upscaling of their collective efforts.

The large number of Transition initiatives has created valuable experience and learning. Being part of this network means we can create change much more quickly and more effectively because we can draw on others' experience and insights. Those engaged in Transition are learning in many different settings. The learning is chaotic and emergent. Conventional academic or scientific research and experiment/dissemination tends to be much slower.

This is a real-time, real-life social experiment, with learning and growing together in many places and cultures, made possible by the sheer number of initiatives and modern communications. Ten years ago, Transition would have been far less possible.

You could think of Transition as being like Open Source software. It is based on some simple principles and then invites participation, inclusion and creativity, the results of which are then shared and go on to further shape the model.

An evolutionary approach such as this develops where the best ideas and practices succeed and are copied. For instance, there is much material about people's experience of awareness raising.

It is discussed in training, at conferences and at regional gatherings. It features in this book and on Transition Network's Projects Directory.[5] There is learning from blogs, forums, tweets and through informal meetings.

The more information is shared, the richer the commons. The faster the rate of learning, the more effective the movement. One of the most important features of a commons is to balance giving and taking. Probably the main role of the larger-scale Transition structures, such as Transition Network and the national and regional hubs, is to facilitate this. This book, and its accompanying online version (www.transitionnetwork.org/ingredients) are very much a part of this.

Rather than reinventing the wheel, tap into the pool of accumulated insight the Transition movement has generated, as well as feeding into it and enriching our collective understanding.

You might also enjoy . . .
RESPECTFUL COMMUNICATION (*Starting out* 3, page 100), MEASUREMENT (*Starting out* 6, page 109), BUILDING PARTNERSHIPS (*Starting out* 11, page 132), FORMING NETWORKS OF TRANSITION INITIATIVES (*Connecting* 1, page 198), THE ROLE OF STORYTELLING (*Connecting* 6, page 229).

Community-scale resilience in practice

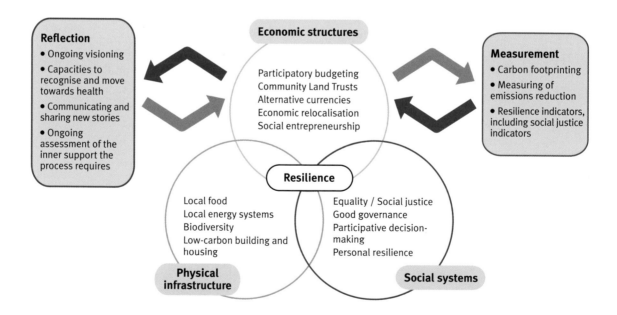

Reflection
- Ongoing visioning
- Capacities to recognise and move towards health
- Communicating and sharing new stories
- Ongoing assessment of the inner support the process requires

Economic structures

Participatory budgeting
Community Land Trusts
Alternative currencies
Economic relocalisation
Social entrepreneurship

Measurement
- Carbon footprinting
- Measuring of emissions reduction
- Resilience indicators, including social justice indicators

Resilience

Local food
Local energy systems
Biodiversity
Low-carbon building and housing

Equality / Social justice
Good governance
Participative decision-making
Personal resilience

Physical infrastructure

Social systems

At the local level, the principle of the learning network can be imagined like this. It is the ability of a Transition initiative to continually reflect on what it is doing (through the telling of stories, ongoing visioning work and reflections on the inner aspects of the process) as well as to measure its impacts (through measurement of its effects on well-being, carbon reduction and resilience), which enable the deepening and evolution of the process, but which can all too easily be ignored.

3. Investing in Transition

with input from Fiona Ward and Peter Lipman

FC United is a supporter-owned football club in Manchester. It aims to raise £1.5 million for a new ground, and has already raised £700,000, in part through a very well-supported share launch.[6]
Photo: Mick Dean, FCUM Matchday Photography

Money isn't a neutral thing. The decisions we make with our investment choices can either prop up and reinforce an economic model rooted in a past of cheap energy oil prices and climate irresponsibility, or they can help to bring forth a new, revitalised and more appropriate way of doing things.

Making the kind of transition that this book has argued for in the time that we have remaining will be an enormous, as well as a historic, venture. As we saw on page 54, successful localisation will require meaningful investment to make it happen. We have already looked at a range of ways of 'plugging the leaks' of our local economy (see Tools for Transition No.19, page 257), but this final ingredient explores how investment on that scale might happen, and looks at a range of possible mechanisms for enabling Transition to scale up sufficiently.

For those of us fortunate enough to have investments, we do have some degree of control over choosing to invest in supporting local enterprises that actually work to strengthen the resilience of our local communities by providing renewable energy, food, transport, building materials and

"OVESCO [see page 249] raises a quarter mil for community solar via people-power finance. If we replicate many times, we can begin to dream."

Jeremy Leggett on Twitter, 1 May 2011

other essential goods and services for which there will always be a demand. Many of these opportunities may already exist. It is early days, but there are many enticing opportunities that feel worth exploring, and could ultimately offer more security than the global financial markets, as well as furthering the aims of Transition. These are as follows.

- **Self-invested personal pensions (SIPPs):** Many people now have pension schemes which allow them to choose where it is invested. You can also transfer traditional pensions funds into a SIPP, which then allows more flexible investment, including into local companies, land, etc. (the rules of SIPPs set out the things that can, and can't, be invested in). Transition offers the exciting possibility that such investment could be done collectively, i.e. a number of people might invest their SIPP funds in a large piece of local land, which is then used to set up a Community Supported Agriculture scheme, or in a community renewable energy project.
- **Local community-owned energy companies:** For example, TRESOC in Totnes, OVESCO in Lewes, Bath Community Energy and others . . . (see Tools for Transition No.18, page 246). These offer the opportunity for investments the results of which are highly visible in, and beneficial to, the community. One model for this would be to raise £100,000 (e.g. find 100 people willing to loan £1,000) then use this to raise more equity (e.g. from a bank) and then buy and install a wind turbine. The profits can be used to pay a reasonable return or interest rate to each

investor, while also generating significant funding for local Transition projects.

- **Community shares and bonds:** Have your Transition initiative issue community bonds, which raise funds for investing in local enterprises for a defined return, or participation bonds, which also give you some equity in the enterprise. Some examples of this have already been seen in Tools for Transition No.20 (see page 267), in so far as they are used to underpin new businesses, but they can also be used for larger projects. The Development Trust Association has a long experience of supporting and informing community bonds or share launches and has some excellent tools available to support you with this (see also resources, on the facing page).
- **A 'Transition Social Investors Fund':** This, currently under consideration, would be a very exciting approach. At the moment most large philanthropic funders have a substantial endowment invested somewhere and then distribute as grants the interest that is generated. However, what might it look like if a significant part of their endowment were invested in local Transition infrastructure, still generating a good return, but enabling Transition at the local level? It could also invest in a range of Transition social enterprises that have to meet social and environmental criteria to be eligible, as well as a viable business case of course. This is a model that Transition Network is currently actively exploring.
- **Urban/rural Transition twinnings:** It might also be worth exploring the 'twinning' of two (or more) Transition initiatives. For example, it might be that a rural Transition community has a great renewable energy asset, for example a powerful local river, or a very windy site, but

** IMPORTANT! You should take expert advice before making any financial investment. The suggestions here are not recommendations to invest in Transition, rather some ideas for further consideration. ******

can't, on its own, raise the revenue to exploit it. At the same time there may well be an urban Transition initiative (or several) who don't have such an opportunity but who would like to invest in community renewables and in supporting Transition. Bringing the two together could be hugely mutually beneficial. This is already being modelled in the River Cottage / British Gas 'Energyshare' initiative, which enables the attraction of investment from a broader 'community' of people interested in investing in community renewables. The same model could also be applied to food, development and construction, or a range of other Transition projects.

- **Transition revolving loan funds:** Here's an evolving idea. Perhaps large investors and businesses out there who want to invest in a way that yields a good social return on their investment (i.e. they can see tangible social benefits arising from those investments) might invest in a 'Transition revolving loan fund'. This would be part of a larger process (such as REconomy (see *Building* 2: Social enterprise and entrepreneurship, page 240) of nurturing new Transition social enterprises and bringing them forward to a point of being investment-ready. The revolving loan fund would lend at below-commercial rates and would create a link between investment and the enabling of a new, resilience-focused economy.

While ultimately it may be the case that 'social returns' of such models may be lower than can be obtained in the markets, through traditional investments (although this is not necessarily so), this book is based on the premise that the current global economic system cannot continue, and that when it ends, so will much of the financial system that many of us rely on to keep our savings safe and growing, especially our pensions.

The Transition movement needs, as it continues to scale up, to think seriously about models that will enable, with confidence, the levels of finance that active Transition will require to come forward. Many models for enabling this already exist, and new ones are emerging.

Resources

The following resources on community bonds and shares may be useful:

Co-operatives UK's document *Investing in Community Shares* offers a detailed guide for the potential investor, and can be found at http://tinyurl.com/44bc83w.

Hill, C, with assistance from Lynch, M. & Curtis, J. (2007) *Community Share and Bond Issues: The sharpest tool in the box.* A good overview guide, from the Development Trusts Association: can be downloaded from http://tinyurl.com/3bhke9w.

A longer list of other useful resources on community shares is at http://www.communityshares.org.uk/resources.

Daring to dream

Epilogue: Where might all this be going?

I have presented in this book the current thinking about what Transition is and how it works – as an invitation to pick it up, try it out, see if it works for you and, if so, to make it yours. It presents no definitive models, but is a snapshot of the collective thinking during the time I wrote it, drawing all I could from the extraordinary stories of people working in their communities to make Transition happen. The next book may look very different. What I'd like to do now is to look forward and to speculate as to where all this might be going.

In its short life, Transition has spread virally around the world, popping up like mushrooms in unexpected places. In some communities it has greatly exceeded expectations; in other places it has struggled. In some places it has engaged widely and deeply; in other places not so. Some initiatives have easily adjusted to the notion of becoming economically viable; others have resisted this, developing other approaches instead. This is not, as I have stressed throughout, something we can guarantee will work everywhere, but it is working well enough to have already created major ripples. It is often referred to as one of the most exciting emerging movements in the world.

It has had its detractors, who usually criticise it for not being sufficiently like them. For the Trapese Collective ('Taking Radical Action through Popular Education and Sustainable Everything!'), Transition is politically naive and its lack of an analysis of power dooms it to ineffectiveness.[1] For writer and blogger John Michael Greer, it will fail because mobilising people on the scale to which it aspires isn't going to happen in time, and the movement is guilty of 'premature triumphalism' for suggesting that such a transition might even be possible.[2]

For Alex Steffen at WorldChanging.com, "the Transition movement seems saturated with . . . 'surplus powerlessness' disguised as practicality"; he argues that a focus on localisation negates the potential of design and human brilliance to create low-carbon, hi-tech new cities.[3] We have already heard Colin McInnes's criticisms – that, by promoting localisation, Transition wants society to return to the Middle Ages[4] (an argument soundly dealt with, I hope, in Chapter 4). All these critiques help to shape Transition. At the same time, it has been remarkable how the movement has often appeared in the mainstream as an accepted part of our culture, as though it has always been there.

In answer to the question "Where does this go next?", my hope is that it continues to grow into one of the most significant forces for change on the planet. I hope that the number of Transition initiatives increases, and that their work deepens.

Transition may well be most successful if it retains its broadness rather than focusing too closely at any one facet of the process. It will do best if based on practical action, community appeal, inner Transition, social entrepreneurship, social justice, careful attention to deep engagement, using the best evidence, creating new economic models for inward investment, and finding skilful ways to involve local businesses and local government. Its strength and resilience will be in its breadth; in its ability to keep moving forward on all those fronts.

Ultimately, it will be judged for how it succeeds, or fails, to make communities more resilient and localised. Throughout this book, the underlying question has been 'How can localisation and resilience shift from being abstract ideas to becoming a tangible, on-the-ground reality?' I posed this question to Michael Shuman, a long-time pioneer of localisation.[5] He identified three highly relevant areas:

> "The first is, I think, that all of us have to go to business school. We have to realise that even if we're going to be advocates of local economies, we have to *be* those economies and *model* those businesses that we want out there and prove the concept wherever possible.
>
> The second thing is that, rather than trying

to beat those on the right [politically] that people just instinctively distrust, I think it's about embracing those with different political views and finding the right ideological and philosophical mix that gets us from here to there.

I think the last piece is seeing ourselves as part of the problem. Our consumption dollars, what drives the system, our investment dollars provide the foundation for the system. The more that we can create alternative systems by channelling our consumption and investment and convince others these are great ways of living, and consistent with what we're trying to achieve long term, I think that's the way we're going to succeed."

This stresses that the task now is to step forward, to add new skills and a new element of practicality and maturity to a movement that has often, largely, felt happier campaigning against stuff than creating new, viable businesses and organisational models. We need both, but the practical building of a new economy and a new infrastructure needs to start today, and it needs to be underpinned by a sense of the extraordinary timeliness of what we are doing.

Milton Friedman, the father of neoliberal economics and once described as "the most influential economist of the second half of the twentieth century . . . possibly of all of it"[6] once said:

"Only a crisis – actual or perceived – produces real change. When that crisis occurs, the actions that are taken depend on the ideas that are lying around. . . . That, I believe, is our basic function: to develop alternatives to existing policies, to keep them alive and available until the politically impossible becomes politically inevitable."[7]

Unfortunately, at present, times of crisis and shock tend to be capitalised on by those with dubious motivations to grab, privatise and redirect wealth to fewer and fewer people – something we are increasingly seeing. Our hope lies in the extent to which Transition, or something like it, is able to inspire and to hold more appeal than less desirable approaches.

This will be a quiet revolution, a humble revolution, one that gently but surely changes culture and shifts the stories we tell about the people and places around us. It is not about rejecting progress, or *choosing* austerity and misery; rather, about facing up to the possibility of increased austerity and circumstances that some might see as being miserable, and looking at them with fresh eyes, and seeking solutions that celebrate what makes us feel alive and best meets our needs.

As I complete the writing of this book, the oil price is again rising towards $120 a barrel, the UK government is talking about the need for an 'oil emergency plan',[8] public spending is being slashed, 'localism' is all the rage politically, and there is much discussion as to where economic activity is going to come from in the future. I hope that, having got this far in this book, you will agree that the approach set out here could well be the response we are increasingly floundering around looking for. A conference about Transition and food localisation held in Colorado in February 2011 was subtitled 'food localisation as economic development'. We need to get away from seeing localisation as something that just takes place on the pinboards of wholefood shops, and see it as a key strategy for economic development.

The last five years' experiment in Transition suggests that anything is possible. A report[9] published just before this book went to print, by the World Economic Forum, identified the key areas of risk for governments as being climate change, extreme energy price volatility and fiscal crises – the very areas that Transition has been focusing on. As such, it seems to me that, in many ways, Transition is ahead of government thinking on this, and has much insight and learning to contribute. 'Engaged optimism' may turn out to be a very powerful tool indeed.

Is Transition happening where you live?

There are Transition initiatives now in 34 countries. If you want to get involved, find out about initiatives, projects and the resources you might need in order to take the first steps towards transforming your street, neighbourhood or town, have a look at www.transitionnetwork.org, where you will find everything you need. You can search the site for initiatives, for projects or for people, or enter your postcode to see where there is 'Transition nearby'.

You can also subscribe to our monthly bulletin or put your questions to our forum. There are inspiring blogs from around the world, telling us what's worked and what hasn't, and what it's like to take the bold steps of reimagining and then redesigning your own community. You will also find all of the ingredients and tools that feature in this book there, and much more besides.

Or perhaps you're not ready to get involved yet. We're faced with uncertainties at all levels and with what often feels like a daunting journey in front of us, and we've all at times felt overwhelmed or underqualified for the tasks ahead. So, if you need time to take a few deep breaths, to do a bit more reading, or to bounce some ideas around – that's fine. There's a place in a Transition initiative for everyone, from people who just want to dip their toe in the water to those who want to dive right in. It's over to you.

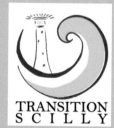

Appendix 1: The advantages and disadvantages of different organisational models

Part A. The following five structure types are the main options for a Transition group with a project-support role. [Note that these apply only within the UK.]

Type	Main attributes	How to set up	Notes
Unincorporated association (non-charity)	Governed by a constitution. Managed by a management committee. Not recognised in law as a legal entity. Liability of members and the governing body is unlimited. Cannot own property in its own right. Cannot enter into contracts (e.g. rental agreements).	Draw up a constitution (also called 'rules'). If there is a membership fee, you are obliged to keep a membership list. No approval or authorisation needed to set it up.	**Advantages:** • Simple and flexible. No need to have the constitution agreed by any outside body (unless you are registering as a charity – see below). • Cheap to run. No need to submit accounts to anyone outside (unless you register as a charity, or funders demand it). • If you have charitable aims, you can register as a charity and gain advantages such as funding that is available only to charities. **Disadvantages:** • Some funders may prefer a more formal structure, especially if you are looking for big sums of money. • Possible personal liability for committee members.
Unincorporated association (charity)	If the association receives more than £5,000 per year and has charitable aims, it must be registered with the Charity Commission.	Submit application form and constitution to Charity Commission. Can 'upgrade' to company limited by guarantee or charitable incorporated organisation (CIO), but this requires re-registration.	As above.
Community interest company (CIC) (cannot be a charity)	Recently introduced (2005) legal form for social enterprises. Private company limited by shares or by guarantee. Can convert directly into a charitable incorporated organisation (CIO – see page 294).	Submit the following to Companies House: • Memorandum and Articles of Association for Community Interest Company. • Community interest statement. • An excluded company declaration. • Usual incorporation forms. • Filing fee. The CIC Regulator will review before assigning CIC status.	Limited company with special additional features created for the use of people who want to conduct a business or other activity for community benefit, and not purely for private advantage. Must have a community interest purpose and an asset lock, to ensure that the CIC is established for community purposes and that the assets and profits are dedicated to these purposes. A CIC cannot be a registered charity and will not have the benefits of charitable status, even if the objects are entirely charitable in nature. See www.cicregulator.gov.uk for more information.

Type	Main attributes	How to set up	Notes
Company limited by guarantee (charity)	A limited company which cannot distribute profits or assets to its members. Must register with the Charity Commission. Can enter into contracts and own land. Directors of the company are trustees of the charity and act as management committee. Directors have limited liability. Can convert directly into a charitable incorporated organisation (CIO – see below) when available.	Draw up Memorandum and Articles of Association for Company Limited by Guarantee and submit to Companies House, along with usual incorporation forms and filing fee. Apply for charitable status with the Charity Commission (unless not registering as a charity – see Part B, right).	**Advantages:** • Suitable for a larger organisation which has considerable assets (e.g. equipment, a building) and employs more than a few staff. The company can take on legal obligations and buy property in its own name. The organisation and not its members is responsible for any debts. However, directors do have a legal duty to act prudently and to ensure that the company manages its finances carefully. • Many funders regard this structure as more stable than an unincorporated association, as they know the company will continue to exist even if there is a change of people involved. • Some funders will give grants only to registered charities. **Disadvantages:** • Complex and usually expensive to set up. • Time consuming to run and annual accountancy fees can be high. • Regulated by both Companies House and the Charity Commission. You have to notify them of every change of directors/trustees and draw up a particular form of annual accounts and reports.
Charitable incorporated organisation (CIO) (charity)	Brand new legal that will be available in late 2011. Must register with the Charity Commission, but don't have to register with Companies House.	See Charity Commission website: www.charity commission.gov.uk	**Advantages (compared with company limited by guarantee):** • Less onerous requirements for preparing accounts. • Less onerous reporting requirements – one annual return. • Less onerous filing requirements. • Less onerous requirements relating to reporting of constitutional and governance changes. • Simpler constitutional form. Codified duties for directors and members which reflect the charitable nature of the CIO. **Disadvantages (compared with company limited by guarantee):** Seemingly none.

Part B. Structures suitable for running a social enterprise such as a community-owned shop or a wind farm.

Type	Main attributes	How to set up	Notes
Cooperative (cannot be a charity) Has the following rules: • Open membership. • One member one vote. • Investment should not carry control. • Dividends distributed among members fairly. • Must include educational and social objectives. • Co-ops should cooperate with each other. • Concern for community.	Unregistered.	Apply rules to a group of people and call yourselves a co-op.	**Advantages:** • Quick, cheap and easy. • Can raise money by issuing shares. **Disadvantages:** • No limited liability (members can have assets seized if co-op is bankrupt).
	Registered as an industrial & provident society.	Register with the Registry of Friendly Societies.	**Advantages:** • Limited liability. • Can raise money by issuing shares. • Cannot demutualise (always a co-op). **Disadvantages:** • Costs between £350 and £700 to register. • High annual fees. • Tight limitations on range of activities.
	Registered with Companies House as 'company limited by guarantee'.	Submit usual company incorporation forms and filing fee to Companies House.	**Advantages:** • Limited liability. • High credibility with other traders and banks. • Can raise money by issuing shares. **Disadvantages:** • Can be demutualised by later members.
Community interest company (CIC) (cannot be a charity)	See Part A, page 293.	See Part A, page 293.	See Part A, page 293.
Company limited by guarantee (non-charity)	Same as Part A, page 294, except no need to apply to Charity Commission.	Same as Part A, page 294, except no need to apply to Charity Commission.	Same as Part A, page 294, except regulated only by Companies House.

Prepared by Patrick Andrews of Riversimple LLP.

Appendix 2: Types of insurance cover for organisations

The following is a brief overview of the types of insurance cover you will need, or could take out, to protect your group, with the order of importance from top to bottom.

- **Employers' Liability**
  This will cover your group against accidents at work, to both staff and volunteers, for which you are legally liable. This is a statutory requirement, and a certificate of Employers' Liability insurance must be displayed at your main residence. Your insurers will need to know what your annual wageroll is for paid staff and how many volunteers you have working on your Transition initiatives. You are liable as an employer whether or not someone working for you is paid or not. Depending on the activities your group is involved in, it may be prudent to check the credentials of your volunteers with regard to undertaking activities with a general degree of risk – if any.

- **Public Liability**
  This protects your group against third-party property damage and/or bodily injury during everyday activities anywhere in the UK. Though not a statutory requirement, it would be extremely inadvisable not to take out this insurance. Both this and Employers' Liability insurance should be viewed as essential.

- **Professional Indemnity**
  Protecting your group from advice given to third parties that causes property damage and/or bodily injury or financial loss.

- **Personal Accident**
  Cover for injury to volunteers and staff that does not follow from legal liability (Employers' Liability) insurance.

- **Renewable energy assets**
  In taking advantage of the Feed-in Tariffs on solar PV or other small renewable energy systems, your group will need to insure the Public Liability risk and against the potential material damage emanating from its operation. Cover can additionally be obtained for loss of revenue and mechanical breakdown too.

- **Other assets**
  Cover for office contents, computers, sheds, exhibition equipment, etc.

- **Machinery, plant and tools**
  Cover for any of these used by your group to carry out everyday Transition initiative business.

At the initial stage you will likely need only Employers' Liability and Public Liability insurance, but over time, as your initiative grows, you will need to add to this. Ask your preferred insurance provider to assist you with these.

Prepared by Matt Criddle of Naturesave Insurance (www.naturesave.co.uk).

Notes and references*

page 2
1   Rubin, J. (2009) *Why Your World is About to Get a Whole Lot Smaller: What the price of oil means for the way we live.* Virgin Books.

Introduction
1   Alexander, C., Ishikawa, S. & Silverstein, M. (1977) *A Pattern Language: Towns, buildings, construction.* Oxford University Press. Alexander's observation was that any built environment is like a 'language', it is composed of different identifiable elements, some obvious, some subtle, and like any language, it can be used to write beautiful poetry or doggerel. Alexander put it like this: "the elements of this language are entities called patterns. Each pattern describes a problem which occurs over and over again in our environment, and then describes the core of the solution to that problem, in such a way that you can use this solution a million times over, without ever doing it the same way twice."

PART ONE
Chapter 1: The emergence of an idea: a potted history of Transition
1   www.kinsalefurthered.ie.
2   The 'grandfather' of peak oil, and the first to repopularise the work of M. King Hubbert through a 1998 paper co-authored with Jean Laherrère called 'The End of Cheap Oil', published in *Scientific American*, 278(3): 78-83.
3   Can be downloaded from http://tinyurl.com/4s9z7y5.
4   The Kinsale part of the early story of Transition is told in more detail in *The Transition Handbook: From oil dependency to local resilience* (Green Books, 2008).
5   http://thelewespound.org.
6   Which you can watch in full at http://vimeo.com/8029815.
7   www.transitionnetwork.org/news/2011-04-05/announcing-movie-transition-20.
8   You can read Miliband's reflections on the experience at http://tinyurl.com/5u4gn6k.
9   There is a short film about Open Space which captures the spirit of the 2007 conference at http://tinyurl.com/63q4ule; a film about the 2008 conference at http://tinyurl.com/6d28yzo; and Part 1 of a film about the 2010 conference at

http://tinyurl.com/4tfhgvo.
10 You can read the script in full at http://tinyurl.com/69mgfhj.
11 Which you can read at http://tinyurl.com/2cgnlll.
12 A very touching film celebrating the project's first birthday can be found at www.youtube.com/watch?v=pWDerzFiqOo.
13 You can read a write-up of the day at http://tinyurl.com/yjtv3bt.

Chapter 2: Why Transition initiatives do what they do
1   www.transitionnetwork.org/blogs/steph-bradley.
2   Snyder, G. (1974) 'Four changes', in *Turtle Island*. New Directions Publishing, p.101.
3   Most clearly and forcefully set out in Wilkinson, R. & Pickett, K. (2010) *The Spirit Level: Why equality is better for everyone.* Penguin.
4   Ibid.
5   Figures from David Strahan at http://lastoilshock.com/map.html.
6   www.worldenergyoutlook.org/docs/weo2010/WEO2010_es_english.pdf.
7   Owen, N. A., Inderwildi, O. R. & King, D. A. (2010) 'The status of conventional world oil reserves – hype or cause for concern?' *Energy Policy*, 38(8): 4743-9.
8   Vidal, J. (2011) 'WikiLeaks cables: Saudi Arabia cannot pump enough oil to keep a lid on prices: US diplomat convinced by Saudi expert that reserves of world's biggest oil exporter have been overstated by nearly 40%'. *The Guardian*, 8 February 2011, http://tinyurl.com/6dqnjnq.
9   Hirsch, R. L., Bezdek, R. & Wendling, R. (2005) *Peaking of World Oil Production – Impacts, mitigation and risk management.* National Energy Technology Laboratory, US Department of Energy.
10 http://tinyurl.com/3a2ec9d.
11 http://tinyurl.com/2a6xp9n.
12 http://tinyurl.com/2fpwjm4.
13 'New study links severe storm increases, global warming'. *Pasadena Star News*, 27 December 2008.
14 http://tinyurl.com/2c85q46.
15 Shakhova, N., Semiletov, I., Salyuk, A., Yusupov, V., Kosmach, D. & Gustafsson, O. (2010) 'Extensive methane venting to the atmosphere from sediments of the East Siberian Arctic', *Science*, 327(5970): 1246-50.

16 'Even soil feels the heat: soils release more carbon dioxide as globe warms'. *Science Daily*, 25 March 2010, http://tinyurl.com/6a9ratd.

17 Bellamy, P. H., Loveland, P. J., Bradley, R. I., Lark, R. M. & Kirk, G. J. D. (2005) 'Carbon losses from all soils across England and Wales 1978-2003'. *Nature*, 437: 245-8. doi: 10.1038/nature04038.

18 http://tinyurl.com/6khm46t.

19 Grudgings, S. (2011) 'Amazon drought caused huge carbon emissions'. *Reuters*, 2 February 2011, http://tinyurl.com/5slxs6g.

20 Kolbert, E. (2007). *Field Notes from a Catastrophe: A frontline report on climate change*. Bloomsbury Publishing.

21 Meinshausen, M., Meinshausen, N., Hare, W., Raper, S. C. B., Frieler, K., Knutti, R., Frame, D. J. & Allen, M. R. (2009) 'Greenhouse-gas emission targets for limiting global warming to 2 degrees C'. *Nature*, 458: 1158-62.

22 Helm, D., Smale, R. & Phillips, J. (2007) 'Too good to be true? The UK's climate change record', www.dieterhelm.co.uk/sites/default/files/Carbon_record_2007.pdf.

23 Sample, I. (2010) 'UK import emissions are the highest in Europe, figures show: Study finds 253m tonnes of CO_2 are released annually in the manufacture of products bound for UK shores – mostly in the developing world'. *The Guardian*, 8 March 2010, http://tinyurl.com/6estzj6.

24 Munich Re Insurance (2010) press release, 27 September 2010: 'Two months to Cancun climate summit / large number of weather extremes as strong indicator of climate change', http://tinyurl.com/5r4socu.

25 Rubin, J. (2009) *Why Your World is About to Get a Whole Lot Smaller: What the price of oil means for the way we live*. Virgin Books, p.206.

26 Rushe, D. (2011) 'Oil prices may threaten global economic recovery, says energy agency: as crude oil prices hit $95 a barrel, it is in a "danger zone" which may derail recovery, says chief economist at Paris's IEA'. *The Guardian*, 5 January 2011, http://tinyurl.com/4befnje.

27 Porritt, J. (2005) *Capitalism: As if the world matters*. Earthscan Publications, p.63.

28 Monbiot, G. (2008) 'Population bombs', www.monbiot.com/archives/2008/01/29/population-bombs, 29 January 2008.

29 Homer-Dixon, T. (2007) *The Upside of Down: Catastrophe, creativity and the renewal of civilisation*. Souvenir Press.

30 Smith, R. A. 'Carpe Diem: The dangers of risk aversion'. Lecture to the Royal Academy of Engineering, 29 May 2007. Reprinted in *Civil Engineering Surveyor*, October 2007.

31 http://tinyurl.com/62z6z6g.

32 Jackson, T. (2009) *Prosperity Without Growth: Economics for a finite planet*. Earthscan Publications.

33 http://news.bbc.co.uk/1/hi/business/7766057.stm.

34 http://postgrowth.org/japan-the-worlds-first-post-growth-economy.

35 Farrell, S. (2011) 'King says living standards may never recover from the crisis: Bank of England Governor strikes dovish note on timing of interest-rate increase'. *The Independent*, 2 March 2011, http://tinyurl.com/4flddvj.

36 You can hear the talk she gave at the 2010 Transition Network conference at http://tinyurl.com/23p4uxc.

37 Daly, H. E. (1977) *Steady-state Economics: The economics of biophysical equilibrium and moral growth*. W. H. Freeman and Company.

38 For more on this see http://tinyurl.com/6he37v6.

39 Shields, R., 'Moss's £60 high street frock is named Dress of the Year: the model beats fashion greats such as Galliano and Gaultier'. *The Independent*, 3 May 2009, http://tinyurl.com/cza6er.

40 Nordhaus, T., & Shellenberger, M. (2009) *Break Through: Why we can't leave saving the planet to environmentalists*. Mariner Books.

41 Seyfang, G. (2009) 'Transition Norwich: A fine city in Transition'. Report of the 2009 Membership survey, University of East Anglia, http://tinyurl.com/63vnakr.

42 Thompson, S., Abdullah, S., Marks, N., Simms, A. & Johnson, V. (2007) *The European unHappy Index: An index of carbon efficiency and well being in the EU*. new economics foundation.

43 http://tinyurl.com/6c59gae.

44 The UK Office for National Statistics, www.statistics.gov.uk/cci/nugget.asp?id=206.

45 See, for instance, Putnam, R. D. (2000) *Bowling*

Alone: The collapse and revival of American community. Simon & Schuster.

Chapter 3: Where we might be headed: the power of future scenarios

1 One of the most active proponents of this position, a largely North American phenomenon, is Michael Ruppert, who made the film *Collapse* and publishes www.collapsenet.com.

2 John Michael Greer's concept of the 'Green Wizard', again in the US, is about the gathering and spreading of advice and insight, much of it from the original 1970s oil shock period, which saw a huge flowering of research and practice in terms of practical sustainability.

3 For example, Alex Steffen at http://worldchanging.com, or Stewart Brand's *Whole Earth Discipline: Why dense cities, nuclear power, transgenic crops, restored wildlands, radical science, and geoengineering are necessary* (Atlantic Books, 2010).

4 http://tinyurl.com/6dorbu9.

5 http://tinyurl.com/38kg8u5.

6 Recently updated in David Holmgren's *Future Scenarios: How communities can adapt to peak oil and climate change* (Green Books, 2009). David Korowicz's *Tipping Point: Near-term systemic implications of a peak in global oil production. An outline review* (FEASTA & The Risk/Resilience Network, 2010) also has some very insightful analysis of different possible versions of the 'collapse' scenario.

7 Speth, J. G. (2008) *The Bridge at the Edge of the World. Capitalism, the environment and crossing from crisis to sustainability*. Yale University Press.

8 One example of this is 'To Plan for Emergency, or Not? Heinberg and Hopkins debate', which appeared on Transition Culture, 27 May 2009, http://tinyurl.com/nxa9r7.

9 Gallopin, C. G. (2002) 'Planning for resilience: scenarios, surprises and branch points', in: Gunderson, L. H. & Holling, C. S. (eds), *Panarchy: Understanding transformations in human and natural systems*, Island Press. Holmgren, D. (2003) 'What is Sustainability?', Sustainability Network Update 31E, 9 September 2003. Heinberg, R. (2004) *Powerdown: Options and actions for a post-carbon world*, Clairview

Books. Curry, A., Hodgson, T., Kelnar, R. & Wilson, A. (2005) *Intelligent Future Infrastructure: The scenarios towards 2055*, Foresight, Office of Science and Technology. FEASTA (2006) *Energy Scenarios Ireland*, FEASTA.

Chapter 4: Resilience and localisation

1 Walker, B. & Salt, D. (2006) *Resilience Thinking: Sustaining ecosystems and people in a changing world*. Island Press, p.9.

2 Adger, W. N., Kelly, P. M., Winkels, A., Huy, L. Q. & Locke, C. (2002) 'Migration, remittances, livelihood trajectories and social resilience'. *Ambio*, 31(4): 358-66.

3 Adger, W. N. (2003) *Building Resilience to Promote Sustainability: An agenda for coping with globalisation and promoting justice*. IHDP Update Newsletter of the International Human Dimensions Programme on Global Environmental Change, February 2003, p.3.

4 Edwards, C. (2009) 'Resilient Nation'. DEMOS, p.18.

5 Which you can read in full at http://tinyurl.com/yzp8ky4.

6 http://tinyurl.com/2urp2av.

7 North, P. (2010) 'Eco localisation as a progressive response to peak oil and climate change – a sympathetic critique'. *Geoforum* 41(4): 585-94.

8 Rubin, J. (2009) *Why Your world is About to Get a Whole Lot Smaller: What the price of oil means for the way you live*. Virgin Books.

9 Kunstler, J. H. (2005) *The Long Emergency: Surviving the converging catastrophes of the 21st century*. Atlantic Monthly Press, p.239.

10 Something I wrote about at http://tinyurl.com/234f3w5.

11 Monbiot, G. (2010) 'An eruption of reality'. *The Guardian*, 20 April 2010.

12 Norberg-Hodge, H. (2002) *Bringing the local Economy Home: Local alternatives to global agribusiness*. Zed Books.

13 http://tinyurl.com/5v86t36.

14 http://tinyurl.com/2urp2av.

15 Spratt, S., Simms, A., Neitzert, E. & Ryan-Collins, J. (2009) *The Great Transition: A tale of how it turned out right*. new economics foundation, p.16.

16 Walker, B. & Salt, D. (2006) *Resilience Thinking: Sustaining ecosystems and people in a changing world*. Island Press.

Chapter 5: A taste of a powered-down future

1   Orr, D. (2009) *Down to the Wire: Confronting climate collapse*. Oxford University Press.

2   Berry, W. (2010) 'The pleasures of eating', in: Berry, W. (ed.) *What Are People For? Essays*. Counterpoint Publishing, p.35.

3   Modelled on StroudCo, which began in 2009. See www.stroudco.org.uk.

4   For a clear argument as to the role of grass-fed livestock in a sustainable agricultural system, see Fairlie, S. (2010) *Meat: A benign extravagance*. Permanent Publications.

5   Ramachandran Nair, P. K., Nair, V. D., Gama-Rodrigues, E. F., Garcia, R., Haile, S. G., Howlett, D. S., Kumar, B. M., Mosquera-Losada, M. R., Saha, S. K., Takimoto, A. N. G. & Tonucci, R. G. (2009) 'Soil carbon in agroforestry systems: an unexplored treasure?' *Nature Precedings*, hdl:10101/npre.2009.4061.1.

6   McKibben, B. (2007) *Deep Economy: The wealth of communities and the durable future*. Times Books, p.66.

7   Heinberg, R. & Bomford, M. (2009) *The Food and Farming Transition: Towards a post-carbon food system*. Post Carbon Institute.

8   Simms, A., Moran, D. & Chowla, P. (2006) *The UK Interdependence Report*. new economics foundation.

9   www.fifediet.co.uk.

10 www.growingcommunities.org.

11 Transition Stroud (2008) *Food Availability in Stroud District: Considered in the context of climate change and peak oil*. For the Local Strategic Partnership Think Tank on Global Change, 16 December 2008.

12 You can find an article I wrote on the subject of 'building miles' at http://tinyurl.com/664okmm.

13 Kemp, M. (ed) (2010) *Zero Carbon Britain 2030*. Centre for Alternative Technology Publications.

14 A fascinating piece of research looked at the potential for using straw bales to retrofit existing buildings and concluded that it is a technique that could be appropriate to around 5% of UK housing stock. See Le Doujet, K. (2009) *Opportunities for the large-scale implementation of straw-based external insulation as a retrofit solution of existing UK buildings*. MPhil dissertation, University of Cambridge Engineering Centre for Sustainable Development, August 2009. Can be downloaded from http://tinyurl.com/6hjqs45.

15 Shah, D. (2009) 'Council to build houses of straw'. BBC News, 20 January 2009. Retrieved from http://tinyurl.com/5vdtxk6 on 22 January 2010.

16 Clarke, S. (2002) 'Final Report on the Construction of the Hemp Houses at Haverhill, Suffolk'. Client Report, Suffolk Housing Society Ltd.

17 MacKeown, T. (2008) 'Straw bale panels', in: Hall, K. (ed.) (2008) *The Green Building Bible, Vol 1: Essential information to help you make your home, buildings and outdoor areas less harmful to the environment, the community and your family*. Green Building Press.

18 Hulme, J. & Radford, N. (2010) *Sustainable Supply Chains That Support Local Economic Development*. Prince's Foundation for the Built Environment.

19 Ibid., p.12.

20 Some fantastic work is going on with developing roundwood pole building by Ben Law: see Law, B. (2010) *Roundwood Pole Building*. Permanent Publications.

21 See, for example, Bevan, R. & Woolley, T. (2008) *Hemp Lime Construction: A guide to building with hemp lime composites*. IHS BRE Press.

22 You can read more about this, including the full interview I did with Justin Bere, at http://tinyurl.com/63y4bm3.

23 Oliver, P. (2003) *Dwellings: The vernacular house worldwide*. Phaidon Press.

24 How this could be achieved is set out in Kemp, M. (ed) (2010) *Zero Carbon Britain 2030*. Centre for Alternative Technology Publications.

25 Willis, R. (2006) *Grid 2.0: The next generation*. Green Alliance, for example, calls for a 'Grid 2.0' of small, decentralised grids.

26 For example, in 2009 the European Energy Agency showed that the economically competitive potential of European wind energy generation is 7 times greater than the electrical demand projected for 2030.

27 Kasser, T. (2002) *The High Price of Materialism*. The MIT Press.

28 Shuman, M. (2000) *Going Local: Creating self-reliant communities in a global age*. Routledge.

PART TWO
Chapter 6: Framing Transition

1   Meadows, D. H., Randers, J. & Meadows, D. L. (2005) *Limits to Growth: The 30-year update.* Earthscan Publications.

2   Hawken, P. (2008) *Blessed Unrest: How the largest social movement in the world is restoring grace, justice and beauty to the world.* Penguin, p.4.

3   Crompton, T. (2010) *Common Cause: The case for working with our cultural values.* WWF.

4   From a post on Transition Culture: An Interview with Michael Shuman: 'If we're serious about localisation, all of us have to go to Business School . . .', 14 February 2011, http://tinyurl.com/5v86t36.

5   DiClemente, C. C. (2003) *Addiction and Change: How addictions develop and addicted people recover.* Guilford Press.

6   One of the best books on this is Leadbeater, C. (2009) *We Think: Mass Innovation, not mass production.* Profile Books.

7   Brafman, D. & Beckstrom, R. A. (2006) *The Starfish and the Spider: The unstoppable power of leaderless organisations.* Portfolio Books.

8   A great reference on this is Maturana, H. R. & Varela, F. J. (1992) *The Tree of Knowledge: Biological roots of human understanding.* Shambhala Publishing.

9   Macy, J. & Brown, M. Y. (1998) *Coming Back to Life: Practices to reconnect our lives, our world.* New Society Publishers.

10 Seligman, M. (2006) *Learned Optimism: How to change your mind and your life.* Vintage Books.

11 Layard, R. (2006) *Happiness: Lessons from a new science.* Penguin.

12 Abdallah, S., Thompson, S., Michaelson, J., Marks, N. & Steuer, N. (2009) *The (Un)Happy Planet Index.* new economics foundation.

13 Jackson, T. (2009) *Prosperity Without Growth: Economics for a finite planet.* Earthscan Publications.

14 Shirky, C. (2009) *Here Comes Everybody: How change happens when people come together.* Penguin.

15 The best reference on this is Hock, D. (1999) *Birth of a Chaordic Age.* Berrett-Koehler.

16 Albert, M. (2004) *Parecon: Life after capitalism.* Verso Books.

17 I still think the best book on the Natural Step is James, S. & Lahti, T. (2004) *The Natural Step for Communities: How cities and towns can change to sustainable practices.* New Society Publishers.

18 Hoverstadt, P. (2008) *The Fractal Organization: Creating sustainable organizations with the viable system model.* John Wiley & Sons Publishing.

19 See, for example: Mollison, B. & Holmgren, D. (1990) *Permaculture One: A perennial agriculture system for human systems*, Tagari Publications; Holmgren, D. (2003) *Permaculture: Principles and pathways beyond sustainability*, Permanent Publications; and Whitefield, P. (2004) *The Earth Care Manual: A permaculture handbook for Britain and other temperate climates*, Permanent Publications.

20 Gillespie, E. (2011) 'Hypocrisy of champagne environmentalists is deceitful and distracting', *The Guardian* Green Living blog, 2011, http://tinyurl.com/3fj3fwr.

21 A fascinating film about the 'Amen Break', one of the world's most sampled breakbeats, looks at how these new musical forms can emerge from cutting up old ones and reassembling them in new ways. http://www.youtube.com/watch?v=5SaFTm2bcac.

22 In particular those set out in Holmgren, D. (2003) *Permaculture: Principles and pathways beyond sustainability.* Permanent Publications.

23 'To be a pilgrim'.

24 Trippi, J. (2004) *The Revolution Will Not Be Televised.* Harper Collins.

25 http://tinyurl.com/6b259lz.

26 The clearest setting out of the 12 Steps of Transition can be found in Hopkins, R. (2008) *The Transition Handbook*, pp.147-75.

Chapter 7: The story of four Transition initiatives told using ingredients and tools

1   www.sustainablebungay.com/library-courtyard-garden.

2   www.sustainablebungay.com/category/projects/biodiesel.

3   www.sustainablebungay.com/bungay-community-bees-2.

4   www.sustainablebungay.com/stow-park-pig-club.

5   www.sustainablebungay.com/an-abundance-of-fruit.

6   Hopkins, R. 'Life after oil: Designing pathways for energy descent'. *Permaculture Magazine*, no.45, 27-30, http://transitionculture.org/wp-content/uploads/LIFEAFTE.PDF.

PART THREE
Starting out

1   Khan, N. (2010) 'From Big Society to Little Society and back again, and how diversity can help . . .' A presentation given to the Cultural Leadership Seminar hosted by Huddersfield Creative Arts Network, 18 November 2010. Full text available at www.naseemkhan.com/huddersfield.doc.

2   CABE (2005) *Decent Parks? Decent Behaviour? The link between the quality of parks and user behaviour*. Commission for Architecture and the Built Environment. Available at http://tinyurl.com/4wgpl4u.

3   Williams, C. & Windebank, J. (2002) 'The uneven geographies of informal economic activities: a case study of two British cities'. *Work, Employment and Society*, 16(2): 231-50.

4   Cohen, D. M. K. (2010) *Reaching out for resilience: exploring approaches to inclusion and diversity in the Transition movement*. MSc dissertation, University of Strathclyde, Glasgow. See http://tinyurl.com/3ppcm4a.

5   www.transitionnetwork.org/blogs/catrina-pickering.

6   As set out in the first permaculture book, Bill Mollison and David Holmgren's *Permaculture One* (Tagari Publishing, 1987).

7   Sapiro, V. (1999) 'Considering political civility historically: a case study of the United States'. Unpublished Paper, International Society for Political Psychology.

8   Reagan, M. (1997) 'Reagan: bye to the GOP'. *USA Today*, 17 April 1997.

9   Undertaken for Hopkins, R. (2010) *Localisation and resilience at the local level: the case of Transition Town Totnes*. PhD thesis, University of Plymouth. Available at http://tinyurl.com/655lg9a.

10 www.london-transition.org.uk.

11 For example, that produced by Leeds University: http://tinyurl.com/237mppq.

12 A useful guide to running focus groups can be found at http://tinyurl.com/65rbv5t.

13 See http://transitionnetwork.org/support/training/training-transition.

14 Some great short films capturing people's reactions to having done the Transition Training can be found at http://tinyurl.com/5tty63h.

15 Hodgson, J. & Hopkins, R. (2010) *Transition in Action: Totnes and District 2030. An Energy Descent Action Plan*. Transition Town Totnes / Green Books.

16 You can watch a film of the Eco-Circus at www.transitiontownshaftesbury.org.uk/index.php?n=Main.Video.

17 DiClemente, C. C. (2003) *Addiction and Change: How addictions develop and addicted people recover*. Guilford Press.

18 http://tinyurl.com/ykcput8.

19 Via the Transition Network website: http://tinyurl.com/6fa2hfh.

20 http://transitionnorth.net.

21 http://tinyurl.com/6ealg7u.

22 Which can be read in Hodgson, J. & Hopkins, R. (2010) *Transition in Action: Totnes and District 2030. An Energy Descent Action Plan*. Transition Town Totnes / Green Books.

23 You can read a write-up of this exercise and how to do it at http://tinyurl.com/4lapp4.

24 Roszak, T., Gomes, M. E. & Kanner, A. D. (eds) (1995) *Ecopsychology: Restoring the Earth, healing the mind*. Sierra Club Books.

25 Macy, J. & Brown, M. Y. (1998) *Coming Back to Life: Practices to reconnect our lives, our world*. New Society Publishers.

26 www.rainforestinfo.org.au/deep-eco/johnseed.htm.

Deepening

1   http://tinyurl.com/34xasxh.

2   http://the-hub.net.

3   http://emptyshopsnetwork.com.

4   www.incredible-edible-todmorden.co.uk.

5   www.transitionnewtonabbot.org.uk/?cat=12.

6   http://tinyurl.com/6hc8wn6.

7   http://tinyurl.com/6fhfwns.

8   There is a great film about this project at www.youtube.com/watch?v=_EjTmyQY9XM.

9 http://transitiontownworthing.ning.com/ group/reskillinggroup.

10 www.transitionworcester.org.uk/?cat=6 cycling.

11 http://tinyurl.com/5rllac8.

12 www.recoverywirral.com/?p=2306.

13 http://tinyurl.com/69lgw3h.

14 There is a great film of Sustainable North East Seattle's 'Skills Fair' at www.youtube.com/ watch?v=5tqnvJ6_CU8.

15 http://transition.putney.net/index.php?ID=49.

16 http://tinyurl.com/6kqeoex.

17 http://tinyurl.com/6jnvypv.

18 www.schoolofartisanfood.org.

19 http://contemporaryagriculture.com/index.html.

20 http://cat.org.uk.

21 A great short film about Stroud's potato day can be found at http://tinyurl.com/4peylzl.

22 Here's a piece I wrote about this: http://tinyurl. com/387nmf3.

23 www.transitionus.org/blog/resilient-nonprofits.

24 Transition Network and Julia Ponsonby of Schumacher College in Dartington have produced a guide to making cakes for Transition events, which can be downloaded as a pdf at http://tinyurl.com/6zal845.

25 Taken from a post on Transition Culture called 'Reflections on when a Transition Initiative stalls', 22 September 2009, http://tinyurl/63b6goz.

26 http://tinyurl.com/yzmgr45.

27 http://tinyurl.com/65f2ho3.

28 http://tootingfoodival.blogspot.com.

29 http://tinyurl.com/2g8z2th.

30 http://tinyurl.com/6yc8akf.

31 http://tinyurl.com/6bnwmkm

32 www.transitioncityallotment.blogspot.com.

33 http://tinyurl.com/6xqzupv.

34 http://tinyurl.com/6fvolqd.

35 http://tinyurl.com/6d3qfre.

36 http://fifediet.co.uk.

37 http://tinyurl.com/6h96y8p.

38 http://tinyurl.com/5ucthqh.

39 http://tinyurl.com/6yswt53.

40 http://tinyurl.com/5uj7qf2.

41 http://tinyurl.com/5tkq5yz.

42 http://tinyurl.com/6xqglzh.

43 http://tinyurl.com/5voa9fa.

44 www.youtube.com/watch?v=XRCFDOdXAbg.

45 http://tinyurl.com/677cfk5.

46 More detailed advice on how to set up a garden-share scheme can be found in Pinkerton, T. & Hopkins, R. (2009) *Local Food: How to make it happen in your community*, Transition Books (now out of print), or at www.transitiontowntotnes.org/content/ gardenshare-3 or www.transitiontowntotnes.org/ gardenshare/startupscheme.

47 http://tinyurl.com/66tduum.

48 http://tinyurl.com/66rsstc.

49 http://tinyurl.com/6at94c2.

50 http://tinyurl.com/5wu6m45.

51 http://tinyurl.com/2vuknkg.

52 www.foodfromthesky.org.uk, and here is a short piece about the project from the BBC: www.bbc.co.uk/news/10424392.

53 You can keep up to date with the Transition Scilly orchard on their blog, http://tinyurl.com/ 6frbevw.

54 http://tinyurl.com/64r5h49.

55 http://news.bbc.co.uk/1/hi/wales/8573006.stm.

56 http://tinyurl.com/654htud.

57 Pinkerton, T. & Hopkins, R. (2009) *Local Food: How to make it happen in your community*. Transition Books. (Now out of print.)

58 The farm has its own blog, www.underlanche. blogspot.com.

59 This is described very well in Kabat-Zinn, J. (2001) *Full Catastrophe Living: How to cope with stress, pain and illness using mindfulness meditation*. Piatkus Books.

60 The Totnes Unleashing makes a passing appearance in Transition Network's film *In Transition 1.0*.

61 You can see a film of my talk at the Lewes Unleashing at http://tinyurl.com/5rtlvym, and my write-up of the event at http://tinyurl.com/ 5sf7uwj.

62 You can read a more detailed account of both at http://tinyurl.com/642ea9.

63 The evening was captured in a film: http://tinyurl.com/5wchbyq.

64 For a report see http://tinyurl.com/6xzhr4x.

65 Captured in a great YouTube film: http://tinyurl.com/6da62md.

66 You'll find that film at http://tinyurl.com/6y9rvs2.

67 Shaun Chamberlin's review is at http://tinyurl. com/2wzhnco.

68 http://tinyurl.com/26hge45.
69 http://tinyurl.com/35dns3n.
70 http://tinyurl.com/6ahd96b.
71 A review from the local media: http://tinyurl.com/6hjkxnj.
72 Which you can hear at http://tinyurl.com/5vvsgu7.
73 Captured in film at http://tinyurl.com/68ztrmq.
74 For a film of a wander round the party, see http://tinyurl.com/6x4nllt.
75 There is a good write-up of the Unleashings of Transition Bloomington, Transition Carrboro-Chapel Hill and Transition Laguna Beach at http://tinyurl.com/3yzxnuj.
76 http://helpguide.org/mental/eq8_conflict_resolution.htm.
77 Louv, R. (2010) *Last Child in the Woods: Saving our children from Nature-deficit Disorder*. Atlantic Books. In addition to this you might also find useful Richard Louv's interactive website that is posting evidence of the positive effect of nature on young people: www.childrenandnature.org.
78 www.bicton.ac.uk.
79 www.kinsalefurthered.ie/permaculture_course_level2.htm.
80 www.schumachercollege.org.uk/courses/ma-in-economics-for-transition.
81 This is already happening in a number of universities; see, for example, Smithers, R. 'Will students dig Allotment Soc? Among the clubs vying for freshers' attention at many universities this year is the allotment society.' *The Guardian*, 4 October 2010, http://tinyurl.com/2vukvvx.
82 http://carbonconversations.org.

Connecting
1 www.london-transition.org.uk.
2 www.transitiondurham.org.uk/index.php/northeasttransitiontownactivistsnetwork.
3 http://southeasttransitioninitiatives.ning.com.
4 You can see a short film of the event at http://tinyurl.com/yjtpyws.
5 www.transitionscotland.org.
6 'Transition Scotland Support Project Report 2008-2011: Our achievements and lessons learned'. www.transitionscotland.org/~transiti/tss-end-project-report.
7 You can hear audio files of the event at http://transitionnorth.net.
8 BBC News Somerset (2011) 'Somerset Council urged to drop green Transition status', www.bbc.co.uk/news/uk-england-somerset-13013145.
9 http://transitioncircleeast.blogspot.com.
10 This report can be downloaded from http://tinyurl.com/67bysb8.
11 www.transitioncornwallnetwork.org.uk.
12 www.transitionnc.org.
13 This group runs a Google group at http://tinyurl.com/6l93vyy.
14 You can read David Johnson's review of the day at http://tinyurl.com/39vor9q.
15 www.transitionstreets.org.uk.
16 http://transitionnorwichnews.blogspot.com/2009/06/transition-circles_16.html.
17 http://cambridgecarbonfootprint.org/action/carbon-conversations.
18 www.christian-ecology.org.uk/ecocell.htm.
19 Rowell, A. (2010) *Communities, Councils and a Low-carbon Future: What we can do if governments won't*. Transition Books.
20 Gautier, A. (2009) *Green Up! Five ways to work with your council on the environment and sustainability*. Community Development Foundation.
21 Told in more detail at http://tinyurl.com/l8ktpv.
22 http://trashcatchers.blogspot.com.
23 http://transitionfinsburypark.org.uk/welcome.
24 http://vimeo.com/10549724.
25 http://vimeo.com/11235581.
26 http://transitionculture.org/in-transition.
27 www.transitionstroud.org.
28 http://transitionlangport.org/media-library.
29 http://transitionalnwick.blogspot.com.
30 http://ealingtransitioncommunitygarden.wordpress.com.
31 www.transitionus.org/blogs/joanne-poyourow.
32 You can read a précis of their first year at http://transitionnorwich.blogspot.com/2010/10/looking-back-looking-forward-year-of.html.
33 You can see an archive of Transition Cambridge's bulletins at http://tinyurl.com/66hq5qz.
34 www.stories.transitionnetwork.org.
35 An archive of newsletters can be found at http://tinyurl.com/6dakqr2.

36 http://tinyurl.com/67ldbyd.
37 http://newforesttransition.ning.com.
38 www.hebdenbridgetransitiontown.org.uk.
39 www.transitiontownlewes.org.
40 http://transitionfinsburypark.org.uk/
    OurApproach.
41 www.letslivelocal.co.uk.
42 Find out more about the community microsites
    offered by Transition Network at www.transition
    network.org/web-options-transition-initiatives.
43 Transition Network page about social media:
    www.transitionnetwork.org/syndication-and-
    social-media, and our Facebook page is
    www.facebook.com/transitionnetwork.
44 http://newforesttransition.ning.com.
45 http://tinyurl.com/3ye4mill.
46 http://tinyurl.com/38hwn7j.
47 Froggatt, A. & Lahn, G. (2010) *White Paper:
    Sustainable energy security. Strategic risks and
    opportunities for business.* Lloyds / Chatham
    House.
48 http://totnesedap.org.uk/book/part2/stories.
49 Most usefully described in Owen, H. (1993)
    Open Space Technology: A user's guide.
    Berrett-Koehler Publishers.
50 http://mychickens.primaryblogger.co.uk.
51 You can hear their piece at http://transitionnorth.
    net/voxpop.
52 http://tinyurl.com/6grla5j.
53 http://transitionnetwork.org/projects/
    transition tots.
54 http://www.foodmapper.org.uk.
55 Chamberlin, S. (2009) *The Transition Timeline:
    For a local, resilient future.* Green Books.
56 www.transitionnetwork.org/blogs/steph-bradley.
57 You can read my report of the evening at
    http://tinyurl.com/37alrnt.

Building

1   This can be downloaded in full from
    http://tinyurl.com/4s9z7y5.
2   http://transitionforestrow.ning.com/notes/EDAP.
3   See http://totnesedap.org.uk.
4   http://tinyurl.com/5s6awnw.
5   www.sse.org.uk.
6   www.mondragon-corporation.com/ENG.aspx
7   www.thevillage.ie.
8   www.esrad.org.uk/resources/vsmg_3.
9   www.awelamantawe.co.uk.
10 You can download the full prospectus for the
    share launch at www.ovesco.co.uk/assets/
    files/offerdoc.pdf; it is a very useful model for
    other communities.
11 You can see a film of this launch event at
    http://youtu.be/3dCGReVTWdo.
12 Keep up to date with developments at
    www.tresoc.co.uk.
13 Ward, B. & Lewis, J. (2002) *The Money Trail.* new
    economics foundation.
14 North, P. (2010) *Local Money: How to make it
    happen in your community.* Transition Books.
15 For a detailed overview see North, P., op. cit.
16 Molly Scott Cato blogs at www.gaianeconomics.
    blogspot.com.
17 www.capitalownership.org/lib/TurnbullSelecting
    ACommunityCurrency.htm.
18 http://theswopshop.org.
19 You can read more about Transition Chichester's
    Tchi at http://tchidirectory.wordpress.com/
    about.
20 Department for Environment, Food and Rural
    Affairs (2008) 'English Organic Action Plan
    Steering Group (OAPSG) Strategic Paper on
    Public Procurement', www.sustainweb.org/
    pdf2/org-238.pdf.
21 www.foodforlife.org.uk.
22 Morgan, K. & Morley, A. (2002) *Relocalising the
    Food Chain: The role of creative public procure-
    ment.* The Regeneration Institute, Cardiff
    University.
23 North, P. (2010) *Local Money: How to make it
    happen in your community.* Transition Books.
24 www.ragmans.co.uk.
25 Wyler, S. (2009) *A History of Community Asset
    Ownership.* Development Trusts Association.
26 www.coinstreet.org.
27 British Association of Settlements and Social
    Action Centres, www.bassac.org.uk.
28 Pinkerton, T. & Hopkins, R. (2009) *Local Food:
    How to make it happen in your community.*
    Transition Books. (Now out of print.)
29 www.sustainweb.org/realbread.
30 Transition Stroud (2008) *Food Availability in
    Stroud District: Considered in the context of
    climate change and peak oil.* For the Local
    Strategic Partnership Think Tank on Global Change.

31 http://tinyurl.com/34bwklu.

32 It can be downloaded from http://tinyurl.com/3yn6ann.

33 You can read the current draft of this at www.eafl.org/Documents/NorwichFoodPlan.pdf.

34 There is an excellent archive of peak oil resolutions and peak oil preparedness plans at http://postcarboncities.net/resources.

35 http://postcarboncities.net/node/2194.

36 http://postcarboncities.net/node/3754.

37 http://postcarboncities.net/node/3888.

38 http://postcarboncities.net/bloomington-ind-recognize-peak-oil-and-need-prepare.

39 http://postcarboncities.net/node/3750.

40 Chen, Y., Deines, M., Fleischmann, H., Reed, S. & Swick, I. (2008) *Transforming Urban Environments for a Post-Peak Oil Future: A vision plan for the city of San Buenaventura.* City of San Buenaventura.

41 Portland Peak Oil Task Force (2007) 'Descending the Oil Peak: Navigating the transition from oil and natural gas'. Report of the City of Portland Peak Oil Task Force.

42 Lerch, D. (2007) *Post Carbon Cities: Planning for energy and climate uncertainty, a guidebook on peak oil and global warming for local governments.* Post Carbon Institute.

43 www.bristol.gov.uk/ccm/content/Environment-Planning/sustainability/climate-change.en?page=2.

44 http://tinyurl.com/5tmu2tn.

45 In response to a question from George Monbiot, as described in Monbiot, G. (2009) 'Cross your fingers and carry on: why does the government refuse to make contingency plans for peak oil?', *The Guardian*, 14 April 2009, http://tinyurl.com/6jowqpw.

Daring to dream

1 Bunting, M. (2009) 'Beyond Westminster's bankrupted practices a new idealism is emerging: progressive politics will take root from the rubble of a Labour defeat. The Transition movement is giving us a glimpse now'. *The Observer*, 31 May 2009.

2 McDonald, M. (2009) *The role of Transition Initiatives in local authorities' responsiveness to peak oil: A case study of Somerset County Council*. MSc dissertation in International Planning, University College London. Available at http://tinyurl.com/6hxztfj.

3 Hurring, D. (2009) *Transition Audit of Somerset County Council*. Somerset County Council in association with Transition Somerset.

4 http://barrierbusting.communities.gov.uk.

5 http://transitionnetwork.org/projects.

6 www.fc-utd.co.uk/communityshares.

7 www.energyshare.com.

Epilogue

1 Their document, *The Rocky Road to Transition*, can be downloaded from http://tinyurl.com/6ylm54d.

2 http://tinyurl.com/8nhzxu.

3 You can read his critique of the Transition approach at http://tinyurl.com/5w4llyk in which he states that "the Transition movement seems saturated with what Michael Lerner called 'surplus powerlessness' disguised as practicality". I responded to Alex's critique at http://tinyurl.com/yb706g3.

4 http://tinyurl.com/2urp2av.

5 'An interview with Michael Shuman: if we're serious about localisation, "all of us have to go to Business School". . .'. Transition Culture, 14 February 2011, http://tinyurl.com/5v86t36.

6 'Milton Friedman, a giant among economists'. *The Economist*, 23 November 2006. www.economist.com/business/displaystory.cfm?story_id=8313925, retrieved 20 February 2008.

7 Friedman, M. (1962) *Capitalism and Freedom*. University of Chicago Press.

8 Helm, T. (2011) 'Oil prices: urgent steps needed to wean UK onto other energy sources, MPs say. As Middle East conflicts cause oil prices to rise dramatically, government spells out plans for radical energy shift'. *The Guardian*, 5 March 2011.

9 World Economic Forum (2011) *Global Risks 2011, sixth edition. Executive Summary.* www3.weforum.org/docs/WEF_GlobalRisks_ExecutiveSummary_2011_EN.pdf.

Resources

Key Transition organisations

Transition Network
43 Fore Street, Totnes, Devon, TQ9 5HN, UK
+44 (0)5601 531882
www.transitionnetwork.org

Transition Training & Consulting
43 Fore Street, Totnes, Devon, TQ9 5HN, UK
+44 (0)5601 531882.
www.ttandc.org.uk

National Transition Hubs

Brazil: http://transitionbrasil.ning.com

Denmark: http://transitiondenmark.ning.com

France: www.transitionfrance.fr

Germany: www.transition-initiativen.de

Ireland and Northern Ireland:
http://transitiontownsireland.ning.com

Italy: http://transitionitalia.wordpress.com

Japan: http://transition-japan.wikispaces.com,
www.transition-japan.net

The Netherlands: http://transitiontowns.nl

New Zealand: www.transitiontowns.org.nz

Norway: www.transitionnorway.org

Portugal: http://tinyurl.com/transition-portugal

Spain: http://movimientotransicion.pbworks.com

Sweden: http://transitionsweden.ning.com

United States: www.transitionus.org

DVDs

A Crude Awakening: The oil crash by Lava
Productions AG. www.oilcrashmovie.com

In Transition 1.0, the film about Transition, made
by people doing Transition, is available from
http://transitionculture.org/in-transition, or can
be watched online at http://vimeo.com/8029815.

*The End of Suburbia: Oil depletion and the collapse
of the American dream* by The Electric Wallpaper Co.
www.endofsuburbia.com

*The Power of Community: How Cuba survived
peak oil* by Community Solution.
www.powerofcommunity.org

*The Powerdown Show: The powering up of
community, creativity and culture.* The Cultivate
Living and Learning Centre. Available from http://
transitionculture.org/shop/the-powerdown-show.

What a Way to Go: Life at the end of empire by Tim
Bennett/VisionQuest Pictures.
www.whatawaytogomovie.com

There is also a large collection of Transition-related
films available on the Transition Network YouTube
channel at www.youtube.com/user/TransitionTowns.

Transition books

Bird, C. (2010) *Local Sustainable Homes: How to
make them happen in your community.* Transition
Books

Chamberlin, S. (2009) *The Transition Timeline: For a
local, resilient future.* Green Books

Hodgson, J. & Hopkins, R. (2010) *Transition in Action:
Totnes and District 2030. An Energy Descent Action
Plan.* Transition Town Totnes / Green Books

Hopkins, R. (2008) *The Transition Handbook: From
oil dependency to local resilience.* Green Books

North, P. (2010) *Local Money: How to make it happen
in your community.* Transition Books

Pinkerton, T. & Hopkins, R. (2009) *Local Food: How
to make it happen in your community.* Transition
Books. (Now out of print.)

Rowell, A. (2010) *Communities, Councils and a
Low-carbon Future. What we can do if governments
won't.* Transition Books

Other useful Transition stuff

Transition Voice magazine. 14, S. Washington
Street, Staunton, VA 24401, USA, +1 (540) 466-6128,
http://transitionvoice.com

Hopkins, R. (2010) *Localisation and resilience at
the local level: the case of Transition Town Totnes.*
PhD thesis, University of Plymouth. Available from
http://tinyurl.com/655lg9a.

Hopkins, R. & Lipman, P. (2009) *Transition Network:
Who we are and what we do.* Transition Network.

Höynälänmaa, A. S. A. (2010) *Spreading seeds of
sustainability: factors affecting the development
of the Transition movement in Dorset.* BSc dissertation in Environmental Protection, University of
Bournemouth.

McDonald, M. (2009) *The role of Transition Initiatives in local authorities' responsiveness to peak oil: a case study of Somerset County Council.* MSc dissertation in International Planning, University College London. Available at http://tinyurl.com/6hxztfj.

Pir, A. (2009) *In search of a resilient food system: a qualitative study of the Transition Town Totnes Food Group.* MPhil dissertation in Culture, Environment and Sustainability, Centre for Development and the Environment, University of Oslo.

Seyfang, G. (2009) 'Transition Norwich: A Fine City in Transition. Report of the 2009 Membership Survey'. University of East Anglia.

Transition Network (2010) *Embedding Transition in the Political Process: A hustings primer from the Transition Network 2010.* Transition Network. Available at http://tinyurl.com/66ptzmu.

Transition Town Totnes (2010) *So, What Does Transition Town Totnes Actually Do? The story so far, 2006-2010.* Transition Town Totnes.

Wreford, L. (2008) *Transition Towns: cultivating grassroots innovations for sustainability.* MSc dissertation in Environmental Science and Society, University College London.

Peak oil

Bentley, R. W. (2002) 'Global oil & gas depletion: an overview'. *Energy Policy*, 30(3): 189-205.

Campbell, C. J. & Laherrere, J. (1998) 'The end of cheap oil'. *Scientific American*, 278(3): 78-83.

Heinberg, R. (2003) *The Party's Over: Oil, war and the fate of industrial societies.* New Society Publishers.

Hirsch, R. L., Bezdek, R. & Wendling, R. (2005) *Peaking of World Oil Production: Impacts, mitigation and risk management.* National Energy Technology Laboratory, US Department of Energy.

ITPOES (2010) *The Oil Crunch: A wake-up call for the UK economy. The second report of the UK Industry Task Force on Peak Oil and Energy Security.* Industry Taskforce on Peak Oil and Energy Security.

Klare, M. T. (2004) *Blood and Oil: The dangers and consequences of America's growing dependency on imported petroleum.* Metropolitan Books.

Kunstler, J. H. (2005) *The Long Emergency: Surviving the converging catastrophes of the 21st century.* Atlantic Monthly Press.

Muttitt, G. (2011) *Fuel on the Fire: Oil and politics in occupied Iraq.* Bodley Head.

Owen, N. A, Inderwildi, O. R. & King, D. A. (2010) 'The status of conventional world oil reserves – hype or cause for concern?' *Energy Policy*, 38(8): 4743-9.

Rubin, J. (2009) *Why Your World is About to Get a Whole Lot Smaller: What the price of oil means for the way we live.* Virgin Books.

Simmonds, M. R. (2005) *Twilight in the Desert: The coming Saudi oil shock and the world economy.* John Wiley.

Sorrell, S., Speirs, J., Bentley, R., Brandt, A. & Miller, R. (2009) *Global Oil Depletion: An assessment of the evidence for a near-term peak in global oil production.* UK Energy Research Centre.

Climate change

Dumanoski, D. (2010) *The End of the Long Summer: Why we must remake our civilisation to survive on a volatile Earth.* Three Rivers Press.

Goodall, C. (2007) *How to Live a Low-Carbon Life: The individual's guide to stopping climate change.* Earthscan Publications.

Hamilton, C. (2010) *Requiem for a Species: Why we resist the truth about climate change.* Earthscan Publications.

Hansen, J. (2009) *The Storms of my Grandchildren: The truth about the coming climate catastrophe and our last chance to save humanity.* Bloomsbury.

Hansen, J., Sato, M., Kharecha, P., Beerling, D., Masson-Delmotte, V., Pagani, M., Raymo, M., Royer, D. L. & Zachos, J. C. (2008) 'Target atmospheric CO_2: where should humanity aim?' *The Open Atmospheric Science Journal*, 2:217-31.

Hawkins, R., Hunt, C., Holmes, T. & Helweg-Larsen, T. (2008) *Climate Safety: In case of emergency.* Public Interest Research Centre.

Henson, R. (2006) *The Rough Guide to Climate Change: The symptoms, the science, the solutions.* Rough Guides.

Hoggan, J. & Littlemore, R. (2009) *Climate Cover-Up: The crusade to deny global warming.* Greystone Books.

Lynas, M. (2007) *Six Degrees: Our future on a hotter planet.* Fourth Estate.

McKibben, B. (2010) *Eaarth: Making a life on a tough new planet.* Knopf Canada.

Monbiot, G. (2007) *Heat: How to stop the planet burning.* Penguin Books.

Oreskes, N. & Conway, E. M. (2010) *Merchants of Doubt: How a handful of scientists obscured the truth on issues from tobacco smoke to global warming.* Bloomsbury.

Pearce, F. (2010) *The Climate Files: the battle for the truth about global warming.* Guardian Books.

Shakhova, N., Semiletov, I., Salyuk, A., Yusupov, V., Kosmach, D. & Gustafsson, O. (2010) 'Extensive methane venting to the atmosphere from sediments of the East Siberian Arctic'. *Science*, 327(5970): 1246-50.

Spratt, D. (2007) 'The Big Melt: Lessons from the Arctic summer of 2007'. Carbon Equity, www.carbonequity.info.

Resilience

Cork, S. (2009) *Brighter Prospects: Enhancing the resilience of Australia.* Australla 21.

Edwards, C. (2009) 'Resilient Nation'. Demos.

Haxeltine, A. & Seyfang, G. (2009) *Transitions for the People: Theory and practice of 'Transition' and 'Resilience' in the UK's Transition movement.* Tyndall Centre for Climate Change Research, Working Paper 134.

Holling, C. S. (1973) 'Resilience and the stability of ecological systems'. *Annual review of Ecology and Systematics*, 4:1-23.

Homer-Dixon, T. (2007) *The Upside of Down: Catastrophe, creativity and the renewal of civilisation.* Souvenir Press.

Masten, A. S. (2001) 'Ordinary magic: resilience processes in development'. *American Psychologist*, 56(3): 227-38.

Wilding, N. (2011) *Exploring Community Resilience in Times of Rapid Change.* Carnegie UK / Fiery Spirits.

Energy descent / Transitions

Douthwaite, R. & Fallon, G. (2010) *Fleeing Vesuvius: Overcoming the risks of economic and environmental collapse.* FEASTA.

Gilding, P. (2011) *The Great Disruption: How the climate crisis will transform the global economy.* Bloomsbury.

Gladwell, M. (2000) *The Tipping Point: How little things can make a big difference.* Abacus.

Green New Deal Group (2008) *The Green New Deal: A user's guide to the end of the industrial age.* new economics foundation.

Greer, J. M. (2008) *The Long Descent: A user's guide to the end of the industrial age.* New Society Publishing.

Kemp, M. (2010) *Zero Carbon Britain 2030.* Centre for Alternative Technology Publications.

McKibben, B. (2007) *Deep Economy: The wealth of communities and the durable future.* Times Books.

Odum, H. T. & Odum, E. C. (2001) *A Prosperous Way Down: Principles and policies.* University Press of Colorado.

Orr, D. (2009) *Down to the Wire: Confronting climate collapse.* Oxford University Press.

Solnit, R. (2004) *Hope in the Dark: The untold history of people power.* Canongate.

Spratt, S., Simms, A., Neitzert, E. & Ryan Collins, J. (2009) *The Great Transition: A tale of how it turned out right.* new economics foundation.

Walker, G. & King, D. (2009) *The Hot Topic: How to tackle global warming and still keep the lights on.* Bloomsbury.

Permaculture design

Holmgren, D. (2004) *Permaculture: Principles and pathways beyond sustainability.* Holmgren Design Press.

Mollison, B. (1988) *Permaculture: A designer's manual.* Tagari Press.

Whitefield, P. (2000) *Permaculture in a Nutshell.* Permanent Publications.

Whitefield, P. (2005) *The Earth Care Manual.* Permanent Publications.

Also highly recommended is a subscription to *Permaculture Magazine* (www.permaculture.co.uk) and to The Permaculture Activist (www.permacultureactivist.net).

The Permaculture Association's excellent website can be found at www.permaculture.org.uk and has a very thorough resources section, and listings of local groups and projects, including the LAND network of demonstration projects.

Food, gardening and growing

Ableman, M. (1998) *On Good Land: The autobiography of an urban farm*. Chronicle Books.

Astyk, S. (2008) *Depletion and Abundance: Life on the new home front*. New Society Publishers.

Bartholemew, M. (2006) *All New Square Foot Gardening: Grow more in less space!* Cool Springs Press.

Carey, J. (2011) *Who feeds Bristol? Towards a resilient food plan: production · processing · distribution · communities · retail · catering · waste*. Bristol Green Capital.

DuPuis, E. M. & Goodman, D. (2005) 'Should we go "home" to eat? Towards a reflexive politics of localism'. *Journal of Rural Studies*, 21(3): 359-71.

Fairlie, S. (2007) 'Can Britain feed itself?' *The Land*, 4 (Winter): 18-26.

Heinberg, R. & Bomford, M. (2009) *The Food and Farming Transition: Towards a post-carbon food system*. Post Carbon Institute.

Jeavons, J. (2005) *How to Grow More Vegetables Than You Ever Thought Possible on Less Land Than You Can Imagine,* Ten Speed Press.

Kloppenburg, J., Hendrickson, J. & Stevenson, G. W. (1996) 'Coming in to the foodshed'. *Agriculture and Human Values*, 13(3) (Summer): 33-42.

Lawrence, F. (2008) *Eat Your Heart Out: Why the food business is bad for the planet and your health*. Penguin Books.

Lucas, C., Jones, A. & Hines, C. (2007) 'Fuelling a Food Crisis: The impact of peak oil on food security'. A free download from http://tinyurl.com/yrg67n.

Morgan, K. & Sonnino, R. (2008) *The School Food Revolution: Public food and the challenge of sustainable development*. Earthscan Publications.

Peters, C. J., Bills, N. L., Wilkins, J. L. & Fick, G. W. (2009) 'Foodshed analysis and its relevance to sustainability'. *Renewable Agriculture and Food Systems*, 24: 1-7.

Pretty, J., Ball, A., Lang, T. & Morrison, J. (2003) 'Farm costs and food miles: an assessment of the full cost of the UK weekly food basket'. *Food Policy*, 30(1): 1-20.

Tudge, C. (2003) *So Shall We Reap: What's gone wrong with the world's food – and how to fix it*. Penguin Books.

Natural building and insights for post-peak-oil construction

Alexander, C. (2002) *The Nature of Order: An essay on the art of building and the nature of the universe* (4-volume series). Centre for Environmental Structure, Berkeley, California.

Alexander, C., Ishikawa, S. & Silverstein, M. (1977) *A Pattern Language: Towns, buildings, construction*. Oxford University Press.

Bevan, R. & Woolley, T. (2008) *Hemp Lime Construction: A guide to building with hemp lime composites*. IHS BRE Press.

Broome, J. (2007) *The Green Self-build Book: How to design and build your own eco-home*. Green Books.

Clifton-Taylor, A. (1987) *The Pattern of English Building* (4th edn). Faber and Faber.

Evans, I., Smith, M. & Smiley, L. (2002) *Hand Sculpted House: A practical and philosophical guide to building a cob cottage*. Chelsea Green.

Jones, B. (2009) *Building with Straw Bales: A practical guide for the UK and Ireland* (2nd edn). Green Books.

Kennedy, J., Smith, M. & Wanek, C. (eds) (2002) *The Art of Natural Building: Design, construction, resources*. New Society Publishers.

Le Doujet, K. (2009) *Opportunities for the large-scale implementation of straw-based external insulation as a retrofit solution of existing UK buildings: how much of a good idea is it to externally insulate existing UK buildings with straw bales?* MPhil dissertation, University of Cambridge.

Roaf, S., Crichton, D. & Nicol, F. (2005) *Adapting Buildings and Cities for Climate Change: A 21st century survival guide*. Architectural Press.

Roy, R. (2003) *Cordwood Building: State of the art*. New Society Publishers.

Woolley, T. (2006) *Natural Building: A guide to materials and techniques*. Crowood Press.

Thinking approaches, tools and change processes

Atlee, T. (2003) *The Tao of Democracy: Using co-intelligence to create a world that works for all*. The Writers' Collective.

Brafman, D. & Beckstrom, R. A. (2006) *The Starfish and the Spider: The unstoppable power of leader-less organisations*. Portfolio Books.

Holman, P. & Devane, T. (1999) *The Change Handbook: Group methods for shaping the future*. Berrett-Koehler.

James, O. (2008) *The Selfish Capitalist: Origins of affluenza*. Vermilion.

James, S. & Lahti, T. (2004) *The Natural Step for Communities: How cities and towns can change to sustainable practices*. New Society Publishers.

Johnstone, C. (2006) *Find Your Power: A toolkit for resilience and positive change*. Permanent Publications.

Klar, M. & Kasser, T. (2009) 'Some benefits of being an activist: measuring activism and its role in psychological well-being'. *Political Psychology*, 30(5): 755-77.

Leadbeater, C. (2009) *We Think: Mass innovation, not mass production*. Profile Books.

Macy, J. & Brown, M. Y. (1998) *Coming Back to Life: Practices to reconnect our lives, our world*. New Society Publishers.

Owen, H. (1993) *Open Space Technology: A user's guide*. Berrett-Koehler.

Seligman, M. E. P. (2006) *Learned Optimism: How to change your mind and your life*. Vintage.

Shirky, C. (2009) *Here Comes Everybody: How change happens when people come together*. Penguin.

World Café Community (2002) *Café to Go! A quick reference guide for putting conversations to work*. Whole Systems Associates.

Zerubavel, E. (2006) *The Elephant in the Room: Silence and denial in everyday life*. Oxford University Press.

Social enterprise and entrepreneurship

Baderman, J. & Law, J. (2006) *Everyday Legends: The stories of 20 great UK social entrepreneurs*. WW Publishing.

Crutchfield, L. & McLeod Grant, H. (2007) *Forces for Good*. Jossey-Bass Publishers.

Dearden Phillips, C. (2008) *Your Chance to Change the World: The no-fibbing guide to social entrepreneurship*. Directory of Social Change.

Dees, G. (1998) *The Meaning of Social Entrepreneurship*. Duke University.

Elkington, J. & Hartigan, P. (2008) *The Power of Unreasonable People*. Harvard Business School.

Johanisova, N. (2005) *Living in the Cracks: A look at rural social enterprises in Britain and the Czech Republic*. FEASTA.

Leadbeater, C. (1997) *The Rise of the Social Entrepreneur*. Demos.

Mawson, A. (2008) *The Social Entrepreneur*. Atlantic Books.

Nicholls, A. (2008) *Social Entrepreneurship: New models of sustainable change*. Oxford University Press.

Young, C. & Edwards-Stuart, F. (2007) *Leadership in the Social Economy*. School for Social Entrepreneurs.

Insights on resilience and its historical disappearance

Berger, J. (1992) *Pig Earth*. Chatto & Windus.

Brown, A. (2009) *Just Enough: Lessons in living green from traditional Japan*. Kodansha International.

Callandar, R. (2000) *History in Birse* (volumes 1-4). Birse Community Trust.

Collis, J. S. (1973) *The Worm Forgives the Plough*. Penguin Books.

Dartington Rural Archive (1985) *Horsepower*. Spindle Press.

Drummond, J. C. & Wilbraham, A. (1958) *The Englishman's Food: A history of five centuries of English diet*. Readers Union/Jonathan Cape.

Gardiner, J. (2004) *Wartime Britain 1939-45*. Headline Book Publishing.

Hammond, R. J. (1954) *Food and Agriculture in Britain 1939-45: Aspects of wartime control*. Stanford University Press.

Hyams, E. (1952) *Soil and Civilisation*. Thames and Hudson.

Jones, S. R. (1936) *English Village Homes*. Batsford.

Norberg-Hodge, H. (2000) *Ancient Futures: Learning from Ladakh*. Rider Publishing.

Rackham, O. (1995) *Trees and Woodlands in the British Landscape: The complete history of Britain's trees, woods and hedgerows*. Weidenfeld & Nicolson.

Reader, J. (1988) *Man on Earth*. Penguin Books.

Sturt, G. (1963) *The Wheelwright's Shop*. Cambridge University Press.

Zweiniger-Bargielowska, I. (2000) *Austerity in Britain: Rationing, controls, and consumption 1939-1955*. Oxford University Press.

Rethinking economics

Boyle, D. (2002) *The Money Changers: Currency reform from Aristotle to e-cash*. Earthscan Publications.

Cato, M. S. (2006) *Market Schmarket: Building the post-capitalist economy*. New Clarion Press.

Douthwaite, R. (1996) *Short Circuit: Strengthening local economies for security in an unstable world*. Green Books.

Douthwaite, R. (1999) *The Growth Illusion: How economic growth has enriched the few, impoverished the many and endangered the planet*. Green Books.

Fleming, D. (2005) *Energy and the Common Purpose: Descending the energy staircase with Tradable Energy Quotas*. Lean Connection Press.

Greco, T. (2001) *Money: Understanding and creating alternatives to legal tender*. Chelsea Green.

Hamilton, C. (2004) *Growth Fetish*. Pluto Press.

Heinberg, R. (2011) *The End of Growth: Adapting to our new economic reality*. New Society Publishers.

Lietaer, B. (2001) *The Future of Money: Creating new wealth, work and a wiser world*. Century.

Simms, A. (2005) *Ecological Debt: The health of the planet and the wealth of nations*. Pluto Press.

Localisation

Cavanagh, J. & Mander, J. (2004) *Alternatives to Economic Globalisation: A better world is possible*. Berrett-Koehler.

Goldsmith, E. & Mander, J. (2001) *The Case Against the Global Economy and For a Turn Towards Localisation*. Earthscan Publications.

Hines, C. (2000) *Localisation: A global manifesto*. Earthscan Publications.

Norberg-Hodge, H. (2002) *Bringing the Local Economy Home: Local alternatives to global agribusiness*. Zed Books.

North, P. (2010) 'Eco-localisation as a progressive response to peak oil and climate change – a sympathetic critique'. *Geoforum*, 41(4): 585-94.

Porritt, J. (2008) *Globalism and Regionalism*. Black Dog Publishing.

Sale, K. (1980) *Human Scale*. Coward, McCann & Geoghegan.

Shuman, M. (2000) *Going Local: Creating self-reliant communities in a global age*. Routledge.

Shuman, M. (2006) *The Small-mart Revolution: How local businesses are beating the global competition*. Berrett-Koehler.

Woodin, M. & Lucas, C. (2004) *Green Alternatives to Globalisation: A manifesto*. Pluto Press.

Some essential websites

www.transitionculture.org. Where the concepts in this book are explored in more depth.

www.energybulletin.net. Essential – make it the one website you visit every day.

www.theoildrum.com. Quite technical, and not really one for the novice, but an excellent source of up-to-date analysis.

www.postcarbon.org. The Post Carbon Institute.

www.casaubonsbook.blogspot.com. Sharon Astyk's excellent blog.

Index